The Subtle Logics of Knowledge Conflicts in China's Foreign Enterprises

Constanze Wang

The Subtle Logics of Knowledge Conflicts in China's Foreign Enterprises

Springer VS

Constanze Wang
Köln, Germany

Dissertation, Universität zu Köln, 2015

ISBN 978-3-658-14183-7 ISBN 978-3-658-14184-4 (eBook)
DOI 10.1007/978-3-658-14184-4

Library of Congress Control Number: 2016939368

Springer VS

Printed on acid-free paper

This Springer VS imprint is published by Springer Nature
The registered company is Springer Fachmedien Wiesbaden GmbH

Acknowledgments

Phenomena are quickly explained with some sort of “culture”. Trying to thoroughly understand what indeed is cultural about them is, by contrast, a complicated and lengthy process. The present study is the result of such a process. It provides an alternative picture of “Chinese culture” in many ways by deeply engaging with one of the most controversial topics of doing business in contemporary China.

The study was pursued in the framework of the research project “Intellectual Property in Sino-German Cooperation” carried out by Bremen University of Applied Sciences and funded by the German Federal Ministry of Education and Research. It has been accepted as dissertation by University of Cologne’s Faculty of Arts and Humanities.

While I am grateful to each and every one who directly or indirectly inspired or motivated me along the way, I would like to express my deepest gratitude to Thomas Scharping, Björn Ahl, Monika Schädler, Renate Krieg, Minyan Luo and Joachim Freimuth for their particular support. I also wish to thank the participating enterprises and interviewees who made the data collection possible.

September 2015
Constanze Wang

Contents

Abstract

Foreign businesses investing in China face severe problems surrounding the handling of valuable knowledge. Critical issues are the excessive leakage of knowledge and insufficient knowledge sharing. The way knowledge is handled by Chinese employees is widely believed to be induced by a "Chinese culture" at the national level, most prominently by Confucianism or collectivism. Against this background, the present study investigates the actual role of culture within knowledge conflicts in German-invested manufacturing enterprises in China. Qualitative interviews with Chinese and German employees reveal that culture essentially provides orientation for the daily handling of knowledge. The evolving of the enterprise into a stable space over time is the crucial criterion for Chinese employees when deciding about sharing and disclosing valuable knowledge. For German employees, in contrast, the enterprise with its formal organizational structures *a priori* is the most decisive reference point. Distracted by a national "Chinese culture", many German employees focus on the Chinese environment in search for explanations for knowledge conflicts, whereas Chinese employees focus on the enterprise as a stable space. By embracing an understanding of knowledge interactions being strongly contingent on an enterprise's stability, however, managers can take action to solve knowledge conflicts.

Keywords: Chinese culture, culture as practice, knowledge sharing, knowledge leakage, knowledge conflict, trade secret, knowledge worker, intermediary, foreign enterprise

Figures and Tables

Abbreviations

AIC	Administration of Industry and Commerce
CIAJ	China Institute of Applied Jurisprudence of the Supreme People's Court
FDI	Foreign direct investment
FIE	Foreign-invested enterprise
GDP	Gross domestic product
HGB	Handelsgesetzbuch (German Commercial Code)
HSBC	Hong Kong and Shanghai Banking Corporation
JV	Joint Venture
KW	Knowledge worker (group)
LUC	Law against Unfair Competition
NBS	National Bureau of Statistics of the PRC
OECD	Organization for Economic Co-operation and Development
PRC	People's Republic of China
SAIC	State Administration of Industry and Commerce
SIPO	State Intellectual Property Office of the PRC
SPC	Supreme People's Court
SOE	State-owned enterprise
TRIPS	Trade-related Aspects of Intellectual Property Rights
WFOE	Wholly-foreign-owned enterprise
WTO	World Trade Organization

1 Introduction

This introduction clarifies why the present study's endeavor is important (1.1), what the study aims for (1.2), what is already known (1.3), how the study touches upon several academic disciplines and fields (1.4), as well as how it is structured (1.5).

1.1 Rationale

"The Confucian Challenge to Intellectual Property Reforms"[1]

"The Influence of Confucius on Intellectual Property Rights in China"[2]

"The Dissonance between Culture and Intellectual Property in China"[3]

"Impact of Chinese Cultural Values on Knowledge Sharing"[4]

"National Cultural Influences on Knowledge Sharing"[5]

For foreign businesses investing in China, valuable knowledge is a most challenging issue. Economic espionage and intellectual property infringements have become rampant in China during the last decades. China has become the country of top concern for Europe and the United States. More than two thirds of the suspected infringing goods originate from China as detected at European Union borders.[6] For the United States, China has become a dominant threat in intellectual property violations with trade secrets infringements being the greatest concern.[7] Losses due to the theft of trade secrets can amount to 114 billion US Dollars for a single case as the trade secrets case of the British-Australian mining group Rio Tinto has shown.[8] Enormous economic gains are at stake in the Chinese market.

---

1 Yu Peter K. 2012.
2 Chou Justin A. and Ratner 2011.
3 Gisclair 2008.
4 Li Wei et al. 2007.
5 Michailova and Hutchings 2006.
6 European Commission 2013: 18.
7 US-China Business Council 2012: 12.
8 Xiao Yunduan 2010: 150, Hein 2009.

This comes at a time of a quest for knowledge-derived competitiveness. After the industrial era has turned into a knowledge era, enterprises around the world struggle for gathering and using knowledge in order to increase their technology-intensity and their level of innovation. As knowledge ever more quickly becomes obsolete, enterprises are easily left behind in the global competition as soon as they do not carefully pay attention to constantly updating their knowledge. Only by embracing a focus on valuable knowledge enterprises are able to sustain and enhance their competitive advantage.

In China's upcoming knowledge economy, knowledge also gains currency as a critical resource. As more sophisticated goods and services are produced in China by Western enterprises,[9] valuable knowledge is increasingly transferred to China. Protecting this valuable knowledge from leaking to infringers within the Chinese business environment is crucial for maintaining the foreign enterprise's competitive advantage.

Not only protecting an enterprise's knowledge but enriching the enterprise's knowledge base with the personal knowledge of Chinese employees has become an inevitable component for being competitive in the Chinese market. The focus of FIEs in the last two decades has shifted from a focus on exporting goods to serving the huge interior market. Goods and services now have to be tailored or adapted to the Chinese market.[10] This entails engaging even deeper in the highly competitive business environment in which localization should take place.[11] Chinese employees' knowledge of the Chinese market appears to be crucial in supporting the FIEs in this endeavor and enhancing a foreign enterprise's competitive advantage. Being familiar with the cultural and political particularities, their important bridging role between FIEs and the Chinese business environment is increasingly acknowledged in the literature.[12] Foreign expatriates can hardly fulfill this task in the same manner in an environment which they perceive as truly obscure.[13] Making use of Chinese employees' knowledge in the increasingly competitive Chinese market thus ranks high on the agenda of foreign enterprises.

Yet accessing the personal knowledge of local employees proves difficult as well. A tendency to hoard information and a reluctance to share knowledge with

---

9 *Economist* 2012, European Union Chamber of Commerce in China 2012: 7, Naughton 2007: 403-418.

10 Mayer-Kuckuk 2010.

11 US-China Business Council 2011: 8, Wexler 2011.

12 *Shanghai Daily* 2012a, Ordish and Adcock 2008: 156, Cucco 2008, Zhang Xueyuan and Reinmoeller 2007: 56-59, Breznitz and Murphree 2011: 47, Li Cheng 2000: 105, Yang Keming 2007: 203, Zhang Wenxian et al. 2010, Buckley et al. 2010: 185.

13 Tse (2010: 159) argues that China will remain an intransparent place to operate in for many years to come.

fellow employees is observed among Chinese employees,[14] allegedly holding a "knowledge is power" [15] attitude. This additional knowledge of Chinese employees can thus not easily be made available for business purposes, causing a significant loss of profit.

Despite such severe knowledge-related hazards to maintaining and enhancing competitiveness, foreign businesses cannot opt for setting the Chinese market aside. For many Western enterprises, most of their sales volume is derived from the rich market opportunities.[16] To be further able to satisfy their economic interests and at the same time secure and enlarge the knowledge base, the question arises of why the handling of valuable knowledge is particularly critical in China and what can be done about it.

Literature aiming at providing explanations and practical advice has flooded bookshelves in recent years. As indicated by the titles exemplary cited above, explanations are sought in the realm of "Chinese culture". Both the intellectual property and the knowledge sharing literature see a collectivist attitude at the roots of the controversial handling of knowledge. This collectivist attitude allegedly provokes the sharing or disclosing of knowledge in the interest of an arbitrarily defined "in-group" rather than in in the interest of one's enterprise.

Within the intellectual property literature on China, Chinese people are said to be collectivist in character and hence, put the benefit of the group above the individual's benefit. Similarly, knowledge, ideas and know-how are not viewed as the property of the individual but rather the property of the group.[17] It is therefore often assumed that the Chinese way of thinking does not support the profound implementation of intellectual property laws, which ascribes the property of knowledge to an individual entity. Both Western[18] and Chinese[19] scholars attribute this to Chinese philosophy, asserting that the philosophical foundations are not encouraging or even inhibit the development of due respect for intellectual property.

Such claims are often underpinned by Confucius' saying to "transmit rather than create" (述而不作)[20]. This saying is interpreted in a way that Confucius refrained from possessing knowledge or creating knowledge on one's own. It prompts scholars to conclude that intellectual property cannot take hold in China due to a "basic incompatibility between modern Western views of intellectual

14 Michailova and Hutchings 2006, Ramasamy et al. 2006, Huang Qian et al. 2008.
15 Huang Qian et al. 2008, Li Shenxue and Scullion 2006: 80, Frank 2008.
16 See e.g. *Süddeutsche* 2012.
17 Fuchs 2006: 65-67.
18 See e.g. Alford 1995, Lehman 2006, Gisclair 2008.
19 See e.g. Qu Sanqiang 2012, Li Luo 2010, Nie Jianqiang 2006.
20 *Lunyu* VII,1. Brought forward as argument in the intellectual property debate e.g. by Alford 1995: 9 and 25, Nie Jianqiang 2006: 178, Qu Sanqiang 2012: xlvi.

property and traditional Chinese ethical and social thought"[21] and because "the idea of intellectual property is absolutely counterintuitive to Chinese"[22]. Such kinds of statements have led to the widespread impression in the West that the notion of knowledge being legally ascribed to an entity is alien to Chinese people.

For the hoarding of knowledge, collectivism also appears to be used as a popular explanation. In many business management studies on knowledge sharing in China, culture is operationalized with Hofstede's popular individualism/collectivism dimension. While collectivism is found to lead to intensive knowledge sharing among "in-group" members, high barriers for knowledge transfer beyond the "in-group" exist.[23] "Chinese culture" in the form of a collectivist orientation is thus supposed to trigger the sharing of knowledge in the "in-group's" interest rather than in the interest of the enterprise.

The controversial handling of knowledge has become received wisdom through guidebooks and articles on the topic.[24] With statements like "the Chinese are quite unique in their attitude toward knowledge transfer and the disclosure of information"[25] Chinese people are described as a seemingly homogenous collective, which can clearly be distinguished from other nations. As the infringement or hoarding of valuable knowledge is a frequent issue in China, such catchy explanations seem intuitive.

This assumed collectivist attitude also carries a nationalist connotation. Trade secrets leakage and economic espionage by Chinese people are often assumed to be motivated by a nationalist Chinese culture. The whole Chinese nation is often perceived as forming a collective within which valuable knowledge is easily disclosed. Fostered by rampant newspaper articles and reports on economic espionage, this picture is all too often in the heads of foreign employees. In Germany, for instance, a general suspicion directed toward Chinese people was raised by the German high-circulation weekly news magazine *Der Spiegel* with an edition titled "Gelbe Spione"[26] [Yellow Spys]. By using the word "yellow" the title alone generally suspects Chinese people of spying. The word "yellow" also reminds of the picture of the "The Yellow Peril" from more than a hundred years ago and hence creates an image of "the Chinese" whose alleged inclination to harm Western interests is deeply rooted in the past.

---

21 Lehman 2006: 1.
22 Li Luo 2010: 277. See also Shao Ke 2006.
23 See e.g. Wilkesmann et al. 2008, Shin et al. 2007, Michailova and Hutchings 2006.
24 See e.g. Fuchs 2006, Frank 2008.
25 Ramasamy et al. 2006: 131.
26 *Der Spiegel* 2007.

These essentialized cultural attributes offer convenient explanations for the handling of valuable knowledge. Being supposedly deeply rooted at a Chinese national level, these cultural attributes manifest the impression of an "inherent Chinese culture". This culture is thought to invoke a handling of valuable knowledge sharply deviating from what is expected by foreign enterprises investing in China. In fact, however, the cultural attributes are hitherto only *ascribed* to causing the controversial behavior observed among Chinese employees. Within all the references to "Chinese culture" in the realm of valuable knowledge in enterprises, it remains unclear whether such conventional cultural attributes *indeed do inform* employees in their daily work.

The drawing on conventional explanations is most severe against the background of daily cooperation of Chinese and foreign employees. Where the handling of valuable knowledge is pictured as being inherently Chinese, foreign employees tend to simply accept that conflicts can hardly be solved. Many of them believe to be unable to impact the allegedly customary, established thinking. Thus, they remain in a state of reluctance or distrust during knowledge interactions. Reluctance and distrust yet are more detrimental to cooperation in China's upcoming knowledge era, where communication is vital in daily work in most positions. Such strong impediments to cooperation quickly lead to the ultimate failure of investments.

It is thus high time to investigate the role culture plays for the handling of valuable knowledge in the practical setting of an enterprise. The criteria which inform Chinese employees in their knowledge interactions might give clues about how knowledge is shared and disclosed. Knowing about those criteria could prevent foreign managers being confronted with the knowledge issues in their enterprises from too quickly resorting to advice such as this one: "this [knowledge] situation does not mean foreign companies should wait for Chinese thinking to change; rather, they should be proactive in learning about Chinese culture and the significance of Confucian doctrine."[27] Before foreign managers swiftly adhere to Confucius' sayings to interprete the daily knowledge conflicts with their Chinese employees, the actual role of culture should well be explored.

1.2 Objectives, Research Questions and Subject Matter

This study's overall objective is to foster an understanding of the role culture plays within knowledge conflicts in China's foreign-invested enterprises (FIE). Conflicts most widely reported by foreign employees working in China are rampant knowledge leakage as well as a reluctance to share knowledge. With these

27 Gisclair 2008: 184.

conflicts as point of departure, the criteria for the setting of knowledge boundaries by Chinese employees are to be identified as well as how these may cause conflicts. These insights should contribute to understanding the actual role of culture in these conflicts and illuminate the (ir)relevance of the all too often superficially consulted "Chinese culture".

The study's ambition is also strongly of a practical nature. By putting emphasis on the Chinese perspective, it is assumed that foreign employees who come to know what in fact informs Chinese employees when drawing the boundaries of knowledge within daily work might be better prepared to encounter knowledge conflicts. Besides understanding the perspective of the "other side", concrete solutions should be provided as well.

In order to achieve these objectives, the largely inductive research process has been guided by the following research questions:

- How do Chinese employees draw the boundaries of valuable knowledge in FIEs?
- How does the boundary drawing cause Sino-German conflicts?
- What role does "Chinese culture" play?
- How can Sino-German knowledge conflicts be solved?

The subject matter of this study is knowledge conflicts in China's FIEs. "Knowledge" refers to valuable knowledge (as opposed to common knowledge) in the business realm, which does not fit into the category of registered intellectual property. This kind of knowledge is valuable considering people's economic interests (either now or potentially value-able in future), yet its boundaries are not legally defined in advance compared to registered intellectual property. Registered intellectual property, such as patents, trademarks, and copyrights, is thus excluded in the present study. Rather, valuable knowledge which could at most be recognized as trade secrets is the object under scrutiny. Even in case of a possible recognition as trade secrets, this officially recognized value of a certain piece of knowledge only becomes clear to actors in retrospect. Only after an infringement has occured, it can be said that a piece of knowledge indeed falls into this category. During the lifetime and use of this valuable knowledge, it remains unclear whether it is legally deemed valuable. With regard to precisely this kind of knowledge boundaries are hard to draw, and it is the employee's crucial task to define these boundaries by himself in daily knowledge interactions.

FIEs in this study exclusively refer to German-invested enterprises in China. German-invested enterprises are to a large extent representative for FIEs in

China in regard to valuable knowledge as is further outlined in the research design and methods section.

1.3 Literature Review and Research Gap

The most obvious literature stream touching upon the intersection of valuable knowledge and culture departs from the angle of intellectual property and Chinese culture. This stream's most prominent work consists of the book "To Steal a Book is an Elegant Offense"[28] by the American legal scholar William Alford. Alford argues that only a weak understanding of intellectual property can be found in China due to Confucianism having invoked a thinking focused on the past. This thinking contradicts the strife for new creations and the ascription of knowledge to an individual. Alford has largely contributed to the widespread impression in the West that intellectual property as a concept is alien to the Chinese people.[29]

Even more vehement than Alford, Lehman[30] argues that in traditional Chinese thinking intellectual property did not exist. Rather, a general belief prevailed that knowledge could not be owned. To profit from producing art and knowledge was immoral and low-class. He even states that intellectual property cannot take hold in China because of a "basic incompatibility between modern Western views of intellectual property and traditional Chinese ethical and social thought"[31]. This is echoed by some Chinese scholars published in English language literature. Qu[32] interprets Confucianism as a philosophical system against individual rights in general and opposed to creativity of individuals in particular. Li[33] even concludes that "the idea of intellectual property is absolutely counterintuitive to Chinese"[34].

This claim is vividly debated in the scholarly world. In response to Alford and his followers, Yu[35] warns that the connection between culture and intellectual property has been "grossly oversimplified"[36]. He alleviates the cultural argument by scrutinizing Chinese philosophical accounts more closely as well as by arguing that Western notions are not that individualist as shown by the develop-

28 Alford 1995.
29 See also Shao Ke 2006.
30 Lehman 2006.
31 Lehman 2006: 1.
32 Qu Sanqiang 2012: xliv-xlvi.
33 Li Luo 2010.
34 Li Luo 2010: 277. See also Shao Ke 2006.
35 Yu Peter K. 2012.
36 Yu Peter K. 2012: 9.

ment of creative commons and open source licenses. Compared to Alford, Ivanhoe[37] provides a more philosophically and historically centered account of why certain aspects of traditional Chinese society and thought have made the development of intellectual property conceptions less likely. Yet he puts his results in perspective by questioning the relevance of Chinese philosophical accounts for past as well as present economical issues.

Other studies put less emphasis on the cultural aspect or even neglect a cultural influence altogether. According to Yang[38], intellectual property issues are not only influenced by cultural aspects rooted in philosophy but also by the political context, the legislative framework, and economic factors. Shi[39] goes further in neglecting the cultural argument as put forward by Alford and instead emphazises the importance of current political and legal institutions. Shao[40] also neglects such cultural factors and points to the fact of explicit economic complications inherent in IP *per se*.

The intense debate on the connection between intellectual property and "Chinese culture" is carried out in the Western hemisphere. Despite intellectual property being a topic widely covered,[41] Chinese academic literature is hardly occupied with the question of an influence of Confucianism on intellectual property in China. The most prominent Chinese legal scholar Zheng Chengsi[42], who is regarded as the ultimate authority on intellectual property in China, was rather occupied with finding traces of an understanding of intellectual property in history instead of explaning possible barriers imposed by traditional culture.

Despite the interesting fact that the debate is limited to Western publications and that even within Western publications various different views on the influence of "Chinese culture" exist, the notion of intellectual property infringements being rooted in a supposedly Chinese Confucianist, Taoist and collectivist society has found its way into guidebooks on intellectual property or business in China.[43] Most widely cited among German language publications is Fuchs'[44] guidebook for instruments and strategies against product piracy in China. It clearly ascribes a collectivist attitude to the property of knowledge. In contrast to the individualist West, Chinese are said to be collectivist in character and supposedly put the benefit of the group above the individual's benefit. According to

37 Ivanhoe 2005.
38 Yang Deli 2003.
39 Shi Wei 2006.
40 Shao Ke 2006.
41 The author's search yielded 25,701 articles in the China Academic Journal Database with "知识产权" [intellectual property] in the title as per Aug 8, 2014.
42 See e.g. Zheng Chengsi and Pendleton 1991, Zheng Chengsi 1987.
43 See e.g. Kotte and Li Wei 2007: 99-100, Witte 2010: 36-37, Thaler 2009: 96-100.
44 Fuchs 2006: 65-67.

Fuchs, intellectual property, meaning knowledge, ideas, and know-how, is traditionally not viewed as individual property but rather as the property of a group.

These guidebooks intend to provide catchy explanations for managers and focus mainly on the interest of Western businesses of having practical advice at hand for preventing intellectual property theft. As intellectual property infringements are particular rampant *in China*, it seems rather intuitive to attribute them to cultural particularities.

In both studies and guidebooks culture is always treated in the sense of an ideological system inherited from the past. Given the strong interest in how Chinese *thinking* differs in regard to intellectual property, it is striking that the thinking itself has not been concentrated on. It has not been scrutinized whether those cultural parameters really inform people. While it might be difficult to scrutinize the thinking of pirates illegally copying patented products, those who in daily business handle valuable knowledge – potentially classified as trade secret – could well be the objects of empirical scrutiny.

Empirical research is yet pursued in another literature stream touching upon the intersection of valuable knowledge and culture. Apart from the realm of intellectual property, "Chinese culture" is also commonly drawn on within the knowledge sharing debate. In business management studies on knowledge sharing in China published in English language journals, culture is seen as national and most often operationalized for Hofstede's "national cultural dimensions"[45] of which the individualism/collectivism dimension is mostly applied by scholars published in English language journals.[46] Michailova and Hutchings[47] found that collectivism leads to intensive knowledge sharing among in-group members. Shin et al.[48] also found that collectivism positively correlates with information sharing within work groups. In their study of knowledge transfer in Hong Kong, Wilkesmann et al.[49] confirm that employees support knowledge transfer within the "in-group" but that simultaneously high barriers for knowledge transfer beyond the group exist. Knowledge sharing with the "outgroup" was also found to

45 Hofstede 1984.

46 Apart from this popular dimension, Wilkesmann et al. (2008) argue that the dimensions "power distance" and "uncertainty avoidance" also inhibit knowledge sharing. Other cultural factors mainly include "face" (面子) with face saving as a barrier to sharing (Huang Qian et al. 2008, Voelpel and Han 2005), whereas face gaining is seen as fostering knowledge sharing (Huang Qian et al. 2008). But see Chow et al.'s study (2000) where nationals of the United States rather than Chinese nationals emphasize a concern for face, which deems "face" as a cultural attribute questionable. These studies thus similarly built on cultural factors typically associated with China.

47 Michailova and Hutchings 2006.

48 Shin et al. 2007.

49 Wilkesmann et al. 2008.

be an obstacle to sharing by Voelpel and Han[50] as well as Chow et al.[51]. All studies conclude that a collectivist orientation, meaning sharing knowledge in the (in-)group's interest rather than according to self-interest, is a decisive factor for knowledge sharing.

However, Michailova and Hutchings[52] also indicate that "Chinese national culture" is becoming more individualist, inducing a more self-centered knowledge sharing behavior. Li and Scullion[53] assert that due to the emergence of "new individualism" and the belief that "knowledge is power", the Chinese tend to hoard knowledge rather than share it in contrast to the pre-reform era. Drawing on several other studies, Ramasamy et al.[54] conclude that a "knowledge hoarding culture" is the largest obstacle to knowledge sharing. Similarly, Huang et al.[55] found the loss of knowledge power being an important factor which has a negative effect on the attitude toward knowledge sharing. They suggest that employees have realized that knowledge power is critical and are unwilling to share their experience and core knowledge with others. Where self-interest is concerned, the loss of knowledge power is more important and hence hard to overcome. By providing evidence for Chinese placing self-interest above group-interest, these results at least question the "collectivist culture" brought forward as an explanation for knowledge sharing behavior by previous studies.

Recent empirical studies published in Chinese academic journals shed more light on this ambiguous issue. Most illuminating is Yu's[56] survey with 400 employees from First Automotive Works in Changchun. While the author likewise takes the individualism/collectivism dimension as a starting point, she criticizes the simplistic inferences drawn by previous research (such as by Hofstede and his followers) that Chinese people are collectivist whereas Westerners are individualist. Instead, she found that within a single (national) cultural context, different cultural orientations in regard to individualism and collectivism exist simultaneously. She does not equate individualist cultural orientation with self-centeredness (as suggested by previous English studies) but sees the individually oriented person as socially embedded in relationships.

This individualist or collectivist orientation is not intrinsically personal as Zhang's[57] survey with 317 employees in enterprises in Guangdong shows. He found that perceived organizational support enhances trust and pride in the or-

50 Voelpel and Han 2005.
51 Chow et al. 2000.
52 Michailova and Hutchings 2006: 399.
53 Li Shenxue and Scullion 2006.
54 Ramasamy et al. 2006: 133.
55 Huang Qian et al. 2008.
56 Yu Mi 2011.
57 Zhang Chunhu 2013.

ganization and also exerts an indirect positive influence on knowledge sharing behavior. More specifically, Liu and Fu[58] acknowledge the important role of the superior in creating an autonomous working atmosphere necessary for knowledge sharing. Their survey with 267 employees and 96 superiors in enterprises in Guangdong revealed that empowerment of employees by the superior can increase the level of knowledge sharing.

Relationships are also seen as playing a role. Yin et al.'s[59] survey, with 389 employees in mainly small and medium sized enterprises in Zhejiang Province, found that the closer and more trustful the relationship (关系) between the knowledge sharer and the knowledge receiver, the stronger the willingness to share and the better the quality of knowledge sharing. Li and Wang's[60] survey with 540 employees in Tianjin pursuing research and development found that "guanxi trust" (关系信任) – a special form of trust which is established in the family – has a positive influence on the motivation for knowledge sharing.

Like the Western studies, Chinese studies also consider their results to be culturally specific and not easily applicable to Western contexts.[61] Both consider a specific local Chinese culture as having explanatory power regarding the differences in Chinese and Western knowledge sharing behavior – yet in a different way. Whereas English language studies tend toward a dichotomic usage of the individualism/collectivism dimension at the national level, Chinese language studies indicate that Chinese culture influences knowledge sharing in a more complex way then the typical cultural dimension suggest. Not only discovering both orientations in a single national context and even in a single enterprise, they also do not regard individualist oriented person necessarily as selfish but as embedded in social relations. Unlike Western studies, they focus on more than one factor influencing knowledge sharing such as organizations, superiors, and social relations. Apparently, similar to the field of intellectual property, the spheres of

58 Liu Chao and Fu Jinmei 2012.
59 Yin Hongjuan et al. 2011.
60 Li Wenzhong and Wang Liyan 2013.
61 Yu Mi (2011: 149) asserts that her study's findings result from localized research and are not applicable for Westerners. Zhang Chunhu (2013: 64) notes that his study's results are to be seen against the Chinese cultural background. Liu Chao and Fu Jinmei (2012: 189) point out that whereas loyalty and commitment to the organization are excessively in the focus of Western scholars, loyalty to the superior is of special importance in the Chinese social and cultural context. Yin Hongjuan et al. (2011: 178) use Confucian culture as vantage point in their study on *guanxi*. Further, the authors often put the term *guanxi* in their study in quotation marks, signifying that the term is not used in its general meaning as "relationship" but has been ascribed to a special meaning in the Chinese context. Li Wenzhong and Wang Liyan (2013: 102) refer to the theories of Chinese sociologists as they see a distinct difference between Chinese and Western culture. Chinese people are to a strong degree influenced by *guanxi*, which has a special localized meaning.

English language and Chinese language literature provide a different picture. Pursuing more thorough research is therefore promising.

Most consequential is the opposed normative usage of cultural explanations. Whereas Chinese studies rather view culture as an *enabler* or vehicle of knowledge sharing, English studies often explicitly[62] or implicitly[63] see cultural specificities as *barriers* or obstacles to sharing knowledge. This picture in the West of a normatively inhibiting culture, drawn by scholarly and popular literature in the realm of intellectual property, is thus empirically sustained by Western knowledge sharing studies. This gives more rise to catchy cultural explanations for obstacles with regard to the valuable knowledge of China's FIEs.

Yet the knowledge sharing studies only deductively depart from common cultural parameters. Following the procedure typical for management research in general, these empirical studies all adhere – without saying – to a positivist deductive paradigm. The more handy and streamlined results stemming from positivist research rather enable researchers to quickly derive practical managerial implications.[64] Similarly, the studies cited above do not endeavor to *inductively* elaborate on the perspective of Chinese employees. They neither leave room for alternative roles of culture to emerge nor show how this more empirically grounded reality indeed leads to conflicts with Western managers.

Not only has the perspective of Chinese employees on the handling of valuable knowledge only been superficially investigated, the protagonists themselves scarcely appear in the scholarly world. Most scrutinized in existing accounts on work of the reform era is the group of – mostly female – migrant factory workers. Among the issues addressed are risks and opportunities of a deregulated labor market and the strife for upward social mobility,[65] the continued role of state and party in regulating daily life and the new required flexibility in the household for fulfilling work demands,[66] as well as oppressive working conditions and employer's control extending to private lives.[67] Proliferating accounts on trade unions and worker's representation account for changing labor relations in China.[68] Apart from factory workers, migrants work in various segments of the service industry, such as a restaurant,[69] a karaoke bar,[70] a department store,[71]

62 Li-Hua and Peng Jian 2007: 147, Ramasamy et al. 2006, Burrows et al. 2005: 76, Voelpel and Han 2005: 53.

63 Wilkesmann et al. 2008, Huang Qian et al. 2008, Shin et al. 2007.

64 Eriksson and Kovalainen 2008: 17-19.

65 See e.g. Tomba 2011, Chang Leslie T. 2009.

66 See e.g. Xu Feng 2000, Fan C. Cindy 2009.

67 See e.g. Pun Ngai 2005, Pun Ngai and Li Wanwei 2008, Chan Anita 2001.

68 See e.g. Oakley 2002, Chan Anita 2001, Chan Chris King-Chi 2010, Lee Lai To 1986, Lee Ching Kwan 2007a.

69 Griffiths 2010, Hsu Carolyn L. 2005.

domestic work,[72] with gender- and other identity-related aspects being the primary issues of interest. The working conditions of workers in constructions are also covered in terms of the temporariness of their work.[73]

Similarly, workers of (former) state-owned enterprises (SOE) are often scrutinized in terms of working conditions and their consequences for daily life. Among the topics covered are workers staging protests against the nonpayment of wages and pensions,[74] pressure and bureaucratic control,[75] the losing of positional and institutional advantage and redefining of positions in relation to work itself,[76] the continuing role of the work unit in producing and maintaining inequality[77] as well as the fate of losing connection to the former work unit.[78]

This exemplary account of the groups being the major objects of interest clearly shows that what has been researched to date often surrounds weak and underpriviledged occupational groups. In contrast, empirical literature on employees who can be referred to as white collar workers, professionals or managers is scarce. An exception is Michelson[79] who scrutinizes gender inequality and the strife for justice among Chinese lawyers. Further, Chan's[80] ethnographic investigation of foreign and Chinese life insurance companies in Shanghai reveals that the institutional dilemmas of commercial life insurance necessitate ideological work by sales agents. Also, Peng's[81] study shows that counterproductive work behavior is induced by personality variables rather than demographic variables.

The two remaining studies are more similar to this study's endeavor. Ross[82] scrutinizes skilled Chinese employees and their managers in FIEs in the information technology services and manufacturing sector in Shanghai and the Yangtze Delta. He found that foreign managers largely attribute frictions at the workplace to the "cultural burden" of mainland Chinese, whereas Chinese employees find it easier to distinguish between frictions caused by the cultural otherness of their managers and frictions caused by contradictory demands.

70 Zheng Tiantian 2007 and 2009.
71 Hanser 2006.
72 Yan Hairong 2009.
73 See e.g. Lei Guang 2007, Swider 2011.
74 Lee Ching Kwan 2007a and 2007b.
75 Junghans 2006.
76 Tomba 2011, Liu Siân Victoria 2007.
77 Xie Yu et al. 2009.
78 Solinger 2009.
79 Michelson 2007 and 2009.
80 Chan Cheris Shun-ching 2007.
81 Peng He 2012.
82 Ross 2007.

Kessler's[83] study on management strategies draws on a hundred qualitative interviews of engineers, entrepreneurs, and government officials of foreign and Chinese enterprises in the information industry of Taipei, Beijing and Shanghai. It is shown that engineers who change employers to obtain salary increases are less likely to develop long-term commitment. Foreign managers do not blame their own wage policies but attribute the turnover to a lack of loyalty of Chinese engineers. They also believe that the nationalism of Chinese engineers contributes to the theft of sensitive technologies. Chinese engineers, however, prove to have relatively few ties to the propaganda but are driven by rational economic decisions. Still, foreign managers adopt measures to protect the enterprise from theft of sensitive technologies including the restriction of an engineer's opportunities within an enterprise. This leads to an even stronger desire to leave the enterprise. The last two studies both point to cultural as well as knowledge conflicts arising from a more intense cooperation at a higher level in foreign-invested enterprises in China in an advanced stage of economic reform.

Apparently, only specific groups of workers are covered to date. Migrant workers, factory workers, (former) SOE workers as well as (urban) service workers are widely scrutinized. As the most palpable groups in terms of workplace changes resulting from economic reform, they have triggered more scholarly (and funding institutions') interest. By contrast, employees in upper white collar and management positions have not been explored to a large extent, neither in foreign nor in Chinese enterprises. Hence, there is not much information on them available which could help to explain why they handle valuable knowledge the way they do. Thanks to widespread publications in the West, such as those of Pun Ngai,[84] one knows about the perspective of Chinese female migrant workers, but those cannot be deemed valid for all kinds of workers in China. After all, upper white collar workers and managers are also exposed to the changing environment of economic reform as indicated by the few existing studies.

In general, such workers can be found to be covered by the conceptual literature on knowledge work. This literature stream mainly focuses on an economic or business angle. This is not surprising considering that the concept of the knowledge worker has been coined by economic and business interests. The Austrian-American economist Fritz Machlup, who observed this development in American society in the mid-20th century,[85] introduced the concept of knowledge work – albeit without specifically using the term knowledge worker – into the discipline of economics.[86] Promoting the idea that knowledge was a major item of production

83 Kessler 2007.
84 Pun Ngai 2005, Pun Ngai and Li Wanwei 2008.
85 Pyöriä 2005: 116.
86 Machlup 1962, Joseph 2005: 249.

within the U.S. economy,[87] he determined its value for national accounting. He argued that although knowledge has always played a part in economic analysis, it was – with the exemption of the theory of patent protection – long treated as an exogenous variable. Instead, he advocated treating knowledge as an endogenous variable for measuring and projecting economic growth. While admitting that the idea already originated with Adam Smith and was also emphasized by Friedrich List, Machlup pointed out that the significance of these ideas in his time lies in the strong interest in the analysis of economic growth and development.[88]

For this purpose, Machlup began identifying knowledge workers,[89] drawing attention to "all the *'transmitters'* of knowledge in the economy"[90] who "will eventually come into the focus of our analysis of the production and distribution of knowledge"[91]. Apart from the growing workforce in both politics and business management, Machlup included "the so-called nonproductive workers" in many industries, being those "who shuffle papers and give signals, who see to it that others 'know' what to do"[92]. That the idea of considering those workers indirectly occupied with production was new at the time is further underscored by Machlup's concern that the inclusion of "this sort of 'knowledge production' may look strange to most readers at first blush".[93] Hence, he established a broad inclusive concept of knowledge workers.

In the sociological realm, the concept was criticized as being too broad. Within his formative work "The Coming of Post-Industrial Society" the American sociologist Daniel Bell[94] forecasted the change in the social framework of Western society. In the post-industrial society, he saw the professional and technical class emerging as the predominant group. Referring to engineers and scientists as well as to what he defined as skilled population,[95] he defined knowledge workers more narrowly than Machlup did. This rather narrow understanding has become the one which is rather accepted nowadays.

Apart from economics and sociology, the concept also entered the field of business management. Basically at the same time with Machlup, the Austrian-American management scholar Peter F. Drucker coined the term for business managers. He devoted several books to this concept and strongly contributed to

87 See also Cortada 1998a: xvi.
88 Machlup 1962: 3-5.
89 Cortada 1998a: xvi.
90 Machlup 1962: 7 [emphasis added].
91 Machlup 1962: 7.
92 Machlup 1962: 6.
93 Machlup 1962: 6.
94 Bell 1974.
95 Bell 1974: 212-265.

its popularization.[96] His point of reference is Frederick Taylor's "scientific management" in the 20th century, which "made the manual worker productive"[97]. Taylor concentrated on the task of each worker and focused on each motion which constituted the task. By applying this knowledge to industrial work, Taylor for the first time organized the so far simple, unskilled, and repetitive motions.[98] Whereas Taylor focused on making manual work productive during his time, the "central challenge" for Drucker was to "make knowledge workers productive"[99]. In terms of contribution of management, Drucker asserted that in the 20th century the increase of manual worker's productivity was the most important contribution of management, whereas he forecasted for the 21st century that the knowledge worker would be most significant.[100] Hitherto, the knowledge worker has been investigated overwhelmingly in the realm of business management,[101] with the vast majority of scholars elaborating on the concept of knowledge work or using it in empirical research building on or referring to Drucker's works.

After literature on the subject increased substantially in the 1980s and 1990s,[102] a significant contribution in the United States of the 21th century was made by the American business and knowledge management scholar Tom Davenport. Similar to Drucker who aimed at finding ways of increasing the knowledge worker's productivity, he is concerned with the issue of how to improve his performance.[103] Although Davenport believes that his book at the time of writing was "by far the broadest, most comprehensive collection of knowledge on the topic of knowledge work and its improvement", he considers it – just as Drucker regarding his book in 1969 –[104] as "just scratching the surface"[105] of this broad topic. Apparently, even in the American context, where the concept was first developed, it is acknowledged that the knowledge worker is not yet sufficiently understood.

In Europe, while the knowledge economy has also been under way in recent decades, the knowledge worker has only recently been markedly considered. In

---

96 Joseph (2005: 247-248) argues that Drucker considered the term knowledge worker unknown until he coined it in his book in 1959 (Drucker 1959), which is in line with the author's observation that the concept is commonly attributed to Drucker within the literature. However, Cortada's (1998b: 14) observation that the concept originated with Machlup at least as much as with Drucker, who just stronger popularized the term, is more convincing.

97 Drucker 1990: 136.

98 Drucker 1990: 135-141.

99 Drucker 1990: 141.

100 Drucker 1990: 135 and 157.

101 Joseph 2005: 246.

102 Cortada 1998b: 17.

103 Davenport 2005.

104 Drucker 1969: 357.

105 Davenport 2005: 10.

the late 1990s, the German scholar Helmut Willke[106] referred to knowledge work (*Wissensarbeit*) in his "systemic knowledge management" as the interplay of personal and organizational knowledge, with the aim of transferring personal knowledge to the organizational level. Klaus North's book from 1998[107], coming strongly from the organizational angle, advocates the traditional view that the knowledge of an organization is in the head of the knowledge carrier (here the knowledge worker), and the organization is concerned how to add it to the organizational knowledge base.[108] Together with Stefan Güldenberg, North in their book from 2008[109] gives suggestions for the knowledge worker himself on how to design his own knowledge work or how to cope with knowledge work within the organization, as well as its implementation, for instance with self-management or intelligent use of communication media. They offer practical strategies, methods and tools for designing human and productive knowledge work, such as coping with information overload, support of information and communication technology. They also build on Drucker – for example on his six factors of enhancing the knowledge worker's productivity.[110] Other recent works originating in Europe mostly tackle the use of information technologies, education and the non-routine nature of work,[111] or analyze knowledge in a work and an organizational context.[112] It becomes apparent that in works originating in the United States and in Europe, concerning both the manager's and the knowledge worker's perspective, most of this interest is triggered by the desire to manage the knowledge worker on the part of the organization and to make him more effective. This is a logical consequence attributed to the growing consciousness in the West regarding the importance of knowledge and people for a competitive advantage in the 21st century.

In China, the concept of the knowledge worker likewise exists. Interest in the knowledge worker almost dates back to the introduction of reform and opening up, as the first academic article in Chinese language was published in 1981.[113] To date, more than 1,100 articles exist on the topic.[114] An exemplary

106 Willke 2001 (2nd edition of the 1998 publication).
107 North 2011 (5th edition of the 1998 publication).
108 North 2011: 121-172.
109 North and Güldenberg 2008.
110 North and Güldenberg 2008: 135-140.
111 Pyöriä 2005.
112 Alvesson 2004.
113 Yang Wanchun 1981.
114 The author's search on July 6, 2012, with the search function in the China Academic Journal Database yielded 1,110 articles. The search was pursued with the parameter "precise" and required the keyword "知识工作者" [knowledge worker] being at least in the body text of the document.

analysis of the first article of 1981, two recent articles of 2012 which both employed 知识工作者 [knowledge worker] in their title, and one article of 1996 as being in the middle of this time span, revealed that all authors build on Peter F. Drucker, and are likewise concerned with the question of how to enhance the productivity of knowledge workers,[115] how to make them more effective[116], as well as how to make them voluntarily participate in management issues.[117] In a similar vein, academic books in Chinese language – for instance published by Qinghua University – mention the knowledge worker from a management angle briefly on two pages.[118] This shows that the concept of the knowledge worker, which originates in the West, has already been introduced to China, yet neither with a significant adaption or amendment nor has it been tried to empirically understand his work. The (cultural) sociological understanding of the knowledge worker from his own point of view instead of from the angle of his economic effectiveness is still open to investigation.

The synthesizing of the above literature streams reveals a research gap in form of an alternative perspective to be gained by applying an inductive method to an under-researched group. The perspective shows whether the cultural attributes ascribed indeed inform the Chinese employees' handling of valuable knowledge. Culture is hitherto treated as a given entity or an ideological construct and is largely imposed on certain phenomena without yielding significant explanatory benefit. Eventually, it is still impossible to determine whether the said culture is indeed relevant for an employee in his daily knowledge work or what cultural knowledge alternatively informs his behavior. An inductive approach to finding the relevant cultures emerging from a Chinese point of view is still missing.

The practice of ascribing common cultural attributes is even more severe as there is another gap concerning the (sociological) understanding of the people these cultural attributes are ascribed to. Research agendas, to date, are largely determined by an interest in the underprivileged groups. If anything, the (non-manual) employees are researched and conceptualized as knowledge workers from an economic or business angle without applying a thorough (cultural) sociological perspective. Approaching the question of controversial handling of knowledge in China's foreign enterprises in a very different way potentially yields much deeper insights compared to those existing to date. These new insights might challenge the conventional mainstream thinking about the nexus of the handling of valuable knowledge and Chinese culture.

115 Wang Lijun 1996.
116 Zhu Bo 2012, Yang Wanchun 1981.
117 Du Jingjing and Tang Youjun 2012.
118 Liu Jisheng 2003: 104-105, Zhang De 2001: 393-394, Chan Jiankun and Li Shichun 2006: 40-41.

1.4 Disciplines and Fields

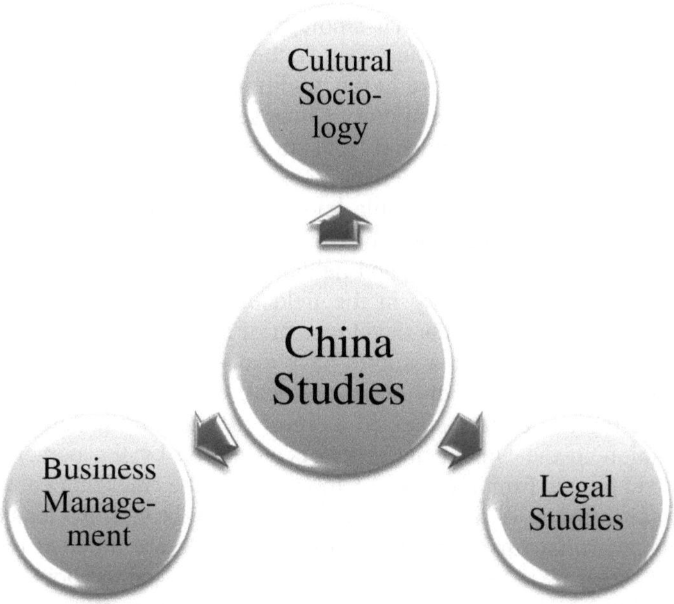

Figure 1: Disciplines and fields of the present study.

Source: Author's own illustration.

The present study examines this topic through a multidisciplinary lens with the field of *China studies*[119] taking center stage (see Figure 1). The research interest precisely surrounds the China-related question of why the handling of knowledge is that controversial *in China,* and what is specifically "Chinese" about this phenomenon. In light of this research interest, the anchoring in this field suggests itself at first glance, yet should be strongly emphasized in two regards.

First, China studies constituting the main field should be emphasized against the background of existing studies on the topic. Studies on the topic of valuable knowledge in China are mainly anchored in the field of business management[120] or the discipline of legal studies[121] using China as a specific envi-

---

119 China studies (commonly also referred to as "Chinese Studies") here refer to social science research on China's contemporary politics, economy and society.

120 See e.g. Yang Deli 2003, Lehman 2006.

ronment for enhancing the knowledge stock of their particular field or discipline. To employ a China focus, such studies often draw pragmatically on cultural specificities derived from traditional sinology. Traditional sinology, however, embraces a philological and historical focus rather than a social sciences research perspective.[122] Referring to culture in this traditional sense without examining it within the social reality of contemporary China serves the often more pragmatic interests of business management and legal studies. This procedure has arguably led to culture as a convenient explanation for differences between Chinese and Western people's handling of valuable knowledge. Against this background, a stronger emphasis is put on the field of China studies beyond being an umbrella term connecting various disciplines and fields.

Second, anchoring the study in the field of China studies is emphasized against the broader context of the development of area studies in general, where China studies form part of. Area studies have evolved in the 20th century by the perceived need of knowing more about political, economic and social circumstances of the regions being perceived as most *different* from the West.[123] The field's evolution in the United States has been driven by the perceived direct challenges and threats from the Soviet Union, China, the emerging cold war, and the decolonialization in Africa and Asia.[124] If looking through the lens of studying such an unfamiliar or even volatile region, people are inclined to look for differences to their own national context. This strife has led to adopting a thinking of monolithic "cultural containers"[125] easily serving the interests behind this research. Even though area studies over the last decades have emancipated themselves to a visible extent from the "national interest" of the country in which they receive their funding,[126] economic interests in the course of China's opening up followed suit and renewed the search for handy cultural explanations. Hence, research agendas on China are often still shaped by the point of departure from China as the "cultural other". This is especially true for the phenomenon under investigation, where the narrative of a unitary culture diametrically opposed to that of the West with a deeply rooted alien attitude to intellectual property and other valuable knowledge prevails.

This study shares the basic assumption that this phenomenon is specific to China. Yet it does not jump on the bandwagon of China as a homogeneous cultural entity. Rather, following Szanton's[127] understanding of area studies, seeking

122 Scharping 2003.

123 The "West" here refers to the United States where this field originates and some Western European countries who have adopted it some decades later.

124 Szanton 2004.

125 Beck 1998: 13-14.

126 Szanton 2004.

127 Szanton 2004.

to understand a certain area is considered an "act of translation"[128] or the attempt to "make the assumptions, meaning, structures and dynamics of another society and culture comprehensible to an outsider"[129]. This attempt calls for focusing on the very essence of China studies: studying China from the inside under the constant assumption that the context – historical as well as current – strongly matters.

Embracing China studies in this sense prompts considerations such as the following: Which part of Chinese society is concerned when regarding a particular phenomenon? What are the multiple and changing contexts within China a certain group is embedded in? Are the political, societal, or economic contexts all equally concerned? To which extents and in what ways are these relevant? How does the phenomenon look like from a Chinese perspective? All this has to be translated for "outsiders", while constantly being aware of what might be lost in translation. This is considered the intrinsic value of China studies and should be more emphasized than it has been the case hitherto in studies covering the topic of valuable knowledge in China.

It is further drawn on the discipline of *cultural sociology* which provides the theoretical perspective fundamental to this study. This perspective paves the way for focusing on the contextualized cultural analysis of the phenomenon in question rather than reducing culture to abstract descriptions of reified values, norms, or ideologies. In that it differs from the sub-discipline of "sociology of culture". As a sub-discipline of sociology, the subject matter of "sociology of culture" is "culture" in the form of coherent and generalized systems of symbols and meanings, explained by the hard facts of social structure. By contrast, "cultural sociology" itself is a sociological perspective which scrutinizes the cultural aspects of social phenomena.[130] Culture within cultural sociology is seen a resource which provides orientation and help for solving daily problems in certain surroundings.[131] In this study, the controversial handling of knowledge in China's FIEs is regarded as a social phenomenon for which culture is a resource informing actions.

The discipline of *legal studies* serves to analyze how valuable knowledge is dealt with in China. Chinese judicial and administrative practice shows which conflicts surrounding the handling of valuable knowledge currently arise among Chinese businesses and between them and their employees as well as between Chinese and foreign businesses. This provides insights into how boundaries of valuable knowledge are currently set in the Chinese business environment.

128 Szanton 2004: 1.
129 Szanton 2004: 1.
130 Halas 2010, Eberle 2011.
131 Alexander 2003: 12.

The field of *business management* provides the concepts which are needed for an analysis of the handling of valuable knowledge in a business setting. Conceptualizing Chinese employees as knowledge workers most adequately illuminates the role of (non-manual) Chinese employees in FIEs in China. Concepts of knowledge as the object of interest show the ambiguous nature of knowledge. Not least, for fulfilling the study's practical objective, the findings are transferred back into business practice in a transdisciplinary manner. Setting itself apart from many business management studies which refer to the "mysteries of Chinese culture"[132], the present study enhances the field of business management on China in a more comprehensive way.

1.5 Structure and Sources

This book is organized into ten chapters. The present first chapter introduces the study by pointing out the rationale for it, its objectives, the relevant literature streams as well as the disciplines and fields concerned. Furthermore, with the present sub-chapter it clarifies how the study is structured and which sources has been used for each of the following chapters.

Chapter two lays out the study's conceptual framework. It draws on conceptual literature from the field of business management as well as theoretical literature from the discipline of cultural sociology. Concepts and theories have largely been borrowed from English language literature (with authors largely coming from the United States and Europe), after ensuring that the existing Chinese sources reflect Western literature and take the same perspective. Concepts and theories are operationalized for analyzing the role culture plays for knowledge conflicts in China's FIEs. This conceptual framework informs all following chapters.

The third chapter is devoted to the research design and methods used during the investigation. It takes on a philosophical and methodological perspective and clarifies the sample, the data collection and analysis process. The validity, reliability, objectivity, as well as the generalizability of data is commented on in this part of the study as well. Finally, the investigation is briefly contextualized into the broader Chinese economic, political and legal environment. This environment is constituent to the investigation as a whole, yet has been extensively covered elsewhere.

The following three chapters specifically focus on the group of people under scrutiny. Chapter four and five consider the Chinese employees in FIEs in their role as intermediaries between the FIE and the business environment. Chap-

132 Goodman 2007: 175.

ter four analyzes the comprador as being the harbinger of Chinese employees in FIEs in contemporary China, while chapter five presents the social and economic contexts of Chinese employees in FIEs. Chinese biographical literature, Chinese statistical sources and Chinese and Western secondary sources are used to show the past and present context of people mediating between foreign businesses and the Chinese business environment.

Chapter six considers the people scrutinized in this study in their role as knowledge workers. Primary statistical data of Chinese official sources are used to estimate the number of knowledge workers in China as well as their contribution to the Chinese economy. Their role in society is analyzed by using Chinese and Western sources on Chinese society.

After having covered the group of interest itself, chapter seven and eight carve out the criteria according to which the boundaries of valuable knowledge are set in China. Chapter seven traces the drawing of property boundaries of valuable knowledge in Chinese philosophy, history and law. It is based on primary literature, such as Confucius' *Lunyu* or Chinese court cases, as well as on secondary literature on Chinese philosophy, history and law from both a Chinese and a Western perspective.

The empirical chapter – chapter eight – takes center stage. It explores in detail the cultural resources informing Chinese employees in their immediate working context. From the empirical qualitative data derived from extensive interviews with Chinese and German employees the implicit criteria and strategies arise which inform the sharing and disclosing of valuable knowledge.

Chapter nine discusses the empirical findings and puts them in a broader context. The tacit rationale underlying all criteria and strategies is discovered and the roots of knowledge conflicts in China's FIEs are discussed. The findings are further embedded in Chinese secondary literature the relevance of which only emerges from the empirical data and could not have anticipated beforehand. Emanating from the assumption that "Chinese culture" has some explanatory power for the controversial handling of knowledge, the role "Chinese culture" really plays is scrutinized. Limitations are acknowledged in this part of the study as are the methodological and theoretical implications. It is further sketched out how these findings surrounding the role culture actually plays can provide solutions to knowledge conflicts. From the previous investigation, four main conclusions are finally drawn in chapter ten.

2 Conceptual Framework

This chapter carves out and operationalizes the concepts and theories this study is based upon.[133] Chinese employees in the present study are conceptualized as knowledge workers (2.1) rather than as "employees" in order to approach knowledge conflicts from a new angle. While the concept's central concern is to make the knowledge worker more productive,[134] it essentially points to the fact that knowledge is crucial not only to the organization but also to the knowledge worker himself. Applying this concept thus is suitable to draw attention to the issue of knowledge property between the two parties.

As the object of the conflicts in FIEs is valuable knowledge, knowledge itself is conceptualized. Considering that the present study takes place within a business environment, knowledge is conceptualized from a business management angle (2.2). In order to understand the role culture actually plays when drawing the boundaries of knowledge, this study's understanding of culture is further illuminated (2.3). Finally, the concepts and theories are integrated and applied to the present study (2.4).

2.1 Knowledge Worker

Knowledge workers are mostly defined by activity.[135] In terms of activity, they can be differentiated from manual workers. Although activities of knowledge

---

133 Note that concepts and theories implicitly reflect the environment and circumstances in which they have been coined. The concepts and theories used currently do not have a specific Chinese counterpart. The existing concepts and theories of Western (North American and European) origin are found suitable. Yet their application to China is not regarded critical as the concepts and theories are in essence relatively open, being comparatively less anchored in the context they have been created in and not severely loaded with contextual assumptions. For an example for a theory being strongly anchored in the context in which it has been created see e.g. Tsui (2012: 41) who regards agency theory as being based on strong assumptions about American culture. In contrast, the latitude of the knowledge worker rather than pursuing specific tasks is one of the concept's constituting elements. The concept of knowledge is rather abstract than specific by nature and so are the theories relating to culture which are inherently open for cultural differences.

134 See chapter 1.3.

135 In line with Pernicka et al. (2010) and Pyöriä (2005), the author observed that no matter which context or discipline, no straight-forward or unitary definition of the knowledge worker exists

and manual workers often overlap, knowledge workers can be characterized by predominantly being concerned with knowledge.[136] This is observable by activities such as negotiating, making phone calls, taking notes or calculating.[137] The common thread in most of the scholarly definitions analyzing activity and what takes the most part of the knowledge worker's daily working time is *communication*.[138] This thread is also taken up by the present study.

The most striking feature of the knowledge worker in contrast to the manual worker is his *latitude* in determining his tasks and pursuing his work. Tasks are inherently emerging and situations are rather unique, novel, rare, and complex. Only the knowledge worker himself[139] is able to define what the task is or should be, determine the processes he follows to fulfill the task, and specify the outputs of his work. He thus needs to be able to work autonomously with only scarce interference by his superiors.[140] This entails that a knowledge worker may know the details of his or her area much better than their superior or their employer.[141]

For autonomously determining and pursuing their work, knowledge workers first and foremost need information. They have to define their individual information need and pursue their own information management. With the growing variety of products and services, more and more information have to be gained externally. Especially if a tailor-made and complex product is to be produced, communication and interaction with the customer is becoming ever more necessary.[142] These developments make gathering information increasingly challenging.

In contrast to the manual worker, who, of course, also needs knowledge for pursuing his work, knowledge has a distinct significance to the knowledge worker. Knowledge is both input and output of his work. Knowledge as input constitutes his means of production and enables him to perform. Not only is certain knowledge required before being able to start work, additional knowledge has to

---

to date. The concept apparently doesn't fit into a strict and closed definition or categorization. Indeed, it is particularly this indefiniteness which allows for condensing and highlighting existing ideas for particular research purpose as it is done here.

136 North and Güldenberg 2008: 22, Davenport 2005: 10, Machlup 1962: 326.

137 Machlup 1962: 41.

138 Machlup 1962: 326, North and Güldenberg 2008: 22, Davenport 2005: 10-11, Willke 2001: 21.

139 The study refers to both male and female knowledge workers. For the purpose of standardization, the male form is generally used for the first person singular.

140 Davenport 2005: 12-17, North and Güldenberg 2008: 27-30, Alvesson 2004: 1 and 23, Drucker 1999: 142-146.

141 Davenport 2005: 1-4 and 20-21, Drucker 1990: 217, Alvesson 2004: 23.

142 North and Güldenberg 2008: 72, Drucker 1999: 123-125 and 130-132, Adams and Oleksak 2010: 35, Alvesson 2004: 24-25.

be permanently acquired and updated in rapidly changing business environments.[143]

Knowledge has also a distinct significance as output. How the output is evaluated determines the knowledge worker's future career. But the crux is that this output is hardly visible or measurable. Knowledge is produced through communication, and its quality is more important than quantitative concerns. The quality of knowledge can only be measured in a subjective way based on the judgments of persons directly engaged with it, that is, rather by the knowledge worker himself than by his superior.[144]

The relationship to the organization is another important point of differentiation from manual workers. The traditional understanding of the relationship between an employee and an organization is a simple vertical one, being strongly informed by hierarchy as expressed by the organization chart. This relationship is generally referred to as employer-employee relationship.[145] This expression strongly relates to the legal agreement between both sides, where their rights and duties are described which can be enforced with the relevant laws. Although still in use, this employer-employee concept rather suits the context of mass production where it has originally been coined.[146]

Knowledge work makes an organizational hierarchical structure flexible. It is the task rather than the organization chart or work descriptions that decide which person is in charge, for which period, and for which purpose. Organization structures suitable for knowledge work are informed both by the necessity of command as well as *the logic of the situation.*[147] The organization alone thus cannot determine work structures in a uni-directional way.

A relationship to the organization which is of horizontal rather than vertical nature seems adequate considering that the knowledge worker is an *asset* for the

143 Scholars disagree on the amount of knowledge required beforehand. For Davenport (2005: 12) education plays a leading role in this regard. Knowledge workers must be highly educated or expert, as it would be difficult to perform without a college degree. Drucker (1990: 141 and 146-154) goes even further by stating that the knowledge *required* for a certain job eventually determines whether a job qualifies as knowledge work. For instance, a surgeon although doing mostly manual work requires highly advanced and thorough theoretical knowledge. Machlup (1962: 326) disagrees with the importance Drucker ascribes to the knowledge needed beforehand. Instead, the amount of communication during working life should be the focus of knowledge work (see Joseph 2005: 249). Davenport 2005: 12-13 and 21-22, North and Güldenberg 2008: 71-72, Willke 2001: 21-23.

144 North and Güldenberg 2008: 139, Drucker 1999: 142, Drucker 1969: 269-270, Davenport 2005: 48-49, Alvesson 2004: 23.

145 This is even more pointedly expressed by the German "Arbeitgeber/Arbeitnehmer" (literally "work provider"/"work taker") terminology.

146 North 2011: 121.

147 Drucker 1969: 271, Alvesson 2004: 23.

organization rather than a cost. Costs need to be controlled and reduced, whereas assets need to be developed. This need shifts the knowledge worker in the position to demand not only the securing of his livelihood, but also the organization's contribution to his development.[148] The future development of knowledge workers therefore always plays at least a latent role during their current work, be it with the current or a future organization.

In contrast to traditional means of production, a certain part of knowledge is essentially "owned" by the knowledge worker alone and not by the organization, simply by being in the employee's head.[149] Knowledge workers thus have significant power to decide to which extent they make use of their knowledge for contributing to the organization's success. As knowledge is their competitive advantage on the labor market, it is viewed as highly valuable property and used carefully. It is generally only shared to the extent that the own position is not threatened. One will be reluctant to share it without being assured that one still has a stake in it while using it within the organization.[150]

The "ownership" of knowledge further allows knowledge workers to be mobile. If manual workers have valuable experiences, these are virtually only valuable at the place where they work. Most often, manual workers need the job and the organization much more than the job needs them. In contrast, the own knowledge makes knowledge workers independent from a certain organization.[151] As a result of this potential mobility and a generally good labor market, employers are often more dependent on their (non-manual) employees than vice versa.[152] The relationship between knowledge worker and organization is thus increasingly complex. All these idiosyncratic features complicate the setting of the boundaries of knowledge in an organization.

These features also complicate the identification of the amount of knowledge workers in a certain country. While workers have traditionally been identified by the industries in which they work, knowledge workers do not necessarily work in knowledge-intensive industries only. In fact, many knowledge workers are employed by manufacturing enterprises, where they generally carry out tasks not directly related to the manufacturing activity itself.[153] Instead of industries,

148 Drucker 1969: 135, Drucker 1999: 148 and 163, North and Güldenberg 2008: 136.

149 Drucker 1999: 159.

150 Davenport 2005: 21-22.

151 North and Güldenberg 2008: 140, Drucker 1999: 149, Davenport 2005: 12-13, Drucker 1990: 218-219.

152 Davenport 2005: 16, North and Güldenberg 2008: 140.

153 Machlup (1980: 229) observed that knowledge-intensive industries employ workers of many kinds of occupations, many of which are not knowledge occupations. Likewise, knowledge workers contribute to industries other than knowledge-intensive industries. Davenport (2005: 5-11) confirms that in traditional industries, high proportions of workers in manufacturing

most countries use occupation as a statistical indicator. In Germany, occupations such as engineers, scientists, teachers, consultants, bankers, managers, journalists, doctors, lawyers, and artists among others count as knowledge workers, accounting for approximately one third of total employed persons.[154] The United States employ a similar definition by occupation, whereas the United Kingdom defines knowledge-based jobs according to skills and education figures in terms of college degrees. In contrast, Canada's definition is less strict, including all sorts of managerial, professional, technical workers and even clerks.[155] Still, the identification of knowledge workers by occupation remains arbitrary, making it difficult to specify the exact number of knowledge workers in a particular country.[156] Scholars' opinions also deviate. While most scholars adhere to the more obvious knowledge-intense occupations,[157] Machlup strongly extends the occupations associated with knowledge work including "the entire body of executive, administrative, supervisory, technical, and *clerical personnel*, from the chairman and president of the firm to the switchboard operator and stock *clerk*"[158]. Within existing definitions, the occupation which apparently is most contested is the clerk who is explicitly excluded by some countries or scholars and included by others.[159] When identifying China's knowledge workers below, it will turn out to be most suitable for the present study to use a definition which includes clerks and related workers and to only consider persons with a college degree or above.

2.2 Knowledge

Knowledge is the critical object of this study. Especially in a business context, the knowledge property question easily causes conflicts. Both the employee and the organization have a stake in the knowledge within and surrounding a certain enterprise and workplace. Most severely, knowledge can only hardly be ascribed to an entity, neither to the knowledge worker nor to the organization. This derives from the following properties of knowledge.

---

firms never touch the manufacturing process, but instead provide knowledge-based services such as marketing, distribution, or customer service. Drucker (1990: 217) estimates that many knowledge workers, maybe even the majority, will continue working in industrial enterprises. Cortada (1998a: xiii) extents this even to agriculture, making the traditional separation between agriculture, industry and services less meaningful for identifying knowledge workers.

154 North and Güldenberg 2008: 9-11.

155 Davenport 2005: 5-7.

156 Davenport 2005: 6-12, Machlup 1980: 229.

157 Davenport 2005: 11-12, North and Güldenberg 2008: 27-28 and 33.

158 Machlup 1962: 41 [emphasis added].

159 Also observed by Davenport (2005: 6) and Cortada (1998a: xiv).

Knowledge can be located on an individual as well as a collective level and is therefore also hard to ascribe to a certain entity. On the one hand, knowledge is constructed by individuals and cannot exist independent of them.[160] On the other hand, the subjective thoughts of an individual can only be considered knowledge if it can be shared with others.[161] This dual character of knowledge particularly manifests itself in the organizational context. Whereas the traditional research perspective aggregates individual knowledge to a collective knowledge carrier, modern research advocates that both individual and collective knowledge exist simultaneously and accordingly focuses on the interaction of individual and collective knowledge structures.[162] Knowledge is not static but in a constant flow between these two levels.[163] What follows is that knowledge can at most *temporarily* reside either at an individual or at a collective level, as it is eventually only of use when flowing between these levels.

The location of knowledge can be further assessed with the intangible capital[164] approach. Intangible capital comprises the *non-physical sources of future economic benefit*, including many items that are important to the creation of future value to an organization but are not generally reported on the balance sheet.[165] The concept of intangible capital has been coined to break down the abstract concept of knowledge into identifiable categories and components. In the present study's empirical investigation as well, the components proved valuable for operationalizing knowledge.

The traditional and most commonly used categories are human, social and structural capital.[166] Human capital is seen as an organization's total workforce and its knowledge about the business.[167] It is embodied in the skills, knowledge, and experience of employees and mostly refers to the tacit knowledge embedded in people's minds.[168] As the potential value of intangibles lies in the eyes of the beholder,[169] it is thus the employee's skills, knowledge and experiences which allow him to identify and unfold the value for the organization.

Social capital is embedded in relationships between people (of the same enterprise or with supplier, customers etc.) as well as in networks being constituted

160 Berger and Luckmann 2007, Knoblauch 2005: 352, Schnettler 2007: 168.

161 Knoblauch 2005: 348.

162 Drepper 2007: 599-602, see Alvesson 2004: 46.

163 Gupta et al. 2008: 3.

164 In the present study, the tem "intangible capital" is treated synonymously with "intangible assets" and "intellectual capital", following e.g. Ariely (2008: 2966) and Adams and Oleksak (2010: 39).

165 Hunter 2006: 67, Ostrom and Ahn 2009: 19

166 Reinhardt et al. 2001: 795-796, see e.g. Ariely 2008: 2966, Adams and Oleksak 2010: 49.

167 Reinhardt et al. 2001: 796.

168 Hunter 2006: 67, Edvinsson 2003: 153, Hsu and Mykytyn 2008: 2049.

169 Ariely 2008: 2967-2971.

by relationships of people.[170] The use of social capital can facilitate the achievement of individual aims. Core organizational capabilities can also be developed through cooperating individuals.[171]

When knowledge is captured by and institutionalized within the organization or otherwise precipitates at the organizational level, structural capital is formed. Structural capital refers to items such as intellectual property,[172] processes, routines, corporate structure, and corporate culture.[173] It is largely embodied in the organization and rather unlocked from individuals. In case of individuals leaving the organization, structural capital can – in contrast to the other parts of intangible capital – stay with the organization.

The composition of capital as just described is in stark contrast to the industrial era, in which physical assets created most of the value, most of which could be owned and controlled by the enterprise. In the knowledge era, an enterprise not only relies on employees to complete daily work, but employees themselves are a part of the capital, which is needed for identifying and unfolding the value of an enterprise's intangible capital.[174] With increasing competition, it is precisely this interaction between the different components of intangible capital which provides the unique competitive edge. Although some aspects of the organization might be imitated or misappropriated by competitors, the whole system can hardly be duplicated.[175] Even though knowledge can be identified as intangible capital, the ascription of a certain piece of knowledge to either the organization or individuals remains a challenging endeavor.

The form in which knowledge occurs makes is also hard to ascribe it to a certain entity. Knowledge can occur in an explicit, implicit or tacit form. What is referred to as explicit knowledge occurs in a symbolic form of codification, verbalization or documentation. Whereas explicit knowledge can be readily articu-

170 See e.g. Patulny 2009. Social capital is also often referred to as relational or customer capital (Hsu and Mykytyn 2008: 2048, Ariely 2008: 2966, Adams and Oleksak 2010). In this study the term social capital is preferred as it also includes the relationships and networks within an enterprise

171 Reinhardt et al. 2001: 805-806.

172 The part of structural capital – and of intangible capital as a whole – which is easiest to capture is knowledge qualifying as intellectual property. With the explication as a precondition, valuable information can be protected as trade secrets, and patentable knowledge, trademarks and copyrights can be registered with the relevant authority. Patents, trademarks, and copyrights even share a common bond with physical capital, as they assert an ownership right that can be defended against unauthorized use by others. Possession of such property rights provides their owners with a potential form of competitive advantage, which cannot be freely be used by others.

173 Hunter 2006: 67.

174 See also Adams and Oleksak 2010: 46-47, North 2011: 56, Reinhardt et al. 2001: 804-805.

175 Adams and Oleksak 2010: 31 and 46, Reinhardt et al. 2001: 796, see Edvinsson 2003: 153.

lated, other forms of knowledge cannot. The most prominent contribution to these other forms of knowledge is Michael Polanyi's "tacit dimension". The Hungarian polymath's starting point in his book "The Tacit Dimension"[176] is the fact that "we can know more than we can tell"[177]. Putting forward the example of face recognition, he asserts that although human beings can recognize a face among plenty of others, they are not able to describe it in a way that other persons are able to easily recognize this person. When focusing too strongly on details, people are not able to see the whole entireness. Only "tacit knowing"[178] allows for shifting the attention from the parts to the whole, which involves recognizing relations between the parts. Likewise, human beings are able to recognize a complex problem by focusing on the relations between single pieces of information rather than on each single piece. They are able to approach the solution by being directed by one's sense of orientation, and to anticipate the still vague implications of one's discovery.[179] Based on indwelling and empathy,[180] tacit knowing can hardly be articulated.

Knowledge management scholars as well as scholars from other disciplines have frequently built on Polanyi for establishing the dualism of explicit and tacit knowledge.[181] Scholars apply the terms tacit and implicit interchangeably as they only need a tool for (roughly) analyzing a non-explicit form of knowledge.[182] In

176 Polanyi 1966.

177 Polanyi 1966: 4.

178 Polanyi 1966: 1.

179 Polanyi 1985: 14-30.

180 Polanyi 1985: 24.

181 For Willke (1998: 12-13), the human being must not necessarily know that he possesses this kind of knowledge, and he must not be able to explain how he applies it. Activities such as riding a bicycle, skiing or diagnosing a mechanical problem are rather hard to explain in terms of how they are performed. Note that Willke further describes tacit knowledge as experience, history, practice, and learning "in the sense of know-how" (1998: 13), while Polanyi's (1985: 16) tacit knowing provides the basis for both practical knowledge (knowing how/"Können") and intellectual knowledge (knowing that/"Wissen"). North and Güldenberg (2008: 24) refer to the human being's personal knowledge being based on ideals, values and feelings. Deeply embedded in the individual's actions and experiences, it unconsciously informs subjective insights and intuition. Being stored in human heads it is only very hard to articulate and transfer. These scholars – albeit the latter without citing Polanyi – tie in with Polanyi's "tacit knowing" for establishing a form of knowledge which in contrast to explicit knowledge is hard to articulate.

182 Strikingly, the above mentioned German scholars use the German term "implizites Wissen" [implicit knowledge] instead of the literal translation "stillschweigend wissen" [tacit knowing] (tacit literally is "silent"; from the Latin verb *tacere*, which means to be silent). At first glance, this is not surprising as the translator of Polanyi's book likewise uses "implizites Wissen", without referring to why he considers this the more adequate translation. In fact, however, "implicit" is the antonym of "explicit" and means (in both English (*Webster's Revised Unabridged Dictionary* (1913: 736)) and German (*Duden* (Wermke et al. 2006: 443)) language) being involved or implied, but not being expressly articulated.

contrast, Li and Gao[183] sharply distinguish between "implicitness" and "tacitness" of knowledge. Implicit knowledge might not be articulated and rests implicit for the organization due to various reasons, including employees not willing or not being motivated to reflect on their work while actually being able to articulate this knowledge. Since the present study pays most attention to knowledge in its non-explicit forms, the three-fold distinction is thus more helpful than the conventional dualism.

Furthermore, knowledge is hard to ascribe to either the (non-manual) employee or the organization, as it is inherently practical and embedded in its context. When information is integrated into a practical context, it is refined through practice and thus knowledge develops. Knowledge itself is practice, and this practice originates in communication and is further reassured by communication. Theoretical and any other abstract knowledge *de facto* does not yet constitute knowledge. Practical knowledge on how to apply theories and abstractions and a context of experiences are what can be considered to be real knowledge. Without the practical context, development or transfer of knowledge would be impossible.[184]

Conventional knowledge management approaches do not consider the contextuality of knowledge. Knowledge is rather seen as a *functional resource* with the underlying assumption that knowledge can be instrumentalized and detached from its context.[185] Meanwhile, numerous (knowledge) management scholars cast serious doubts that knowledge can be managed – at least in a simple, direct, rational, hierarchical, or controlling manner.[186] Knowledge in its ambiguity indeed appears hardly to be managed as it often occurs in a tacit and uncodified form, is embodied in individuals to a large extent,[187] takes place inside the individual's mind[188] and is possessed[189] and owned[190] by individuals in organiza-

183 Li Meng and Gao Fei (2003) take the usage of "tacit" by Nonaka and Takeuchi (1997) as point of departure who developed a famous model according to which "tacit knowledge" can be externalized. Yet Li Meng and Gao Fei argue that the study, which was pursued in the context of Japanese manufacturing enterprises, in fact denotes implicit knowledge, as it can be articulated through proper knowledge management by middle managers. Li and Gao rightly see the reference to Polanyi as inadequate, as Polanyi focuses on hard-to-articulate knowledge.

184 Willke 2007: 28-34.

185 See e.g Gupta et al. (2008: 3) who define knowledge management as the collection of processes that govern the creation, dissemination, and utilization of knowledge, and Probst et al. (2006) who identify further components of knowledge management, that is, the identification, acquirement, development, sharing, use, and preservation of knowledge. Schilcher 2006: 134-137, Alvesson 2004: 41.

186 See e.g. Reinhardt et al. 2001: 794, Land et al. 2008: 29, Schilcher 2006: 134-137, Alvesson 2004: 166-187, Schanz 2006: 124, Kakabadse et al. 2003: 85, Rooney and Schneider 2005: 33, Ariely 2008: 2969.

187 Ariely 2008: 2968-2969, Schilcher 2006: 134.

188 Gelepithis and Parillon 2008: 1484.

tions. Processes of knowing, learning, and sharing depend to a large extent on the employees' motivation, willingness, and ability and can only be supported by the management of the environment.[191] As a matter of fact, only the context of knowledge rather than knowledge itself can be managed. Due to its ambiguous nature, it is generally hard to determine to whom knowledge belongs within an organization.

2.3 Culture

The question of what "culture" is has been put forward and has been answered in endless ways.[192] Within various conceptualizations of culture, the author identified three themes along which culture appears to be usually defined. Accordingly, culture is defined by its spatial unit of reference, by its (im)materiality, as well as by its relation to the human being.

The ascription of a *spatial unit of reference* to culture originates in cultural anthropology of the 19th century. Culture refers to the whole way of life of a collective – an ethnic group, a community, or a nation. It is the "complex whole which includes knowledge, belief, art, moral, law, custom, and any other capabilities and habits acquired by man as *a member of society*".[193] Accordingly, as a member of society a human being is automatically subject to the influence of the respective culture. This internal homogeneity and seclusion from the outside triggers the impulse to pronounce its uniqueness in comparison to other cultures.[194] Although cultural anthropologists and other (ethnographic) researchers are rather interested in a collective *per se*, they essentially search for its particularities, which are only particularities in comparison to other collectives.

More recently, cultural collectives have mostly been equated with nation states. As the state has come to be understood as being the self-evident and quasi-natural unit of authority, the political boundaries are used to mark every sphere of a society including its culture. Nation states have become "cultural containers"[195] considered homogenous from the inside and different to the outside with cultural differences being mostly derived from the specific historical

189 Ariely 2008: 2969.
190 Ariely 2008: 2969, Adams and Oleksak 2010: 43.
191 Sollberger 2006: 67, Kakabadse et al. 2003: 86, see Rooney and Schneider 2005: 33-34.
192 Thorougly defining "culture" is particularly necessary, as it is among the words used most frequently in society as well as in social sciences and humanities (Nünning 2009).
193 Famous definition of the cultural anthropologist Edward Burnett Tylor, quoted from Kroeber and Kluckhohn 1952: 81 [emphasis added].
194 See Reckwitz 2004: 5-6.
195 Beck 1998: 13-14.

origins.[196] This territorialization of culture has been reinforced by comparative empirical investigations, which ascribe "cultural dimensions"[197] or "cultural standards"[198] to certain nations, making the cultural differences between nations seemingly measureable and comparable. Locating culture at the level of the nation state easily leads to the use of cultural arguments for the sake of "essentializing differences"[199].

To overcome the territorial ascription of culture and the cultural segregation of nation states, concepts such as inter-, multi-, and transculturality have been created. These, however, are still based on the premise of the nation state and more or less take it as reference point. The same applies to the convergence theory which assumes that national culture will converge into a global culture, diminishing local differences. Others see the global cultural system as *strengthening* differences, albeit providing a global reference system to communicate about the differences.[200] In any event, the discourse reflects the ongoing search for a definite spatial unit of reference for culture, that is, global, regional, national, local, including the intercultural communication between or the transcultural transcending of each.

The question of the *(im)materiality* of culture or its "substantialization"[201] comes to light in various approaches to culture. In the context of the Enlightenment and partly even up to the 20th century, culture was seen as a "material" or "visible" artifact. The bourgeoisie culturally distinguished itself from the gentry and the proletariat, referred to as "high culture" (*Hochkultur*). Similarly, cultural anthropologists, mostly of the 19th and 20th century in their effort to study the whole way of life of a collective, concentrated on artifacts such as laws and customs.[202] In the 20th century, culture was regarded as a specialized system of society related to intellectual and "visible" activities such as art, education, and science.[203]

A stronger immaterial understanding of culture became prevalent mostly in the second half of the 20th century. Culture was viewed as a mentality, a readable text, a nexus of meanings or values and norms, a symbolic code,[204] or the "col-

196 Beck 1998.
197 Hofstede 1984, Hall 1989, Trompenaars and Hampden-Turner 1997, House et al. 2004.
198 Thomas 2005.
199 Beck 1998: 54.
200 Beck 1998: 59-60 (referring to the American cultural anthropologist Richard Wilk).
201 Hörning and Reuter 2004: 9.
202 See e.g. the definition of the cultural anthropologist Tylor, quoted from Kroeber and Kluckhohn 1952: 81.
203 Reckwitz 2004: 4-6.
204 Hörning and Reuter 2004: 9-10, Hörning 2004: 139-141.

lective programming of the mind"[205]. The cultural anthropologist Clifford Geertz, for instance, defined culture as a system of symbols and meaning, as "webs of significance he [man] himself has spun"[206], and man being "an animal suspended in those webs"[207]. This shift triggered more attention to culture as an invisible category, and loaded with this meaning culture spread across many disciplines.

A connecting thread within conceptualizations until recently – and most obvious in the latter approach – is that culture is mostly defined as a rather fixed, abstract and generalized[208] whole or system, operating detached from human beings and determining their behavior. These culture-as-system approaches[209] largely neglect that culture only exsists in *relation to the human being*. More often than not it is far from clear if norms and rules *indeed* prove relevant for an actor, how they influence actions, and what the preconditions for such an influence are.[210] Indeed, the most apparent flaw of culture conceptualized in this rather abstract way is the neglect of how culture is actually connected to human beings and vice versa.

For an elaboration on this link it proves useful to draw on social theory, and, more concretely, on practice theories. Practice theories seek to overcome the dualisms in social theory, such as individual and society, action and structure, subjectivism and objectivism. Although no unitary and coherent theoretical approach to practices exists,[211] the hitherto existing practice accounts provide useful and complementary ideas about the nature of practices in social life, and accordingly how the link of the individual and the social can be established. In the following, the link is established by alluding to the most relevant practice accounts of the sociologists Bourdieu and Giddens as well as to Schatzki's more philosophically informed account on social practice.

For Bourdieu[212], the link between the individual and the social is basically what he refers to as "habitus"[213] – a system of permanent dispositions inculcated in early childhood by the group of society (e.g. class) the individual has been born into. Although every individual has made his own experiences in the past, individuals from a specific group are *more likely* to have faced similar situations

205 Hofstede 1984: 82.
206 Geertz 2008: 31.
207 Geertz 2008: 31.
208 Reckwitz 2010: 189.
209 Sewell 2008.
210 Hörning 2004: 143.
211 Schatzki 1996: 11-12 and 2001: 2.
212 See Bourdieu 1977: esp. 15-23 and 78-95, Bourdieu 1987: esp. chapter 3 and 5, Bourdieu 1994: esp. 15-51.
213 Bourdieu 1977: 17.

or circumstances compared to individuals from other groups. The subjective past experiences form an "immanent law"[214], which constantly functions as a matrix for perception and judgment of present experiences. Instead of "mechanically"[215] acting according to a fixed set of objective and explicit rules, however, it allows the individual to strategically cope with an infinite number of situations and fulfill an infinite number of different tasks. The individual (consciously) decides how to (re)act in a specific situation within the (unconscious) range of the historically and socially conditioned possibilities and limitations. The habitus tries to reproduce structures in order to ensure the practice's inherent logic and consistency or their "practical sense"[216].

In Giddens'[217] theory of structuration, the individual is conceptualized as a reflective and knowledgeable actor, whose actions are informed by his discursive and practical consciousness. While discursive consciousness involves the ability to consciously reflect upon actions, practical consciousness refers to (tacitly but not unconsciously) knowing the rules and tactics of practical conduct. This practical knowledge leads to routines which invoke the formation of structures. These again affect actors via their "positioning"[218] in time and space. At the same time, actors are positioned in daily life, in their life spans, and in institutional time, as well as in multiple social relations with the respective identities ascribed to them. Social practices are "ordered through time and space"[219]. As actors move through time and space, starting with their practical day-to-day routine, they reproduce and transform the structures. The greater the distance of time and space of social systems, the more resistant social structures prove to be against the transformation by an actor.

While Bourdieu and Giddens posit that both the individual and the social are the result of practices, Schatzki[220] develops an account of practice which – on the basis of Wittgenstein's works – furthers existing accounts by paying substantial attention to practices *per se*. He defines a practice as "a temporally unfolding and spatially dispersed nexus of doings and sayings"[221]. The attributes of "doings" and "sayings" are expressions of the human body. Doings and sayings constitute a nexus, also described with "context" or – even in Schatzki's English language work – best expressed with the German word "Zusammenhang". Prac-

214 Bourdieu 1987: 111.
215 Bourdieu 1987: 287.
216 Bourdieu 1994: 45.
217 Giddens 1984: esp. 41-92.
218 Giddens 1984: 84.
219 Giddens 1984: 2.
220 Schatzki 1996: esp. 88-110.
221 Schatzki 1996: 89.

tices can be categorized as "dispersed"[222] among different sectors and situations of social life, such as describing, reporting, and following rules. A second category of practices is "integrative"[223], which, in contrast, relates to particular domains of social life, such as business practices, industrial practices, and teaching practices. Armed with these links between the individual and the social, it is possible to further query into how "culture" is related to human beings.

Hitherto, only the contours of a praxeological theory of culture exist.[224] The most comprehensive approach is Hörning's culture-as-practice approach[225], on which this study is largely based, while also drawing on the above mentioned practice accounts.[226] In Hörning's approach, culture is understood as a *resource* of the human being taking the form of knowledge. Essentially it is knowledge about the social world, allowing for *orientation* in social life.

Hörning refers to cultural knowledge in its explicit and implicit form. *Explicit cultural knowledge* is most similar to the notion of culture-as-system.[227] It includes general and apparent cultural knowledge, or Bourdieu's "system of dispositions"[228], such as rules and norms or symbols and meanings either existing in written form or being regularly articulated. These rather stable knowledge stocks function as cognitive background knowledge or previous knowledge, providing the human being with a framework of possibilities and limitations.[229]

Yet in modern pluralized and complex societies explicit knowledge stocks cannot be thought of as homogenous, orderly and straightforward "systems" anymore. With ongoing differentiation of society, cultural knowledge stocks become more and more disordered and fairly ambiguous. Rules and norms "inculcated"[230] in childhood cannot serve as clear-cut instructions guiding the actions of an individual, assisting in clearly separating right from wrong. They become less influential compared to norms or rules of professional life or the other manifold practical contexts the human being becomes continuously entan-

222 Schatzki 1996: 91.
223 Schatzki 1996: 98.
224 E.g. Reckwitz 2004: 18.
225 Hörning 2004.
226 Within Chinese academia, merely practice theories as such appear to have been analyzed in Chinese academia to date (see e.g. Xiao Junming 1996). The culture-as-practice approach neither has been reflected upon nor used for empirical research. The author's search on Aug 6, 2013, with the search function in the China Academic Journal Database yielded ten articles with the keyword "文化" [culture] and the keyword "实践理论" [practice theory] both in the article title. Yet none of them proved relevant considering the culture-as-practice approach.
227 See also Sewell (2008) who posits that a culture-as-practice approach does not necessarily exclude a culture-as-system approach, but can complement it in a dialectical way.
228 Bourdieu 1977: 85.
229 Raphael 2004: 269.
230 Bourdieu 1977: 15.

gled in during his life.[231] In fact, concrete actions often do *not* resort to official codes or explicit norms. And even if actions conform to these codes and norms, it is still open to question if they *de facto* informed the actual behavior.[232]

Due to this reasoning, Hörning proposes to consider *implicit cultural knowledge*. These are more practical norms in the sense of know-how.[233] This know-how allows to cope with practical situations by providing criteria on how to act; it judges which (re)action is adequate in a certain concrete situation. It thus consists of common criteria which develop when people act together, providing the human being with his rather subtle competencies and strategies. This kind of cultural knowledge exists mainly within practices, but, in the sense of Giddens' "discursive consciousness"[234], can without much effort be reflected upon and made explicit. Yet there is usually no need and no occasion to consciously reflect upon it in depth and externalize it within daily life.

For the purpose of this study, Hörning's understanding of culture as a "two-sided repertoire"[235] is (re-)constructed as a three-fold cultural resource, which more sharply distinguishes between cultural knowledge in its explicit[236], implicit, and tacit[237] form, with the latter being informed by Polanyi's "tacit knowing"[238]. Tacit cultural knowledge provides even less discursive criteria for the judgment of adequacy of social actions. Individuals act in an intuitive way following their instinct and senses. Intuition does not originate – as colloquially referred to – "by the seat of one's pants"[239], but from an unconscious combination of facts that have been formerly absorbed from the environment. Corresponding to Bourdieu's "forgetting of history"[240], historical and social facts are absorbed in such a self-evident way that there is no necessity to consciously reflect upon them. Through tacit knowledge the individual is provided with the tactfulness and

231 While Bourdieu in his former research puts weight on disposition from early childhood, he later pays more attention to other fields, such as professional life (Raphael 2004: 271). Hörning (2004: 149) also emphasizes the multiple practical contexts building up the cultural repertoire.

232 Hörning 2004: 147 and 150.

233 See Hörning 2004: 148.

234 Giddens 1984: 41.

235 Hörning 2004: 145.

236 In contrast, Hörning (2004: 149) also extends his explicit rules to what is generally not known explicitly but can be made explicit. In this study, this cultural knowledge is put into the category of implicit knowledge.

237 Like many German knowledge management scholars (see chapter 2.2), Hörning (2004), while referring to Polanyi's "tacit knowing" and using "implizit" in his German account, does not distinguish between implicitness and tacitness.

238 See also chapter 2.2.

239 The German equivalent of this idiom "aus dem Bauch heraus" – literally "out of the stomach" – even more pointedly brings forward the general view according to which this kind of knowledge virtually arises from the individual instead of being informed by the social.

240 Bourdieu 1977: 78.

timing which he needs in practices.[241] In line with Schatzki's "understanding"[242] of what to say and what to do, tacit cultural knowledge connects doings and sayings into practices. Thereby, practices are inhabited by Bourdieu's "practical sense"[243], which is an inner logic of practices existing only within practices. Tacit cultural knowledge can thus hardly be shifted to a discursive level. Alluding to Giddens' "practical consciousness"[244], tacit knowing does not happen on a totally unconscious but on a reflexive level. In order to make practices work coherently in the complex social world, tacit knowledge intends to stay tacit, functioning as an underlying rationale for behavior. Interestingly, it is basically tacit knowledge as the most unarticulated kind of cultural knowledge which preserves the social order.

All three kinds of cultural knowledge constantly interact, and – eventually – only this interaction can picture the complex reality. Bourdieu's[245] empirical research in the traditional French Province of Béarn provides a fertile example for the interaction and necessity of all kinds of cultural knowledge. At a discursive level, every child has the right to inherit a part of the family property. On a practical level, however, lots of subtle strategies of the parents, which primarily result in the eldest son solely receiving the property, prevent the family property of being split among all children, and hence, serve the tacit rationale of protecting the family property. This kind of tacit exploitation of the younger children, however, is only part of the big picture, as at the discursive level, younger children exhibit a sense of duty and feelings for their parents, rationalizing the situation for themselves. As such, considering only one level (which is most often done with the discursive level) would show only a certain part of reality.

Still, such seemingly stable cultural practices as observed in Béarn must not necessarily persist in that way for a long time. Practices consist of both a routine and an innovative character. The routine character – in Giddens' sense –[246] refers to the repetitiveness of activities which provides a sense of trust and ontological security in daily life. Yet Hörning asserts that the repetition of a past action is never the same, metaphorically alluding to Heraclitus' saying "you cannot step twice into the same river".[247] To cope with the contingencies of daily life, practices also productively set change in motion and allow for the continuation of the familiar in a (slightly) new way. Accordingly, practices are also innovative and creative. With implicit and tacit knowledge they judge the adequacy of (past)

241 Hörning 2004: 146.
242 Schatzki 1996: 89.
243 Bourdieu 1994: 45.
244 Giddens 1984: 41.
245 Bourdieu 1987: 264-287.
246 Giddens 1984: xxiii.
247 Hörning 2004: 144.

rules for a certain (present) situation and creatively adapt these rules. Thereby, they even have the power to transform the explicit cultural knowledge. As such, practices are a continuous mixture of routine and innovation, every action both reproduces and transforms.[248] Only with this flexibility culture can serve as an adequate orientation in the complex social life.

As can be seen from the above analysis, the culture-as-practice approach is *not* so much focused on the *spatial unit of reference* of culture and does not primarily ask how specific, different, or alien a certain culture of a certain nation or group in comparison to other nations or groups is. This focus is usually applied in the culture-as-system approach, where the degree to which systems are different is both the starting point of cultural analysis and the determinant of the relevance of the "system" for a certain nation or group. Instead, within the culture-as-practice approach culture is not regarded as fruitful for explaining local phenomena merely on the precondition that it is significantly different from other "cultural containers". Rather, the research interest focuses on how culture actually matters in social life, and how it can provide orientation.

Albeit being less tied to a certain clearly defined spatial unit of reference, the spatial dimension is yet not to be neglected. The body is certainly needed to exert physical and mental processes. Body and mind thus have a natural spatial dimension.[249] Human beings in contemporary societies are "positioned"[250] within a widening range of "fields"[251], such as home, workplace, nation-state, and the worldwide systems at a certain point in time. These provide human beings with a range of the historically and socially conditioned possibilities and limitations. All human beings move in situated contexts limiting the knowledge they have of other contexts which they do not directly experience.[252] Practices can transcend "the local" and "the global" and are independent of national or other boundaries being socially ascribed to certain groups.[253]

As a matter of fact, implicit and tacit cultural knowledge mostly constitute culture. The conventional explicit cultural knowledge usually ascribed to certain phenomena can but do not have to inform the people involved. Only as far as implicit and tacit cultural knowledge take hold of explicit cultural knowledge, it is of relevance within daily life at all. Simply put, culture in this study is the

---

248 Hörning 2004: 145-149.

249 Reckwitz 2010: 190. This logic can be extended to the cyber-spatial dimension, where a human being can likewise only be active within a limited number of domains.

250 Giddens 1984: 83.

251 Raphael 2004: 271.

252 Giddens 1984: 91.

253 See Bourdieu 1977: 4-15 and 1987: 180-204 and 1994: 19, see Giddens 1984: 111, see Schatzki 1996: 91.

spatiotemporal interaction of explicit, implicit, and tacit cultural knowledge within practices.

2.4 Application to the Present Study

In FIEs in China, Chinese employees are often found to leak knowledge externally and to not share knowledge internally, both to an extent being clearly regarded as detrimental to the enterprise's interests. This situation entails significant conflicts over knowledge between the FIE and Chinese employees.

In light of the frequent occurrence of knowledge conflicts, Chinese employees can be assumed to not arbitrarily decide how to draw the boundaries of valuable knowledge but to be informed by overarching criteria beyond the individual. These criteria are usually approached from the angle of culture. As culture – in its most basic sense – informs the behavior of a group of individuals from a higher level, taking up this thread seems intuitive.

Hitherto, knowledge conflicts appear to be usually explained with "Chinese culture" at a *national* level, informed by Chinese philosophy or similar reference systems. In the sense of "culture-as-system", cultural norms and values are seen as determining the behavior of Chinese employees in FIEs. Being clearly ascribed to China as a spatial unit of reference, it is often assumed that everyone being born and raised in the Chinese national context has "automatically" internalized these cultural meaning systems. Yet such inferences to what is conventionally regarded as "Chinese culture" appear to be hardly able to explain the knowledge conflicts in a convincing way.

What is missing within these approaches is the link between the individual and the social. It is still unclear whether "Chinese culture" as conventionally defined indeed informs Chinese employees' knowledge interactions in FIEs. In the spirit of the discipline of cultural sociology, which aims to highlight the social unconsciousness, the task of this research is to bring the rather unconscious and subtle cultural knowledge to light which indeed prompts Chinese employees to handle knowledge in such a controversial way.

This cultural knowledge is assumed to provide employees with an orientation for their actions. In this respect, it is fundamentally different from what is referred to as valuable knowledge above. Whereas valuable knowledge always denotes a property relation to a certain entity (the organization or the employee or both), cultural knowledge is not the property of anyone, but provides *orientation* on how to determine the relation of valuable knowledge to an entity. Hence, cultural knowledge in this study is seen as a resource which provides orientation for drawing the boundaries of valuable knowledge between Chinese employees and their FIE.

In reform-era China, where tremendous changes in the economic and social sphere are under way, orientation is especially needed. This orientation needs to go beyond conventional conceptualizations of "Chinese culture", which treat culture as a homogenous construct and ascribe it to China as a fixed and abstract spatial unit of reference. In the process of reform and opening up, Chinese stocks of explicit cultural knowledge have become more varied and multifaceted and cannot provide orientation in a straightforward way anymore. Conventional concepts of "Chinese culture" now seem hardly applicable in the different spheres of social life.

Especially in the sphere of knowledge interactions in FIEs, explicit cultural knowledge stocks might not provide straightforward and sufficient orientation for Chinese employees. Supposedly, Chinese employees have latitude in doing their work as it is typical for knowledge workers. Especially since FIEs are generally less familiar with the Chinese market, control by foreign superiors cannot strongly be exercised. Chinese employees might hence find themselves in an intermediary role, having considerable latitude externally since only they can pursue exchange with the external business environment. Which part of knowledge exactly is exchanged with the outside as well as which part of knowledge accumulated from the external environment is shared within the FIE is all to be decided by the individual employee.

In contrast to manual workers, who are guided by explicit rules as orientation, Chinese employees in their role as mediating knowledge workers might rather be exposed to implicit and tacit cultures for orientation in daily work. Their work appears to be less structured with a lower degree of routine. Rather, flexible implicit and tacit cultural knowledge provides them with subtle competences and an intuitive underlying rationale of how to behave within knowledge interactions. Explicit cultural knowledge stocks are drawn upon only when deemed adequate. Eventually, the interaction of all three kinds of cultural knowledge within practices might show how Chinese employees in FIEs draw the boundaries of knowledge.

Although these implicit and tacit forms of culture cannot be clearly demarcated into spatial units of reference, they all interact in a certain space at a certain point in time. The non-manual Chinese employee in a FIE in his role as a knowledge worker and intermediary is at least positioned in the following contexts: the Chinese national context, the Chinese economy and society, the industrial sector of his FIE, and the FIE. Through this positioning he is exposed to the explicit, implicit, and tacit cultural knowledge of several contexts.

Although Chinese and German employees are both positioned in the same FIE in China, contexts overlap only to a limited extent. Most significantly, German employees naturally enter China at a later age than Chinese employees. The implicit and tacit cultural knowledge, which mainly informs the actual behavior, can hardly be understood in advance by consulting written accounts. When German employees enter the Chinese context, the context of the Chinese manufacturing sector, as well as in the context of in the FIE, they are exposed to different kinds of cultural knowledge which they can only get in touch with when being physically positioned in the relevant contexts. These different contexts the employees have become entangled in might well contribute to explaining how Sino-German knowledge conflicts are caused and how they can be solved eventually.

3 Research Design and Methods

The process of achieving the study's objective and answering the research questions necessitates a reflection on the study's philosophical stance (3.1), on the sample (3.2), on the data collection (3.3), and the analysis (3.4), as well as on the data's validity, realiability, objectivity (3.5), and generalizability (3.6). Finally, the data are contextualized (3.7).

3.1 Philosophical and Methodological Considerations

This study departs from the philosophical position of realism which is positioned in between the two extremes of positivism and interpretivism. This approach neither follows the ontological assumption of an objective reality completely disconnected from social interactions nor does it take subjective perspectives at face value.[254] Rather, a social reality beyond the individual is assumed which is constituted through social interaction but also anchored in the wider objectively existing context.

From an epistemological point of view, the social reality can be known through employees' views of situations which provide evidence for how cultural knowledge is indeed relevant in terms of orientation in daily life. Apart from these subjective points of view, positivist elements are also viewed to be informative of social reality, such as the objectively given contexts the employees are embedded in. These contexts enrich and contextualize the individual statements.

Methodologically speaking, for scrutinizing the social reality of handling valuable knowledge from an employee's point of view, qualitative research is most appropriate. Qualitative research allows investigating the topic more profoundly "from the inside"[255]. The social reality is grasped as completely as possible by bringing Chinese employees' perspectives into focus. This includes the reconstruction of the logic[256] inherent to the controversial handling of knowledge through inductive and constructivist analysis as well as considering its "particu-

254 Travers 2001: 10-12.
255 Flick 2007a: ix.
256 This is in line with Kruse's (2014: 21-24) understanding of qualitative research.

lar context"[257] through contextualization with secondary material. It is particularly adequate to openly depart from the employees' views regarding the fact that this study precisely aims to search for answers for this phenomenon beyond the explanations hitherto provided.

Among the methods available in qualitative research, conducting interviews proves most suitable for this study. It is often implicit and tacit cultural knowledge which informs the behavior of Chinese employees of which they themselves are not completely aware. This cultural knowledge cannot be anticipated before there is an opportunity for verbal interaction and extensive verbatim responses.[258] Being provided with the chance to elaborate on daily work in a colloquial way by drawing on examples, experiences, and analogies enables the interviewees to unveil much more than the official explicit knowledge available for describing behavior in a specific practical situation.[259]

Especially in a foreign context, such as the Chinese one, it is particularly adequate that qualitative research employs an open and rather unstructured approach in order to avoid ethnocentric outcomes.[260] In a study in which a China-specific phenomenon is investigated, ethnocentric outcomes very likely occur when predetermined Western propositions or hypotheses are applied. As the – usually Western – cultural essentializations should be overcome, an open und impartial research approach is obligatory.

3.2 Sample

Using the sampling technique of purposive sampling,[261] interviewees, enterprises, and locations were selected. Typically, this sampling technique is used to conduct interviews with persons from a population difficult to reach.[262] As the topic of valuable knowledge and its handling by Chinese employees is highly sensitive for FIEs operating in China, accessing enterprises posed a challenge. To enlarge the pool of enterprises potentially willing to participate, the nearly 1,500 German enterprises registered with the German Chamber of Commerce in

257 Mason 2002: 1. See also Cappai 2008: 19-20.

258 For instance, it appears to be self-evident that when someone leaves the enterprise knowledge still belongs to him personally, or that one necessarily cultivates certain pieces of valuable knowledge for competitive advantage (see chapter 8.2 and 8.1).

259 Hörning 2004.

260 See Cappai 2008: 21.

261 See e.g. Bernard 2006: 190-191.

262 Neuman 2000: 198.

the "German Company Directory"[263] were contacted with a short screening questionnaire.[264] The contact person could indicate on the questionnaire whether a follow up with the enterprise was conceivable.[265] Some of the positively responding enterprises were contacted in different field research stages.

Eventually, the sample of the main investigation consists of 14 FIEs in China with the investors all being of German origin. Ten of them are wholly-foreign-owned enterprises (WFOE) and four of them Sino-German equity joint ventures (JV). The sampled enterprises are mostly small and medium-sized, starting from sixty employees to large enterprises with more than 50,000 employees. All enterprises operate in the manufacturing sector. Industries mostly include engineering and automotive. The sampled enterprises are located in Beijing, Shanghai, Jiangsu Province, Guangdong Province, and Jilin Province. All enterprises are located in cities at provincial, prefectural, and county levels. During data analysis, special attention was paid to the sample's diversity in terms of different enterprise types, sizes, industries, and locations.

The study's sample consists of 68 interviewees.[266] The interviews were conducted in September 2009 and April 2010. The interviewees comprise 44 Chinese[267] and 24 German[268] employees. This proportion reflects the weight which is given to the Chinese perspective in this study as compared to the existing literature. The German interviewees are decisive for figuring out how knowledge conflicts occur from their perspective. The sampled Chinese employ-

263 The "German Company Directory" (http://www.german-company-directory.com/) is administered by the German Industry & Commerce, which is the service provider of the German Chamber of Commerce in China.

264 1,463 German-invested enterprises (996 WFOEs, 438 Equity JVs, 29 Contractual JVs; representative offices excluded) in Mainland China as of Jan 17, 2009. According to Chinese statistics, the number of German-invested enterprises totaled 4,723 at the end of 2008 (National Bureau of Statistics of the PRC (NBS) 2010b: 652). Despite the shortcoming that only a certain part of FIEs with German origin might be registered with the German Chamber of Commerce, the directory still proves to be a valuable tool for the study's research purpose. Its strength lies in the listing of contact persons often not being available on the enterprises' websites, which allows the sending of the questionnaire directly to the contact person. Avoiding cross-postings (in case one contact person is in charge of more than one enterprise) and deducting the invalid contact addresses, 1,064 questionnaires had effectively been sent out. 94 valid questionnaires had been returned, yielding a response rate of 8.8%.

265 19 respondents positively answered the last question about the willingness to follow-up the matter in a personal discussion with the research team, while 29 chose "maybe".

266 See appendix 1.

267 Chinese nationality coincides with Chinese ethnicity in this study.

268 All referred to as "German" employees were of German nationality (and ethnicity) except two of them holding a Hungarian and a British nationality. As both of them speak German and had been working in a German working context for years as well as due to the fact that no deviating opinions in regard to the research questions could be observed, they were included in the group of German employees.

ees were aged between 24 and 46 years and 34 years on average (see Table 1), while the German employees were 44 years old on average. In terms of education level, all the Chinese employees held a college degree or above. 70% of the German employees held a German diploma.

Table 1: The sampled interviewees according to nationality, age, gender, and type of FIE.

Nationality	Quantity	Age	Male/Female (%)	WFOEs/JVs (%)
Chinese	44	24-46 (Ø 34)	70/30	68/32
German	24	30-63 (Ø 44)	96/4	46/54

Source: Author's own compilation.

None of the Chinese employees has been abroad for a longer stay, e.g. for studying and the like. At most, very few of the Chinese employees have been to Germany for pursuing a short training in the parent enterprise. They thus have not accumulated work experience in a foreign country for a period exceeding a few weeks.

The German employees have stayed with the Chinese subsidiary between 0.5 and 7 years. On average, they stayed 3.4 years with the FIE. This duration coincides with their stay in China, except 3 interviewees who had formerly been employed at another FIE in China. Hence, all of them have stayed in China for a certain time, but were raised and worked most of their life in the German national context.

The sampled employees worked in different departments, such as sales, purchasing, product management, marketing, research and development, human resources, finances, as well as the legal and the production department. More than half of the Chinese employees held management positions, mostly in lower and middle management. The remaining employees held assistant positions, such as assistant to the general manager or sales assistant. German employees rather held upper management positions such as general manager, plant manager, director operations, or vice president sales and marketing. Taking up the common thread of communication as a primary activity of knowledge workers, the sampled employees encompassed all those workers whose work largely consists of communication.

3.3 Data Collection

Semi-structured interviews were conducted.[269] A rough topic guide[270] was used which ensured that core issues were addressed in each interview, while at the same time encouraging more in-depth interviewing necessary to gain hidden perceptions and attitudes and following new leads.[271] Sufficient depth of the interviews had been ensured by using the topic guide in a flexible manner and having one to two hours time (according to the availability of the interviewees), asking mostly open-ended questions, asking for experiences and examples,[272] and, most significantly, by employing a variety of probes.[273] Particularly in light of the sensitive topic of valuable knowledge, longer questions were frequently asked in order to provoke long answers as proposed by Bernard and Ryan.[274] Approaching the end, the interviewee was given the opportunity to emphasize once more what was most important or what was missing from his or her point of view.[275]

---

269 Interviews were conducted in the framework of the broader research project on the topic of "Intellectual property in Sino-German cooperation" funded by the German Federal Ministry of Education and Research and conducted by Bremen University of Applied Sciences.

270 See appendix 2. In March 2009, 26 exploratory interviews with 20 German and 6 Chinese employees in FIEs had already been conducted as exploratory interviews in the framework of the research project on "Intellectual Property in Sino-Cooperation". These interviews proved helpful in getting first insights on the handling of sensitive knowledge in FIEs in China, which proved relevant for both the research project in general and this study in particular (for more information see Müller and Schädler 2009). These insights helped in creating the interview guide and valuable insights have slightly influenced the findings chapter as well. The interview guide had further been checked in a pilot study in September 2009.

271 Marvasti 2004: 21, Bernard and Ryan 2010: 29-31, Bernard 2006: 212.

272 For instance, an interviewee exemplarily describes how to circumvent barriers at work, thereby implicitly illuminating by his informal way of speaking that barriers are obviously existent at the workplace and that subtle strategies are needed for circumventing them (see chapter 8.4).

273 As stimulating an interviewee to produce more information by himself, Bernard and Ryan (2010: 29-31) and Bernard (2006: 217) view probing as the key to successful in-depth interviewing. Most often, affirmative probes were used, in the sense of ranging from "hmhm" to "oh right, tell me more about that" which proved particularly useful when the interviewee vaguely indicates, for instance, the importance of the enterprise culture and then step by step explains what he actually means by that (see e.g. C/29/JV/SHA(9:29)) (note that interviewees are cited as follows: nationality/age/type of enterprise/location(interview number:quote number); for the dates of conducting the interview and the interviewers involved see appendix 1). Furthermore, silent probes triggered additional comments such as "I feel that actually knowledge mostly belongs to the person" (see e.g. C/36/WFOE/GD(4:4)).

274 Bernard and Ryan 2010: 32. A probe such as "there are different views on relationships, what is yours?" (see e.g. C/36/WFOE/SHA(13:14)) proved useful to assure the interviewee that his/her personal opinion is of interest rather than what is commonly regarded as an adequate answer.

275 See e.g. G/31/JV/SHA(8:37).

The whole research process within a foreign cultural environment deserves special awareness for cultural biases. In this study, the author hopes to reduce cultural biases by conducting empirical research with both Chinese and German interviewees as well as Chinese and German interviewers.[276] A cultural bias was avoided to its utmost extent by discussing the topic guide as well as the empirical findings with both Chinese and German nationals. Pitfalls of indirect and inductive communication patterns employed by Chinese interviewees (where the core statement is often at the end of an answer to a certain question)[277] were addressed. These were addressed by providing the interviewee with the time to describe their opinions extensively as well as by conducting the interviews in a group of two interviewers. In the team, the multiple tasks of asking, listening, and probing were pursued more profoundly. Also, interviews were audio recorded,[278] which proved indispensable for figuring out the subtle criteria and strategies regarded as useful for knowledge interactions.

Especially when tackling a sensitive topic such as valuable knowledge in a commercial context, Chinese interviewees might resort to diverse strategies to avoid answering the interviewer's questions.[279] In this study, this was alleviated by asking to comment on cards and to pursue card sorting according to the importance he/she ascribes to the components. Also, some questions were posed in the form of vignettes. Using hypothetical characters instead of the employee himself, vignettes prove especially fruitful to gain more detailed and contextualized responses in sensitive situations. By these means, it was possible to control the social desirability bias to an extent sufficient for collecting rigorous data.

Additionally, "participatory observation" in Bernard's[280] sense was pursued. One or two entire days have been spent in the sampled FIEs. This provided the interviewers with a couple of opportunities for informal talks with some interviewees, for instance, during lunch or while visiting the production site. This served both the purpose of building up trust as well as gaining additional infor-

---

276 All five members of the research team have participated in data collection. One of the researchers was ethnic Chinese with German nationality, while the remainder is German. With one exception, all the German researchers were fluent in Chinese with a sinologist and business background. Being a German national, the author tried not only to avoid biases with Chinese interviewees but also with German interviewees by critically keeping a distance rather than taking the (seemingly familiar) meaning behind their statements at face value (see also Cappai 2008: 20).

277 Alpermann 2012, see also Cappai 2008: 23.

278 Only one German interviewee did not want to be recorded for a few minutes during the interview, yet this passage was not relevant to the research questions.

279 Alpermann 2012.

280 Bernard (2006: 232-344) includes techniques such as taking field notes and making photographs within the environment where the group under study is usually present and which is decisive for belonging to his group at all.

mation on the topic under investigation, verifying or complementing what has been said in the interviews. Photos and documents of the enterprise contributed to grasping the overall situation of the environment the interviewees are usually situated in.

With the warming up, a more personal atmosphere was created. This included the introduction of the interviewers and the purpose of the interview as well as some small talk. This was most important as interviewees (Chinese as well as Germans) often appeared to be cautious in the light of the sensitive topic and due to being interviewed in their working context. The warming up proved most successful when the interviewers showed their interest and competency in regard to China as well as when commonalities among the interviewers and the interviewee were found. A more trustful atmosphere was continuously created and after the first quarter of the interview, interviewees started to answer questions more openly, forgetting about the audio recorder.[281]

The interviewer is always part of the interview situation and fundamentally influences the answers not only through his interviewing technique but also due to his very presence.[282] Precisely because the interviewers came over from Germany, they were perceived as rather neutral (although the interview was conducted in the setting of a German-invested enterprise). This can be seen from the following: in the last part, interviewees took the chance during the last follow-up part to reflect on the interview as such. Among others, the interview was seen as an opportunity to talk about one's work.[283] Furthermore, in some cases, when one hour was originally planned, interviewees prolonged the interviews, taking more time for it as originally intended.

The interview groups consisted of one male Chinese and one male German and three German female interviewees of different ages, thus, interviewer biases regarding gender or age could largely be avoided. Due to the German ethnicity of at least one interviewer in the group a certain hierarchy seemed to be felt quite often by the Chinese interviewees due to the fact that interviews were conducted in a German-invested enterprise. This was alleviated during the interview process by both using the interviewee's mother language.

The physical environment of the interview situation influenced the interview situation to a certain extent. An influence was observable in open plan offices. In one case,[284] a colleague came to sit at the table where the interview

281 This was the case with both German and Chinese interviewees with the exception of two German 8G/51/WFOE/JS(18), G/45/WFOE/BJ(83) and two Chinese interviewees C/42/WFOE/JS(37), C/35/WFOE/BJ(84) who aimed to give socially desirable answers over a significant part of the interview.

282 See Mason 2002: 7.

283 See e.g. C/28/WFOE/SHA(54:40).

284 C/27/WFOE/GD(3).

was conducted. In this situation, it was indirectly signaled that this was a rather intimate talk which made the colleague leave a few moments later. The overwhelming majority of interviews were conducted in separate rooms and, hence, this influence could be controlled.

The respective enterprise's corporate culture turned out to be most significant regarding the openness of the interviewees. The more open the culture, the more open were the interviewees. Since most enterprises that agree to such an investigation inherently harbor an open culture, most of the corporate cultures positively influenced the interview situation. It is no coincidence that socially desirable responses were given in the four interviews of two FIEs where the research team was only allowed to conduct two interviews each.

Ethical considerations are advisable particularly against the background of a sensitive topic which might influence the career of the interviewees. To avoid the interviewees being disadvantaged by their employer when answering questions surrounding the sensitive topic of valuable knowledge, informed consent was obtained from all interviewees. All interviewees were aware of the purpose of the interview as well as the data use being exclusively for research purposes in an anonymous and confidential manner. Their agreement to conducting the interview was thus based on full and open information.[285]

3.4 Data Analysis

Data analysis was prepared by transcribing the audio files. The data were transcribed by using the transcription software Olympus. A word-by-word transcription was pursued, including verbal signals or pauses. Data were fully transcribed by native speakers in order to ensure – especially in case of the Chinese language interviews – that the whole range of vocabulary used by the interviewee was grasped and mistakes resulting from a necessarily smaller vocabulary of non-native speakers were avoided.[286] In a second round, the Chinese language interviews were fully rechecked by one of the interviewers having participated in the respective interview. Having transcribed this way, mistakes have as far as (realistically) possible been avoided. This allowed for preparing data in a way to read between the lines and to draw reliable conclusions of what is not explicitly said but still is grounded in the data.

Technically, data analysis was pursued by using the Atlas.ti software. In order to roughly structure the data, topic guide issues, cards, and vignettes were de-

285 See Christians 2005: 144-145.
286 See Alpermann 2012.

ductively used as codes for a realist coding.[287] By applying Bernard and Ryan's data analysis techniques[288], repeated words (for instance corporate culture was much more often and more extensively referred to as compared to other parts of structural capital) or the co-occurrence of words (for instance atmosphere or spirit commonly occur together with corporate culture, later forming the particular idea of a corporate culture which cannot be expressed by slogans) were analyzed.

Also informed by Bernard and Ryan's techniques,[289] inductive and constructivist coding was pursued. During the search for indigenous categories, for example, themes such as "entering society" (进入社会) that cut across interviews were identified. A deeper search for theory-related material revealed that the meaning of "entering society" involves the need for learning to grasp the complex reality of relationships to be able to pursue knowledge work. In a further step, the overarching category "investigating relationships" emerged from several codes, especially from those codes which denoted a kind of relationships such as "healthy relationship".

In the last round of analysis, the overarching categories (organized in code families) were put in relation to each other, and comparisons between German and Chinese primary document families within each code family were made. Also in each document family it was searched for missing data, for instance, whether or not the corporate culture played a role for German employees. During this process, the overarching metatheme of a stable space providing orientation emerged from code families. This theme emerged after approximately two thirds of the interviews were analyzed and the saturation of this theme was confirmed during further analysis.

Considering the amount of data, only parts are included in the empirical chapter. Three interviewees are exemplarily cited, which either directly stated or indirectly conveyed the meaning of the respective passage during the interview. Interviewees are cited as follows: nationality/age/type of enterprise/location(interview number:quote number).[290] The exemplary citations show that the findings (if not otherwise stated) concern all types of enterprises, interviewees, or locations involved in the sample.

---

287 Coding and categorizing can be both realist and constructivist (Flick 2007a: 101).

288 Bernard and Ryan 2010: 55-67.

289 Bernard and Ryan 2010: 55-67.

290 For the dates of conducting the interview and the interviewers involved see appendix 1.

3.5 Validity, Reliability, and Objectivity

Although the traditional criteria of validity, reliability, and objectivity originate from quantitative research and their application for qualitative research proves difficult, qualitative researchers argue that they cannot be omitted, yet should be reformulated in a distinct way.[291] While *validity* within quantitative research involves the control over context conditions, qualitative approaches during the whole research process reflexively take into account factors potentially influencing the outcomes.[292] In this study, validity has been ensured by analyzing the interview content for biased responses – such as socially desirable responses – as well as the interview situation, including the relationship between interviewer and interviewee. Mostly by putting the interview in the context of observations made in the respective enterprise environment and by conducting several interviews in the same environment, such influences had been detected and taken into account during data analysis.

In qualitative research, instead of demanding the identical repetition of data, *reliability* ensures a transparent and accurate production of data. Not only the methods should be made transparent but also what is a statement of the interviewees and what belongs to the researcher's interpretation.[293] In the empirical chapter of this study, direct and indirect quotations clarify what has been stated by the interviewees and where interpretation starts.

If *objectivity* is an issue in qualitative research at all, it centers around the question whether two researchers would come to the same conclusions with the same qualitative data set.[294] In this study, subjective interpretation already started when analyzing the data, deciding which pieces of information were worth coding. Since inductive coding was largely applied, other researchers could well have done it differently. Yet the objectivity of this study has been sufficiently enhanced by discussions during the data analysis process within the research team.

3.6 Generalizability

As being a qualitative research endeavor, this study's value lies in identifying the key issues and relating them to their particular context. Generalizing such qualitative data to a wider population is not the study's primary concern and cannot

291 See e.g. Mason 2002: 39, Flick 2007b: 15.
292 See Flick 2007b: 16-18.
293 Flick 2007b: 16.
294 Flick 2007b: 15.

be done as neatly as it would be possible within representative quantitative research. Yet following qualitative researchers such as Mason,[295] the *extent* to which the research could be linked to a wider population is at least specified more clearly.

The group under scrutiny is (Chinese and German) knowledge workers in China's German-invested manufacturing sector in (north)eastern urban China. From the angle of internal generalizability,[296] one has to consider potential variations *among* this population in terms of different ages, education levels, departments, positions, enterprise types, sizes, industries, and locations. The average age of 34 years coincides with statistical data on China's knowledge workforce per age group, which show that their average age is also around the mid-thirties.[297] An average age of 44 for German employees might also reflect the respective population due to the fact that German employees usually have formerly worked in Germany before being sent to China. The education level also reflects the usual situation for non-manual employees within FIEs in China where Chinese employees mostly hold a bachelor degree while Germans hold a diploma. Departments and positions share the common thread of communication and fit well to the education level. The hierarchical difference between German and Chinese employees reflects the current situation in FIEs in China.

Among the types of enterprises, WFOEs and Equity JVs are most prevalent. The proportion of 10:4 mirrors the general proportion of German WFOEs and Equity JV.[298] Despite many differences between both types such as degree of control or autonomy, the fact important for this study shared by both types is that Chinese employees act as knowledge workers with the latitude how to share and disclose valuable knowledge and are needed as intermediaries to the market. They are summarized as FIEs except otherwise specified in the empirical chapter.

German-invested enterprises with a parent company in Germany with more than 1,000 employees dominate the sample (64%), which comes very close to the proportion of 60% for German-invested enterprises in China as a whole.[299] German-invested enterprises are mainly active in manufacturing (as opposed to service and trade), and engineering and automotive are precisely the sectors were

295 See e.g. Mason 2002:39.
296 See e.g. Maxwell 2013: 137.
297 See chapter 6.2.
298 996 WFOEs and 438 Equity JVs in Mainland China as of Jan 17, 2009 (according to the "German Company Directory" (http://www.german-company-directory.com/), which is administered by the German Industry & Commerce (GIC) being the service provider of the German Chamber of Commerce in China).
299 German Chamber of Commerce in China 2007: 11.

most German-invested enterprises operate in.[300] These sectors have in common that they have been highly competitive in China at the time of investigation.[301]

German-invested enterprises are largely representative for FIEs in China in regard to valuable knowledge. All FIEs more or less have to cope with the controversial handling of knowledge by Chinese employees. Yet in terms of technological innovations and valuable knowledge at stake, German-invested enterprises are most representative for Western enterprises, that is, enterprises from Europe and North America. These are followed by Japan with other Asian countries following suit.

In terms of culture, findings must be generalized to FIEs with more caution. Sino-German conflicts might not be the same as Sino-American conflicts or Sino-Japanese conflicts. Only when it comes to cultural knowledge informing the Chinese employees in FIEs, findings can be generalized to Chinese in FIEs no matter the origin. The extent and way how this leads to conflicts with foreign employees in the enterprise, however, strongly depends on the respective foreign culture.

In terms of the location of the sampled enterprises, the cities and provinces form part of the economically more advanced eastern region (东部地区) as well as the northeastern region (东北地区).[302] While the locations in the eastern region reflect the general spatial distribution of German FIEs in China,[303] the northeastern region is not a typical location for German enterprises. Yet, most importantly, in all regions established FIEs can be found, ensuring that cultural knowledge informing employees working in FIEs has potentially evolved over time. During data analysis special attention has been paid to the potential influence of the regional factor.

The external generalizability[304] beyond that group is limited. In the light of the different experiences and educational backgrounds of age cohorts in China, generalization to Chinese employees older than the range of the sample cannot easily be made without further researching that group. Findings cannot be gener-

---

300 German Chamber of Commerce in China 2007: 15.

301 See e.g. Apco Worldwide 2010, *China Daily* 2011, US-China Business Council 2011: 8, Wexler 2011.

302 Following the official division of the NBS (2011a), China's 31 mainland provinces (and municipalities) are grouped into four regions, namely the eastern (东部地区), central (中部地区), western (西部地区), and northeastern region (东北地区). This categorization is popular since the 9th five-year-plan (1996-2000) and has focused on balancing the large regional disparities (Taubmann 2007: 41-44). It is still considered useful for statistical purposes by the NBS (2011a).

303 German Chamber of Commerce in China 2007: 10.

304 See e.g. Maxwell 2013: 137.

alized to employees in departments or in positions mainly occupied with manual work as communication of knowledge is not their main concern.

As valuable knowledge seems to be creating conflicts mostly between China and the West, many people are tempted to easily draw on the simple and dichotomous cultural view of "East versus West". Yet this proves to be oversimplified. Especially in the business realm, the available country-level studies show cultural differences among employees of countries in the Western hemisphere as well as among Asian countries.[305] Findings of Chinese employees can thus not be generalized to other employees of other Asian countries, like findings of German employees cannot be generalized to employees from other countries in Europe or the Western hemisphere.

The municipalities and provinces where the sampled FIEs are located are not representative for the rest of the 26 municipalities and provinces. In China, spatial disparities – both rural-urban and regional – are particularly large. Spatial disparities include a higher overall education level, a much more dynamic and developed economy as well as a more vibrant investment, legal and political climate in eastern urban China.[306] Most significant for the study's topic is that whereas interior provinces tend to have rich natural resource endowment and find themselves at a mid- or pre-industrialization stage, the knowledge economy has already taken hold in the eastern region with high knowledge intensity and innovation capability.[307] Findings can thus not be generalized to the central and western region or rural areas. Even generalization to the eastern and northeastern China is limited as northeastern China is less developed than eastern China and as even within eastern China, disparities are still significant.

3.7 Contextualization

Contextualization of data plays a paramount role in qualitative research.[308] In this study, the sampled employees are entangled in manifold contexts which are constituent to the cultural knowledge they are informed by. The interpretation of the findings against the background of the employees' positioning in these contexts yielded explanations for the phenomenon of increased leakage and insufficient sharing of knowledge in FIEs in China. These contexts are considered in the following three chapters.

305 Hofstede 1984, Hall 1989, Trompenaars and Hampden-Turner 1997, House et al. 2004.
306 See e.g. Lieberthal 1995: 273, Chen Chunlai 2011: 36-46 and 149, Cooke 2005: 25.
307 See e.g. Dahlman and Aubert 2001: 43-44, Naughton 2007: 4, Chen Jiagui and Wang Qin 2010: 67.
308 Cappai 2008: 21-22.

Apart from the contexts under scrutiny below, the empirical findings of handling knowledge in China's FIEs are inevitable shaped by the larger Chinese economic, political, and legal system. To cover these influences in full depths is well outside the scope of this study. It is aimed, however, at providing the reader with a rough idea of the complex environment the conflicts over the handling of valuable knowledge are embedded in.

The Chinese economy is complex. While being still in the midst of transition from a large traditional agrarian economy to an industrialized economy, the knowledge economy is under way. Only with the introduction of Western technology in the 19th century, the industrial economy took hold in China's large traditional agrarian economy. Legacies of the traditional agrarian economy range from family businesses, labor abundance, and localized incremental innovation. China's innovation capacity is still very much locally embedded with quick reaction to market changes by imitation, experimentation, and adaptation at the borderline or in breach of intellectual property laws. The upcoming knowledge economy is yet largely pushed by FIEs as the main technology providers.

For more than three decades now, China is undergoing another transition from a socialist command economy toward a market economy. The influx of the Soviet state industrial ownership structure after 1949 is mirrored in parts by the multifaceted ownership structure in today's China. The current Chinese business landscape is still characterized by state intervention combined with gradual liberalization of the market. These time-lapse transitions unfold into very different uncertain local institutional environments, the managing of which is still crucial to economic progress and business success in China to the present day.[309]

In China, the inter-relatedness of politics and economy is ubiquitous. As a legacy of the past, the political landscape is still characterized by strong personal rule at the top, powerful local bureaucracies, a low degree of institutionalization complemented by informal procedures and exercise of power. Yet the Chinese Communist Party – although still playing the leading role in state, economy, and society – has gradually loosened control in favor of economic modernization in the reform era. In times of rapid economic modernization and global integration as well as pluralization of political interests in state and economy, political regulatory problems have become even more complex.

For handling this complexity of interests, economic decision power has strongly been decentralized. Policy instruments are developed and practiced locally, only vaguely guided by the central government. Most economic matters are exclusively decided and handled by local governments. Local officials share an interest in promoting economic development as they are encouraged by vari-

309 For further reading, refer to Naughton 2007, Rawski 1989, Spence 1990, Hu Albert G.Z. and Jefferson 2008.

ous incentives. For the sake of economic growth, local officials often ignore central policies and goals and make their own rules even when in conflict with centrally defined goals. As a consequence, the discrepancy between central guidelines and local implementation produces an ambiguous political business landscape in which power of local officials is strong and successfully doing business is highly contingent on complex relations with local officials.[310]

Whereas the state traditionally refrained from administering economic activity and only interfered in the case of disruption of public order, the process of developing a concise legal framework after 1978 has sought to cope with the multitude of interests in contemporary China. The Chinese government has recognized that the domestic legal system was in many ways unattractive for foreigners and has put efforts in establishing a separate legal system. During the decades, the focus has shifted to an active consideration of the needs of the domestic economy. Distinctions between the state and the private sector, as well as between domestic and foreign actors, gradually eroded. The strife for alignment of different investment and ownership types in the domestic realm was flanked by the alignment of domestic trading and investment rules with international norms which ultimately led to the entry into the World Trade Organization (WTO).

Despite an aligned and profound legal framework, enforcement in various areas still faces numerous structural problems. The legal framework is often inconcise and suffers from conflicting regulations which make enforcement complicated. The processes of enforcement remain subject to the limitations of bureaucratic politics and the overall leadership of the Chinese Communist Party. Qualification of local judges often proves insufficient. The judiciary at different levels is dependent from the local government, which is responsible for the appointment and dismissal of judges as well as for their salary and benefits. Local governments in many cases have little incentive to enforce national regulations, which can be clearly observed in the realm of the enforcement of intellectual property rights.[311] This overall situation still leaves ample room for uncertainty for business and other actors in contemporaray China.

310 For further reading, refer to Lieberthal 1995, Heilmann and Perry 2011, Shambaugh 2011.
311 For further reading, refer to Clarke et al. 2008, Potter 2011, Heuser 2002 and 2009.

4 Compradors in China's Foreign Enterprises

When the historian Hosea Ballou Morse as early as 1907 observed that "the China of to-day is, with minor differences, the China of the past"[312], he could not have forseen that more than a century later this observation still proves valid. Despite China's rapid and visible change, deeply rooted fundamentals have continued to prevail. Indeed, the need for intermediaries for foreigners doing business in China observable in present times proved to be considerable throughout modern Chinese history. Moreover, the foreigners' concerns arising from the institution of the intermediary – the so-called "comprador" – were also very similar to those of today. The comprador can thus be regarded as *the* harbinger of contemporary Chinese employees in FIEs who act as intermediaries between the FIE and the local business environment. Compradors played not only a pivotal role for foreign businesses (4.1), but also significantly contributed to the Chinese economy (4.2), while inhabiting a rather ambiguous status within Chinese society (4.3). Many similarities to contemporary intermediaries, who are analyzed in the subsequent chapter, can be found.

4.1 The Role of the Comprador for Foreign Businesses

Prior to the Opium Wars, China's economic relations with the global trading system were limited. From the mid-18th century until 1842, foreign trade mainly concentrated in Guangzhou. The right of trading with foreign merchants was exclusively granted to a group of Chinese merchants – Cohong (公行) –, who were appointed by the Qing government. These merchants took care of and bore responsibility for every act of the foreign merchants and their ships. This included engaging a comprador[313] or *maiban* (买办)[314], who supplied the foreign merchant with food and daily necessities and managed his daily private affairs.[315]

312 Morse 1920: vii.

313 A term borrowed from the Portuguese for local Chinese merchants in Guangzhou and Macao (Bergère 1986: 46, Hao Yenping 1970: 44).

314 *Maiban* 买办 literally means "purchaser". It originally referred to the official broker who purchased supplies for the Ming dynasty (1368-1664) government (Hao Yenping 1970: 45, Huang Yifeng et al. 1982: 1-2).

315 Morse 1910: 63-67 and 312, Bergère 1968: 26, Xu Dixin and Wu Chengming 2003: 144-145.

With the Treaty of Nanjing in 1842, the five ports of Guangzhou, Xiamen, Fuzhou, Ningbo, and Shanghai were opened to foreign trade, and the Cohong monopoly was abolished. Foreigners – mostly being agents of large foreign family enterprises – were then able to decisively expand their businesses in China: they could trade goods at prices set by free competition, they could rent and build warehouses and residences, and they were protected by their own national law instead of being subject to Chinese law.[316] In theory, foreigners in the treaty ports were free to trade with any Chinese merchant and pursue all transactions necessary for trading.

In reality, however, direct trading with Chinese merchants posed serious obstacles. Language barriers, the complexity of the currency, varying systems of weights and measures, the obscure financial status of banks or trading partners as well as the extraordinary variety of commercial practices and social customs were among the most obvious impediments. More subtle but even more powerful obstacles were posed upon foreign merchants by the traditional trading system. The limited trading routes available between different regions were controlled by Chinese merchants. Banks only negotiated with Chinese merchants and not with foreigners. Most significantly, market networks and credit institutions were controlled by strong guilds. The powerful Shandong shipping guild, for instance, restricted foreigner's loading of pulse without interference by local officials. These guilds were – apart from commercial ties – first of all characterized by strong familial and regional ties and thus difficult to enter by outsiders from a certain region or family, be they Chinese or foreign. Trading with single guild members was also an obstacle as guilds even had the power to inhibit direct business transactions of their members.[317] Therefore, the foreign merchants, whose crucial task was to establish trade relations in China for their employers in their home countries, had no choice but to pursue this task via compradors, whom they then could freely employ.[318]

Initially, the role of compradors as intermediaries only slowly gained significance. Supplies still exceeded the demand and communication was slow. Only after the conclusion of the Treaty of Tianjin and the further opening of eleven treaty ports in the late 1850s, their role became significantly more important. The extension of telegraphic communication and steamship transportation via the newly opened Suez Canal in the 1860s also contributed strongly to their importance for

316 Morse 1910: 297-312, Morse 1918: 6, Bergère 1986: 33, Xu Dixin and Wu Chengming 2003: 146.

317 Bergère 1986: 33-37, Hao Yenping 1970: 24-25, Morse 1918: 154-156.

318 Hao Yenping 1970: 15-17, Morse 1910: 312.

foreign merchants, who became much more exposed to competition and business risks through enhanced communication and shorter transport times.[319]

This trend is reflected in numbers. Whereas the group of compradors only comprised about 250 compradors in 1854,[320] their number had increased to 10,000 by the end of the 19th century. In 1920, they reached their peak with 40,000 persons in total.[321] With the number of foreigners amounting to nearly 321,000 persons in 1924, one comprador on average could be in charge for eight foreigners. Whereas mostly the British were at the forefront of the treaty negotiations and together with other "Westerners" (in the sense of Europeans and North Americans) are the only foreigners covered by the relevant comprador literature, the large majority of foreigners in the early 20th century were indeed Janapanese or Russian, with "Westerners" only making up less than 10%.[322] Viewed from this angle, the number of compradors seems to have been able to satisfy "Western" demands.

Contractually employed by the foreign enterprise, compradors were in charge of handling the Chinese side of the enterprise's activities, acting as intermediaries for the enterprise's business transactions. They took care of the purchase of products from the interior, which were to be exported by the foreign enterprise, with tea and silk being the commodities exported the most. They also provided market information, such as price fluctuations and the competitors' situation.[323] For the import business, such as woolens and cotton, compradors analyzed the demand on the Chinese market and introduced the foreign goods to Chinese customers.[324] They were also responsible for the transport of goods, mainly in the shipping business, where they dealt with customs reporting and with Chinese officials in different ports. They even acted as interpreters and mediators, helping to settle disputes between merchants in different ports.[325] Their tasks also included the hiring and employing of Chinese staff, which was larger in number than the foreign employees.[326] Compradors thus completely managed all tasks which connected the foreign enterprise with the Chinese environment. As the vast majority of foreign enterprises were active in trade, the comprador *de facto* pursued the enterprise's main business activities.

319 Xu Dixin and Wu Chengming 2003: 148 and 769, Morse 1910: 342 and 562-563, Hao Yenping 1970: 20-44.
320 Hao Yenping 1970: 101.
321 Xu Dixin and Wu Chengming 2003: 148 and 769.
322 Morse and MacNair 1967: 1033-1034.
323 Hao Yenping 1970: 17 and 74-83, Morse 1918: 400-406, Chan Kai Yiu 2006: 51.
324 Huang Yifeng et al. 1982: 36-37, Xu Dixin and Wu Chengming 2003: 148.
325 Hao Yenping 1970: 74-75, Chan Kai Yiu 2006: 50, see Hao Yenping 1970: 154-159, see Bergère 1968: 27.
326 Hao Yenping 1970: 24.

The most outstanding feature of the comprador system in China was their guaranteeing of safe business transactions of their foreign principals. This included the guaranteeing of provision of cash, granting of credits as well as bearing of responsibility for insolvency of local merchants or banks. They also were held liable for disloyalty of staff.[327] By such means, foreign enterprises could effectively minimize the business risks in an environment they perceived as obscure and uncertain. The comprador was not only the *de facto* manager of the foreign enterprise but also secured its business.

This large responsibility and latitude in doing business provided the comprador with many opportunities to be active in business himself. The significance of these opportunities for him is reflected by his income structure. The salary from their foreign employer indeed only constituted 17.6% of their income. Trading on the interior market gave the comprador the opportunity to take part in the commission system, which constituted the main source of his income (36.8%).[328] In addition to their contractual agreement, many compradors simultaneously conducted their own independent business.[329] In fact, only a very small part of his income came from his foreign employer. The large part was earned through the comprador's activitiy outside. This indicates that the identity of an independent businessman must have been much stronger than the identity of an employee.

The comprador's strife of doing business on his own account also resulted in business activities at the expense of his foreign employer or even included betraying him. Functioning as treasurers, compradors could secretly use their employer's funds to finance their own businesses,[330] such as the well-known comprador Chen Lianbo (陈廉伯) who used the capital of the Hong Kong and Shanghai Banking Corporation (HSBC) to finance his silk business.[331] Compradors also conducted their own businesses by using the seal of the foreign enterprise. Some of them forged a higher price list of local products and kept the surplus money for themselves.[332] Also, products were manipulated before delivering them to the employer. For instance, after a British enterprise returned tea of minor quality to the famous comprador Xu Run (徐润) which he had previously purchased for them, the comprador mixed it a year later with tea of excellent quality and successfully sold it again to the British merchants.[333]

327 Bergère 1968: 27, Hao Yenping 1970: 49 and 65-68, Chan Kai Yiu 2006: 50-51.
328 Xu Dixin and Wu Chengming 2003: 147-148 and 175.
329 Hao Yenping 1970: 12, Hou Zhigang 1996: 327.
330 Hao Yenping 1970: 94-95.
331 Hou Zhigang 1996: 328.
332 Hao Yenping 1970: 94-95.
333 Cao Wenjuan 1996: 8.

Embezzlement, forging, and deceit must be seen, however, against the background of modern Chinese economy, where such practices were common among businessmen in general. In regard to compradors, the boundaries were particularly blurred as their activities for enterprises were hard to distinguish from their independent business transactions. Under the system of "complete responsibility", a distinction between personal and enterprises' funds was even harder to make.[334] The difficulty of drawing this line is also reflected in court decisions. Foreign enterprises sued their comprador for such malpractices but did not necessarily win the suit since the comprador might have acted as an independent merchant according to the Sino-German mixed court's verdict.[335] As the behavior was common in the business environment and the boundaries of funds and activities were hard to draw, the comprador's behavior is again to be seen in the context of his special intermediary identity. This identity in fact resembled an independent businessman rather than an employee.

This identity made it also inevitable that the comprador possessed a certain kind of knowledge monopoly.[336] As intermediary, the comprador possessed both information on the business environment and exclusive information on the enterprise and the products of his foreign employer. In this exclusive position, he could easily make use of them for grasping business opportunities. Chen Liangbo, for instance, gathered the HSBC's business information regarding the government's intent to buy silver and made use of this information by quickly importing silver in advance to be the first to satisfy the government's need.[337]

On the part of foreign enterprises, these incidents raised the questions of trustworthiness and loyalty. Mutual trust between foreign employers and compradors was merely prevalent in the 1850s and 1860s, when doing business was perceived as being impossible without trusting the comprador. Some foreign businesses were strongly dependent on compradors such as Xu Run who developed the interior market for them.[338] Those foreigners who were able to recruit high quality compradors appeared to be the most successful and competitive ones. Foreign enterprise thus had to maintain good relations with the compradors and to secure efficient compradors in order to conduct business smoothly.[339] As a consequence, foreign merchants made concessions such as paying a commission in addition to salary. Also, they acknowledged the comprador as a merchant in

334 Hao Yenping 1970: 150-151. See also chapter 4.2.
335 Hao Yenping 1970: 168-170.
336 See Liu Yunsheng 2007: 56.
337 Hou Zhigang 1996: 326-327.
338 Cao Wenjuan 1996: 7.
339 Hao Yenping 1970: 26.

the first place and usually gave consent for trading transactions on his own account, except when interfering with the enterprise's transaction.[340]

When the foreign merchant's confidence was betrayed and the comprador's activities had been found detrimental to the enterprise's interests, the foreign merchant not necessarily sanctioned his comprador but, quite the contrary, even continued to support him. When the comprador Tang Tingshu (唐廷枢), for example, took 80,000 taels (两) from his foreign enterprise's account for private purposes, his boss – although being shocked and absolutely unsatisfied with the situation – still praised his work.[341] In the first two decades, foreign merchants were virtually completely dependent on the comprador, having no choice but to entrust him with their business even in case of misbehavior.

With the rapid development of steamships and communication methods and a regional shift to new treaty ports since the 1860s, the personal ties continuously weakened. In the 20th century, the relationship became rather impersonal in nature. Compradors' trustworthiness was then deemed insufficient by the foreign business community which depicted them as unscrupulous bargainers. Foreign enterprises then saw the need for putting mechanisms in place in order to control the compradors. Methods such as requiring a cash deposit, checking the cashbook, and obtaining information via third persons were employed – albeit in a cautious way in order to avoid too much distrust.[342] The relationship of trust thus changed into one of relative control.

While compradors were still growing in numbers and in economic strength at the beginning of the 20th century, foreign enterprises had already induced the transformation of the comprador system by employing different measures. Compradors were, for instance, employed as high-level employees. Their activity level, however, soon deteriorated and the foreign employer returned to pay them commission, which shows that in fact the comprador system was still in place. Alternatively, the comprador's status was changed into that of a partner or an independent purchaser. Foreign enterprises with a monopoly on a certain product or in a certain region installed independent distributors, who had essentially the same function as compradors but were closely connected and relied on the foreign enterprise's monopoly.[343] Some companies only effectively gained control by integrating salaried Chinese employees in their corporate hierarchy. They put much effort into cultivating the Chinese employees for adequately serving the enterprises' needs.[344] As a matter of fact, when the latitude of the former com-

340 Hao Yenping 1970: 161, Xu Dixin and Wu Chengming 2003: 147-148 and 163-164.
341 Tang Kemin 1996: 47-48.
342 Hao Yenping 1970: 160-168, see Chan Kai Yiu 2006: 49.
343 Xu Dixin and Wu Chengming 2003: 785-799.
344 Cochran 2000: 12-43, Chan Kai Yiu 2006: 162.

prador was restricted externally by the regional monopoly or internally by cultivating Chinese employees, the ambiguity of the comprador institution could be alleviated to a certain extent.

These attempts were only possible against the background of a changing market and institutional landscape. Becoming smaller in size and making smaller profits, foreign enterprises could no longer afford the comprador's commission, finding it more difficult to control the compradors and with it their own financial resources. What is more, the capacity of the traditional comprador system proved to be limited for enterprises aiming at further developing the interior market. As more and more market players emerged, compradors were hardly able to reduce the risks emerging from their responsibility as guarantors.[345] At the same time, foreign merchants – who in the beginning were largely ignorant toward Chinese language, customs, and money systems –[346] became more and more knowledgable about China. They learned about Chinese customs and trading practices and were encouraged by their enterprises to take courses in Chinese language,[347] which enabled them to directly trade with Chinese merchants. In the 1930s, institutional reasons, such as the simplification of the currency, further induced the comprador's decline. Compradors ultimately disappeared with the signing of the "equal treaties" in 1943.[348]

In summary, as an intermediary in modern China, the comprador was well positioned in foreign enterprises due to the difficulties these faced in the Chinese environment, presenting virtually the only real connection to the environment. Foreign enterprises depended on the comprador so heavily that they accepted paying a high commission as well as fraud. Only in a changing market and institutional environment were foreign enterprises able to alleviate the difficulties and reduce the dependency on the comprador.

Most significantly, the comprador was in fact an independent businessman rather than an employee just working for a certain employer and being "in between" the employing enterprise and other market players. This identity allowed him to know both the foreign business and the domestic market very well and, most importantly, enabled him to use this knowledge for his own business. Along with a distinct business culture where embezzlement and the like were not uncommon, as well as an uncertain market and institutional environment, this identity paved the way he set the boundaries of knowledge between him, his foreign enterprise and other businesses.

345 Xu Dixin and Wu Chengming 2003: 776-779, Chan Kai Yiu 2006: 75.

346 Bergère 1986: 46.

347 Hao Yenping 1970: 61, Xu Dixin and Wu Chengming 2003: 782.

348 Hao Yenping 1970: 62-63.

4.2 Compradors in Chinese Economy

In line with the rise of compradors, their direct and indirect contributions to the Chinese economy became more and more visible. Their indirect contribution was visible in the increase of foreign trade and investment. A more direct contribution was their own investment activity, their knowledge and innovation capacity, without which China's industrialization and modernization would not have taken place the way it did.

With foreigners being active in China with trading as their main activity especially in the first decades, China's foreign trade volume increased during the comprador period. Exports almost doubled between 1867 and 1905, and imports into China nearly tripled in this period.[349] The share of trade in national income rose from 5% to 16% between 1871 and 1929.[350]

Chai[351] puts these figures in perspective by comparing them to the crucial role of foreign trade in early Japanese development. Viewed in this light, China's trade potential might not have been far from being fully grasped. A large part of the Chinese domestic market was surely not reached by foreign influence, taking the absence of any trade promotion policies as well as the tight traditional trading system into account.

Yet the fact that foreigners could participate in the trading system at all can clearly be attributed to the compradors. It was only through their bridging function that regional trade between the interior and the treaty ports as well as between southern and northern coastal areas became possible. In fact, the compradors connected two separate trading systems, that is, the one of foreigners trading between ports and overseas with that of Chinese trading between treaty ports and the interior.[352] Against this background it can be said that trade did not increase tremendously due to foreign presence in China, however, without the institution of the compradors this increase would not have happened.

Investment by foreigners played a more substantial role for the Chinese economy. The number of foreign enterprises increased from 343 in 1875 to 933 at the end of the 19th century and further rose to 7743 in 1925. Whereas most enterprises in the beginning were of British origin, Japanese-invested enterprises – following the Treaty of Shimonoseki – accounted for nearly 60% in 1920. Large Europeans trading houses were followed by smaller enterprises which benefitted from increased transportation. These developments explain why the

349 Morse 1918: 397-402.
350 Chai Joseph C.H. 2011: 64-65.
351 Chai Joseph C.H. 2011: 63-71.
352 Hao Yenping 1970: 112-120, Bergère 1986: 33-38.

foreign direct investment (FDI) increased more strongly than the trade volume.[353]

Whereas trading enterprises initially dominated, the sectors became more diverse after the turn of the century. In the aftermath of the Treaty of Shimonoseki, first the Japanese merchants, followed by other foreignerns, were officially allowed to invest into the manufacturing sector. Not only foreign banks and insurances emerged, but most significantly, foreign industrial and shipping enterprises appeared in China. These were most active in economically important sectors ranging from mining, textiles, machine manufacturing, and the steamship industry.[354]

Nevertheless, the FDI's impact on industrialization has to be put into perspective. Xu and Wu found that more than half of foreign industrial capital was invested into the railway industry, while manufacturing only accounted for one fifth.[355] Chai[356] confirms that the share of foreign capital in the manufacturing sector increased from 10% in 1913 to a still modest 20% in 1936. Furthermore, in view of Chinese industrial investments, Xu and Wu's[357] comparative analysis reveals that the amount of FDI only slightly exceeded the indigenous industrial investment in 1920. Hence, FDI into modern Chinese industries did not play that important a role as commonly expected.

These new industrial enterprises, however, very likely still had their effects on the quality of China's capital stock, industrialization, and structural change. This can, for instance, be judged from the rapid increase of imports of foreign machinery and large equipment. By 1933, more than one third of the total equipment installed in China was imported.[358]

Also, this can be judged from the likely benefits for the Chinese industry from the imported machinery reaped through transfer of the relevant knowledge which took place via compradors. At the end of 19th century, compradors appeared to be not only largely employed by trading enterprises but also of foreign enterprises of various sectors. Chinese enterprises then also began to conduct business with foreigners via compradors.[359] Compradors were thus well positioned for the transfer of technical knowledge. Henceforth, they were not only knowledgeable in trade but gained technical knowledge over time. The comprador Xu Run, for instance, made use of his familiarity with foreign technology to successfully organize foreign machines and engineers for Chinese coal mining

353 Xu Dixin and Wu Chengming 2003: 148 and 768-769.
354 Xu Dixin and Wu Chengming 2003: 148 and 178-183, Hao Yenping 1970: 120-136.
355 Xu Dixin and Wu Chengming 2003: 1066.
356 Chai Joseph C.H. 2011: 76.
357 Xu Dixin and Wu Chengming 2003: 7-9 and 1066.
358 Chai Joseph C.H. 2011: 67.
359 Xu Dixin and Wu Chengming 2003: 148, Bergère 1968: 27.

plants.[360] Only via his direct technical knowledge input, Chinese enterprises could benefit from the availability of foreign machinery and equipment at all.

Knowledge spillovers must have taken place as can be seen by the foreign trade structure. As usually the case during catch-up industrialization, the imports of machinery had – albeit slowly – been substituted in part. Whereas manufactures – both light and heavy industrial products – made up 72% of imports in 1912, they accounted for only 54% in 1933.[361] Yet the following phase of catch-up industrialization, that is, the exporting of heavy industrial goods, only happened to a limited extent. The export structure shows that exports were still dominated by light industrial products. Still, more fixed capital investment would have been required to produce machinery and equipment and difficulties in technological absorption and experiences remained.[362]

Indeed, a lack of capital prevailed. As it is typical for underdeveloped economies, capital was scarce anyway. Confronted with high interest rates, it was difficult to secure capital for long-term investments. Foreign investment in the form of foreign loans existed, yet can be neglected in its role for capital formation. It was basically used for post-war indemnity payments and rather contributed to the capital formation of the creditor countries rather than to indigenous capital formation.[363] Not only Chinese but also foreign enterprises were in demand of capital.

Against this background, investments by compradors played a remarkable role. Compradors had acquired considerable wealth and investment capacity through lengthy associations with foreign merchants. Their contacts with foreigners placed them at the forefront of investing in foreign enterprises, even before other groups of society dared to invest or were fully aware of the profitability of these opportunities. Compradors thus invested nearly half of their income in enterprises. Their investment flew into diverse sectors and especially into those crucial to modernization. A smaller part was even invested into traditional Chinese enterprises, directly assisting them in catching up with their foreign counterparts.

Chinese investors – of whom a great number was compradors – held around 40% of the shares of foreign enterprises. In extreme cases, such as the Chinese government sponsored steamship enterprise "China Merchants' S.N.", the shares of compradors even amounted to nearly 80%.[364] A significant part of capital formation can thus directly be attributed to the comprador.

360 Cao Wenjuan 1996: 27.
361 Chai Joseph C.H. 2011: 69-71.
362 Chai Joseph C.H. 2011: 67-69.
363 Chai Joseph C.H. 2011: 71-74.
364 Hao Yenping 1970: 120-136, Xu Dixin and Wu Chengming 2003: 178-183.

Another contribution to modern Chinese economic development was the managerial knowledge the comprador acquired via close collaboration with foreign managers. Compradors were eager to learn foreign knowledge and ideas. Basic managerial abilities, such as planning, pricing, calculating were acquired and improved. These abilities provided them with an enormous advantage over traditional gentry members or officials who were knowledgeable in Confucian classics instead of business management. These abilities indeed proved very valuable as compradors were even appointed to manage SOEs, which were formerly administered by officials. Most importantly, these abilities could hardly be acquired otherwise.[365] This was an important channel for knowledge transfer, and it is only due to the comprador that this knowledge could have been transferred to the Chinese economy.

Yet this did not linger on the level of pure transfer and spillovers. Instead of being only a transmission belt for knowledge and technology, the comprador developed a discrete innovation capacity. His deep knowledge of the conditions of various sectors of the Chinese economy as well as being knowledgable in foreign products, technology, and management provided him with extraordinary input for innovative ideas. As a matter of fact, compradors quickly responded to new situations and grasped business opportunities. They innovatively promoted the foreign trade by, for instance, purchasing in the interior, like directly from tea growers. They found new ways of raising large amounts of capital, realized the importance and profitability of modern enterprises, were not reluctant to enter new fields of business before any other groups had this intention, and innovatively combined new factors of production and distribution.[366] Compradors also had important effects on the modernization of Shanghai's banking system.[367] Accordingly, compradors' innovative capacity contributed in multiple ways to China's economic modernization and industrialization. This contribution is even more significant in the light of the fact that the traditional economic system generally hampered modernization.[368]

After 1920, opportunities for direct business interactions precipitated, leading to a decline of the economic strength and influence of compradors.[369] Foreign merchants started to grasp opportunities to trade directly with Chinese merchants. Chinese merchants, too, increasingly gained experiences in trading with foreigners and approached foreigners or engaged in foreign trade themselves. This was only possible against the background of the development of modern

365 Hao Yenping 1970: 136-146.
366 Hao Yenping 1970: 9 and 114-120 and 146-148.
367 Yi Jicang 2006.
368 Bergère 1986: 38.
369 Xu Dixin and Wu Chengming 2003: 784.

Chinese banks and a prospering Chinese local industry.[370] Hence, the comprador's role was most crucial in a transitional period in general and in the Chinese transition in particular.

In the developmental state of the Chinese local economy, quantitative contributions of the foreign presense were visible, yet not enormous. Yet qualitative contributions can indeed be considered remarkable: benefits reaped through modernization are clearly attributable to activities of and experiences with foreigners. As it were the compradors who were at the forefront of foreign knowledge, experiences, and advice, and truly engaged with the local economy as well, the comprador can, in retrospect, truly be seen as an agent of economic modernization.

4.3 Compradors in Chinese Society

In Ancient China, merchants ranked at the bottom of the traditional social hierarchy with scholars at the top, followed by farmers and artisans. However, the merchant's role *de facto* had already become significant for China's society in the 18th century. Population growth had started to accelerate and the balance between population and resources had become difficult to sustain. More and more Chinese switched from agriculture to artisanry. Handicrafts were traded on the simultaneously emerging hierarchical network of regional markets consisting of major commercial centers and intermediary markets. Private banks satisfied the newly emerging demand for money. Markets and banks were connected by and functioned thanks to merchants, and hence, their role became indispensable for the rural society.[371]

Another consequence was that merchants, despite theoretically being at the bottom of the hierarchy, were in fact often wealthier than scholars, farmers, and artisans.[372] Their wealth helped the merchants to improve their social status. In addition, merchants had the opportunity to purchase examination degrees and official titles – encouraged by the Qing government, which sought to improve its financial situation. This proved to be a lucrative vehicle for merchants obtaining gentry status without passing the conventional examinations.[373] Merchants could then become part of the urban elite.

370 Hao Yenping 1970: 62.

371 Bergère 1986: 21-32.

372 Tanner 2009: 103.

373 Hao Yenping 1970: 184-186. Influential compradors almost always possessed titles in late Qing (Hao Yenping 1970: 184), such as comprador Xu Run whose social status thereafter visibly increased (Cao Wenjuan 1996: 9-10).

After 1842, the urban elite pluralized into import-export merchants, bankers, officials with contact to foreigners, returned overseas Chinese, and compradors. Among them, compradors were best prepared to grasp the numerous opportunities for becoming rich in the treaty ports and to make use of the foreigners for their purposes. Compradors thus were generally rich, some of them even being among China's richest merchants.[374]

Within modern Chinese society, the group of compradors enjoyed a high social status. They generally played an active role in Chinese local affairs by raising funds for infrastructure, education, public health, and disaster relief activities.[375] They also played a leading role in social organizations. In Shanghai, for instance, they were among the leaders of geographical and commercial guilds. In 1911, seven of the 21 directors of the Shanghai Chamber of Commerce were compradors.[376]

The group of compradors was not particularly large in size. While the comprador group only comprised about 250 persons in the middle of the 19th century, the gentry, in comparison, amounted to 1.1 million members.[377] Totaling 40,000 in 1920, with the majority being located in Shanghai, they were neither significant in numbers compared to Shanghai's total population of 1.3 million in 1910 and 2.6 million in 1927.[378] Accordingly, compradors formed a new small but significant group within the urban elite, being rich and enjoying a high status in modern Chinese society.

Compradors could be further distinguished from the rest of the urban elite in terms of exposure to foreign culture. They communicated by using "Pidgin English" – a mixture of Chinese, English, Indian, and Portuguese. In addition to their Chinese name they had foreign given names. Usually wearing the Chinese silk gown, they occasionally opted for Western suits instead. The Western-style buildings they lived in were being furnished by the foreign employer but decorated in Chinese-style and surrounded by a Chinese garden. The foreign settlement where they worked and lived was located within a Chinese-populated area.[379] These visible artifacts alone show that compradors were most probably influenced by foreign culture to a certain extent.

Apart from these visible artifacts, foreign cultural values were also partly adopted. On the one hand, they were still influenced by traditional Chinese val-

374 Bergère 1986: 46-51, Hao Yenping 1970: 99-101.
375 Hao Yenping 1970: 186-188.
376 Bergère 1986: 47, Hao Yenping 1970: 189. For example, the comprador Xu Run was one of them (Cao Wenjuan 1996: 32).
377 Bergère 1986: 28 (gentry refers to those possessing a mandarin title).
378 Bergère 1986: 47 and 106-107.
379 Hao Yenping 1970: 180-183, Bergère 1986: 54. See, for example, Xu Run who possessed houses in both Western and Chinese styles (Cao Wenjuan 1996: 37-38).

ues and customs, such as Buddhism, Confucianism, familism, and regionalism.[380] Especially for successfully doing business they relied heavily on traditional values and institutions. Their guaranteeing of safe business transactions – being already common in the Qing dynasty before the Opium Wars –[381] was part of a larger system of responsibilities. In this system a person was held responsible for the acts of a person connected to him, for instance the father for the acts of the son, the village for thefts and murderers occurring there, and so forth.[382] Due to their far reaching responsibilities, compradors were forced to recruit those whom they could trust and accordingly recruited them from people from their family or region. In contrast, it was difficult to conduct business in regions where compradors from the home province were few in numbers.[383]

On the other hand, judged by their activities, compradors neglected or questioned Confucian values. Their profit making aspirations rivaled orthodox Confucianism. They sent their children to Western schools instead of encouraging them to study Confucian classics. Some compradors converted to the foreigners' religions or imitated their cultural values and ideas.[384] Although a partical identification with foreign culture can clearly be observed, this hybrid of cultural artifacts and values might not have led to a homogenous social group in clear distinction from Chinese society as a whole.

Yet even this partial identification with foreigners raised questions about the extent to which compradors actually identified with Chinese national interests. This question was particularly relevant as the foreign impact on China between 1842 and 1943 was widely regarded by the Chinese as detrimental to the national economy. Playing a pivotal role in keeping the foreign business running and helping foreigners to sell opium among others, the comprador was viewed as a traitor and as a collaborator in foreign colonialism and economic imperialism by modern Chinese society.[385]

Indeed, some compradors collaborated with foreign governments.[386] Some were charged with collaborating in human trafficking, that is, for sending Chinese people to the United States to build the American railroad under inhumane

---

380 Hao Yenping 1970: 182-183.

381 Chan Kai Yiu 2006: 50, see Hao Yenping 1970: 49.

382 Morse 1910: 114-115.

383 Hao Yenping 1970: 171-177, Bergère 1986: 47. For example, Ningbo merchants were known for their fierce loyality to their native place, they preferred to confine their dealings to fellow natives (Cochran 2000: 16).

384 Hao Yenping 1970: 8 and 182-189 and 205-206, Bergère 1986: 55. See, for example, Xu Run's children who studied abroad (Cao Wenjuan 1996: 37-38).

385 Huang Yifeng et al. 1982: 29-38, Hao Yenping 1970: 106-112, see Wang Guangwu 2003: 63.

386 Hao Yenping 1970: 194-195.

conditions.[387] The comprador Chen Lianbo escaped to Japan after being condemned as traitor.[388] Especially in the 20th century, among the increasingly nationalist population the comprador's reputation deteriorated to such an extent that foreign enterprises changed the comprador's professional title into "Chinese manager" (华经理).[389]

However, it is also to acknowledge that the comprador also supported the Chinese government in dealing with foreigners. In the Cohong period, compradors were supposed to keep a close watch on the foreign merchants' conduct and political intentions. During the Opium Wars, they played an important role in Sino-foreign negotiations. When foreigners set up factories in treaty ports from 1895 onwards, the compradors gave advice how to cope with the situation. In addition, they helped with internal dealings by, for instance, financing and organizing a mercenary force against the Taiping.[390] Furthermore, together with other members of the bourgeoisie they participated in boycotts of American products as an answer to the discrimination of Chinese or in campaigns against the foreigners' control of strategically important infrastructure such as China's railway system.[391] Hence, compradors displayed nationalist sentiments and even used their experiences with foreigners for Chinese nationalist purposes.

Still, it was the anti-nationalist attitude which was first sustained by Chinese Marxist historians,[392] who have applied ideological criteria for distinguishing the "comprador class" (买办阶级) from the "national bourgeoisie" (民族资产阶级). Thereby, they sustained the general suspicion of the "comprador class" as traitors to the nation.[393] Decades later, this has been alleviated by Chinese contemporary historians[394] who have used the neutral concept of the "comprador stratum" (买办阶层) to scrutinize the comprador's social and economic strength.[395] The French historian Bergère[396] even deems the distinction between a national and a comprador bourgeoisie artificial, since the whole bourgeoisie was econom-

387 Huang Yifeng et al. 1982: 39-40.
388 Hou Zhigang 1996: 332.
389 Xu Dixin and Wu Chengming 2003: 785, Hao Yenping 1970: 63.
390 Hao Yenping 1970: 190-193.
391 Bergère 1968: 47-51.
392 See e.g. Huang Yifeng et al. 1982.
393 Bergère 1986: 247. As an example for a Marxist view on compradors see Huang Yifeng et al. (1982).
394 Bergère 1986: 247 (remark no. 1, p. 325). See also Xu Dixin and Wu Chengming (2003) who pursue research on the comprador in an objective manner.
395 See e.g. Xu Dixin and Wu Chengming 2003: 784-785. Today, both terms *jieji* 阶级 (class) and *jieceng* 阶层 (stratum/strata) mean that a social group is divided according to a certain standard. Scholars today frequently use the concept of *jieceng* due to historical reasons (Li Peilin 2004: 3).
396 Bergère 1968 (esp. 51) and 1986. See also Hao Yenping 1970: 111-112.

ically intertwined with foreigners and the distinction between comprador and independent merchant was usually blurred.

To summarize, although not having necessarily formed a homogenous social group, compradors had a most ambivalent role in harmonizing economic rationale with nationalist sentiments. Dealings for and with foreigners were economically lucrative but easily raised suspicions of being anti-national among the Chinese public. The comprador's position can thus not only be thought of as in between the foreign and Chinese businesses, it can neither be seen as isolated from the social context at a particular point in time.

5 Intermediaries in China's Foreign Enterprises

In contemporary China, the need for foreign enterprises to engage with the Chinese business environment resurfaces. Whereas compradors epitomized the vital link for the first foreigners doing business in China, it is nowadays the Chinese employees in FIEs which function as intermediaries between the FIE and the Chinese business environment. Within FIEs, all Chinese employees who do non-manual work most likely fulfill tasks that involve establishing this connection. Unlike the comprador in the past, these employees have not yet been awarded with a distinct designation. In the present study, these Chinese employees are referred to with the more general term "intermediary". Like the compradors before them, today's intermediaries play a paramount role for their FIEs (5.1) and contribute significantly to the Chinese economy (5.2), while occupying a critical position within Chinese society (5.3). Another identity of the Chinese employees, namely being a knowledge worker in contemporary China, is intimately connected with their intermediary identity and analyzed in the subsequent chapter.

5.1 The Role of Intermediaries in China's Foreign Enterprises

Soon after the comprador system had declined, foreign investment in China came to a halt. During the Mao era, foreign businesses basically had to withdraw from China, and the role of intermediaries in the economy became obsolete. Only China's reform and opening up paved the way for a new era of foreign businesses and revived the need for intermediaries.

Since the establishment of the first FIEs in the form of JVs in 1979 and since 1986 also as WFOEs,[397] Chinese employees working in FIEs have substantially increased in numbers. While in 1985 only 60,000 employees worked in FIEs, accounting for 0.05% of total urban employment, their number exceeded

397 Clegg et al. 2007: 3, Child 2007: 290. Two forms of JVs exist, namely the Contractual Joint Venture (中外合作经营企业) and the Equity Joint Ventures (中外合资经营企业). However, as the significance of contractual joint ventures is very low (3% in 2004) (Zhang Xueyuan and Reinmoeller 2007: 52), only equity joint ventures are relevant for this study.

10 million in 2010[398] (see Table 2: The development of FDI, FIEs, and employees in FIEs (1985-2010).), accounting for 3.04% respectively.[399] Among them, employees with Chinese nationality account for the overwhelming majority, whereas foreigners make up only a very tiny proportion. This can be judged by the fact that foreigners holding a Chinese working permit only accounted for 231,700 persons in 2010.[400] The number of those foreigners working in FIEs is even smaller, as the figure also includes persons not employed by FIEs but pursuing other professions, such as journalists or scholars, or – to a smaller extent – those being employed by a Chinese enterprise. Accordingly, the Chinese employees in this study are part of a larger group of more than 10 million persons who potentially act as intermediaries for FIEs.

Table 2: The development of FDI, FIEs, and employees in FIEs (1985-2010).

Year	Foreign Direct Investment Flows (USD)	Foreign-invested Enterprises[401]	Employees working in Foreign-invested Enterprises
1985	1,956,000,000	3,073	60,000
1990	3,487,000,000	7,273	620,000
1995	37,521,000,000	233,564	2,410,000
2000	40,715,000,000	203,208	3,320,000
2005	60,325,000,000	260,000	6,880,000
2010	105,735,000,000	445,244	10,530,000

Source: Author's compilation based on *China Statistical Yearbook* (National Bureau of Statistics of the PRC, various years).

Throughout the reform era, intermediaries have proved helpful for foreign businesses to cope with the Chinese business environment. Chinese intermediaries' functions comprise providing and interpreting local market information as well as offering access to authorities.[402] Although the Chinese business environment has developed significantly in terms of rules and regulations concerning foreign investment during the last three decades of reform, it still presents itself in a largely obscure and uncertain manner to foreign businesses. Issues range from institutional gaps in law and contracts, unpredictable behavior of officials appears to idiosyncratic business practices. In a constant manner, foreign businesses have to defend

398 Since most of the empirical data have been collected in 2010, this year is used as reference year in this study.

399 NBS 2011a: 110-111.

400 Ministry of Human Resources and Social Security of the PRC 2011.

401 Excluding Hong Kong, Macao or Taiwan-funded enterprises.

402 See Child 2007: 295, see Zhang Xueyuan and Reinmoeller 2007: 52-58.

themselves against business threats inherent in the current regulatory environment.[403]

When dealing with the complexity and uncertainty of the local environment, local embeddedness has proved helpful. Local embeddedness of enterprises is usually realized by building business relationships, or *guanxi* 关系,[404] and networks with other market players and the bureaucracy. The vast literature on *guanxi* in China is largely consensual in that without *guanxi* and networking hardly any business deal is concluded.[405] While *guanxi* and networks are especially crucial for Chinese private enterprises, the success of FIEs' business ventures similarly depends on the relationships involved. Trustful relationships and network memberships prove to facilitate knowledge flows between FIEs and local Chinese enterprises as well as between FIEs and governmental institutions. *Guanxi* and networks thus allow to overcome the problem of asymmetric information existing in nascent markets and to have a platform available to share knowledge.[406]

Employing Chinese nationals appears to be crucial for building up *guanxi* and networks. *Guanxi* and business networks are not only seen as economic institutions or actors in their own right bridging institutional gaps[407] but also as key features of Chinese culture. Barner-Rasmussen and Björkman[408] argue that *guanxi* are both culturally determined and caused by a lack of institutional alternatives. Todeva[409] shows that culture and institutions are no zero-sum game (as the historical assumption implies) but coexist within business networks in China. Wu[410] argues that networks are inevitably influenced by Chinese cultural values such as trust, face, reciprocity, respect for age and authority, harmony, and time. As most scholars – albeit to varying extents – conceptualize *guanxi* as being culturally specific, Chinese nationals seem to be best suited to bridge the FIE with the local Chinese business environment.

With the gradual opening of the domestic markets, the focus of FIEs shifted from low-cost manufacturing for exporting products to penetrating the domestic

403 Tse 2010: 159, Wu Wei-ping 2000: 51, Redding 1990: 95, Hendrischke 2007, Davies et al. 2003: 48, Teo and Wang Karen 2007: 244, Krug 2007: 133.

404 Note that the expression *guanxi* 关系 is not only the Chinese translation of "relationship" but connotes a particular meaning of relationships in the Chinese context, emphasizing mutual obligations and trust.

405 See e.g. Hendrischke 2007: 202, Tse 2010: 188, Krug 2007: 133.

406 Barner-Rasmussen and Björkman 2007: 93, Cucco 2008, Yang Mayfair Mei-hui 2002: 464, Krug 2007: 133, see Child 2007: 295.

407 Hendrischke 2007.

408 Barner-Rasmussen and Björkman 2007: 93.

409 Todeva 2007.

410 Wu Wei-ping 2000: 47.

market. FIEs now mostly aim at adapting existing technologies for the parent enterprise to the local market.[411] This requires being much closer to the local market than producing goods which are sold in the home country where enterprises possess relevant market information.

Being close to the domestic market has become ever more necessary as FIEs have increasingly been exposed to competition. The main competitors are Chinese private enterprises – partly formerly state-owned as well as newly established private enterprises – which have appeared on the market.[412] Following China's entry into the WTO in 2001 and the associated market liberalization, competition has become even fiercer.[413] Rising competition between Chinese enterprises and FIEs as well as among FIEs themselves has resulted in highly competitive industries already experiencing a steady erosion of margins and profitability. Currently, FIEs along with Chinese private and state-owned enterprises are concentrated in competitive industries, such as automobile, machinery, electronics, textiles, and food processing.[414]

In countering competition, FIEs at first usually benefit from higher quality products, yet then fail in responding well to the Chinese market. Smaller Chinese private enterprises, in contrast, are often successful by immediately reacting to market changes. Being inclined to imitation, experimentation, and adaptation, willing to take chances and learning from their experiences, they rapidly move up the learning curve,[415] while utilizing their own incremental technological innovations, their ties to state institutions as well as their superior understanding of the Chinese market.[416] They are adept at making use of China's large and fragmented marketplace, which gives rise to many ways of production and distribution,[417] and are able to adapt products more neatly to the needs of local customers.

With increasing competition on the Chinese market, these qualities increasingly gain importance. Yet cooperation with Chinese enterprises and institutions, which could be useful in assisting FIEs in their localization project, remains weak. FIEs do not fully appreciate knowledge generated locally, do not suffi-

411 Bielinski 2010: 216, European Union Chamber of Commerce in China 2012: 7, Naughton 2007: 403-418, Li Yiqiong and Sheldon 2011: 129.

412 Liao Chun 2009: 93-96.

413 Lardy 2002: 174, Yang Keming 2007: 220, Bramall 2009: 476, Brandt and Rawski 2008: 3.

414 Child 2007: 294, Yang Keming 2007: 220, Krug and Kuilman 2007: 238, Naughton 2007: 10.

415 Tse 2010: 81-85, Nie Winter et al. 2009: 46, see Tan Yinglan 2011.

416 Nie Winter et al. 2009: 46 and 99, Zhou Junqiang 2008: 163-165.

417 Enterprises often start in rural areas on the low end market and move into mid-range urban markets. (Keane 2007: 7, Nie Winter et al. 2009: 46). For example, the Chinese mobile phone companies develop a strategy of serving second and third-tier cities and accumulating capital for serving first-tier cities (Luo Minyan and Müller 2011: 49-52).

ciently learn from the local environment, and do not actively create relationships with a broad range of local partners.[418] Hence, FIEs depend on intermediaries to further these cooperations or search for alternative means for gathering market information and access.

Yet entrusting Chinese employees with such tasks is a double-edged sword. On the one hand, FIEs depend on Chinese employees for building the bridges to other market players. On the other hand, the FIE's valuable knowledge is at risk. Especially as Chinese employees acting as intermediaries are particularly connected to the business environment, the concern for potential knowledge leakage through Chinese employees is strong. While intellectual property concerns are generally strong in recent years in China, the infringement of trade secrets is of highest concern.[419] Trade secret abuses are still difficult to combat due to general enforcement problems of intellectual property laws and of trade secrets law in particular.[420] Yet protecting their valuable knowledge from leakage to infringers within the Chinese business environment is crucial for maintaining the FIE's competitive advantage.

Not only are intermediaries particularly connected to the market, they are easily suspected of making use of this position, motivated by a nationalist Chinese culture. In Germany, for instance, a general suspicion toward Chinese people was raised by the German high-circulation weekly news magazine *Der Spiegel* with an edition titled "Gelbe Spione"[421] [Yellow Spys]. By using the word "yellow", the title alone generally suspects Chinese people of spying. The respective article[422] in this edition basically suspects all Chinese students, trainees, and researchers (especially those working in German enterprises and institutions) to be instructed by a seemingly homogenous "Chinese state" to spy out any information in science and economy they can take hold of. "The Chinese state" in the first instance allegedly achieves this commitment to spying by appealing to their national pride and patriotic responsibility for the well-being of their home country.[423] Although the cited instances of espionage and cheating have surely occurred, *Der Spiegel* used them for creating a general image of "the Chinese" having no choice but giving China's national interests the top priority. Not only the people in Germany but also German managers in FIEs in China might have the image of Chinese employees being driven by their nationalist sentiments (and therefore acting in the Chinese national interests rather than in the interest of

418 Zhou Junqiang 2008: 120-121, Staiger 2007: 538-539, Barner-Rasmussen and Björkman 2007: 92, see Hu Albert G.Z. and Jefferson 2008: 312-313.
419 US-China Business Council 2012: 12.
420 Bai J. Benjamin and Da Guoping 2011: 354-355.
421 *Der Spiegel* 2007.
422 Dahlkamp et al. 2007.
423 Dahlkamp et al. 2007: 26 and 28.

FIEs) in their heads. As a result, FIEs' foreign managers easily doubt the loyalty of their Chinese employees. Particularly those interacting very closely with other market players come into the spotlight.

Besides risking the leakage of knowledge, FIEs equally risk not broadening their knowledge base to a sufficient extent. Chinese employees' knowledge of the Chinese market is crucial in supporting the FIEs in their localization endeavor and enhancing a foreign enterprise's competitive advantage. Yet the sharing of personal knowledge within the enterprise is deemed insufficient. Holding a "knowledge is power"[424] attitude, Chinese employees tend to hoard information and are reluctant to share knowledge with fellow employees.[425] The knowledge of Chinese employees can thus not easily be grasped and made available for business purposes.

What makes both the protection and the enhancing of the FIE's knowledge base even more critical is the difficulty in recruiting and retaining qualified Chinese employees. Insufficient supply of qualified labor has resulted in high employee turnover rates of 14-20%.[426] Employee turnover appears to be particularly prevalent among FIEs. In FIEs, job-hopping appears to be even more strongly seen as a means for advancing the career.[427] As Chinese enterprises have gained in attractiveness over the past few years for middle- and high-level professionals in China,[428] FIEs increasingly have difficulties in retaining employees.

Regarding high turn-over rates, FIEs have partly resorted to poaching, that is, intentionally recruiting employees from a labor market competitor by offering high incentives. This has resulted in fierce competition for local workforce as well as to a destabilized local remuneration structure and the discouragement of FIEs from providing training. This vicious circle has led to an increased employee turnover and higher remuneration levels. In contrast to developed countries where poaching occurs mainly in higher occupations, in China, poaching recently extends to lower skilled university graduates.[429] This has led to a competitive situation for qualified local employees even referred to as "talent war"[430]. A scarce supply of less qualified and often changing intermediaries increases the risk of leakage and inhibits the buildup of a thorough knowledge base.

In summary, in their identity as intermediary, Chinese employees are indispensable for FIEs for acting on the domestic market and building the bridge to other market players. Not only due to the largely unregulated institutional envi-

424 Huang Qian et al. 2008. Li Shenxue and Scullion 2006: 80, Frank 2008.
425 Michailova and Hutchings 2006, Ramasamy et al. 2006, Huang Qian et al. 2008.
426 Cooke 2010: 45, Krotoschak and Kleine 2010.
427 Cucco 2008: 127-128, Oakley 2002: 26, Li Yiqiong and Sheldon 2011: 138.
428 Wang Hongyi 2011.
429 Li Yiqiong and Sheldon 2011: 138-141.
430 *Shanghai Daily* 2012b, Wexler 2011.

ronment but especially in the light of increased competition, localization, and adaptation to local customers, intermediaries are needed for providing relevant market knowledge and connections. For FIE's, this dependency on intermediaries and their knowledge for ensuring embeddedness and localization is a double-edged sword, for intermediaries are precisely positioned where the boundary drawing between the environment, the FIE, and the employee takes place.

5.2 Intermediaries in Chinese Economy

The contribution of intermediaries to the Chinese economy cannot be exactly determined. Yet their contribution can be approached with an analysis of the role of FDI for the Chinese economy. Since intermediaries enable FIEs to operate in China, it can be assumed that Chinese employees acting as intermediaries in FIEs contribute to China's economy in the same manner as FDI.

After the opening up of the Chinese economy to the global market, China has quickly become the largest FDI recipient among the developing economies. FDI inflows increased more than 50 times during the reform era (see Table 2). In 2010 alone, China received 105 billion USD of FDI inflows, whereas Germany, for instance, received less than half (46 billion USD) of this amount.[431] In line with increasing investments, the number of FIEs grew nearly 145-fold between 1985 and 2010 (see Table 2).

The enormous amount of FDI inflows has contributed to the Chinese economy in several ways. In terms of economic performance, FDI inflows accounted for 2.5 of gross domestic product (GDP) on average between 2005 and 2010. Taking China's huge economic size into account, this is a considerable contribution.[432]

In terms of economic growth, Yueh[433] estimates that if China had not attracted FDI, China's annual GDP growth could have been between 0.5 to over 1 percentage point slower (that is, as low as 8.5%) over the past thirty years. Chen[434] estimates that between 1986 and 2005 even 1.5 percentage points of the average growth rate of 11.8% of GDP came from direct and indirect contributions of FDI. Altogether, 0.5 to 1.5 percentage points of economic growth can be attributed to FIEs and their activities in China. This is a recognizable contribution as even a half percentage point each year can translate into significantly higher standards of living over time.

431 OECD 2012.
432 World Bank 2010.
433 Yueh 2013: 12-16.
434 Chen Chunlai 2011: 227-231.

The FIEs' contribution to economic growth mostly results from their activities in the manufacturing sector. The manufacturing sector is the most productive sector in China. Nearly half of the FIEs' activities operate in this sector.[435] This is above average as the proportion of enterprises operating in the Chinese manufacturing sector is only about one quarter in general.

Not only do FIE's operate in the more productive sectors, they also appear to be more productive than Chinese domestic enterprises. FIEs alone account for 30% of industrial output and 22% of profits generated by China's industrial enterprises.[436] The gross industrial output value of a foreign-invested industrial enterprise on average accounted for 329% of the equivalent of the average domestic-funded private industrial enterprise (私营工业企业) in 2010.[437]

This enormous difference can be explained by the weak policy environment for domestic enterprises compared to that of FIEs. Chinese private enterprises have long been disadvantaged in terms of access to capital, infrastructure, and skilled workers. While the vast majority of small and medium Chinese private enterprises still lag behind, only a few large private enterprises and some SOEs have successfully enhanced their productivity. Against this background, FIEs still add much to the productivity of industrial enterprises operating in China.

Being mostly represented in the manufacturing sector, FIEs strongly contribute to augmenting China's trade volume. The trade volume generated by FIEs accounts for half of the country's foreign trade. China's vast trade surplus is also largely contributed by FIEs, with exports exceeding imports since the late 1990s.[438]

FDI have further been beneficial to the country's domestic capital formation. The capital formation marks the increase of total physical capital stock and furthers the growth of China's real economy. Especially during the 1990s, FDI made an important contribution to domestic capital formation with up to 17.3% anually. Although its role has been declining, FDI is still considered a significant additional source for the formation of domestic capital.[439]

FIEs also play a remarkable role in employment creation. Around one third of China's manufacturing labor force is employed by FIEs. Apart from direct effects through the employment of Chinese employees by FIEs, indirect employment effects through opportunities created by the activities of FIEs exist as well in China, yet are difficult to measure.[440]

---

435 NBS 2011a: 245.
436 World Bank 2010.
437 NBS 2011a: 526 and 536.
438 World Bank 2010, Davies 2013: 15-17.
439 Chen Chunlai 2011: 214-216.
440 Chen Chunlai 2011: 216.

There is another indirect – yet most important – contribution to the economy, resulting from technical spillover effects. FIEs are the main technology providers, with almost half of the output of FIEs related to high-technology industries compared to around one fifth for Chinese enterprises.[441] With their technology and know-how, FIEs are predestined to contribute to the economy indirectly via spillovers.

Spillovers take place via different channels. FIEs can assist domestic enterprises, such as suppliers, in strengthening their performance or function as learning models for domestic enterprise who adopt similar techniques. Employees trained by FIEs are another means to transfer skills and knowledge to domestic enterprises. It has become widely acknowledged that technical spillovers have indeed strengthened the competitiveness of Chinese enterprises to a certain extent.[442]

Yet the precise spillover effects are scarcely covered by the existing literature due to the difficulties of measuring them. Deng's[443] recent study on spillovers shows the negative and positive effects of spillovers. He found that the absorptive capacity and level of productivity of domestic Chinese enterprises is decisive for determining the extent to which spillovers are effective in enhancing their productivity. Absorptive capacity of Chinese enterprises is given in enterprises which export, invest in human capital or research and development, or have already made some experiences with innovation. While SOEs in the 1990s did not benefit from spillovers, Chinese private enterprises did. This can be explained with the tight bureaucratic control of SOEs that time. In the 21st century, the situation changed with large SOEs developing the necessary preconditions for absorbing spillovers. In his manufacturing firm-level analysis, Deng examines the role of different spillover channels. It is shown that whereas exporting FIEs have spillover effects on all exporting domestic enterprises regardless of ownership type, horizontal spillover effects within the same industry have only positive effects for SOEs. Also, the sampled productive large-scale SOEs take advantage of knowledge embodied in workers which were transferred from FIEs. On private domestic enterprises, labor transfers could in contrast have a negative effect. This results from the higher recruiting costs of employees with work experiences in FIEs, which do not yield the expected benefits due to the enterprise's low absorptive capacity.[444]

Also using manufacturing firm-level data, Chen's estimation indicates that a 1 percentage point increase in the industrial share of foreign investment may

441 Nolan 2011: 45, Zhou Junqiang 2008: 120, Hu Albert G.Z. and Jefferson 2008: 332.
442 See e.g. Child 2007: 294, Jarrett and Wendholt 2010.
443 Deng Ziliang 2011.
444 Deng Ziliang 2011: esp. 24-39.

initially cause an increase in productivity of domestic firms of 0.124% on average. When the FDI share exceeds a critical threshold, the competition effect could become larger then the positive effects and the net effect of spillover could turn out to be negative.[445] If any, spillovers only produce marginal productivity increases.

In brief, the role of FDI for the Chinese economy in terms of contribution to economic growth, productivity, foreign trade, capital formation, and employment creation suggests that the intermediary's contribution is significant. Yet what can be absorbed by the local economy is still marginal. Considering the still small spillover effects of FDI to China's economic growth, Chen[446] suggests that apart from improving local economic and technology conditions to attract more FDI inflows, the Chinese government should encourage cooperation and knowledge exchange between FIEs and domestic enterprises and strengthen industrial linkages.

The bridging role of intermediaries for Chinese economic transition and modernization is indeed increasingly recognized. The Chinese government tries to mobilize professionals, who are positioned at the intersection of politics and management at different levels, to contribute to ongoing modernization. They are regarded as vehicles through which "soft" technology – including new standards of efficiency and new managerial models – can be disseminated outside the enterprise's boundaries and serve as interfaces between state and non-state actors including FIEs.[447] As there is still much leeway for knowledge spillovers, the contribution of intermediaries to the Chinese economy is likely to further increase.

5.3 Intermediaries in Chinese Society

In contemporary Chinese society the enterprise where one works constitutes an important stratifying element. This is a legacy of the Mao era, where 98% of urban labor force was allocated to, employed and nurtured by work units or *danwei* (单位).[448] The *danwei*, a social institution combining work and residence in Chinese urban society, was located at four levels, that is, province, prefecture, county, and town. The higher the level the richer was the *danwei* and the better was the welfare for its employees. The remuneration for the same job could vary

445 Chen Chunlai 2011: 232-248.
446 Chen Chunlai 2011: 231.
447 Cucco 2008: 129-131.
448 Hebel and Schucher 2007: 285, Bian Yanjie 1994: 23, Cai Fang et al. 2008: 169.

greatly between two *danwei* of the same kind but being located at different levels.[449] The social position was thus largely determined by one's workplace.

Hitherto, the *danwei* remains an important stratifying element in China.[450] Many *danwei* still persist more or less to enable employees to participate in the state welfare system, and also non-state units often take over functions similar to a *danwei* by providing dormitories and food.[451] For the urban youth looking for employment, the enterprise or work unit still plays a more important role than the occupation itself.[452]

Lu Xueyi[453] also employs the enterprise as an indicator of social status. The size of the employing enterprise qualifies for either the upper, upper middle, or middle stratum. A manager of a large enterprise (i.e. formerly state-owned or multinational enterprise) is ascribed to the upper stratum, whereas a manager (of the same rank) of a small and medium enterprise (including FIEs) belongs to the upper middle stratum. Likewise do heads of China's few large private enterprises belong to the upper stratum, whereas heads of mid-sized enterprises are ascribed to the upper middle and owners of small enterprises to the middle stratum.[454] Hence, Chinese employees working in FIEs occupy the same stratum as employees of the same rank working in a Chinese enterprise of equivalent size.

In contrast, which ownership types are associated with high social prestige in Chinese society is less straightforward. The reputation and attractiveness of enterprises' ownership types has changed during the reform era. Increasing liberalization of the labor market – at least theoretically – made the choice of workplaces possible.[455] Since the 1990s, the option of working for a FIE has become considerably more appealing, when the pace of enterprise reform has led to mass lay-offs within the formerly highly attractive state sector.[456] Many university graduates have been attracted by the generally higher wage level, the relatively high level and variety of structured training and development as well as advancement depending on performance. Furthermore, FIEs being more integrated into the global economies and operating in the most modern sectors have been valued for providing the opportunity to learn advanced Western management

449 Li Yi 2005: 172-180.

450 Apart from *hukou*, cadre status, educational and political credentials, the *danwei* can still serve to explain social inequality (Lin Thunghong and Wu Xiaogang 2009: 105-106).

451 Li Yi 2005: 172-180.

452 See Bian Yanjie 1994: 73.

453 Lu Xueyi 2002.

454 Lu Xueyi 2002: 9-16.

455 In practice, university graduates have difficulties in finding employment (see chapter 6.3) and for some parts of the population, especially migrant workers, labor mobility is still severely constrained (see e.g. Hebel and Schucher 2007, Cai Fang 2010: 88).

456 Howell 1999: 136.

methods and techniques. As particularly FIEs have well-established brand names, being employed by those has been regarded as improving chances for future career advancement.[457]

Apart from FIEs (and a few large Chinese private enterprises which are attractive due to similar reasons), the remaining large SOEs have begun to become attractive for younger employees again. Increased competition has forced SOEs to bring salaries in line with the market and provide access to continued training as well as to opportunities for career development.[458] They also present an alternative to FIEs, where employees often feel that senior level positions are still mostly reserved to foreigners. Here, the state sector presents a means to overcome this barrier and to put into practice the skills and competencies that were acquired during employment in the FIE.[459] Although still remaining less attractive to the highest quality recruits,[460] small and medium Chinese private enterprises are also starting to enjoy a better reputation among the qualified workforce as they ever more often offer various welfare benefits and housing funds as well as numerous other incentives as a means for employee retention.[461] Employees therefore face increasingly diversified opportunities and do not necessarily opt for FIEs anymore for acquiring a high social status. Instead, switching between FIEs and Chinese enterprises of different types becomes increasingly appealing. Thus, Chinese employees in FIEs are not very likely to belong to a particular social stratum or even constitute a particular identifiable group in Chinese society.

Chinese employed by FIEs are exposed to the foreign culture brought to China by foreign employees. In contrast to compradors more than a hundred years before, however, today Western cultural elements have generally become integrated in Chinese lifestyle. The lifestyle of Chinese employees in FIEs might thus not much differ from their peers in Chinese enterprises. Regarding management methods, a hybrid culture can similarly be observed in both FIEs and Chinese enterprises which also increasingly employ Western methods.[462] Furthermore, it has been found out that foreign cultural influence does not complete-

457 Howell 1999: 137-142, Hebel and Schucher 2007: 296-298, Cooke 2005: 24-25 and 106, Chan Anita 2001: 11-13, Zhao Shuming 2005: 115, Li Yiqiong et al. 2011: 124, Wang Hongyi 2011, *Shanghai Daily* 2012b, Cucco 2008: 139.

458 Cai Fang et al. 2008: 208, Cucco 2008: 131, Cooke 2005: 105-106, see Li Yiqiong et al. 2011: 124, Li Raymond 2012. An alternative is also the Chinese state itself. In the light of potential prestige, power, and material rewards, civil servant remains one of the most popular occupations among university graduates (Li Raymond 2012, Cooke 2005: 50-58).

459 Cucco 2008: 141.

460 Li Yiqiong et al. 2011: 124.

461 Cucco 2008: 127-132, Heberer 1999, Cooke 2005: 24 and 154-171, Tang Wenfang and Parish 2009: 115.

462 See e.g. Child and Warner 2003, Cooke 2005.

ly replace basic cultural Chinese values at the workplace.[463] Moreover, cultural clashes and the failure of joint ventures among others show that Chinese cultural values continue to persist within the multicultural working environment of a FIE.[464] As such, Chinese employees working in FIEs cannot be said to form a group with its own particular cultural values different from Chinese society as a whole.

Nevertheless, working for a FIE while being part of Chinese society could potentially trigger conflicts which do not concern employees in Chinese enterprises. Working for foreigners bears the potential of provoking nationalist sentiments of Chinese citizens. Within East Asia, national identity plays the most important role in China. Nationalism has been spurred by exogenous shocks, such as the Western imperialism or the Japanese invasion. The perceived threat to China's sovereignty in regard to territorial disputes still spurs nationalist sentiments today.[465] Although the relation to Japan in historical respect is one of the most sensitive, the recently erupting protests over disputed islands involving boycotts and smashing of Japanese products[466] yet show the potential for the unfolding of nationalist attitudes in contemporary Chinese society.

Toward FIEs, nationalist attitudes are likewise observable. When foreign enterprises attempt large or even hostile acquisitions, nationalism erupts in most countries. In China, however, in the light of these historical events, people rhetorically make use of them for arousing nationalist sentiments in the public. This is shown, among others, by the struggle over ownership and control of the French Danone and the Chinese Wahaha 娃哈哈 joint venture where Wahaha accused its French partner of having imperialist intentions.[467]

---

463 Most prominently, different cultural backgrounds are investigated by Hofstede who identified five fundamental classification schemes that distinguish members of different cultural groups from one another, whereby culture is defined as "collective programming of the mind" (Hofstede 1984, Hofstede and Hofstede 2005). While Hofstede's data collection in China took place in the 1980s and 1990s (Hofstede 2009) and was since much criticized, the more recent and notable GLOBE study (Fu Ping Ping et al. 2008, Brodbeck and Frese 2008) still suggests differing deeply embedded cultural values in the Chinese organizational context. While the use of such country-level require utmost caution, He Saiying et al. (2002: 143) provides more pertinent evidence that the multicultural environment in FIEs does *not* exert a significant influence on basic cultural values of the Chinese staff compared to Chinese employed by SOEs.

464 Take, for instance, the failure of the Danone/Wahaha JV where fundamentally different assumptions and expectations on ownership and control (Zhang Pingying and Van Deusen 2010) as well as disputes not only at the institutional but at a more personal level (Barboza 2009) suggest cultural differences being at the root of the problem.

465 Rozman 2012.

466 Spegele and Nakamichi 2012.

467 Zhang Pingying and Van Deusen 2010: 89-90, *Taipei Times* 2007.

While nationalist sentiments are chiefly directed against the FIE, its Chinese employees could also be targeted. In the Rio Tinto case,[468] Chinese employees of the British-Australian mining group Rio Tinto were charged with bribery and the theft of trade secrets of Chinese (majority) state-owned steel enterprises. On the Chinese internet, they were referred to as *yang maiban* 洋买办 – literally "foreign compradors" – who threatened Chinese national economic security and interests.[469]

Furthermore, a negative view of Chinese people working for FIEs can be found in Chinese popular literature. The term of the comprador was used for the agents (*daily* 代理) of the first foreign businesses in China after reform and opening up. At that time, foreign businesses were more dependent on their agents or representatives, a position which bestows the agent with power, wealth, and a high social status. Describing what they contributed to Chinese economy is an attempt to rehabilitate the agent's reputation.[470] Meanwhile, however, foreign businesses have more or less set up their own enterprises and increasingly employ Chinese people as employees. This trend alleviates the negative connotation of the early reform era.

Still, the discourse shows that working for FIEs remains an issue. It provides fertile ground for nationalist sentiments in case Chinese employees act in a way detrimental to Chinese national interests. While Chinese employees in FIEs cultural-wise do not differ from Chinese society in general and working for a FIE can lead to a high social status, their workplace – depending on the FIE's country of origin and business sector – could prove disturbing for fellow Chinese citizens. The more conflicting the interests of the FIE and Chinese national interests, the more critical the Chinese employee's intermediary position is perceived by public opinion.

468 For further details to the case refer to chapter 7.3.
469 See e.g. Zhuang Xulong 2010, Jiang Ruqin 2009.
470 Liang Xiaosheng 2010: 149-200.

6 Knowledge Workers in China

The Chinese employees in this study not only function as intermediaries. Since their work consists predominantly of communication and considering the latitude with which they pursue their work, they can also be regarded as knowledge workers. This chapter sheds light on the larger group of knowledge workers in China to which Chinese employees in this study belong. Knowledge workers in contemporary China are identified along established Western concepts (6.1). Furthermore, their contribution to the Chinese economy (6.2) as well as their status in Chinese social hierarchy is scrutinized (6.3).

6.1 Identifying China's Knowledge Workers

Hitherto, an officially determined or otherwise established Chinese concept of the knowledge worker does not exist. In Western countries, knowledge workers are usually conceptionalized and counted by drawing on occupational statistics.[471] Chinese statistical data,[472] however, only provide a classification of employed persons into broad occupational groups. These comparatively broad occupational groups[473] very likely comprise both knowledge and manual work. However, under the assumption that each of the categories of unit heads, professional and technical personnel as well as clerks and related workers largely comprises knowledge workers and the remaining categories mostly include manual workers, these categories still prove adequate to identify the number of China's

---

471 See chapter 2.1.

472 Chinese statistics are to be used in a cautious way. Inconsistencies and inaccurate figures are a common phenomenon. One of the most significant sources of inconsistencies is data manipulation of economic growth rates and reform efforts as these, among others, serve as benchmarks of the career and reputation of political cadres (Fischer 2002). Occupational categories, especially knowledge worker categories, might also be lower to a certain unknown extent. Since the incentives for data manipulation continuously persist, a trend observed over a certain time period can yet be considered reliable.

473 Whereas in Western market economies, detailed classifications of occupations are available, official Chinese statistics, in contrast, provide detailed information on the distribution of the labor force across sectors, types of organizations, and administrative regions reflecting their (former) rationale of catering to central economic planning (see also Zhou Xueguang 2004: 99).

knowledge workers. Informed by different established Western concepts,[474] four groups of knowledge workers are proposed (see Table 3).

Table 3: Overview of the four knowledge worker groups (KW1-4).

<table>
<tr><th>Occupational categories</th><th colspan="2">All qualifications</th><th colspan="2">College degree or above</th></tr>
<tr><td>Unit heads (单位负责人)</td><td rowspan="3">KW1</td><td rowspan="2">KW2</td><td rowspan="3">KW3</td><td rowspan="2">KW4</td></tr>
<tr><td>Professional and technical personnel (专业技术人员)</td></tr>
<tr><td>Clerks and related workers (办事人员和有关人员)</td><td></td><td></td></tr>
<tr><td>Business and service personnel (商业, 服务业人员)</td><td colspan="2">-</td><td colspan="2">-</td></tr>
<tr><td>Agriculture and water conservancy laborers (农林牧渔水利业生产人员)</td><td colspan="2">-</td><td colspan="2">-</td></tr>
<tr><td>Production, transport equipment operators and related workers (生产运输设备操作人员及有关人员)</td><td colspan="2">-</td><td colspan="2">-</td></tr>
<tr><td>Others (其他)</td><td colspan="2">-</td><td colspan="2">-</td></tr>
</table>

Source: Author's own compilation based on *China Labor Statistical Yearbooks* (National Bureau of Statistics of the PRC, various years).

The first group (KW1) which can be identified in China is the broadest and most similar to Machlup's concept. It comprises the three occupational categories of unit heads, professional and technical personnel as well as clerks and related workers, all of which Machlup explicitly refers to. In 2010,[475] the number of knowledge workers in China according to this definition amounted to 98,175,450 persons, accounting for 12.9% of total employed persons.[476]

The second group (KW2) only considers unit heads as well as professional and technical personnel. It excludes clerks and related workers, which are also excluded by all scholars other than Machlup. Unit heads are still included in this and the following groups (though these are – except Machlup's "chairman" – not

474 See chapter 2.1 and 1.3.

475 Since most of the empirical data have been collected in 2010, this year is used as reference year in this study.

476 NBS 2011b: 59 and 2 (see also appendix 3). Note that for every year (see appendices 3, 4, 6 and 7) the number of total employed persons in the respective yearbook functions as the basis (not considering later adjustments subsequently obtained from census figures). The figure of the respective yearbook is assumed to have served as the basis for calculation of an occupational category's proportion of total employed persons in the respective year and accordingly is also used in this study to calculate the absolute numbers of occupational categories.

explicitly alluded to) since basically all occupations in Western definitions such as lawyers, architects, managers, and the like could well be unit heads (without being categorized as such). Accordingly, KW2, comprising unit heads as well as professional and technical personnel, adds up to 65,450,300 knowledge workers or 8.6% of total employed persons in 2010.[477]

Whereas all qualifications are included in both groups KW1 and KW2, the third group (KW3) only captures persons with a college degree or above (大专及以上程度). Some concepts, such as Bell's concept, and some statistical calculations, such as the one of the United Kingdom, explicitly only consider academically qualified knowledge workers. Also, this limitation is already given in Western countries where occupations like engineer, lawyer, or architect necessitate a certain qualification. With the further inclusion of clerks and related workers, which is for example the case in the less conservative Canadian calculation, 52,632,696 knowledge workers are included in group KW3 in 2010, accounting for 6.9% of total employed persons.[478]

The narrowest group is the fourth one (KW4), considering only workers with a college degree and above as well as excluding clerks. This group is most congruent with the term "knowledge worker" as it is usually understood. Anecdotal evidence suggests that occupations such as researcher, engineer, architect, or lawyer are commonly associated with this term. These occupations are also in the focus of North and Güldenberg's as well as of Davenport's concept. Moreover, they constitute the statistical parameters used in the United States and Germany. Measured by these criteria, knowledge workers in 2010 account for 37,120,975 persons, constituting 4.9% of total employed persons in China.[479]

By comparison, the size of the four groups varies substantially. The narrowest group KW4 only accounts for approximately one third of the broadest group KW1. The proportion of knowledge workers ranges from 4.9% to 12.9% of total employed persons. Accordingly, the inclusion or exclusion of academic qualifications and the category of clerks have to be thoroughly reflected upon when quantifying China's knowledge workers.

The fact that the groups KW1 and KW2 (including all qualifications) are both larger than KW3 and KW4 shows that inclusion or exclusion of qualifications is more consequential than the inclusion or exclusion of the category of clerk and related workers. If only qualifications like college degrees and above are considered as it is the case in KW3 and KW4, these groups only account for half the size of KW1 and KW2, respectively. In fact, closer scrutiny of the distri-

477 NBS 2011b: 59 and 2 (see also appendix 3).

478 NBS 2011b: 59, 58 (incl. college (大学专科), bachelor (大学本科) and master (研究生) graduates) and 2 (see also appendix 4).

479 NBS 2011b: 59, 58 and 2 (see also appendix 4).

bution of qualifications within an occupational category reveals that lower middle school (初中) and upper middle school (高中) graduates make up a significant proportion within each of the relevant three occupational categories.[480]

Compared to the remaining occupational categories in Chinese statistical data, however, knowledge workers of the above three occupational categories are significantly better qualified. Within the remaining occupational categories, persons with a college degree and above only accounted for 11.4% or less in 2010.[481] Clerks and related workers are in line with other knowledge worker occupational categories considerably better qualified than the remaining categories. Hence, including clerks into China's knowledge work force (as it is the case in KW1 and KW3) is advisable as these in terms of qualification are more similar to professional and technical personnel as well as to unit heads compared to business service, agricultural and production workers.

Comprehensive occupational data are available from 2002 onwards.[482] Between 2002 and 2010, the hierarchy of the four groups in terms of their size has not changed, with KW1 constantly being the broadest and KW4 the narrowest (see Figure 2). This shows that qualifications and the category of clerks and related workers are significant factors for quantifying knowledge workers during the whole time span, with the inclusion or exclusion of qualifications always being more decisive than the (non-)consideration of clerks and related workers.

480 In 2010, for instance, unit heads who graduated from lower or upper middle school accounted for 55.4% of total unit heads, professional and technical personnel accounted for 36.5%, and clerks and related workers accounted for 47.7%, respectively (NBS 2011b: 58).

481 NBS 2011b: 58.

482 Prior to 2002, only in 1988 data had been collected in 1107 enterprises for what was referred to as "type of persons" (人员类型) where both engineers and technical workers (工程技术人员) and managers (管理人员) have been included, of which 40.5% held college degrees and above (NBS 1989: 50). Since then, workers have over time been defined – as it was traditionally the case in the West – by industries rather than occupations. Except for 2001 and only for urban occupations additional data are available (NBS 2002: 60 and 61).

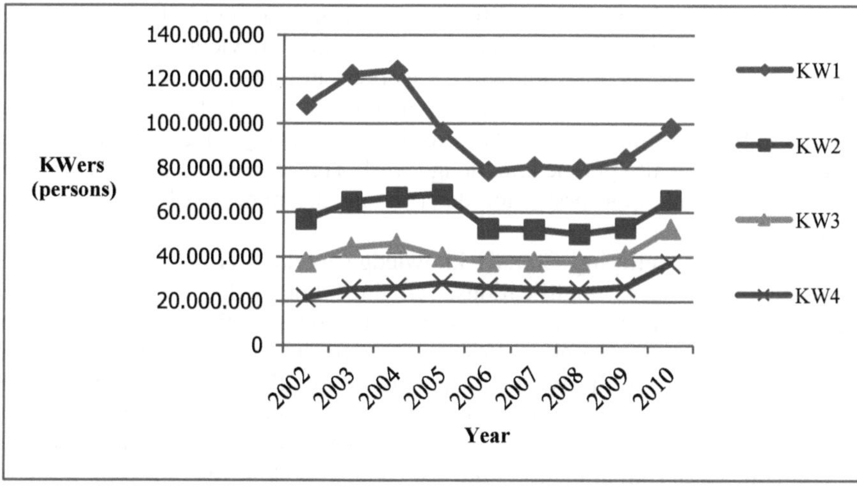

Figure 2: China's knowledge workers in absolute numbers (2002-2010).

Source: Author's own illustration based on *China Labor Statistical Yearbooks* (National Bureau of Statistics of the PRC 2003-2011). For calculation of relevant numbers see appendices 3 and 4.

Increases in knowledge workers (see Figure 2) result from the first expansion of higher education enrollment in 1999[483] as well as adjustments following the population census in 2010. Decreases mostly result from the category of clerks and related workers, presumably due to an adjustment of criteria for this rather vague category. Also, professional and technical workers with degrees below college were less considered over time, showing a trend toward the mere inclusion of higher qualifications into the knowledge worker categories.[484]

Altogether, the proportion of knowledge workers in China varies between 4.9% and 12.9% of total employment according to the calculation method applied, and consequently the suitable method should be carefully chosen. Clerks and related workers should not be as easily neglected as it is done by most Western definitions. In China, occupational categories are much broader than in the West, with total employment merely broken down into seven occupational categories, most of which very likely contain both knowledge and manual work. In contrast, in the West, "clerks" or "clerical workers" are an occupation among many other more precise occupations, and whether they are included or excluded

483 Chen Shuang-Ye 2012: 104.

484 For more details regarding the fluctuations see appendix 5.

might not even make a significant difference in the outcome of the different calculations. China's clerks' qualification level also sustains the fact that this category of clerk and related workers might contain knowledge workers. Being roughly as qualified as other knowledge workers in relevant categories and significantly better qualified than those belonging to non-knowledge worker occupational categories, most of the persons in the category of clerks and related workers might actually pursue knowledge work. Hence, calculating with KW1 or KW3 rather seems appropriate for determining the number of China's knowledge workers.

Cautiously identifying China's knowledge workers is also advisable with regard to their diverse qualifications. All three knowledge worker categories include lower and upper middle school graduates to a significant extent. As such, China's occupational categories do not automatically imply a certain qualification as it is the case in the West. It seems to be intuitive to include only higher qualifications when calculating the number of knowledge workers in China (especially since data are available). However, in the light of the comparatively low overall educational attainment[485] and the relatively low overall skill level of China's large labor force[486] with the vast majority of Chinese workers aggregating at the lower end,[487] knowledge workers to date still display a relatively low education and skill level. Therefore, including all qualifications – and clerk and related workers (KW1) – proves adequate for identifying the number of people pursuing knowledge work in contemporary China as a whole. Yet even when calculating with the largest group (KW1), knowledge workers only constitute 12.9% of China's total employment. The group of China's knowledge workers is thus small compared, for instance, to Germany's knowledge workers, who account for approximately one third of the country's total employed persons.[488]

For the purpose of this study, however, which focuses on knowledge workers being positioned in FIEs, KW3 is most appropriate. Knowledge workers in FIEs – as it is the case in the sample – generally hold a college or university degree. Also, FIEs are almost always located in urban areas. Along the lines of the above calculation and considering urban areas only, knowledge workers with a tertiary education (KW3) located in urban areas account for 50 million per-

485 Only 4.6% of China's population between 25-64 years of age received tertiary education while the average of OECD countries was 30% in 2009 (or latest available year) (OECD 2011: 217).

486 Demographic developments during the next decade predict a significant increase in labor force, for which it will prove challenging to provide sufficient education and work opportunities (Scharping 2007: 69). Consequently, the overall skill level might not be remarkably enhanced in the near future.

487 Cooke 2005: 87-88.

488 See chapter 2.1.

sons.[489] Therefore, the employees in this study are part of a larger group of 50 million unit heads, professional and technical personnel as well as clerks and related workers located in urban areas and having received a tertiary education.

6.2 Knowledge Workers in Chinese Economy

With the economy of the United States growing in the 19th century, the emergence of new industries and the service sector, and the expansion of organizations in size and numbers, workers being occupied with knowledge have strongly increased in numbers and in variety.[490] In the late 1950s, a small group of American scholars came to draw attention to the increasing significance for knowledge to the economy. In the following decades, American and European scholars endeavored to capture the economic contribution of knowledge work. This proved to be a challenging enterprise as knowledge is hard to measure. The real value of knowledge work lies in its quality rather than in its quantity.[491] Even today, the exact contribution of knowledge workers to a certain economy remains difficult to determine.

In China, the significance of knowledge workers for the economy has come to light comparatively late. This is due to the fact that highly labor-intensive agriculture and traditional manufacturing prevailed in the traditional Chinese economy.[492] Only when industry, technology, and the related knowledge took hold in China with the introduction of Western technology in the 19th century,[493] occupations such as modern industrial workers, managers, administrators, clerks, and technicians developed.[494] Soon after, however, the initial development of a knowledge workforce again came to a halt. In the Mao era, labor was considered a national resource and lost its character as a commodity, an ideology which totally eliminated market allocation of labor. Instead of acquiring a workplace according to skills and talent, the urban labor force was allocated to "work units" or *danweis* (工作单位) by the state. During working life, individual qualification was largely decoupled from salary, and the career path was controlled by the

489 For calculation of KW3 (urban) see appendix 7.
490 Cortada 1998a: xiv-xv, Cortada 1998b: 3-14.
491 See chapter 1.3 and 2.1.
492 Chai Joseph C.H. 2011: 13 and 32, Rawski 1989: 346, Naughton 2007: 34-35, Spence 1990: 95.
493 See Naughton 2007: 44, Rawski 1989: 5-6. Well-developed and efficient non-mechanized processes in agriculture and industry, which made capital investments in mechanization unprofitable, together with technological constraints and institutional failure led to the absence of an industrialization as experienced by Western countries (see e.g. Hu Albert G.Z. and Jefferson 2008: 289-209, Chai Joseph C.H. 2011: 50-59).
494 Tang Wenfang and Parish 2009: 115, Xu Xiaoqun 2004: 1-2, Shaffer 1981.

Chinese Communist Party, provoking passive work attitudes and low labor productivity.[495] This system was diametrically opposed to what knowledge workers are expected to do in order to be productive: defining and fulfilling their tasks as well as managing their development actively on their own.

Since the start of economic reform and opening up in 1978, China has first build on its comparative advantage in labor-intensive manufacturing. In the 1990s, FDI inflows indicated the shift toward the technology-intensive and capital-intensive sector.[496] Since the beginning of the 21st century, knowledge and innovation have strongly appeared on the government's agenda. The Chinese government intends to reduce the reliance on foreign knowledge and technology by transforming China into a global leader in science and technology by 2015 as well as into an innovation-oriented country by 2020.[497] For this transition from a labor-intensive and still industrializing economy to a knowledge-based economy in a comparatively short period of time, knowledge workers are of particular importance to China.

As the contribution of knowledge workers to the Chinese economy is hard to measure, only estimations on the quantitative contribution of human capital to China's economic growth are available. These cater to the research interest of explaining the growth rates achieved in the reform era. Challenging the widespread assumption that technical progress is exogenous, these accounts regard human capital as crucial as a source of endogenous growth, driven by improvements in education and skills. Jamison et al.[498] scrutinize the contribution of education to economic growth. They estimate that the educational attainment for adults has accounted for 5-8% of economic growth in China between 1970 and 2000. Other existing studies include measures such as student-teacher ratio, spending on education and science, and the number of science and technology workers when calculating human capital and differentiating it out from other forms of capital. The results vary from human capital contributing 11% to China's economic growth (for the period of 1978-1999),[499] 13% (1990-2000),[500] to 15% (1978-1998).[501] According to these estimates, education and human capital account for 5-15% for China's economic growth.

495 Hebel and Schucher 2007: 285-297, Bian Yanjie 1994: 23 and 51-71, Naughton 2007: 61, Cai Fang et al. 2008: 169.

496 Grewal and Sun Fiona 2002: 206, Chen Chunlai 2011: 206-207, Zhou Junqiang 2008: 49.

497 Release in 2006: 国家中长期科学和技术发展规划(2006-2020) [National Medium- and Long-term Program for Science and Technology Development (2006-2020)] (*Renminwang* 2006). Xie Wei and Li-Hua 2009: 8, Schüller 2008: 64-65, Williams and Mihalkanin 2011.

498 Jamison et al. 2010.

499 Wang Yan and Yao Yudong 2003.

500 Qian Xiaolei and Smyth 2006.

501 Arayama and Miyoshi 2004.

Other studies indicate that the contribution of human capital to the Chinese economy might well exceed the above estimations. Besides direct and indirect positive effects of human capital on physical capital investment, productivitiy growth and innovation have also been observed.[502] The output factors for innovation capacity – such as patent applications and scientific publications – can further serve as an indicator for the contribution of human capital as an input factor. While still showing the persisting reliance on foreign technology, both patent applications as well as citations in international journals rapidly increase in China.[503] Moreover, some analyses raise awareness for qualitative factors, such as the effect of high levels of education on products or efficient production organization.[504]

Regarding the contribution of China's knowledge worker to the economy, a further consideration on qualifications and experiences per age group is illuminating. Although not being properly researched, the value of human capital might very likely differ according to age. First of all, knowledge workers are rather young, with the majority being between 25 and 39 and the size of groups continuously decreasing starting at the age of 40 (see Figure 3).[505]

502 See e.g. Chi Wei 2007, Fleisher et al. 2010.

503 See Schüller 2011.

504 See e.g. Sonobe et al. 2004, Fleisher and Wang Xiaojun 2004.

505 The size of each age group has been calculated according to the occupational data of age groups. As these are available for *urban* employment only, the following investigation is confined to knowledge workers in urban areas. KW1 (urban) along the lines of the calculation in chapter 7.1 consists of 87,064,370 persons in 2010 (see appendix 6). With 88.7% of knowledge workers located in urban areas, the following investigation still considers the vast majority.

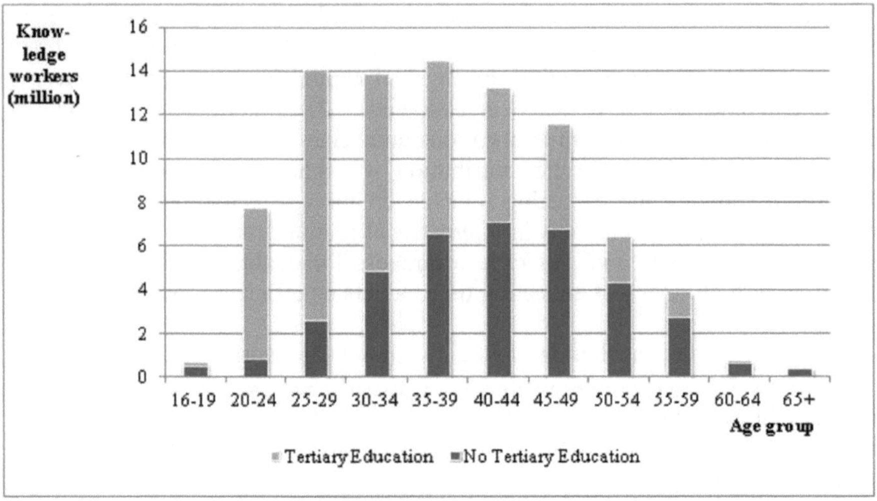

Figure 3: Number of knowledge workers (urban) by age group and education received (2010).

Source: Author's own illustration based on *China Labor Statistical Yearbook 2011* (National Bureau of Statistics of the PRC 2011b). For calculation of relevant numbers see appendix 8.

In terms of tertiary education, the older age groups received higher education to a lesser extent than the younger ones (see Figure 3).[506] Workers born in 1970 and before (40 years of age and older in 2010) are still influenced by the educational situation during the Mao era. With the founding of the People's Republic of China (PRC) in 1949, China was endowed with relatively good human capital, as – for instance – skilled individuals had been trained abroad. From 1952 onward, however, educational institutions were reorganized along the Soviet model and controlled by the state. Universities became highly specialized while strongly reducing the number of comprehensive universities, and academic freedom was restricted. From 1958, Mao Zedong put strong emphasis on primary education in rural and urban areas. Education was heavily politicized. Mass education programs stressing political consciousness caused a deterioration of quality standards, mostly in upper secondary and tertiary education, bringing about a lack of medium and highly skilled workers. Manual work was favored over theoretical

506 For more details on the calculation see appendix 8. Note that the proportion of qualification per age group is only available for total – instead of urban – employment. Nevertheless, in relative terms, it can well serve as a reference for the distribution of tertiary education among knowledge workers.

work, leading to workers participating in technical and on-the-job training provided by enterprises rather than continuing their formal education. Most significantly, China's education system was hampered in the period of the Cultural Revolution (1966-1976). Chinese universities became almost dysfunctional, and many schools were closed for several years. Although some schools reopened in the first half of the 1970s, they could not provide an adequate education for producing skilled workers.[507] Even today, more than 40% of knowledge workers[508] are potentially influenced by this educational situation.

The disruption of formal education and the focus on manual work of the Mao era was most consequential for urban youth born in 1955 or earlier, being 55 years of age or older in 2010. With 5.1 million these senior workers form the smallest group.[509] In regard to the official retirement age of 55 years for women and 60 years for men, it is not surprising that this group is small and mostly consists of male workers.[510]

Among the senior workers, an estimated 4.1 million (or 80%) had not entered upper middle school directly after graduating from lower middle school.[511] The reason is that these age groups were most likely part of the "send-down" episode during the Cultural Revolution, when urban youth were sent to rural areas in order to participate in farm work. As the probability of being "sent down" was significantly higher precisely for those with an intellectual family background or a father having graduated from college, the "send-down" policy potentially more concerned knowledge workers than manual workers. "Sending down" of urban youth – after completion of lower middle school or above – began in 1967 and peaked in 1968, with most sent-down youth living in rural areas for six years on average. One fifth returned after more than ten years.[512]

Despite this episode, these knowledge workers frequently occupy high positions. One reason is that since 1977, a significant number of them – but rather those with a shorter duration in rural areas – took college entrance examinations in order to resume their disrupted education. As 1.4 million senior workers of the total 5.1 million senior workers have received tertiary education[513] and an estimated 4.1 million had not entered upper middle school directly after graduating

507 Chen Shuang-Ye 2012: 102, Staiger 2007: 523, Naughton 2007: 51-66, Stone 2011: 73, Fairbank and Goldman 2006: 362, Wang Xiufang 2003: 9-10, Hebel and Schucher 2007: 230, Bramall 2009: 209-110, Hannum et al. 2008: 218.

508 See appendix 8. Knowledge workers from 40 of age upwards are considered, making up 41.7% of all knowledge workers of KW1 (urban).

509 See appendix 8.

510 See NBS 2011b: 70.

511 See appendix 9.

512 Zhou Xueguang 2004: 128-141.

513 See appendix 8.

from lower middle school,[514] approximately 400,000 knowledge workers among the latter must have resumed their education. Another reason was the favorable state policy. Workers who have been "sent down" account for proportions in government, public organizations such as cadres or professionals similar to those of urban youth who stayed in urban areas.[515] Furthermore, in addition to qualification, attainment of a certain position by seniority status rather than by qualification continued to a certain extent during the reform era among older workers within state-owned and majority state-controlled enterprises. Hence, in China, people with a lower or often disrupted formal education often occupy high knowledge worker positions. Due to their long work experience, however, their contribution to the Chinese economy as human capital might be larger than those of the educated new workforce entrants.

For those born after 1955, although having at least part of their education deferred or negatively influenced, both attainment of upper middle school and tertiary education increases. For the age group of 40-44 years nearly half have a tertiary education. These workers (40-54) are better educated than the older workers, and in contrast to new workforce entrants possess valuable work experiences.

Within the age group of 30-39, more than half have received a tertiary education.[516] These knowledge workers born in 1971 or later have received their education after the turbulences of the Cultural Revolution came to an end and received an education similar to the new workforce entrants. Although they are likewise affected by problems of the education system, in contrast to the new workface entrants, they have already gained valuable work experiences. Additionally, it is this age group which most likely received management training. Severe shortage of managers and the value employers place on managerial skills for organizational development have pushed Chinese and foreign enterprises to make use of a variety of managerial training programs, ranging from in-house training, mentoring and coaching, training in regional training centers, local outsourced training programs, and overseas training. MBA and Executive MBA programs offered by Chinese universities as well as joint and international programs also play a role in promoting business education and training.[517] Also, compared to workers aged 40 and above, this group is found to be more willing to adapt to major work changes.[518] Hence, these 28.3 million persons form a most valuable part of China's human capital.

514 The estimation is based on Tanigawa (2005: 12-14) (see appendix 9).
515 Zhou Xueguang 2004: 145.
516 See appendix 8.
517 Li Yiqiong et al. 2011: 121-122.
518 Tang Beibei 2011: 84.

Another valuable part of China's current human capital consists of the overseas returnees. The so-called "sea turtles" or *haigui*[519] received (part of their) tertiary education in a foreign country and returned to China for work. During the reform era, 632,200 persons returned to work in China until the end of 2010.[520] Whereas during the first decades of reform only one third to one fourth of Chinese students abroad returned to China, the number of returnees has steadily increased in recent years, with more than 70% choosing to return to China for work.[521]

Yet only those with work experience abroad easily find employment in China. The most successful "big sea turtles" (*da haigui* 大海归)[522] return at the age of 35 on average.[523] They generally possess the skills that are currently needed in China's upcoming knowledge economy such as experimenting, exploring, observing, and communicating.[524] The lack of creativity and practical experiences faced by knowledge workers having exclusively received Chinese education has been alleviated to a certain extent by the experiences gathered abroad.

The less successful "small sea turtles" (*xiao haigui* 小海归), also called "sea weed" (*haidai* 海带),[525] comprise mainly those who left for a foreign country after the year 2000 and who stayed only for studying and returned after one or two years. Since they face employment difficulties similar to their local counterparts,[526] it appears that it is mostly the international work experience in a foreign country which makes overseas returnees successful. Hence, although *haigui* are such a tiny fraction of China's human capital – and the successful among them constitute an even smaller proportion –, they are worth considering as they show that work experiences in contrast to (even overseas) education raises the value of human capital.

519 They are conventionally referred to as "sea turtles" (*haigui* 海龟). This is a pun on *haigui* 海归 which is an abbreviation for *haiwai guilai* (海外归来) – literally "returning from overseas".

520 Wang Huiyao 2012.

521 Staiger 2007: 535, Duan Yu 2012.

522 Mei Liumei 2012.

523 Lu Jiangyong et al. 2012: 7.

524 According to the returnees' self-assessment in the framework of a comprehensive survey conducted by Beijing University's Guanghua School of Management (Lu Jiangyong et al. 2012), their consciousness of creativity has been fostered in the foreign country. More than 75% like experimenting and exploring as well as considering themselves as being good at observing and communicating (Lu Jiangyong et al. 2012: 92-93, Wang Huiyao 2012). Also, a majority thinks that they can more easily gather technical and commercial information from overseas, and can better develop foreign markets. More than half assert having an advantage in management (Lu Jiangyong et al. 2012: 100).

525 *Haidai* 海带 is a pun on *haidai* 海待 (Lu Jiangyong et al. 2012: 21), an abbreviation of *haigui daiye* (海归待业) – literally "returned from overseas and awaiting employment".

526 Lu Jiangyong et al. 2012: 21.

Knowledge workers up to 29 years of age, who have only recently entered the workforce, account for the large majority of knowledge workers with a tertiary education (see Figure 3).[527] This is a consequence of the expansion of higher education enrollment since 1999, which aimed at building on China's comparative advantage of its vast population and to turn it into human capital.[528] This caused a more than eight-fold increase of graduates between 1998 and 2012.[529]

Yet these inexperienced workers benefit from the education received only to a comparatively limited extent. The Chinese education system suffers from significant structural weaknesses. Traditionally, education in China has been highly valued, aiming at personal advancement.[530] The state, however, realized that the promotion of education could strengthen good government. It therefore played the key role in establishing, funding, and controlling of educational institutions. The purpose of education was then to become a civil servant, and education as a whole aimed at preparing for the examinations.[531] Due to the need of a standard reference for the civil service examinations, (rote) learning of classics became the paramount feature of the education system.[532]

Nowadays, passive rote learning of standard knowledge without questioning content or relevance is still prevalent. Throughout the whole educational career strong emphasis is put on formal theoretical subjects.[533] This trend has been strengthened further by the traditionally poor reputation of apprenticeship or practical learning within vocational schools. Skepticism toward any education which is not directly relevant for theoretical examinations is still widespread.[534]

As a consequence, the offer of qualifications does not match the demand of employers across enterprises of different sizes, ownership types, and sectors.[535] Employers have difficulties to fill job vacancies due to an inappropriate knowledge base, a lack of practical expertise and operational capacity, low moral standards,

527 See appendix 8.

528 Chen Shuang-Ye 2012: 104.

529 Li Chunling 2012: 164. Despite this expansion, tertiary education provision is even in quantitative terms not sufficient yet (Hebel and Schucher 2009: 237-238).

530 Thoegersen 2007: 102, Lee 2000: 2-16.

531 Lee 2000: 11-53.

532 Lee 2000: 20-29.

533 Thoegersen 2007: 103, Seffert 2003: 580 and 588, Groeger 2010, Yin Pumin 2012.

534 Thoegersen 2007: 103, Cooke 2005: 89, Li Yiqiong et al. 2011: 118-119. But see Lin Jing and Sun Xiaoyan (2010: 239) who assert that the form of higher education today is meeting the expectations of the masses if not the elites with specialized knowledge, communication skills, computer skills, and a wide exposure to information from official and inofficial channels.

535 Li Yiqiong et al. 2011: 115-120, Cheng Tsung-Mei 2012, Li Yiqiong and Sheldon 2011: 132, Hebel and Schucher 2009: 240, Cooke 2005: 29 and 175.

and an inadequate sense of social responsibilities.[536] The severe skill shortage[537] is exacerbated by the rising demand of FIEs as these have increasingly focused on higher quality, more sophisticated products, more complex manufacturing technologies, and more efficient production in recent years.[538] As such, when entering the workforce and before having gained work experience, the quality of this part of human capital is rather low compared to other knowledge workers of other age groups in China as well as to their peers in foreign countries.

To conclude, not all of China's knowledge workers are currently well positioned in China's economy. They strongly differ qualitatively in terms of education, work experience, and position on the labor market. Most significantly, new workforce entrants can only partly counterbalance the strong need for skilled knowledge workforce. Education alone is far from providing the skills of managing themselves and autonomously defining one's own task. Their contribution to the Chinese economy might be low even though they are – at first glance – the most qualified generation.

What is most valuable in the Chinese labor market is obviously work experience. Mid-aged employees with several years of work experience are well positioned in the Chinese economy. The most qualified overseas returnees only make up a tiny proportion. Being still relatively young but having received a tertiary education and having already gained some work experience, Chinese knowledge workers in their thirties (including some successful *haigui*) generally constitute the most valuable part of China's human capital and are best positioned in current Chinese economy. These knowledge workers do not only have latitude in their jobs but most probably have most latitude in choosing their jobs from a broad spectrum.

6.3 Knowledge Workers in Chinese Society

Knowledge workers are generally identified by occupation, which allows for drawing inferences about their social status. Occupations most clearly defined social status in ancient China. Society was simply structured into four occupations with scholars (士) at the top, followed by farmers (农), and artisans (工), with merchants (商) at the bottom. Mental labor enjoyed a higher status than

536 Morgan and Wu Bin 2011: 4-5, Hebel and Schucher 2007: 298-299, see *China Daily* 2010. The need for human capital pertains to all educational levels as apart from higher qualifications there is a considerable demand for a technically trained mid-level workforce (Hebel and Schucher 2009: 237-238).

537 Shenkar 2005: 4, Chow 2004: 64. Naughton 2007: 5 and 15, Cooke 2005: 31-32, Hebel and Schucher 2007: 298, Krotoschak and Kleine 2010, Cucco 2008: 127.

538 Li Yiqiong and Sheldon 2011: 129.

manual labor. This is in stark contrast to the Mao era, where – after the short interval of a multi-faceted workforce in the Republican era – manual labor was highly valued and mental labor even discarded, while social status was also largely determined by political credentials.

With the (re-)differentiation of Chinese society during the reform era, occupation has again become the most important structuring principle for contemporary Chinese society by Chinese sociologists.[539] The reason is that the differentiation of workers is increasing. They can be differentiated into workers who rely on their physical strength and those who do not. Furthermore, they can be differentiated into those who manage other workers and those who do not.[540] This implies that the difference between knowledge workers and manual workers is becoming clearer within Chinese society, and that their number and social status can be more sharply identified using occupational categories.

In their influential social stratification study,[541] Lu Xueyi, a sociologist with the Chinese Academy of Social Sciences (CASS), and his colleagues, identified ten occupation-based strata (阶层), to each of which they ascribed a certain socio-economic stratum. The social position of each occupation-based stratum and the ascription of a socio-economic status are determined by the capital available. Organizational capital (组织资源) enables to control and allocate societal resources of administrative and governmental organizations and is considered most important. Economic capital (经济资源) mainly refers to the property right as well as the right to use and operate production resources, which has become important since the reform and opening up. Educational capital (文化资源) implies the possession of officially acknowledged knowledge and skills which have played an increasingly important role since the beginning of the 1990s.[542]

Knowledge work-related occupations occupy the upper half of the social hierarchy (see 4). Cadres rank at the top by benefitting from their organizational capital. They are followed by managers who are either former cadres of state-owned or collective enterprises, or managers of private enterprises. With their relatively high educational background and their high political and social status, they allocate the resources of China's large and medium enterprises. Further down the hierarchy, private entrepreneurs with their economic capital conduct businesses with more than eight employees. Thereafter, professional and technical personnel owe their status to their educational capital, while clerks occupy

539 Li Peilin 2004: 7-8, see Cheng Li 2010: 68.
540 Lu Xueyi 2002: 7.
541 Lu Xueyi 2002.
542 Lu Xueyi 2002: 7-10.

the lowest knowledge worker status with a small amount of organizational and educational capital.

All these occupations are categorized by Lu Xueyi and his colleagues as belonging to the upper, upper middle, or the middle strata of the social hierarchy. Professional and technical personnel as well as private entrepreneurs can potentially belong to each of the three socio-economic strata. Cadres and managers either belong to the upper or upper middle strata. Clerks are merely ascribed to the middle class stratum.[543]

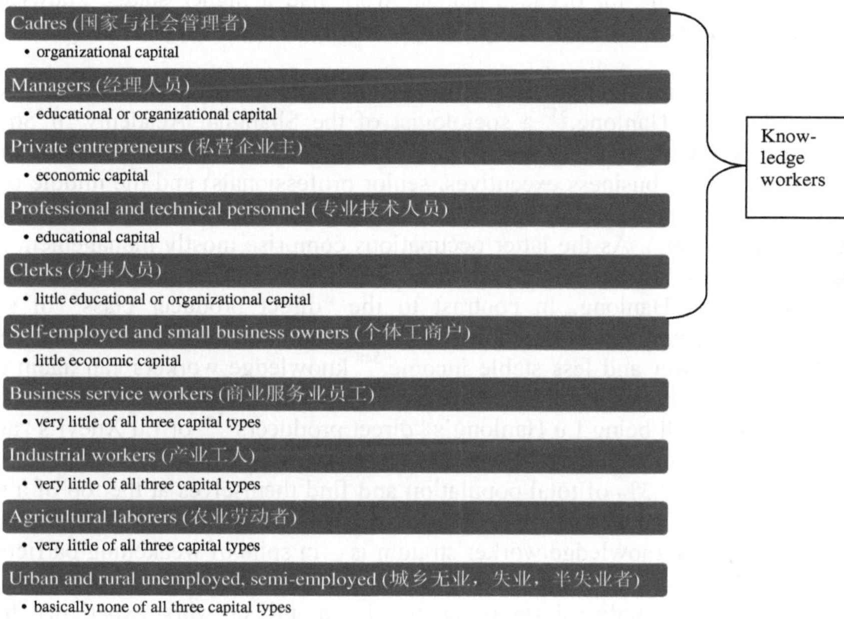

Figure 4: Knowledge workers within Chinese society's ten strata.

Source: Author's own compilation based on Lu Xueyi (2010: 9).

In contrast, self-employed persons and small business owners have only little economic capital available. Even if they employ a few persons, they themselves labor and operate production,[544] which allows for categorizing them as manual workers. This categorization is opposed to the rather positive notion of "self-employed" in the West, which often refers to typical knowledge worker occupa-

543 Lu Xueyi 2002: 9-18.
544 Lu Xueyi 2002: 18.

tions such as architects and consultants. The Chinese term *getihu*, however, rather connotes small shop owners or street food sellers. Along with business service workers, industrial workers, and agricultural laborers who can more clearly be categorized as manual workers, self-employed and small business owners have only very few capital available. Those workers are ascribed to the middle, lower middle, or lower strata of society.[545] Taking the huge ideological role of the working class in the Mao era into account, it is remarkable that Lu Xueyi as the first Chinese scholar has clearly put the working class at the lower end of the hierarchy.[546] While for decades manual work had a higher status, knowledge worker occupations are officially recognized as being on top of the hierarchy ever since.

Similarly, in the five-class structure of China's social stratification constructed by Lu Hanlong,[547] a sociologist of the Shanghai Academy of Social Sciences, knowledge workers form part of the elite class (that is, party and government leaders, business executives, senior professionals) and the middle class (that is, government and office clerks, white collar workers in corporations, general professionals). As the latter occupations comprise mostly management and knowledge service, the middle class is also referred to as knowledge service groups by Lu Hanlong. In contrast to the "direct producer class" of self-employed, manual and semi-manual workers, retail service assistants, and peasants with a lower and less stable income,[548] knowledge workers can again and even more definite be ascribed to one of the (two) upper classes. With the majority of people still being Lu Hanlong's "direct producers"[549] or Lu Xueyi's "agricultural laborers and industrial workers"[550], knowledge workers (KW1) make up a proportion of 7.3% of total population and find themselves at the top of a still pyramid-shaped rather than olive-shaped society.[551]

To reach a knowledge worker stratum is – in spite of weakening barriers to social mobility in the reform era –[552] not easy for a large part of society. For the older generation, political status, economic capital, or work experience have largely been decisive for reaching such an occupation. With the acknowledgment of knowledge being more important since the beginning of the 1990s, the young-

545 Lu Xueyi 2002: 9 and 18-23.
546 Cheng Li 2010: 66.
547 Lu Hanlong 2010: 116.
548 Lu Hanlong 2010: 116-117.
549 Lu Hanlong 2010: 127-128.
550 Lu Xueyi 2010: 394.
551 KW1 in % of total population (NBS 2011b), Cheng Li 2010: 66.
552 Lu Xueyi 2004: 178-179.

er generation increasingly relies on the higher educational credentials.[553] Yet these can be earned only with successfully mastering China's highly competitive education system.

As a legacy of the past, Chinese education institutions form a hierarchical and performance-oriented system with institutions differing substantially in quality. From the start, examination results completely determine the educational and professional career.[554] The score of the primary school graduation exam determines the lower middle school which can be attended and so forth. Most decisive is the *gaokao* (高考) – the national higher education entrance examination – as it determines which university can be attended.[555] The quality of the higher educational institution then largely determines future occupation and social status.

In order to help their (only) child to attain a high social status in their future life, parents are no longer satisfied with admittance to any common university and put extreme pressure on their children to study hard for the sake of admission to a top university. Despite large workloads and extensive homework burdens from schools, parents push their children to perform at an ever higher level, including the learning of additional languages and playing of musical instruments, by making considerable financial sacrifices. Attempts made by schools to reduce homework are not appreciated by parents due to the fear that their children might not pass the exam for the next level of the educational ladder.[556] For students, parents' efforts and expectations result in enormous pressure to perform, as well as in a fierce competition with their peers.

After graduation, the potential knowledge worker faces an extremely competitive labor market and the danger of facing unemployment. This is a recent phenomenon, appearing only after the abolishment of the job assignment (分配) system in the late 1990s. Under the system, every graduate has been assigned a workplace, and the phenomenon of unemployed university graduates was virtu-

553 Lin Jing and Sun Xiaoyan 2010: 238, Lu Xueyi 2004: 157 and 192, Hsu Carolyn L. 2007: 167-177.

554 Thoegersen 2007: 103, Seffert 2003: 580 and 588, Groeger 2010, Yin Pumin 2012.

555 Li Yi 2005: 165-167, Liu Jinghui 2007: 518-519, Staiger 2007: 532-533, Seffert 2003: 580. At the bottom of the hierarchy are colleges (高等专科学校) and higher vocational schools (高等职业学校) with a duration of two to three years (Liu Jinghui 2007: 519), which can be attended with lower *gaokao* results, coming along with a faltering reputation within society compared to universities with a duration of generally four years (see Staiger 2007: 536-537, Cooke 2005: 90, Hebel and Schucher 2009: 237-238, Liu Jinghui 2007: 501). The middle part of the hierarchy is occupied by the provincial-level universities, which usually educate their students up to bachelor degrees and pursue little research. These universities require a mid-level *gaokao* result. At the top are the central-level universities of "project 211" and "project 985" (Chen Shuang-Ye 2012: 103-104, Staiger 2007: 536-537, Yin 2012). Attending one of these roughly 100 universities requires excellent *gaokao* results.

556 Seffert 2003: 588-589, Hsu Carolyn L. 2007: 173-177, Thoegersen 2007: 103.

ally unknown. The competitive situation was excacerbated by the simultaneous expansion of higher education enrollment.[557] Currently, only about 70% of the graduates or even less find work each year. Even graduates from elite universities appear to be anxious about their future employment.[558]

The prevalence of this competitive situation in contemporary Chinese society is reflected by several discourses having emerged in recent years. For instance, the *kenlaozu* (啃老族) discourse – literally "gnawing the old"-group meaning adults still living with and depending on their parents – reflects the current struggle to find work and to survive in China's big cities.[559] They are also referred to as "ant tribe" (*yizu* 蚁族), reflecting the graduates' unavailing efforts to find work and their poor living conditions.[560] One part of the "ants" is underemployed. For instance, nearly a third of Beijing's "ants" is employed in "sales in private business", such as selling low-end computer parts for wholesalers.[561] Another part of the "ants" is unemployed, though chances improve in the first six months upon graduation.[562] Nevertheless, together with *xiagang* (下岗) workers (those laid off from SOEs) as well as rural migrant workers (where unemployment is traditionally highest[563]) graduates may recently find themselves at the lowest rank of society (see figure 4). This leads to the paradoxical situation that China's "newest underclass"[564] does not move up the social hierarchy stratum by stratum but is aspiring to jump to the knowledge worker occupation strata directly.

Once having found work and officially belonging to the knowledge worker strata, pressure and competition are likely to continue. The upper social strata are associated with white collar workers.[565] The term "white collar worker" and its counterpart "blue collar worker" emerged during the industrialization process in Western countries, addressing the evolving dichotomy between office and factory workers.[566] In China, "collars" have become important social status markers. White collars are associated with a higher social status. This higher social status does not merely include the obligatory purchase of a house or an apartment before getting married (on the part of men), but the burden of continuous expenses such as pur-

557 Li Yi 2005: 155, Hurst 2014: 333. See also chapter 6.2.
558 Lin Jing and Sun Xiaoyan 2010: 230, Seffert 2003: 589.
559 Lin Jing and Sun Xiaoyan 2010: 230.
560 *China Daily* 2010. Feng Sue 2009. See also Morgan and Wu Bin 2011: 4-9, Chen Shuang-Ye 2012: 107, Hebel and Schucher 2007: 298-299, Hebel and Schucher 2009: 237-238.
561 *China Daily* 2010.
562 Lin Jing and Sun Xiaoyan 2010: 231.
563 Schucher 2009. Rural migrant workers were also mainly referred to in 2002 in Lu Xueyi's (2002: 23) study.
564 *China Daily* 2010.
565 See e.g. Lu Xueyi 2004: 19 and 158.
566 See e.g. Mills 1951.

chasing at least a middle-sized car, sending children to special courses, and inviting friends for costly dinners.[567] More measurable and even harsher criteria for fitting into this category have been established by Chinese internet users, according to which white collar workers are supposed to possess an apartment with at least two bedrooms as well as a car worth around 150,000 RMB, and should earn a monthly salary of 20,000 RMB.[568]

Meanwhile, *de facto* compliance with these clearly defined standards proves complicated for many employees whose occupation falls into the white-collar category.[569] Although the average monthly income for the upper half of Lu Xueyi's ten occupation-based strata is the highest,[570] the average monthly starting salary for graduates in Beijing is only 2,655 RMB,[571] accounting only for 13% of the expected white collar standard. Salary increases do not necessarily alleviate the problem, as prices, especially for housing, are constantly on the rise, not leading to significant, if any, purchasing power effects for employees.[572]

Furthermore, as it is common in other countries,[573] white collar workers in China are associated with the middle class. In the United States, the middle class accounts for the majority of the American population and comprises what is referred to as "common people". In China, in contrast, a decisive criterion for belonging to the middle class is the purchase of luxury goods and the ownership of two houses or apartments.[574] Following an announcement of the official figure of 37% urbanities belonging to the middle class, the majority of white collar workers have found themselves *bei zhongchan le* (被中产了) – having been pushed into middle class – while *de facto* not fulfilling the associated standards.[575] This gap between expected and real social standard is bound to create a constant pressure among white collar workers.

Mastering the highly competitive education system, competing for work, and being forced to fulfill the associated living standards – at least in the eyes of the public –[576] triggers a strong competitive mentality. Several indications can be found that this is the case in Chinese society in general and for Chinese knowledge workers in particular. According to the *Annual Report on Social Mentality of Chi-*

567 Qian Minhui 2011: 71-72.
568 *China Daily* 2012.
569 *China Daily* 2012.
570 Lu Xueyi 2010: 186.
571 Lin Jing and Sun Xiaoyan 2010: 230.
572 Qian Minhui 2011: 48-50.
573 See e.g. Mills 1951.
574 Cheng Li 2010: 68-69.
575 Qian Minhui 2011: 57-63 and 71, see Lin Jing and Sun Xiaoyan 2010: 230.
576 Qian Minhui 2011: 71-72.

na 2011, social pressure in Chinese society has increased.[577] Peng Kaiping, Director of the Department of Psychology at Qinghua University, argues that the greatest pressure for urban Chinese results from social competition.[578] Also, the general trust level in society has dropped to 60 points out of a full mark of 100 points in 2010 according to the *Annual Report on Social Mentality of China 2012-2013*.[579] With simultaneously decreasing trust and increasing pressure, it is no doubt that substantial social competition pervades Chinese urban society.

For Chinese citizens being socially competitive seems to be highly desirable. China's free content-encyclopedia *Baidu Baike* (百度百科), which currently exceeds the English language Wikipedia by roughly two million articles, includes an entry on "social competitiveness" (社会竞争力), which is explained as a personal ability for survival in society.[580] Advice how to achieve social competitiveness is also given online as well. According to this advice, one should develop a consciousness for social competition as well as "adapt to social competition", which can be achieved – among others – by continuous learning.[581] These online sources reveal the general belief that social competition cannot be avoided.

Another underlying assumption is that coping with or rather "adapting to" competition requires an ability which can be trained rather than being naturally inherent in people. This conviction is well in line with the results of Whyte's[582] national representative sample survey on the perception of inequalities in China. Whyte found that the majority of Chinese society views current social differences as primarily due to merit and less due to an unfair social structure. Accordingly, it is widely believed that hard work will be rewarded, and that ordinary citizens are able to get ahead and prosper based on hard work.[583] People are convinced that hard work helps in coping with social competition which is further shown by the *guolaosi* (过劳死) phenomenon – literally "death from overwork" –, which concerns young white collar workers below forty years of age. It has become increasingly common since the turn of the century with 600,000 persons dying every year due to overwork and 70% of white collar workers being at risk.[584] Thus, the attitude that someone is able to influence his social status through hard work is widespread in contemporary Chinese urban society.

577 Wang Junxiu 2011: 3.
578 China International Conference on Positive Psychology 2012.
579 Wang Junxiu 2013: 9.
580 Baidu 2013.
581 Mop.com 2012, 360doc.com 2012.
582 Whyte 2010.
583 Whyte 2010: 84-91.
584 Qian Minhui 2011: 69, *China Labor Bulletin* 2006, Chelala 2012.

Knowledge workers are particularly exposed to social competition. Online advice given is directed to knowledge workers. In order to provide help for the adaptation to competition, topics such as the choice of being generalist (全才) or specialist (专才) are discussed.[585] Also, Wang and Yang[586] assert that while status attainment is a factor that increases the pressure in workers' lives in a market economy in general, knowledge workers in particular are likely to respond to these pressures. On the one hand, their motivation for self-realization and success makes them work more. On the other hand, if a knowledge worker's abilities are not sufficient to solve a certain task, they are also inclined to work even harder.[587] For increasing the living standard and countering social pressure, knowledge workers tend to overwork, making full use of their latitude in managing themselves and their future development.

It becomes clear that it is not only workers of lower classes who are inclined to be exposed to social competition, but that also – or rather primarily – the upper knowledge worker strata are concerned. Needless to say that this phenomenon only applies to a part of each stratum rather than a stratum as a whole, such as single strata or "the middle class" are not homogenous in perceptions regarding needs, values, life satisfaction, and so forth.[588] Just as their contribution to economic growth might be different,[589] knowledge workers might differ in social status. For instance, experienced overseas returnees are likely to perceive social competition less severe, taken their position on the labor market into account. Yet despite their – according to objective criteria – distinguished position in the current social hierarchy, a significant part of knowledge workers within different (upper and middle) strata finds itself in a (subjective) state of constant social competition within Chinese society.

The knowledge worker strata, which might experience most social competition, are managers, clerks, and professional and technical personnel rather than cadres who have a rather secure position or private entrepreneurs whose concern might rather be economic competition. Knowledge workers in FIEs thus rather belong to the three strata most exposed to social competition. Hence, Chinese employees might draw knowledge boundaries carefully. Not only due to their identity *per se* do they pay attention to keep their means of production updated but due to the competitive social situation in China. This situation could even more likely influence their boundary drawing in a way that makes them able to increase their social competitiveness.

585 360doc.com 2012.
586 Wang Dan and Yang Heqing 2012.
587 Wang Dan and Yang Heqing 2012.
588 See e.g. Li Cheng 2010: 10, Wang Jianying and Davis 2010.
589 See chapter 6.2.

7 The Property of Knowledge in Chinese Philosophy, History, and Law

This chapter traces the drawing of property boundaries of valuable knowledge in Chinese philosophy, history, and law. Since Chinese philosophy is strongly concerned with practically trying to help people to live good and moral lives,[590] it is scrutinized whether it provides behavioral norms for the issue under investigation as well (7.1). Premodern Chinese history reveals how valuable knowledge was indeed handled in economic life (7.2). The application of China's trade secrets legislation to the Chinese business reality provides insights on the handling of valuable knowledge in current business practice (7.3).

7.1 Knowledge Property in Chinese Philosophy

The two dominant schools of Chinese philosophy are Legalism and Confucianism. The Legalists with their two leading figures Shang Yang (390-338 BCE) and Han Fei (280-233 BCE) were concerned with preserving and strengthening the state. This was to be achieved by a strict focus on farming and military, a centralized bureaucracy ruling by law, strategy and power as well as by employing strong rewards and severe punishments. Property was advocated by the Legalists only in terms of private ownership of land. Legalists were not strongly concerned with property in general or the property of knowledge in particular. This is not astonishing as Legalists addressed themselves exclusively to the ruler. Only in terms of their usefulness to the ruler were private individuals and their lives an issue at all.[591]

Rather than Legalism, Confucianism provides moral norms potentially more directed to society as a whole. Ancient Confucian thinkers were generally concerned with seeking moral cultivation of oneself and society. The most influential work of the Confucian tradition – the *Analects* or *Lunyu* (论语) – focuses on cardinal virtues such as benevolence, righteousness, honesty, and integrity and thus reveals the main concerns of Confucians.[592] This is also figuratively illuminated by

590 See e.g. Wen Haiming 2012, Cua Antonia S. 2009, Fung Yu-Lan 1947.
591 Fu Zhengyuan 1996, Watson 2003, Lai Karyn L. 2008: 172-198.
592 Wilhelm and van Ess 2005, van Ess 2003: 21, Rainey 2010: 30-31, Wen Haiming 2012: 28.

the construction of the moral ideal of the "gentleman" or *junzi* (君子). The gentleman always acts right and works at overcoming his own selfishness and at helping others becoming better people. In contrast, the "small man" (小人) is concerned with his own benefit instead for the public good, being motivated by his own greed and desires.[593] To a limited extent, the Confucian opposition to private interests in favor of public interests can serve as an indicator that the matter of private property was not a major concern of Confucianism.

Nevertheless, the reluctant attitude considering private interests does not necessarily imply that property is seen as unacceptable. Confucius (551-479 BCE) did not object to wealth as long as it had been attained in a moral way and was not hoarded for oneself.[594] Profit or possession was something which should not be strived for or concentrated on,[595] but if attained, one had the duty to share it with others.[596] It was consensus among Confucius, Mencius (372-289 BCE), and Neo-Confucianists that property should be tolerated as long as it benefits society and not only the individual. Only absolute property rights were opposed.[597] Apart from these vague statements, Confucian thinkers paid no further attention to more concrete questions of the handling of knowledge property.

But does the frequent reference to Confucius' saying to "transmit rather than create" (述而不作)[598] of the *Lunyu* not point to references in Chinese philosophy? Within the intellectual property debate, this saying is referred to for proving that Confucius was against the creation of new knowledge but instead only transmitted existing knowledge. Yet putting the saying in context, it becomes clear that it can hardly be interpreted in a way that Confucius was against individual knowledge property. In China's Imperial past, it was usually sought after the knowledge of ancient sages to solve the problems of that era. This knowledge has been regarded as common heritage instead of being an individual endeavor. Indeed, in China – such as in many other countries – producing texts was understood as preserving or disseminating what was regarded as ancient

593 See e.g. *Lunyu* IV, 12 and IX, 4 (Wilhelm and van Ess 2005: 33 and 76), Rainey 2010: 31 and 42-43, Zhang Dainian 2002: 311-318.

594 See e.g. *Lunyu* IV, 5 and VI, 4 (Wilhelm and van Ess 2005: 31 and 48-49), Zhang Dainian 2002: 311-312, Rainey 2010: 35.

595 See e.g. *Lunyu* IV, 11 and 16 and XI, 16 (Wilhelm and van Ess 2005: 33, 34 and 100), Rainey 2010: 42-43.

596 See e.g. *Lunyu* XIV, 13 and XVI, 10 (Wilhelm and van Ess 2005: 131 and 159).

597 Confucius (Bell 2003, Zhang Dainian 2002: 311-312), Mencius (Bell 2003, Ivanhoe 2002: 14), Neo-Confucianists (Ivanhoe 2002: 30-32).

598 Lunyu VII,1. Put forward for instance by Alford 1995: 9 and 25, Nie Jianqiang 2006: 178, Qu Sanqiang 2012: xlvi.

(and eternal) truth.[599] Those citing Confucius do not differentiate between knowledge used as common reference for all people – such as the Bible or the Koran – and knowledge or ideas of an individual entity created in daily life. Against this background an attitude counterintuitive to individual knowledge property cannot be derived from this saying of Confucius.

Such references often come with the quick assumption that Confucian thinking is highly relevant in contemporary China (while the extent to which this provided guidance in the past also open to question).[600] Judging from the current state of Chinese society, the assumption that Confucian norms provide strong guidance for daily behavior in general appears less likely. Taking, for instance, the discourse on the "moral void"[601] within Chinese society into account: as revealed by Chinese and Western (social) media, there is a lack of public morality among Chinese people. This discourse is mainly invoked by instances of ignorance on streets when injured people require help.[602] The discourse is not only present within society but the Chinese government is involved as well, counting on Confucian ethics, traditional faiths, and moral models to enhance public morality.[603] The search for orientation within contemporary society is further reflected by the remarkable popularity of Yu Dan and the Yu Dan phenomenon (于丹现象). The professor of media studies at Beijing Normal University published popular accounts on Chinese philosophy in an effort to make Confucius' thoughts understandable for the general public.[604] Such evidence of the lack of a unitary reference system within society casts doubts of why Chinese people overly adhere to or are strongly influenced and guided by a certain philosophical system.

To summarize, direct hints of how to handle knowledge property in Chinese philosophy are scarce. This is not astonishing in view of the fact that ancient Chinese philosophers formed part of the elite and were concerned with how to organize the state and how to cultivate a moral society while refusing to bother with the private interests of individuals. Anyway, explaining behavior (exclusively) with philosophical norms in contemporary Chinese society generally requires caution.

599 See e.g. Hesse 2002. In medieval European monastries, for instance, scribes copied sacred texts for eternal preservation (Hofmann and Katzenbach 2006: 9, see Röttgers 2010: 181).
600 See e.g. Fuchs 2006: 63-64, Witte 2010: 36.
601 Lim and Blanchard 2013.
602 See e.g. Siemons 2011, Zhang Lijia 2011.
603 See e.g. Yang Yao 2013, He Dan 2013.
604 Yu Dan 2009.

7.2 Private Knowledge Protection in Premodern China

The concern for private protection of valuable knowledge is clearly observable in historical accounts. Among premodern China's population, keeping ideas privately and excluding others from using this knowledge was wide-spread. Attempts were made of keeping manufacturing formulas, processes, and techniques of certain products secret. Famous examples include Jingdezhen porcelain-making, Guizhou Maotai ingredients, as well as traditional Chinese medicine and acupuncture techniques.[605] For differentiating a product line and its associated quality from that of competitors, commodities were labeled into various subtypes as well as brand names identifying area of production (e.g. Jingdezhen porcelain), the producer's name (e.g. "Made by family Zhang") or the seller's name (e.g. "Tongren Temple" medicine) with the earliest traces in Tang dynasty.[606] As a matter of fact, people protected their knowledge for the sake of gaining reputation and profit.

Several forms of protection existed. First and foremost, knowledge was protected via keeping it secret within the boundaries of the family. Sayings, such as "passing on a secret recipe from generation to generation" (祖传秘方) and "passing on to the daughter-in-law instead of the daughter" (传媳不传女),[607] suggest that knowledge ideally should stay within the family, preferably the lineage. Yet within clans competition was prevalent as well. For instance, core families differentiated themselves from the rest of the clan with a different brand name such as "Made by big family Zhang" or similar.[608] In any event, the family – in line with their functioning as unit of production and joint holder of family property –[609] also ensured effective protection of a knowledge monopoly for its own benefit.[610]

In extension to the family, guilds and related groups formed the second most important unit of protection in late Imperial Chinese society. The commoditized economy was flourishing in an increasingly competitive environment. Fierce economic competition took place between different regions in China.[611]

605 Shan Hailing 2008: 3, Hamilton and Lai Chi-kong 1986: 4-15 (quoted from Alford 1995: 16).

606 Hamilton and Lai Chi-kong 1989: 257-262, Chen 2008: 58, Liu Yunsheng 2007: 55, Shi Wei 2006: 8. Zheng Chengsi (1987: 21) even asserts that according some historical records, brands first appeared in late Zhou Dynasty (1046-256 BC).

607 Chen Hefang 2008: 58, He Saiying 2002: 26, Wang Yu 2006: 16, Liu Yunsheng 2009: 12-13, Liu Yunsheng 2007: 55, Bai Yunfei and Jia Yuping 1997: 39.

608 Liu Yunsheng 2007: 55, see Hamilton and Lai Chi-kong 1989: 265.

609 Spence 1990: 95, Bell 2003: 230.

610 Chen Hefang 2008: 58, Liu Yunsheng 2009: 12, Liu Yunsheng 2007: 55.

611 Hamilton and Lai Chi-kong 1989: 256, van der Sprenkel 1977: 611-612, Golas 1977: 555, see Skinner 1977b: 278-297.

For countering interregional competition, guilds strived for monopolization of a certain artisanry or trade. The most effective means for preserving this monopoly was limiting access to knowledge to guild members while keeping it secret from outsiders.[612] This need for preserving secrecy to counter regional competition might have been much less pronounced in Medieval Europe, where the populace was supplied by local guilds only.[613]

To keep knowledge within the guild, new guild members were carefully selected through pursuing an apprenticeship for a period of three to five years. The apprenticeship system was sometimes limited to sons and nephews of members, accepting no more than one family member of one master at a time as well as just one apprentice for each technique at a time. In other cases, a new apprentice could only enter the guild by paying a fee and working without being paid for a certain time. After completion of the apprenticeship, the master was supposed to ensure that the apprentice stayed with the guild.[614] As a means of protecting complex technical knowledge, membership was thus granted only by status (by adhering to the inheritance principle similar to a family system) or by agreement (by treating knowledge as a commercial good the access to which has to be paid for).

Within guilds, strict internal rules similarly prevented the diffusion of knowledge. Luring away workers or apprentices of fellow members was prohibited. Brand names and symbols were protected from use by fellow members. Disputes between members were settled internally, and misconduct was sanctioned.[615] With these sophisticated internal and external protection measures, more or less effective knowledge communities in addition to the family as unit of protection had been established.

Yet knowledge was not only protected at a collective or community level. The large amounts of sojourners characteristic for late imperial China's economic centers concentrated in native-place associations (*Landsmannschaften*) for mutual support and as a front against discrimination by locals.[616] As different locations often specified in a certain trade or artisanry, most of the associations equally specified in this certain economic activity and most often eventually became guilds.[617] Although the importance of the native place tended to diminish in favor of membership by economic activity (in extreme cases even leading to

612 Skinner 1977a: 541, Morse 1967: 2-3, Liu Yunsheng 2009: 13, Golas 1977: 565-570.

613 Hamilton and Lai Chi-kong 1989: 254.

614 Morse 1967: 37-38, Liu Yunsheng 2009: 13-14, Golas 1977: 565-570.

615 Liu Yunsheng 2009: 13-16, Golas 1977: 561-580, van der Sprenkel 1977: 614-617, Hamilton and Lai Chi-kong 1986: 4-15 (quoted from Alford 1995: 16).

616 Skinner 1977a: 538-539, Golas 1977: 556, see van der Sprenkel 1977: 614.

617 Golas 1977: 563, van der Sprenkel 1977: 611-612. Native-place associations and guilds were hard to disentangle with native-place associations sometimes consisting of guild-like sub-divisions among others (Skinner 1977a: 543).

the refusal of admission for persons from the same native place (同乡) who pursued a different economic activity), the importance of native places remained, being one of the most significant particularities of guilds in late Imperial China compared to the local guild structures in Medival Europe.[618]

Most consequential was the fact that "native place" as a category could refer to particular counties, prefectures, or provinces (and each with the adjacent counties, prefectures, and even provinces respectively), leading to an overlapping of localities of many native-place associations in one economic center.[619] Accordingly, memberships of a single person could be manifold as well, for instance, a sojourner from Ningbo in Beijing could among others be affiliated with the Ningbo Prefecture association and adjacent prefectures associations, as well as with the Zhejiang Province association.

With increasing competition, native-place associations became even more diverse, through, for instance, sharing a monopoly in a certain trade with completely different native associations, or through intermarriage with locals or assimilation of immigrants from other places.[620] Groups thus increasingly overlapped and became more heterogeneous. These specific *multilayered group affiliations* differentiated an artisan or merchant from his fellows in a particular group.

Every group possessed its own special knowledge, often drawn from a geographically specific and distant knowledge reservoir. Individual knowledge must have been a combination thereof corresponding to the *individual mix of affiliations* to different and changing groups. The individual artisan or merchant might thus have decided in which groups to tactically and strategically share his particular knowledge and make use of his family and at least one or more native place (associations) or guilds as multiple units of protection. In this sense, the individual can – in retrospect – also be seen as unit of knowledge protection with his *unique combination of knowledge*.

Apart from being affiliated with different groups, merchants and artisans frequently acted as *intermediaries* for connecting groups and people. The intermediary was a considerable institution in Chinese society. According to van der Sprenkel "probably few commercial transactions of any consequence in traditional China were either impersonal or casual"[621] since "one got nowhere until a relationship of trust had been established"[622]. Prior to any commercial transaction – be it conducting purchases, hiring staff, or granting credits – a personal

618 Golas 1977: 558-563.
619 Skinner 1977a: 538-539.
620 Golas 1977: 565.
621 van der Sprenkel 1977: 620.
622 van der Sprenkel 1977: 620.

relationship had to be established. If no direct personal relationship existed, an intermediary was used. The intermediary arranged the terms of an agreement and usually not only guaranteed the good faith of the parties involved but their proper fulfillment of the agreed terms. This involved the guaranteeing of payment as well as mediating between the two parties in case of difficulties.[623] Apart from receiving commission for bearing the risks involved, the intermediary was involved in the detailed terms of the specific transaction.[624] With no doubt, the latter gave him a knowledge monopoly, knowing more about the transaction than each party of the agreement.

It is very unlikely that the groups were informed of all the details regarding the occasional activities of each of their members as intermediaries or of the particular knowledge acquired through mediating a transaction. This situation must have provided an intermediary with a certain latitude for tactically and strategically making decisions regarding his knowledge. He was surely able to decide to either protect or (carefully) share his particular knowledge (or parts thereof) and – most importantly – with whom he shares knowledge in his personal intricate network. All this most likely allowed for certain specific privately protected knowledge stock not only at a community but also at an individual level.

Private knowledge protection was hardly hampered by the state. The economic sphere in general was characterized by low interference from officials.[625] This gave a considerable latitude to the self-organization of Chinese society into various groups, often with tacit consent from the government.[626] Guilds hold almost unrestrained control over commercial activities, effectively exercised via customary law. Their activities, such as the enforcement of standards of weights and measures, also complemented the bureaucratic state affairs. The power of guilds was even further reinforced by their coordination of various public functions, for instance organizing fire fighters, which the state was often not able to provide.[627] Hence, the state not only refrained from interference into guilds' activities but was rather given the incentive to support guilds including their cultivation of knowledge monopolies.

623 Accounts differ on whether the middleman and the guarantor had been one single or two separate roles, but presumably roles differed locally (van der Sprenkel 1977: 621).

624 van der Sprenkel 1977: 621.

625 Morse 1967: 24-25, van der Sprenkel 1977: 631. Alford (1995: 16) supposes that in case of rampant imitation of goods not much successful support was provided by local officials, which further suggests that the government was not too much in involved in commercial affairs.

626 Chen Hefang 2008: 58, Golas 1977: 580, Hamilton and Lai Chi-kong 1989: 265, van der Sprenkel 1977: 614.

627 Morse 1967: 2 and 24-29 and 57, Skinner 1977a: 547-553, Golas 1977: 575, Morse 1918: 154-156.

As a matter of fact, the extent and way of privately protecting valuable knowledge in premodern China was mostly determined by the dense social fabric. It was subject to diverse relationships and group affiliations within the family and society. The orientation along the complicated social fabric for individual ends was most decisive for drawing boundaries between one's own knowledge and that of the respective other groups. In contrast to Medieval Europe, which exibited a social structure with more rigid class boundaries and a more limited social mobility, late Imperial China's social structure was much more complex.[628] What follows is that Chinese employees nowadays potentially have a distinct awareness of the knowledge acquired from the affiliation with several groups and the private knowledge monopoly gained as a result. Due to the legacy of a more straight-forward and simple guild structure in past times, Europeans might rather be focused on drawing the boundaries of knowledge only between themselves and one particular and clearly defined organization.

7.3 Valuable Knowledge in Chinese Law and Practice

In the late 19th century, the first norms governing valuable knowledge appeared in Chinese legislation. While the Qing government focused on controlling its printing monopolies for government materials and was not interested in legally granting private knowledge protection,[629] domestic pressures demanding modernization as well as foreigners pressuring for trademark protection forced the government to issue laws and regulations.[630] Western advice – of both anglo-american and continental lawyers – influenced the drafting processes to a great extent. The Qing government, the government of the northern warlords, and the nationalist government each came to pass some kind of intellectual property legislation, encompassing patents, trademarks, copyright, and trade secrets.[631] Yet in times of political turmoil promulgation of legislation was slow, and it was hardly implemented and enforced.[632] During the Mao era, the concept of intellec-

628 Hamilton and Lai Chi-kong 1989: 263.

629 Chen Hefang 2008, Pelzer 2012: 16, Liu Gang 2011: 36-37, Hesse 2002: 29-30. Zheng Chengsi (1987: 86-87) views these developments as an early form of copyright protection, whereas Alford (1995: 13-17) disagrees.

630 Alford 1995: 34-36.

631 Yang Deli 2003: 17-21, Kong Qingjiang 2005: 5-6, Zheng Chengsi 1987: 21-22 and 51-52 and 87-88.

632 Alford 1995: 35-50. For inventions and creations see e.g. Shan Hailing 2008: 3 and Yang Deli 2003: 18, for patent law see e.g. Yang Deli 2003: 20-21, for copyright see e.g. Pelzer 2012. Nonetheless, some legislation was put into practice. For instance, Chinese authors and publishers took advantage of copyright law through use of the registration system and copyright nota-

tual property contradicted the Marxist ideology with the ideal of property belonging to the people instead of the individual and virtually left no room for private protection of knowledge at all. In favor of a Soviet style reward system, existing intellectual property laws and regulations were eliminated.[633]

Only within the process of market reforms and opening up to the global economy starting in 1978, a regulatory framework has systematically been established. A wide range of intellectual property laws has been promulgated, including Trademark Law (1983), Patent Law (1985), and Copyright Law (1990). These allowed granting the exclusive rights over the use of valuable knowledge to a private entity. Similar to tangible property, competitors or (former) employees can be excluded from its use.[634]

Such exclusive rights are rather granted for outstanding ideas and significantly novel knowledge. Yet there are many other kinds of knowledge that are not eligible for granting these exclusive rights but can prove to be very valuable for a business as well. In 1993, information not being eligible for protection under Chinese Patent Law was recognized as trade secrets (商业秘密) by the Law against Unfair Competition[635] (LUC).[636] Although the law's main intent is the protection of fair competition, it provides trades secrets with the legal status of an intellectual property right.[637] Knowledge in the form of trade secrets can thus be considered the property of an entity.

In contrast to the more traditional intellectual property of patents, trademarks, and copyright, the property question of trade secrets is most difficult to answer. The property of information is not a zero-sum game belonging exclusively to either person A or person B. The doctrine of balance of interests is most

tions in books. Yet enforcement faced difficulties due to insufficient personnel for seizing the escaping infringers (Pelzer 2012: 26-31).

633 Gale 1978, Yang Deli 2003: 21-25. But see Zheng Chengsi (1987: 22-23 and 88-90) for some shortly existing or less influential regulations on trademarks and copyrights, and Alford (1995: 64) for some trademark registration (accompanied by massive unauthorized copying of product labels). The reward system for inventions also showed slight vestiges of the personal property element, granting a set of privileges to the inventor (Gale 1978, Zheng Chengsi 1987: 52-53).

634 Shan Hailing 2008: 91, Klett et al. 2008: 46.

635 Law against Unfair Competition of the PRC (LUC) (中华人民共和国反不正当竞争法) as of Dec 1, 1993 (Guowuyuan 1993).

636 Han Dekuan 2012: 32, Shan Hailing 2008: 4-13.

637 Liu Xiaohai 1999: 71. With the consideration of trade secrets in line with the traditional intellectual property types in the Criminal Law in 1997, Chinese legislators with no doubt view trade secrets as a part of intellectual property (Liu Yingqun 2008: 44, Liu Xiaohai 1999: 71-73). Another indicator is that trade secrets are considered in the *China Intellectual Property Yearbook* (中国知识产权年鉴) (State Intellectual Property Office of the PRC (SIPO) 2000-2011) as well as in the intellectual property category of the *Selected Cases of the People's Court* (人民法院案例选) (China Institute of Applied Jurisprudence of the Supreme People's Court (CIAJ) 1992-2011).

fundamental in establishing trade secrets legislation. After carefully studying law making in the West, Chinese scholars and judges equally adhere to a combination of property, contract, and tort theories for achieving this balance.[638] While property theory strikes a balance between an individual and society (generally an enterprise and the public), contract and tort theories focus on relationships between persons (generally an employer and his employee or business partner).[639] With a multilayered legislative framework,[640] the interests in valuable knowledge of the general public, of businesses, and of employees should be kept in balance.

As China is a statute law country, the legislative framework for trade secrets is the main source for judicial and administrative organs seeking to resolve disputes over valuable knowledge. This implies that complex conflicts of interests behind the controversial handling of knowledge in China have to be subsumed under abstract norms derived from Western countries.[641] With trade secret cases increasing in China, the law has been complemented by regulations[642] issued by the State Administration of Industry and Commerce (SAIC) by an interpretation[643] of the Supreme People's Court (SPC) based on experience with trade secrets cases in Chinese judicial practice.[644] Further experiences with trade secrets cases in China can be derived from the annually published cases which are considered typical for trade secrets issues in China by Chinese judiciary and administration of all levels.[645] Although decisions by judges as a source for legal practice play a minor role in statute law countries, the typical cases nonetheless

638 Lemley 2008: 319-328, Shan Hailing 2008: 80-93. In China, trade secrets are seen as a special intellectual property, which is most critical among intellectual property cases (Dou Xingya 2007: 65).

639 See also Shan Hailing 2008: 239-240.

640 Apart from unfair competition law, protection arises from contract law, labor law, and labor contract law as well as the general principles of the civil law (Müller and Sprick 2011: 156-162, see Shan Hailing 2007: 153).

641 With China entering the WTO in 2001, the regulatory framework protecting enterprises' intellectual property have basically become consistent with the requirements of the agreement on Trade-related Aspects of Intellectual Property Rights (TRIPS) (Guo Shoukang and Zuo Xiaodong 2007, Yang Deli and Clarke 2005, see Kong Qingjiang 2005: 4-5).

642 "Several regulations on prohibiting trade secret infringements (Amendment)" (关于禁止侵犯商业秘密行为的若干规定(修正)) as of Dec 3, 1998 (State Administration of Industry and Commerce (SAIC) 国家工商行政管理总局 1998). In the following: SAIC Regulations.

643 "Interpretation of the Supreme People's Court on Some Matters about the Application of Law in the Trial of Civil Cases Involving Unfair Competition" (最高人民法院关于审理不正当竞争民事案件应用法律若干问题的解释) as of Feb 1, 2007 (World Intellectual Property Organization (WIPO) 2012). In the following: SPC Interpretation.

644 See *Renminwang* 2007.

645 Typical cases are either published in the *Selected Cases of the People's Court* (CIAJ 1992-2011) or the *China Intellectual Property Yearbook* (SIPO 2000-2011). In the following: typical cases of CIAJ & SIPO.

yield profound insights here: not only are they informative about the way laws and regulations are applied in China's business environment but they illuminate the handling of valuable knowledge in Chinese business reality itself.

How often valuable knowledge in the form of trade secrets had actually been in dispute in China's business environment is hard to determine. Due to their secret nature, the dimension of trade secrets can in general only be estimated by recorded infringements. In China in particular, the exact number is difficult to determine due to different ways of enforcement and statistics compiled by different enforcement institutions. From 1995[646] until the end of 2010[647] 749 cases were administratively enforced with Administrations of Industry and Commerce (AIC) (工商行政管理局) at all levels.[648] Criminal cases from 1998[649] to the end of 2010 amounted to an estimated 513.[650] In regard to civil cases, it is estimated that 6,547 cases were filed by first instance courts at all levels between 1995 and 2005.[651] Starting from 2006, civil trade secrets cases were included in the unfair competition category. As this category did not fluctuate much between 2006 and 2010,[652] the trade secrets cases are assumed to not having substantially fluctuated either. As such, the average number (of the years 1995-2005) of 595 cases is adopted for the years 2006-2010, adding another 2,975 cases to the calculation. In total, trade secrets cases in China according to what can be known from official figures amounted to 10,784 until the end of 2010.

Although the number of trade secret cases has increased to the highest level in history,[653] it is still not significant compared to total intellectual property cases, with 42,931 civil cases having been received by Chinese courts in 2010 alone.[654] Foreign trade secret cases seem to account only for a very small proportion as estimated on the basis of exemplary cases: only six of a total of 74 typical

646 Following the enactment of the Law against Unfair Competition (LUC) on Dec 1, 1993.

647 Since most of the empirical data have been collected in 2010, this year is used as reference year in this study.

648 *Yearbook of Industry and Commerce Administration of China 1996-2011* (工商行政管理年鉴) (Editorial Office 'Yearbook of Industry and Commerce Administration of China' (1996-2011)). (Only the figure for the year 2007 was drawn from the *China Intellectual Property Yearbook 2008* (SIPO 2008).)

649 Following the enactment of the Criminal Law on March 14, 1997.

650 SIPO 2000-2011. Since there were no data available for the years 2005 and 2006, 53 cases are being estimated for each year, presenting the average of the preceding year (52) and the following year (54).

651 Ou Xiuping 2006: 4, Bai J. Benjamin and Da Guoping 2011: 355, Liu Rong 2008.

652 SIPO 2007-2011.

653 Shan Hailing 2008: xvi.

654 SIPO 2011: 698. See also the typical cases of SIPO where only around five out of 200-300 cases per year concern trade secrets.

trade secret cases involve foreign business.[655] This mirrors the situation of intellectual property cases in general where less than 5% of the total cases involve foreign enterprises.[656]

Yet infringements on an enterprise's trade secrets are likely to occur much more often than those numbers might suggest, as obstacles to enforcement are likely to discourage enterprises from filing a complaint. In addition to enforcement problems of intellectual property in general, trade secrets are particularly challenging in China due to a high burden of proof on the part of the trade secrets holder.[657] Furthermore, there is a lack of incentives to enforce trade secrets, for any compensation to be obtained from court is still relatively low in China.[658] Being in such a disadvantaged position, trade secret holders might be reluctant to opt for legal or administrative remedies.

Nevertheless, trade secrets are a significant issue of conflict in China as can be seen from the substantial commercial value of the secrets in the cases available. In most of the typical cases annually published in the *China Intellectual Property Yearbook* from 2000 to 2011 the trade secret's value is located in the range between 100,000 and 4 million RMB. Similarly, other typical cases involving traditional types of intellectual property are also often in this range.[659] In typical cases annually published since 1992 by the Supreme People's Court, economic losses caused by trade secrets range from 80,000 up to more than 8 million RMB, with an average loss of nearly 1.6 million RMB.[660] Taking into account that according to Criminal Law a "significant loss" is assumed starting at 500,000 RMB (penalized with up to three years imprisonment), and "particular serious consequences" of trade secret misappropriation are assumed when a

655 38 typical cases of CIAJ and 36 typical cases of SIPO are concerned with trade secrets.

656 In 2010, for instance, foreign-related cases accounted for 3.19% of all civil cases (SIPO 2011: 699).

657 Not only is it to prove that the information of the infringer is substantially identical with the trade secret and that it falls into the scope of trade secrets, further it is to submit evidence that trade secrets had been obtained by unfair means or by violating an agreement or demand for keeping it secret (LUC (Art. 10 (1)), SPC Interpretation (Art. 14). This proves difficult as only documentary evidence is usually given weight and not witness or expert statements and as evidence is often in possession of the infringer. An effective mechanism to obtain this evidence is not provided (EU-China IPR2 2011: 7-8). As such, proving trade secrets infringement in China is generally more difficult than in Europe (EU-China IPR2 2011). The high burden of proof has also been recognized as an enforcement problem by Chinese scholars (Zang Yunxiao 2010: 51).

658 Müller and Sprick 2011: 157-158.

659 SIPO 2000-2011.

660 Figures are based on all 21 trade secret cases of the *Selected Cases of the People's Court 1996-2011* (CIAJ 1996-2011) in which the economic loss was indicated.

loss of 2.5 million RMB occurs (penalized with three to seven years of imprisonment),[661] trade secrets are of significant value in China.

In an exemplary case, Jinan Lights Equipment Factory Ltd. (济南灯具厂有限公司) sued three of its former employees in 2008 for infringing on its customer list. The employees had joined another enterprise and had redirected the customers of Jinan Lights Equipment, whose turnover shrank to less than 10% of that of the preceding year with a total economic loss of about 2,030,000 RMB.[662] In a similar case with the German enterprise Rosenberger in 2006 – which is considered being a typical German enterprise investing in China –[663] former employees set up a new enterprise and redirected customers by using information Rosenberger deemed its trade secrets, such as product specifications, quantity, and sales prices for specific customers. For Rosenberger the loss incurred was about 3.17 million RMB.[664] For Chinese and foreign enterprises alike, typical cases could involve information on customers worth more than the average value of trade secrets.

The most extreme case in China to date resulted in losses of 700 billion RMB in total.[665] Here, a foreign enterprise – the British-Australian mining group Rio Tinto, which is among the global leaders in the production of iron ore and other commodities – was the infringer. Chinese employees of its Shanghai office had bribed Chinese large (majority) state-owned steel enterprises in order to receive information on Chinese steel industries' iron ore bid prices and steel enterprises' output production plans among others.[666] Knowing in advance the highest price which would be accepted, Rio Tinto had been able to negotiate high purchasing prices for iron ore. Although this is an extreme case, involving a whole industry in China and having economic consequences at a global level, it shows the enormous value trade secrets can possess.

The Rio Tinto case also shows that trade secrets cases do not only touch upon an economic dimension on the level of enterprises. From a Chinese perspec-

661 Criminal Law (Art. 219), Interpretation of the Supreme People's Court and the Supreme People's Procuratorate on Some Matters about the Specific Application of Law in Handling Criminal Cases of Intellectual Property Rights Infringements (最高人民法院、最高人民检察院关于办理侵犯知识产权刑事案件具体应用法律若干问题的解释) as of Nov 2, 2004 (Art. 7) (*Renminwang* 2004). Müller and Sprick 2011: 148-150.

662 CIAJ 2009: 428-435 (No. 4, Case No. 49).

663 The German enterprise "Rosenberger Hochfrequenztechnik GmbH & Co. KG" (http://www.rosenberger.de/de/company/headquarters/) is considered typical, as it is a traditional medium-sized family enterprise founded in 1958 in southern Germany, manufacturing relatively technology-intensive products in China in a WFOE since 1997 ("Rosenberger Asia Pacific Electronic Co., Ltd." (http://www.rosenbergerap.com/page.asp?p=30)).

664 Dong Ying 2007, Beijing Higher People's Court 2007.

665 Xiao Yunduan 2010: 150, Hein 2009.

666 He Junjian 2011: 262, Hein 2009, Barboza 2010.

tive, as the steel sector is a strategic one, the case is a matter of national interest. When being arrested, the respective Rio Tinto employees had indeed been charged with *state secrets* theft until the charge was reduced to trade secrets theft.[667] Still, Chinese scholars and the populace would favor a categorization as state secrets as the information in question is property of the state rather than property of an enterprise.[668] With increasing competition during the reform era, foreign economic espionage has augmented with the Rio Tinto case only regarded as the tip of the iceberg.[669] In this context, Chinese scholars worry about turnover of Chinese employees to foreign enterprises resulting in leakage of Chinese core technology.[670] Conflicts surrounding trade secrets thus potentially touch upon a national dimension.

Further issues of conflict are visible from determining which kind of knowledge actually constitutes a trade secret. The LUC refers to technical and management information which can bring about economic benefits to the holder, is of practical utility, is unknown to the public, and for which secrecy measures have been adopted.[671] In the years following the law's promulgation, these vague indicators needed to be specified. The SAIC regulations contain proposals which kind of information can potentially be subsumed under the law: Technical information includes but is not limited to designs, procedures, formulas of products, manufacturing techniques, and manufacturing methods; management information comprises among others management knacks, customer lists, information regarding suppliers of goods, production and sales tactics, as well as the bottom price of a bid and contents of a bid documents.[672] This specification shows how broad the spectrum of information potentially being recognized as a trade secret is. The fact that this is an open enumeration further shows the difficulties of determining the scope of trade secrets.

This nominal classification only provides a point of reference. For more specifically drawing the legal boundary between knowledge an enterprise can claim as its trade secret and knowledge supposed to be in the public realm, the four statutory elements are supposed to be decisive.[673] Among them, the *econom-*

667 Chen Longxin 2009: 40, Zhang Jiaqing 2011: 138, Barboza 2010.
668 Zhang Jiaqing 2011: 137, Zhu Miaochun and Wang Xiaobing 2009: 15, He Junjian 2011: 262.
669 Chen Longxin 2009: 44.
670 Xiao Yunduan 2010: 150, see Yang Ping 2009: 143.
671 LUC (Art. 10). Criminal law defines trade secrets in the same manner (Criminal Law (Art. 219)). Both technical and management information are also included in the German Act Against Unfair Competition/Gesetz gegen den unlauteren Wettbewerb (Art. 17): Betriebs- und Geschäftsgeheimnisse.
672 SAIC Regulations (Art. 2 (5)).
673 LUC (Art. 10). In the following, the four elements will be elaborated on with the typical cases of CIAJ & SIPO if not otherwise specified.

ic benefit (经济利益) the information should bring to the holder is hardly an issue in legal practice.[674] The actual benefit in monetary terms is not of interest,[675] only the rather subjective – and potential –[676] commercial value (商业价值) is taken into account.[677] The competitive edge required[678] can – in the case of customer lists – easily be achieved by showing that customers have actively been cultivated by the holder.[679] This quick recognition of economic benefit is in accordance with the TRIPS Agreement[680], which reflects a minimum standard agreed upon by the WTO member countries, and follows the trend of broadening the scope of trade secrets protection by many countries in recent years.[681] This shows that the upcoming knowledge era in China in line with other knowledge economies requires a multitude of different kinds of information to be unconditionally recognized as economically valuable.

The element of *practicality* (实用性) is not an issue of conflict either. On a theoretical level, Chinese scholars and judges propose that information deemed eligible as trade secret has to be specific, definite, objectively useful, and can be put into practice. By contrast, simple ideas, general principles, or abstract concepts, and even customer lists are ideally to be excluded.[682] In judicial and administrative practice, however, the element of practicality to date is not an issue.[683] Practicality is mostly considered in unison with the element of economic

674 See typical cases of CIAJ & SIPO.

675 Ascertaining the actual amount of the commercial value becomes only decisive for calculating compensation. Then an objective standard is deemed necessary, which is a controversial issue. Points of reference could be the costs of development, the income from implementing the trade secret, as well as the holders' loss (SPC Interpretation (Art. 17), CIAJ 2010: 30-34 (No. 4, Case No. 8)). The latter could include loss of profits resulting from loss of reputation (CIAJ 1995: 127-134 (No. 2, Case No. 34)). Yet loss of profits is difficult to objectively determine, especially if financial documents contain flaws (CIAJ 2005: 344-358 (No. 2, Case No. 50)).

676 SPC Interpretation (Art. 10 and 17), see SAIC Regulations (Art. 2 (3)).

677 SPC Interpretation (Art. 10), Müller and Sprick 2011: 153. Commercial value could refer, for instance, to information on the basis of which new products or technology could be developed (Liu Xiaohai 2011: 129, see e.g. CIAJ 1999 (No. 4, Case No. 44)), or to customer lists, if during the preceding years a certain amount of profit has continuously been realized with a certain customer (CIAJ 1998: 213-222 (No. 2, Case No. 42), CIAJ 2009: 428-435 (No. 4, Case No. 49), Liang Zhao 2012).

678 SPC Interpretation (Art. 10).

679 SIPO 2010: 912-913 (SAIC Case No. 7), SIPO 2006: 462-467, SIPO 2011: 969 (SAIC Case No. 9).

680 TRIPS (Art. 39 (2)) (WTO 2013).

681 Shan Hailing 2008: 67. In Germany, this is not an issue either, as only the significance of the information for the enterprise's competitiveness suffices to assume that the holder has an interest in keeping it secret (Liu Xiaohai 1999: 30-32 and 218).

682 Shan Hailing 2008: 55-56 and 69, Liu Yingqun 2008: 43, Yu Liping and Yin Xianying 2007: 15, Liu Xiaohai 1999: 56, Han Dekuan 2012: 32, Wu Ming 2008: 90.

683 See typical cases of CIAJ & SIPO, Liu Xiaohai 1999: 57.

benefit,[684] and even in case of the contested customer list, letters of intent or contracts with customers are in practice already deemed suitable for proving practicality.[685] This legal practice is in line with TRIPS and many other countries, such as Germany and the United States, where practicality not even appears in the respective laws and regulations.[686] This reveals that the concern for limiting negative effects for society resulting from too strong a protection of knowledge for individual purposes is present in China. The Chinese business reality concerning the range of information which can practically be of value, however, already resembles that of Western countries.

What is more often an issue of conflict is the statutory element of *unknown to the public* (不为公众所知悉).[687] Whether information is unknown to the public is not always immediately obvious. For more clearly determining what is considered to be known by the general public, the SAIC Regulation and the SPC Interpretation more clearly exclude information which can be directly known via public channels, such as the media or exhibitions.[688]

The typical cases indicate that the question whether or not customer lists are to be considered public is most controversial. The secret nature of customer lists is least pronounced since name, address, and contact details as well as usual needs of the customer are often publicly known.[689] In the Rosenberger case, of all the information in dispute only the price was deemed a trade secret. The remaining customer information was considered market information, as the information of an existing business relationship between Rosenberger and the respective customer can be obtained from Rosenberger's website.[690]

Only in combination with special customer information, the customer list as a whole can be considered as unknown to the public. What is recognized as special customer information are model numbers, quantity, quality standards, terms and conditions of delivery and payment, prices of transactions and so forth. Additionally, the financial situation, purchasing intentions, and even personals de-

684 SPC Interpretation (Art. 10). See e.g. CIAJ 1998: 213-222 (No. 2, Case No. 42), SIPO 2011: 969 (SAIC Case No. 9).

685 CIAJ 2009: 428-435 (No. 4, Case No. 49), CIAJ 2001: 261-269 (No. 1, Case No. 45), CIAJ 2007: 8-20 (No. 4, Case No. 2), CIAJ 1998: 213-222 (No. 2, Case No. 42).

686 TRIPS (Art. 39 (2)) (WTO 2013), Han Dekuan 2012: 32, Shan Hailing 2008: 55.

687 Wu Ming 2008: 91.

688 SPC Interpretation (Art. 9), SAIC Regulations (Art. 2 (2)).

689 Liang Zhao 2012, CIAJ 2009: 428-435 (No. 4, Case No. 49), CIAJ 1995: 138-141 (No. 2, Case No. 36), CIAJ 2005: 344-358 (No. 2, Case No. 50), CIAJ 2009: 2-11 (No. 1, Case No. 1).

690 Dong Ying 2007, Beijing Higher People's Court 2007. The Rosenberger case is also a typical one regarding that the elements "unknown to the public" and "secrecy measures" (see below) usually are the contested issues for customer lists (see e.g. CIAJ 2005: 344-358 (No. 2, Case No. 50).

tails on the contact person, such as character traits and hobbies, are recognized as secret information since these relate to distinct business habits.[691]

A typical case involving a Chinese enterprise where precisely this boundary was in dispute occured when Jinan Lights Equipment sued its three former employees Zhang, Li, and Feng for infringing its trade secrets. Jinan Light Equipment had many stable relationships with foreign customers and regarded its customer list as important management information. Zhang and Li had been in contact with customers personally, and Feng had access to customer contracts in the enterprises' database. All three employees left Jinan Lights Equipment at the same time and joined the enterprise Jinan Zhifu Trade and Commerce Ltd. (济南智富商贸有限公), which had been founded by relatives of Zhang a year before. Customers of this enterprise coincided with those of Jinan Lights Equipment. When Jinan Lights Equipment sued its former employees for trade secret infringement, the first instance court concluded that the customer information met all trade secrets requirements. However, Zhang filed an objection arguing the information was publicly known since he had obtained it himself at a trade fair where it had been publicly available.[692] Zhang actually only referred to parts of the whole package of information which separately considered would indeed constitute market information.

For better identifying which information is considered unknown to the public, the SPC Interpretation further determined other criteria, for instance, stating that the information should not be easily obtained.[693] Regarding customer lists, the SPC Interpretation determined that the relationship with the customer should be considered, meaning that a long-term and stable relationship must have been developed and maintained.[694] This should be judged by the *efforts* which have been put forth. These efforts mainly constitute investment in human and financial resources, such as creativity, time, and energy for the search and cultivation of customers, as well as recommendations, contacts, feedback, communication, advertisement, visited exhibitions, organized annual customer meetings, networking activities, and presents for customers.[695] Also, the existence of mutual trust within business relationships could be taken into account, as trust building cannot be accomplished within just one day[696] and is needed to eventually form-

691 CIAJ 1995: 138-141 (No. 2, Case No. 36CIAJ 2005: 344-358 (No. 2, Case No. 50), CIAJ 2009: 428-435 (No. 4, Case No. 49), SIPO 2006: 462-467, SPC Interpretation (Art. 13), Liang Zhao 2012.

692 CIAJ 2009: 428-435 (No. 4, Case No. 49).

693 SPC Interpretation (Art. 9).

694 CIAJ 2009: 428-435 (No. 4, Case No. 49), CIAJ 2005: 344-358 (No. 2, Case No. 50), SIPO 2010: 912-913 (SAIC Case No. 7), SIPO 2006: 462-467, Liang Zhao 2012.

695 CIAJ 2009: 428-435 (No. 4, Case No. 49), Liang Zhao 2012.

696 CIAJ 2009: 428-435 (No. 4, Case No. 49).

ing a stable business relationship.[697] At least, the development of the customer must have already entered a critical phase. This means that negotiations with the customer have been conducted several times, a prototype has been built with which customers have expressed satisfaction, customers of a certain location have exclusively referred to the advertising material of this particular enterprise, and there has been an intent to cooperate with the phase of signing the documents approaching.[698]

Precisely due to the stronger consideration of the efforts, the second instance court in the Jinan Lights Equipment case reduced the compensation for Jinan Lights Equipment. Despite following the first instance court in considering the customer information a trade secret being not publicly known, the second instance court still reduced the compensation by half. Although Zhang and the other employees infringed on the trade secrets, they had put forth effort in building and maintaining the relationship, too, which resulted in the high turnover they received. The turnover of Jinan Lights Equipment would probably not have been as high as theirs, and their profit is no adequate measure of the loss Jinan Lights Equipment incurred.

In terms of the efforts put into obtaining information, the Chinese legal practitioners follow the general practice of many other countries, including Germany, of recognizing information as the property of the party who invests most time and costs into it.[699] Yet it is striking – at least when compared to typical cases in Germany –[700] that special information on a customer also includes the contact persons themselves. It is also noticeable that the quality of relationships behind customer details is deemed an important indicator for the efforts having been invested. Relationships to contact persons of customers thus determine whether or not a customer list can be considered as unknown to the public and thus can be recognized as trade secret or not. Even though customer lists, being the most easily obtained trade secrets, are also sometimes under dispute in other jurisdictions, the rather subjective indicators of relationship quality and distinct knowledge about the contact person seem to be less recognized elsewhere.

Another controversial statutory element is the *adoption of secrecy-keeping measures* (采取保密措施) by the trade secret's holder. Trade secrets are essentially characterized by their *secrecy*.[701] Their secret nature makes them unique in that they are only valuable as long as they have not been disclosed to the public.

697 CIAJ 2001: 289-300 (No. 3, Case No. 44).
698 CIAJ 2009: 2-11 (No. 1, Case No. 1).
699 Liu Xiaohai 1999: 217.
700 Liu Xiaohai 1999: 24-25.
701 Liu Yingqun 2008: 43, Wu Ming 2008: 91, Lemley 2008: 342-344, Yang Ping 2009: 144.

A broad range of secrecy measures is considered reasonable (合理)[702] for Chinese business practice including but not limited to secrecy systems, such as locking information carriers, adopting passwords or codes, and limiting access of visitors and employees who do not need to know the information.[703]

Yet this is only a relative secrecy as some employees or business partners have to be informed about the secrets or work with them. For those employees and business partners who have to know the information, awareness of secrecy is seen as resonably raised by tagging a secrecy sign on the relevant documents or signing secrecy agreements.[704] Signing a secrecy agreement is the means which is seen as most decisive and has frequently been deemed a sufficient measure in legal practice.[705] In a typical case, the valuable information in dispute was openly lying on a table and hence was accessible for any employee at the enterprise. Regardless of other protections measures in place, the judges still viewed the concluded secrecy agreement alone as sufficient for meeting the statutory requirement of keeping the secrecy.[706]

The content of secrecy agreements, however, is also a matter of dispute. Secrecy agreements or systems are often rather superficial and do not refer to the concrete content and scope of the trade secret in question.[707] Some argue that if secrecy agreements or systems exist, it can be assumed that an employee understands them, and consequently, these measures should be deemed reasonable. Others argue that these measures are not sufficient to assume that employees have been clear about the trade secret's scope.[708] Rather, it should explicitly be stated that, for instance, "customer information" are part of the secret information,[709] and that these are to be kept secret.[710]

The Rosenberger case also shows that the issue in dispute is the awareness of the employees rather than the measures taken. The evidence of employment contracts containing a secrecy clause, a staff manual, evidence of a secrecy system, and job descriptions for each employee was deemed sufficient for meeting

702 Shan Hailing 2008: 62-66, Cui Xuesong 2008: 61.

703 SAIC Regulations (Art. 2 (4)), SPC Interpretation (Art. 11).

704 SAIC Regulations (Art. 2 (4)), SPC Interpretation (Art. 11).

705 Yu Liping and Yin Xianying 2007: 14, Liu Xiaohai 1999: 53, Kisgen 2005: 110, Cui Xuesong 2008: 61. See e.g. CIAJ 2001: 289-300 (No. 3, Case No. 44) where the secrecy agreement is deemed sufficient as well as CIAJ 2001: 261-269 (no. 1, case no. 45) where a general clause for all the employer's trade secrets ('必须严守某公司的业务秘密') in the working contract was deemed sufficient as security measure and similarly with SIPO 2007: 713 (SAIC Case No. 5) and SIPO 2010: 912-913 (SAIC Case No. 7).

706 CIAJ 2001: 289-300 (No. 3, Case No. 44).

707 CIAJ 2009: 428-435 (No. 4, Case No. 49).

708 CIAJ 2009: 428-435 (No. 4, Case No. 49), CIAJ 2005: 344-358 (No. 2, Case No. 50).

709 SIPO 2009: 893, CIAJ 2001: 289-300 (No. 3, Case No. 44).

710 CIAJ 2005: 344-358 (No. 2, Case No. 50).

the statutory requirement by the first instance court. The second instance court, however, dismissed the case on the grounds that Rosenberger failed to submit evidence that the former employees were informed of those. The clause in the employment contract regulating that the staff must abide by the enterprise's secrecy stipulations was considered being too general. Also, the staff manual only contained general principles instead of concrete secrecy requirements, and no additional secrecy agreement was signed. Furthermore, no evidence could be submitted that the secrecy system was *de facto* implemented.[711] The *active* adoption of secrecy measures at an objective level together with the strong will at a subjective level are both considered essential for information being ascribed to a particular enterprise.[712]

The focus on raising awareness is also shown by tolerating secrecy requests orally agreed upon. Judicial and administrative practice takes into account that Chinese enterprises are used to conclude agreements orally.[713] In the Jinan Lights Equipment case, the enterprise secured its digital customer list by password, locked hardcopies in a safe, and established a secrecy system where only specifically appointed persons were in charge of the specific information. Although the secrecy measures were first deemed too broad in terms of content and scope, Jinan Lights Equipment was still able to provide evidence that the employees had been *informed* about the secrecy requirements, and hence, the security measures were deemed reasonable.[714] In another typical case, the employer orally pointed out to his employee several times that drawings must be kept secret, which the judges also deemed a reasonable secrecy agreement.[715] Judges also often accepted that no secrecy agreement has been signed among relatives jointly involved in the same business. Since in traditional Chinese culture, relationships between relatives are assumed to involve a high degree of trust, the disclosure of a trade secret to a family member without concluding a secrecy agreement is considered safe.[716]

711 Dong Ying 2007, Beijing Higher People's Court 2007.

712 See e.g. Ren Jingrong 2005: 45, Dou Xingya 2007: 66, Cui Xuesong 2008: 61, CIAJ 1995: 127-134 (No. 2, Case No. 34).

713 Xing Lujia and Hong Min 2010: 108, CIAJ 2009: 428-435 (No. 4, Case No. 49), Dou Xingya 2007: 66, see Cui Xuesong 2008: 61. Note that the SPC Interpretation (Art. 11) of 2007 already concretely refers to "sign" (签订) in lieu of the rather vague "conclude" (订立) as it is stated in the SAIC Regulations (Art. 2 (3)) of 1998.

714 CIAJ 2009: 428-435 (No. 4, Case No. 49).

715 CIAJ 2001: 269-275 (No. 1, Case No. 46).

716 At least, from this behavior it cannot be concluded that the holder was (subjectively) not eager to protect his trade secrets, especially when he had limited the scope of people only to relatives (Dou Xingya 2007: 66).

competition clause or agreement obviously to be in writing in Germany.[717] In German legal practice, mainly the subjective will of the holder is decisive. It is taken for granted in favor of the holder, which renders the objective proof of secrecy measures virtually obsolete (as long as no counter evidence is submitted by the infringer).[718] Hence, in Chinese business practice increased efforts are required to make the employees aware of the enterprise's trade secrets.

After certain information has been recognized as falling into the scope of trade secrets, one more condition has to be met to successfully claim trade secrets protection: the information must have been made use of in an infringing way. According to LUC, an infringement has occurred if the trade secret is obtained by *unfair means* (不正当手段), such as stealing, luring, or by resorting to coercion among others, or by disclosing, using or allowing another person to use the trade secrets obtained by unfair means.[719] In the Rio Tinto case, for instance, valuable information about price negotiations was obtained by the unfair means of bribing the executives of Chinese steel enterprises.

To confine an infringement of trade secrets to "unfair means" is significant since trade secrets are no absolute secrets but can also be obtained in a "fair" manner by a certain part of employees or business partners. These "fairly" obtained trade secrets are most controversial in China. Trade secret leakage via former employees is considered a "common phenomenon"[720]. Disloyal employees[721] are the source of most trade secret infringements in China.[722] Accelerated by Chinese employee's frequent switching of employers and enterprises facing high employee turnover rates, trade secrets infringement most often happens after employees have left the enterprise.[723]

A common incident is the use of customer information after having resigned. In an exemplary case, an employee set up his own enterprise and used confidential customer information which he had obtained within his former employment period. Although the information had been obtained in a "fair" manner during the employee's previous employment, the local AIC determined this behavior as infringement on the trade secrets of the former enterprise due to the

717 HGB §74 (1).
718 Liu Xiaohai 1999: 22 and 217-218.
719 LUC (Art. 10), Criminal Law (Art. 219).
720 Chen Yu 2010: 99.
721 Although the LUC (Art. 10) only refers to businesspeople (经营者), the administrative rules explicitly include the infringement on trade secrets by employees (SAIC Regulations (Art. 3 (4)).
722 Zang Yunxiao 2010: 48, Shan Hailing 2008: 215-217. See also typical cases of CIAJ & SIPO.
723 Zhu Miaochun and Wang Xiaobing 2009: 15, Wang Xi 2012: 93, Shan Hailing 2008: 223, Müller and Sprick 2011: 160. See also typical cases of CIAJ & SIPO.

fact that non-competition had been contractually agreed upon by the employee and his enterprise.[724]

To protect trade secrets from being disclosed or used by persons having them "fairly" obtained during work or business processes, the LUC considers these seemingly "fair" acts as infringement if they violate an agreement or demand for keeping it secret.[725] Possible agreements include secrecy agreements with business partners and employees as well as non-competition agreements with employees. Employers in China regularly include non-compete clauses or agreements as standard provisions in employment contracts or human resource policies.[726]

This contractual protection – with applicable Chinese statutes ranging from labor law and contract law to labor contract law – complements the statutory protection. Whereas statutory trade secrets protection leans toward the interest of the employer or trade secrets holder (and balancing it with public interest), labor legislation leans toward the interests of the employee.[727] Achieving the balance between employers' and employees' interests is critical. The Labor Law of 1995 only vaguely included but not further specified limitations of the rights of an employer to include contractual clauses on matters concerning the keeping of his trade secrets.[728] Only the Labor Contract Law[729], being effective since 2008, was an important step in regulating the balance at all by inserting limits to what had already become usual practice.[730] Its drafting process – which saw unprecedented deliberations over 18 months on four different drafts with various Chinese and international actors, including the general public, as well as workers and entrepreneurs –[731] particularly shows how contested this balance in China is.

---

724 SIPO 2007: 713 (SAIC Case No. 5).

725 LUC (Art. 10), Criminal Law (Art. 219). Disclosure both by intention *and* negligence is considered a violation (Kisgen 2005: 112).

726 Hewitt Associates 2007: 4, Li Shoushuang 2007, Müller and Sprick 2011: 160.

727 Note that labor legislation also imposes a duty of confidentiality and non-competition (as accessory duties, such as in Germany) on the employee which could be referred to in case there is only a contract but no explicit clause or agreement. Still, this duty is ambiguous in China, which is also a reason why many employers have tried to protect their trade secrets by signing secrecy agreements (Shan Hailing 2008: 212-220).

728 Labor Law of the PRC (中华人民共和国劳动法) as of Jan 1, 1995 (Art. 22) (Gov.cn 2005), Cooney et al. 2007: 799, Kisgen 2005: 124.

729 The Law of the PRC on Employment Contracts (中华人民共和国劳动合同法) (Gov.cn 2007).

730 That this had been usual practice before can be observed within the typical cases of CIAJ & SIPO.

731 Cooney et al. 2007: 789-790, Wang Haiyan et al. 2009: 487-488. The first draft alone received an estimated 191,000 comments (Hewitt Associates 2007: 1, Schucher 2006: 48) with many of them having indeed been considered by the legislators (GIC German Industry & Commerce 2007: 1).

Western businesses exercised a pivotal role in the controversy on non-compete agreements in China. With the reasoning of requiring better protection of their trade secrets and other intellectual property, European and American business groups lobbied for the strongest restriction possible. It was argued that in order to import new technologies and to encourage innovation as well as research and development in China, the rights of the creators of intellectual property should be strengthened.[732]

Demands by Western enterprises have partly been considered in the drafting process. While the first draft had imposed geographical restrictions on the territory in which there would be an actual competitive relationship, the enacted law has reacted to Western criticisms[733] by only stipulating that geographical restrictions are to be determined by the parties.[734] This does not only cater to the demands of Western employers but also to those of Chinese employers as many Chinese enterprises conduct business in all of China. Anyway, the application of too broad geographical restrictions seldom was an issue in judicial practice prior to the enactment of the law.[735]

In favor of employees, the Labor Contract Law limits the kinds of employees that can legally be constrained in their post-employment options. This follows former proposals of Chinese judges. Accordingly, employees without special knowledge or in relatively low positions having no access to trade secrets should not have their employment options constrained, simply because they are not able to disclose trade secrets they are not informed of.[736] This rationale was adopted by the first draft of the Labor Contract Law, which limits the employer's right to restriction of post-employment options to employees having knowledge of the employer's trade secrets.[737] With the second draft of the law non-compete

732 The comments on the first draft of the Labor Contract Law by the US-China Business Council (2006: 1) in regard to non-compete agreements explicitly propose to "strengthen the rights of those who create intellectual property". The European Union Chamber of Commerce in China (2006: 6) similarly underscores that "adequate protection of trade secrets and other intellectual property rights is crucial [...] for import of advanced technology [...] in order to encourage research and development of new technologies". The American Chamber of Commerce in the People's Republic of China (2006: 18) warns that an "unreasonably high compensation" for non-competition would result in employers "giving up efforts to protect their trade secrets" leading to "discouragement of innovation". Following the release of the second draft, the American Chamber (2007: 12) warns again that "the limitation of non-competition agreements [...] may reduce employers' confidence in non-competition agreements as a means of protecting trade secrets".

733 European Union Chamber of Commerce in China 2006: 6, US-China Business Council 2006: 2.

734 Cooney et al. 2007: 799-800, Hewitt Associates 2007: 4.

735 Shan Hailing 2008: 250-251.

736 CIAJ 2004: 641-650 (No. 3, Case No. 85).

737 Labor Contract Law, first draft (Art. 16) (Jincao.com 2013).

agreements have even further been limited to specific categories of employees,[738] such as senior managers and senior technicians, as well as any other personnel having the obligation to keep the employer's secrets.[739]

In reaction to the second draft, Western businesses lobbied for a stronger restriction of employees' post-employment options. They expressed concerns that "distinguishing 'senior' managers and technicians and other employees with access to trade secrets may prove difficult in practice, particularly since an employee's access to trade secrets may not be foreseen when the employee is hired"[740]. This attempt shows that Western enterprises strive to extend non-compete agreements to as many employees as possible in their Chinese subsidiaries. Being clearly aware of the fact that a certain knowledge transfer always takes place when an employee leaves for an employer in the same sector, they hope for the non-compete agreement at least to defer knowledge leakage or to be compensated for what they consider an infringement on their trade secrets. Nevertheless, the law as enacted adheres to the content of the second draft which only allows for restriction of employees in particular positions.

Most significantly, while the duration of three years for non-compete agreements had become usual business practice in several localities,[741] the law has limited the duration to two years for employment in enterprises of the same product or business category.[742] Taking into account that, for instance, German law also only allows a period of two years,[743] Western businesses enjoyed a comparatively strong protection of their interests in China in the past. The vehement controversy when this was amended shows that Western businesses still see a strong need for non-compete agreements to be strengthened, facing strong knowledge leakage via employee turnover in their daily business practice.

On the other hand, the controversy points to an increasing awareness regarding personal knowledge among Chinese employees. In line with Chinese employees, Chinese legal scholars point to the strengthening of the employees' right to personal knowledge. For being able to exercising their right to work – as

738 Hewitt Associates 2007: 4.

739 Labor Contract Law (Art. 24) (Gov.cn 2007).

740 American Chamber of Commerce in the People's Republic of China 2007: 12.

741 Müller and Sprick 2011: 161, Liu Xiaohai 1999: 107. See e.g. three typical cases involving non-compete agreements in Jiangsu Province (CIAJ 2007: 290-297 (No. 1, Case No. 34), CIAJ 2004: 641-650 (No. 3, Case No. 85), SIPO 2007: 713 (SAIC Case No. 5)) where post-employment could be restricted up to three years. As other regulations proposed three years as well (Shan Hailing 2008: 248-249), this period can be regarded as usual prior to the enactment of the Labor Contract Law.

742 Labor Contract Law (Art. 24) (Gov.cn 2007), Cooney et al. 2007: 799, Hewitt Associates 2007: 4.

743 HGB §74a.

granted by the Chinese Constitution –[744] Chinese employees inevitably need some information from their employer. A right to information (知情权) for employees is discussed by Chinese legal scholars, albeit only rudimentary appearing in legislation to date.[745] At least implicitly, a right to information is granted by the Labor Contract Law according to which the employer should notify about job contents and other basic clauses of the work contract, as well as of the economic situation of the enterprise.[746]

Yet the employer might well be reluctant to disclose details on this economic situation to his employees. As important management information, these might fall into the scope of his trade secrets. Chinese scholars emphasize that the information disclosed should at least include all information relevant for the employee's livelihood and development.[747] However, just this basic information could easily overlap with the employer's trade secrets. But even here scholars point to the right to personal knowledge. This indicates the difficulties of differentiating trade secrets from personal knowledge in Chinese business practice.

The right to personal knowledge also extends to receiving training in professional skills from the employer as is granted by the Labor Law.[748] This right implies that an enterprise's knowledge to a certain extent has to be transferred to the employee in order to train him for exercising his job. Additionally, apart from merely fulfilling their tasks, employees shall according to the Labor Law also "improve their professional skills"[749]. Moreover, the State Commission of Science and Technology[750] as early as 1988 was concerned about the spare time employment of scientific and technical personal.[751] It was stipulated that at other (spare time) workplaces no technical results are allowed to be used, but that knowledge, techniques, experiences, and information mastered and accumulated during the general employment could well be used at other workplaces.[752] Consequently, all knowledge acquired during employment through exercising one's job, via training and via improving one's skills cannot constitute property of the employer alone but ideally passes into the employee's personal knowledge stock.

744 Chinese Constitution of 1982 (Art. 42) (Gov.cn 2012).
745 See Du Ningning 2012.
746 Labor Contract Law (Art. 8 and 41) (Gov.cn 2007).
747 Du Ningning 2012.
748 Labor Law (Art. 3) (Gov.cn 2005).
749 Labor Law (Art. 3 (2)) (Gov.cn 2005).
750 The predecessor of the Ministry of Science and Technology of the PRC (until 1989).
751 Note that spare time jobs of scientific and technical personnel have been encouraged by the Chinese government, which has made a distinction between personal knowledge and trade secrets significant (Liu Xiaohai 1999: 98).
752 Guowuyuan 1988.

The right to personal knowledge also comprises the legitimate use of knowledge acquired during previous employment for the subsequent career. This can be derived from the employee's right of choosing occupation granted by the Labor Law.[753] Only if the use of one's own knowledge during post-employment is ensured, employees may pursue a career that they enjoy or that they are expert at. Otherwise, employees will consequently gradually lose their previous knowledge and skills as they are not able to use them regularly.[754]

The right to use knowledge of a previous employment is further implied in the articles concerning non-compete agreements in the Labor Contract Law.[755] This law regards – in line with some other countries including Germany – compensation as essential for the validity of non-compete agreements.[756] The fact that compensation must be awarded to former employees for not being able to exercise a job according to their qualification shows that legislators implicitly acknowledge the legitimate use of knowledge accumulated before.

In an exemplary case, a former vice director of a medicine factory later worked for a competitor even though a non-compete agreement had been concluded. As he could not find a suitable employment except with the competitor, and the compensation granted was too low for his livelihood, the non-compete agreement could not be enforced by his former employer.[757] Chinese legal practice thus confirms in favor of the employee that the use of previously acquired knowledge is the employee's right which can only be constrained if adequately compensated.

The right to use knowledge acquired during previous employment can extend to information critical to the former employer. A recurrent point of contention is the redirection of customers to a subsequent enterprise by unfair means.[758] The SPC Interpretation even devoted an article to that problem. Accordingly, evidence is to be submitted that the customer had "voluntarily" chosen to perform market transactions with the respective employee or the new enterprise he works for.[759] The customer should not have been lured away, but should have actively contacted the former employee on the grounds of being satisfied with the service quality, acknowledging the service standard, or trusting his personal reputation.[760] Hence, in Chinese business practice, using customer information

753 Labor Law (Art. 3) (Gov.cn 2005).
754 Shan Hailing 2008: 234-238.
755 Labor Contract Law (Art. 23) (Gov.cn 2007).
756 Shan Hailing 2008: 255.
757 CIAJ 2004: 641-650 (No. 3, Case No. 85).
758 SIPO 2010: 912-913 (SAIC Case No. 7).
759 SPC Interpretation (Art. 13).
760 Liang Zhao 2012.

within a subsequent employment is rather common and does not necessarily constitute an infringement on the former employer's trade secrets.

The controversial "seaweed quota case"[761] also shows that the judicial practice acts in favor of the employee and the use of what is regarded his personal knowledge in the form of customer information gathered during his previous employment. The case, which was even reviewed by the Supreme People's Court, surrounds the export of seaweed to Japan. Seaweed from China for export to Japan is limited to certain quotas, and export can only be pursued via a designated Japanese trading company. The Shandong Food Company (山东食品公司) seized and made use of this business opportunity for nearly thirty years. The employee Ma worked for Shandong Food Company for twenty years being responsible for seaweed export most of the time. When Ma's contract expired he started to work with Shengkedacheng Company (圣克达诚公司), which his nephew and his spouse had founded shortly before. After the Japanese trading company examined the future trading plans of both companies it decided to shift the seaweed quota and the respective business to the company of Ma and his family. Whereas the first instance court condemned this behavior as "unfair means", the second instance court rejected this judgment, supported by the Supreme People's Court's review.

The latter judgment takes into account that seizing business opportunities *per se* – even by employees – contributes to fair competition. The employee benefitted from the personal trust he had built up over the years with the customer. Although this relationship building took place during the employment at Shandong Foods Company, planning and preparing a future career does not necessarily imply that unfair means have been adopted. An employee's behavior would be deemed unfair, if, at first, a statutory obligation or an agreement of non-competition had been violated.[762] In the seaweed quota case, however, no such agreement had been concluded with Ma. Also, as department manager,[763] he was not affected by statutory obligations arising from company law. Second, the way in which the future career had been planned and prepared shows that the principle of good faith in the LUC[764] had been respected. The principle is respected if what is commonly accepted as business ethics, such as reasonably anticipating and seizing a business opportunity, is observed. Ma acted in an ethical way since he clearly stated that he represented Shengkedachang Company

761 SIPO 2011: 850-864 (IP Judicial Cases No. 15). The case is among the fifty typical cases selected in 2010 (SIPO 2011: 787).

762 While the statutory obligation mainly arises from the Company Law (公司法) and concerns board members and senior managers, the obligation from a non-compete agreement signed with employees arises from the Company Law or the Labor Contract Law.

763 In contrast to board members or senior managers.

764 LUC (Art. 2).

and did not misleadingly let the Japanese trading company to believe that he still worked for Shandong Foods Company.

The seaweed quota case judgment further points out employees inevitably master and accumulate knowledge, experience, and skills in the work process related to their specific position. If knowledge could not be independently used within future employment, employees could not be encouraged to acquire new knowledge, accumulate new experiences, and increase their own professional skills. If the use of this knowledge makes the customer trust the employee and even provides him with a competitive advantage, this still can be seen as a fair use of knowledge. The judgment concludes that this knowledge, experiences, and skills form part of the employee's personality.

While Chinese trade secret legislation is in consistence with the TRIPS agreement and similar to the legislation of the international community,[765] the application of the legislation to the Chinese business environment shows areas of conflict. These conflicts mark discrepancies between the law as enacted and the business reality which has to be subsumed under the legal norms.

The vast majority of conflicts result from the fact that knowledge and personal relations are strongly intertwined in Chinese business practice. This is most obvious regarding the trade secret of the customer list, which is most often the issue of conflict.[766] The knowledge about a customer and the knowledge inscribed in the relationship to a customer are important issues in China, which is why they are even recognized by Chinese legal practice. Certain knowledge, like how the employee interacts with the customer, is important for enterprises, but at the same time is seen as forming part of the employee's personality. This knowledge is considered highly valuable by Chinese judicial and administrative practice and thus might play a strong role in the current Chinese business environment. This is a striking difference to German legal practice, where a person's hobbies or the quality of relationships are not necessarily indicators for the recognition of certain information as a trade secret.

Another obvious difference is the degree to which awareness for trade secrets is to be raised. The German legal practice of simply equating the conclusion of a secrecy agreement with a certain degree of awareness does not suit the Chinese business environment. In fact, in Chinese enterprises, misunderstandings commonly arise from either considering virtually all information of an enterprise

765 With the exception of the element of practicality, which, however, does not play a role in Chinese legal practice.

766 See typical cases of CIAJ & SIPO, of which see e.g. CIAJ 2009: 428-435 (No. 4, Case No. 49) and SIPO 2010: 912-913 (SAIC Case No. 7). Liang Zhao 2012, SIPO 2005: 104, SPC Interpretation (Art. 13) (note that the customer list is the only kind of trade secret which is explicitly referred to in a separate article).

as trade secrets or, conversely, believing that sensitive information exclusively exists in high-tech enterprises.[767] The awareness of the scope of trade secrets thus seems to be less clear in China.

The frequent exchange of sensitive information, for example regarding prices, can be seen as another indicator of a less developed awareness. In the Rio Tinto case, for instance, information on price negotiations had been obtained by what is deemed as unfair means by the Chinese court. Yet according to industry experts, informing each other about prices has been usual business practice in the Chinese steel sector for years.[768] This marks another discrepancy with trade secret legislation which excludes information that was commonly exchanged.[769]

Altogether, the issues of conflict arising in trade secret cases and the way judicial and administrative practice deals with them mirror a specific social fabric most consequential to knowledge interactions in the Chinese business reality. What is considered valuable knowledge is very strongly connected to personal interactions between employees and market players. The strong connection between market players implies valuable knowledge being widely exchanged. It is this strong exchange of knowledge and the significance of the knowledge arising from this exchange itself that characterizes the handling of valuable knowledge in China's current business environment and which might pose conflicts especially with FIEs from Western jurisdictions.

767 Chen Yu 2010: 99, Yang Ping 2009: 143.
768 Hein 2009, Barboza 2010.
769 SPC Interpretation (Art. 9), SAIC Regulations (Art. 2 (2)).

8 Knowledge Practices and Sino-German Conflicts

This chapter delves into the actual knowledge situation in China's business environment and depicts the conflicts arising within daily working practice between Chinese and German employees in FIEs. By analyzing empirical data gathered in FIEs in China, six practices inductively emerged which help to fathom how boundaries of knowledge are currently drawn. These practices illuminate the subtle criteria and strategies which inform the sampled Chinese interviewees when drawing these boundaries and reveal how these easily lead to conflicts with German employees. Although the practices are often simultaneously relevant for a knowledge interaction, they are artificially split up for analytical purposes.

Reference to the different types of enterprises is scarcely made in the following analysis. Admittedly, WFOEs and JVs are very different types of enterprises in various regards. Differences also include the matter of valuable knowledge where the interests in JVs might stronger be opposed with valuable knowledge even more sensitive and more easily leaking to other enterprises the JV is connected to. Nevertheless, the difference appears hardly relevant for the most basic cultural knowledge informing the handling of valuable knowledge. WFOEs also appear to be characterized by many conflicts of interests, and hence, the vast majority of cultural knowledge identified is valid for both types of enterprises in the same manner. Where the type of enterprise plays a role, it is particularly emphasized below.

8.1 Cultivating a Limited Personal Competitive Advantage

Among German employees, a "reluctance in knowledge sharing"[770] on the part of Chinese employees was widely perceived.[771] Knowledge was seen as being not sufficiently shared within the enterprise. As Chinese employees' knowledge

770 See e.g. G/31/JV/SHA(8:20), G/63/WFOE/GD(2:10), G/50/JV/SHA(58:6). Note that interviewees are cited as follows: nationality/age/type of enterprise/location(interview number:quote number). For the dates of conducting the interview and for the interviewers involved see appendix 1.

771 In the following, male and female interviewees are both referred to. As male interviewees form the majority, the male form is used for the first person singular (except when referring to a particular interview with a female respondent).

was regarded as particularly valuable for the FIE's activities on the Chinese market, this caused many conflicts in daily work.

A German general manager at a WFOE reflected on some of his employees in the sales and after-sales department who had to write reports about the interactions with customers. These reports were written only after several requests by the general manager:

> Wenn ich da nicht nachfrage, dann ist manchmal der Informationsfluss sehr spärlich. [...] Wenn ich dann zum Beispiel sage, hier bitte erledige dies und dies, dann erwarte ich irgendwann auch ne Rückmeldung, ist erledigt, oder das und das ist dabei passiert oder sonst was. Da kommt nichts. Erst wenn man nachfragt, hast du das gemacht. Jaja, hab ich gemacht. Also insofern, das ist das ist aber nicht nur bei uns so, das ist allgemein so glaub ich. [...] Im Allgemeinen, ich glaub die Chinesen wollen erst mal nicht ihr Wissen preisgeben. [...] Und äh gerade im Verkauf, wenn Li zum Beispiel, der hat nen Projekt, und er redet aber nicht darüber. Li, du warst doch bei dem und dem Kunden, was ist denn da jetzt los. Da war doch nen Projekt, das war doch da. Jaja, is still ongoing, ne. [...] Sehr vage, ja. [...] Also man muss den Leuten manchmal die Sachen so aus der Nase ziehen. Manchmal kommen sie halt nicht von alleine und sagen irgendetwas.[772]

> [If I do not ask, then the information flow is sometimes very scarce. [...] For example, when I say, please do this and that for me, I eventually do expect feedback, this is done, or this and that has happened and stuff like that. But nothing comes around. Only if you asked, did you do that. Yes, yes, I did. But this is, this is not only the case here in our enterprise, this is the generally the case, I think. [...] In general, I think, the Chinese first do not want to reveal their knowledge. [...] And uhm especially in sales, taking Li as an example, he has a project, and he doesn't talk about it. Li, haven't you been with this and that customer, what is going on there. Wasn't there a project, there was something, right. Yes yes, is still ongoing, right. [...] Very vague, yes. That means you sometimes have to pull every word out of their mouths. Sometimes they do not come on their own initiative and say something.]

This German employee expected his Chinese colleague to actively share his knowledge and to provide feedback without being asked for it. He desired concrete information being provided as soon as possible and found it exhausting to obtain the information by himself through repeated asking.

Being often confronted with this behavior, German employees assumed that Chinese employees are selfishly keeping and using knowledge for their personal advantage.[773] This German head of production at a JV found the keeping of knowledge particularly annoying during daily work:

772 G/63/WFOE/GD(2:10).

773 See e.g. G/50/JV/SHA(58:6), G/51/WFOE/JS(18:9), G/34/JV/JL(53:9).

> Das Eine ist dieses Glauben, ich habe einen persönlichen Vorteil, wenn ich was weiß und nicht weitergebe. Das beobachte ich sehr oft in dieser Firma, nicht nur bei meinen Mitarbeitern, sondern auch bei anderen. Die wissen oft viel mehr, können oft viel mehr, geben das aber nicht preis. Behalten das für sich. Häufig versuchen sie damit auch bestimmte Strategien und Taktiken einzusetzen. [...] Also das ist schon manchmal ärgerlich und kostet unheimlich viel Nerven. Das Zweite ist wirklich, Wissen zu nutzen für sich selbst. Wobei das ist ja auch nicht nur, das gibt es auch in Europa, da gibt es auch Leute, die so agieren, das ist klar. Aber hier ist das noch ein bisschen ausgeprägter, eben aufgrund dieser, wie ich eben sage, sehr, dieses sehr verbreiteten Egoismusses, den es hier gibt.[774]

> [The first thing is the belief that I have a personal advantage if I know something and do not share it. I observe this very often in this company, not only with my employees but also with others. They often know much more, are able to do much more, but do not reveal it. Keeping it for themselves. They frequently try to use it for employing certain strategies or tactics. [...] This is indeed annoying sometimes and costs an awful lot of nerves. The second thing indeed is to use knowledge for oneself. Yet this is not only, this also happens in Europe, there are also people acting like this, without a doubt. But here it is a bit more visible, just due to this, as I just said, this, very, this very wide-spread egoism existing here.]

The quoted German employee evaluated the gap between what Chinese employees pretend to know and what they indeed do know as very large. This gap was supposed to be intentionally maintained and informed by a seemingly selfish nature of Chinese people.

Interviews with Chinese employees revealed the necessity to strife for a personal competitive advantage as well as its limits. Being involved in knowledge interactions on a daily basis, Chinese employees were particularly occupied with gathering information and exchanging knowledge within communication processes. They permanently made decisions what, how, and when which part of knowledge was to be gathered to fulfill a certain task and what could be given away during communication with fellow employees or people in the business environment. These decisions were far from straightforward. Decisions included at least one important consideration: any knowledge interaction was to be viewed against the background of one's own knowledge repository.

A Chinese interviewee working in a purchasing department of a JV even more pointedly expressed that this knowledge is "her" knowledge which she had to protect for herself in order to stay competitive:

---

774 G/50/JV/SHA(58:6).

> 如果你这里讲的是。。。，嗯，**我的** know-how 的话[。。。]那 know-how **是**需要去保护的。因为这是你的核心竞争力。[775]
>
> [If you are talking about…, well, about *my* know-how […] that know-how *does* need be to protected. Because this is your core competitiveness.]

Although she clearly and explicitly stated that keeping know-how as one's core competitiveness was absolutely necessary and depicted it as "her" know-how, she was yet not able to draw an exact line to narrow down this personal knowledge stock. By probing into her concrete tasks, the knowledge which she considered her core competitiveness came to light. Before a project started, she had to communicate closely with suppliers of electronic devices and adapted the products according to the demands of her enterprise.

These in fact are strong mediating activities including the employees from product development, production, and quality management. It was not the technical know-how *per se* she referred to as this was something she considered necessary to exchange and which enabled her to discuss the exact demands with the various parties on a certain level. Rather, it was the know-how needed to estimate the technical knowledge of the supplier and to anticipate how counterpart will interpret the drawings based on his own technical understanding, whether he might be equipped for this order, and where difficulties to fulfill the various quality demands might occur. Her reflections on these mediation and anticipation tasks and her experiences gathered in the process were what she regards her core competitiveness. Although she could not fully express the range of this core competitiveness, she was very much aware that it had to be protected. The reflections and experiences hence mark the – albeit vague – boundary of knowledge she ascribed to herself and which she was keen on cultivating as her competitive edge.

A Chinese interviewee who worked in the sales department of a JV elucidated a tendency of protecting one's own knowledge and experiences against usage by fellow employees. As point of departure the interviewee was asked about differences between German and Chinese employees in daily knowledge work. In response, the interviewee reflected on the training he received at the German headquarters. He recalled how he observed that knowledge was carefully documented by Germans engineers and praised the usefulness of these documents for systematically evaluating technical problems suddenly occurring in the production process. The interviewee argued that Chinese employees rather (多一点) put a solution in the head – referred to as stomach (肚子) and hand (手上) – instead of writing detailed reports and making them easily accessible to anyone.

775 C/36/JV/SHA(43:19) [emphasis added].

If anything, less detailed reports were delivered. The concrete problem solving process and the reflections following such a process belonged to the part of knowledge which was usually not shared by Chinese employees in contrast to German employees.[776]

A German senior project manager of the same enterprise mentioned the same problem without being asked. From his perspective the situation of documenting processes and procedures appears to be very problematic:

> Wir haben hier außerordentlich große Schwierigkeiten in der Dokumentation, die es in Deutschland so nicht gibt. Das heißt zum einen, erarbeitete Dinge werden nicht dokumentiert. Hier schreibt keiner irgendwo einen Entwicklungsbericht, wo das Ergebnis seiner Arbeit noch später nachgelesen werden kann. Wenn man das Ergebnis der Arbeit wieder braucht, muss man ihn Jahre später noch fragen und hoffen, dass er es noch weiß.[777]
>
> [Here we have enormous difficulties concerning documentation, which do not exist in Germany to such an extent. For one, things that have been worked out are not documented. Somehow no one here writes a development report, where the result of his work can be looked up later on. If you need the results again later on, you need to ask him even years later and hope that he remembers.]

Asked about the reasons for this difference, the Chinese sales employee responded by referring to the proverb "教会徒弟，饿死师傅"[778] [the master will starve, if he passes everything to the apprentice]. Although the interviewee used the proverb with a laughter indicating that it should not be taken literally, it still explains why Chinese employees exhibit a tendency to keep knowledge to themselves. In a figurative sense, "starving" means not being able to cope with the competitive environment. The employee is yet himself responsible for keeping knowledge allowing him to compete with others. Although the advantages of documentation are acknowledged (at least by a Chinese employee having received training at the German headquarters), the strife for cultivating one's own competitive advantage weighs much more.

The constant comparison with fellow employees was directly expressed by another Chinese sales employee at a WFOE, showing that this competitive situation also occurs in WFOEs and not only in JVs:

> 因为只有当我把这些经验公布大家了，他就会感到有竞争，因为他就不能出类拔萃了。[779]

776 C/45/JV/SHA(11:23).
777 G/40/JV/SHA(59:11).
778 C/45/JV/SHA(11:23).
779 C/28/WFOE/SHA(54:19).

> [As only when I make the experiences public, he [I] will feel the competition, as he [I] then cannot stand out from his [my] fellows anymore.]

One's own and individual core competitiveness is accordingly seen as a protection against the prevalent competition at the workplace. As long as an employee does not publicly share knowledge he is able to cultivate his own personal competitive advantage. This advantage could easily be lost by sharing with the consequence of being stronger exposed to the competitive atmosphere at work and to the peers on the Chinese labor market as a whole.

Accumulating information was another main concern for the majority of Chinese employees directly resulting from the conviction of the imperative to cultivate one's competitive edge. Without sufficient information Chinese employees saw themselves unable to fulfill their daily work. Furthermore, there seemed to be a strong consciousness for information channels not being always open and the need to grasp opportunities for accumulating information to be assured to be informed to a sufficient extent.[780]

The extent to which knowledge is accumulated quickly causes conflicts with German employees. It was observed that documents were generally not put on the server to allow fellow employees to read them but on the personal hard disc or usb stick. Instead, information was hoarded to an even unnessary extent, including outdated information. Only certain employees had access rights instead of granting them to all people of certain levels as German employees were used to from the German headquarters or branches in other countries. Who has access was not transparent and thus an important and rare information which had to be gathered first.[781] This mirrors the apprehension of Chinese employees who have to cope with obscure and fuzzy information access. Under these conditions, rather what someone is able to receive instead of what someone really needs is the primary rationale when accumulating information.

Yet the strife for a competitive advantage is not unlimited. While elaborating on their knowledge, almost all sampled Chinese interviewees employed what can be considered a moral boundary.[782] Knowledge sharing was seen as useful for learning from others, and the potential of knowledge to be multiplied through exchange was acknowledged. Only with knowledge exchange an enterprise was seen as able to innovate, and innovations were seen as vital for the development of society. Precisely because it was considered vital for the development of society, knowledge sharing was explicitly or implicitly considered a moral act. A person who shares knowledge was considered a good person, acting in an *altru-*

780 See e.g. C/29/JV/SHA(9:24), C/36/WFOE/SHA(13:14), C/33/WFOE/SHA(49:25).
781 G/40/JV/SHA(59:11), G/51/WFOE/JS(18:14).
782 See e.g. C/38/JV/JL(73:10), C/24/WFOE/SHA(61A:23), C/28/WFOE/SHA(54:19).

istic way. Conversely, intentionally keeping all of one's knowledge to oneself was despised, especially when knowledge needed for the common interest is not shared. Another Chinese interviewee, for instance, who worked in the quality management department of another JV and provided training for other employees (and hence was most concerned with knowledge sharing), directly expressed his thoughts of employees not adhering to this moral boundary:

> 你并不是说，额，你自己有了知识之后，你就把这个知识捂得**很严**，就是说这是我的，我**谁也**不告诉，那么你想问我，我也不告诉你，这样的话，我觉得这个可能就是说，我觉得对于这种人来讲，可能就是，嗯，我觉得就是这个人的这种思想有问题。[783]
>
> [It cannot be that, uhm, after you yourself have acquired knowledge, that you then *very strictly* cover up this knowledge, this is mine, and I don't tell it to *anyone*. If you are asking me, I still don't tell you. In this case, I think this is maybe, how to say, ehm, I think from the angle of this person, maybe this person's way of thinking is problematic.]

The expression of a person's "problematic way of thinking" (思想有问题) has a strong moral connotation. One clearly should share one's knowledge, especially when asked for it.

Yet another important issue the quotation implies is that the interviewee does not opt for *complete* knowledge sharing. It was perfectly acceptable for all interviewed employees if only parts of knowledge are shared with selected persons. In fact, one should always be aware of a certain part of knowledge which is not to be shared. In a strikingly direct way, it was stated that "people *always* have their own part" of knowledge (人**总是**有他自己的一部分)[784]. This intrinsic (固有)[785] part of knowledge only belongs to oneself and should be protected, as this is considered an employee's competitive advantage (竞争优势)[786] or core competitiveness. Chinese employees clearly believed that 100 percent of one's knowledge can never be shared and just enough for sustaining one's competitive advantage was seen as legitimate to be cultivated and protected.

This intrinsic part of one's knowledge was seen as hard to circumscribe. After accumulating knowledge, experiences, and abilities which form one's individual competitive advantage, knowledge sharing only becomes an option. When an employee's own development reaches a certain level after the adaption phase,[787] and the employee has become a comparatively knowledgeable person,

783 C/38/JV/JL(73:8) [emphasis added].
784 C/35/WFOE/JS(66:24) [emphasis added].
785 C/28/WFOE/SHA(48:15).
786 C/28/WFOE/SHA(48:15), C/28/WFOE/SHA(54:19).
787 See also chapter 8.2.

has accumulated experiences, and has a deeper professional understanding, he should share knowledge and keep only a comparatively small part for oneself.[788] These criteria are thus no absolute criteria but relative criteria employed in comparison with fellow employees.

Legitimately protecting one's core competitiveness is a conviction valid not only for oneself but also for fellow employees. When trying to access knowledge from fellow employees, Chinese employees similarly do not expect to receive 100% of what fellow employees know, but respect the minimum level (底线)[789] of personal competitive advantage. Hence, not only is one's own competitive advantage constantly taken into account during knowledge interactions but even the competitive edge of fellow employees. Keeping one's own secrets is considered as legitimate as the keeping of secrets by an enterprise or the state.[790]

Striving for cultivating one's own personal competitive advantage *to a certain extent* is thus morally accepted. This extent includes exactly the amount of knowledge one needs to ensure one's relative core competitiveness or, in other words, to ensure that one does not metaphorically "starve". As long as cultivation of knowledge serves this need, keeping this confined part of it to oneself is perfectly acceptable. Beyond that, all knowledge is to be shared with people who are in need of it. Protecting too much for oneself and not sharing additional knowledge with anyone is seen as morally unacceptable when drawing the boundaries of valuable knowledge in FIEs.

The quotations of the German employees above, by contrast, imply that fully sharing one's knowledge was taken for granted by all interviewees. After having acquired knowledge it should be shared with fellow employees and not kept to oneself. Sharing knowledge within the own enterprise is not seen altruistic, but as a matter of course. Hence, a person not sharing knowledge deviates from the norm and is regarded as egoist and selfish.

As the interview section with the German head of production rightly points out, German employees might hesitate to share their knowledge for the same reasons as Chinese employees, that is, striving to be more knowledgeable compared to other persons of the same department or enterprise. But having (formerly) been exposed to a culture where knowledge sharing within the enterprise is generally expected, German employees would rather see to it that the intention not to fully share knowledge is not that obvious to fellow employees. As such, not everyone necessarily adheres to the norm neither in Germany nor in China.

---

788 See e.g. C/28/WFOE/SHA(48:15), C/35/WFOE/JS(66:24), C/27/WFOE/GD(3:74).

789 C/28/WFOE/JS(14:47). One then would rather use other channels (see chapter 8.4) or indirectly access it from the other one's talk (see chapter 8.5).

790 See e.g. C/35/WFOE/JS(66:24), C/40/JV/SHA(77:26), C/36/WFOE/GD(60:25).

Yet German employees would at least try to make others believe that they are fully sharing their knowledge and not holding anything back.

Thus, even when German employees come to China for work, they most often follow these habits. In the same vein as German employees in Germany would be regarded as egoistic when deviating from the standard of fully sharing knowledge, Chinese employees are likewise regarded as egoistic and selfish when knowledge sharing cannot be observed. As such, German employees draw the boundaries differently, assuming that – in theory – virtually anything has to be quasi automatically shared within the FIE, while in China only altruistic persons would share knowledge that forms part of their (limited) personal competitive advantage. Precisely as this limited part forms a personal competitive advantage, which is not called into question in China, people are *not* regarded as egoist when cultivating it for themselves.

8.2 Evaluating Efforts into Knowledge Application

When Chinese employees enter a FIE, they often stay for a rather short time. A crucial point is that an employee, having acquired knowledge from the enterprise via training and other means, might use this valuable knowledge elsewhere in the Chinese business environment, most probably even at a competing enterprise. Although the sampled enterprises managed to keep their employee turnover comparatively low, they were still facing the problem of employees who were trained well but left the enterprise before the training really paid of.

This situation raises critical questions about the extent of knowledge the FIE discloses to its employees and how this disclosure is reciprocated by the employees. In their daily practice, the sampled Chinese and German employees did not explicitly discuss where to draw the boundaries when sharing valuable knowledge. Instead, they were guided by a subtle point of reference. The point of departure was similar for both Chinese and German employees: both were guided by the implicit belief that who puts *efforts* into knowledge has a stake in it and is eligible of using it.

Yet the understanding of efforts clearly differed among German and Chinese employees. German managers assumed that their investment of efforts starts with employment in the enterprise. During their employment, Chinese employees were expected to make active use of this opportunity by improving their capabilities for fulfilling the designated tasks. German employees particularly emphasized the provision of training for employees especially at the start of their employment.[791]

791 See e.g. G/60/WFOE/SHA(55:3), B/57/WFOE/SHA(16:11,16:13), H/39/WFOE/SHA(17:3).

During daily work, Chinese employees were often viewed as not *actively* using the platform offered and thus not adequately contributing to the enterprise. For instance, they were neither perceived as willing to take on responsibility, nor as actively pursuing tasks or bringing in new ideas.[792] A German engineer at a JV was surprised about not seeing his well educated Chinese colleagues taking on resonsiblity or actively searching for solutions:

> Also wo ich von einem deutschen Ingenieur erwarte und ich es auch bekomme, ist Eigenständigkeit, Verant… und Verantwortungsübernahme. Und dieses Thema fehlt hier komplett. Das sind nur ganz wenige, … wo ich merke, dass die Leute nachdenken, wo sie selber ne Lösung suchen. […] Und das macht mich auch immer so ein bisschen … upset. […] Das versteh ich nicht. Also das ist mir so ein …, das ist mir zu hoch. Und was dann wiederum als Output kommt, ist auch nicht so.[793]

> [What I expect from German engineer and what I indeed receive is self-reliance and respon… and the taking over of responsibility. And this topic is completely missing here. Only a very few, … I notice that very few people reflect or search for a solution. […] And that always makes me a little … upset. […] I do not understand that. That for me is such a…, that is beyond me and my mind. And regarding the output isn't that good either.]

Taking on responsibility and actively contributing to solving problems were clearly expected by this German employee. His Chinese colleagues, however, did not live up to the expectations, neither in terms of their behavior nor regarding the output they achieved. Even worse, those employees who performed well soon left the enterprise.

To encourage responsibility and active behavior, efforts were put into providing in-house training in nearly all sampled FIEs. Yet before having applied the knowledge acquired, it happened Chinese employees switched their employers. A British employee at a WFOE vividly expressed his anger about a former employee of his who left the enterprise soon after having been thoroughly and personally trained on a particular project:

> Hab ihn trainiert, hab ihm alles gezeigt, alles meine Wissen um diese project, dass es wirklich reibungslos läuft, war immer frustriert, weil ‚ja, ja, wir machen mit' und er hat nichts getan, aber ist egal, das ist the Chinese way, ne, und dann komm ich letztes mal, war hier, hab ich ihm noch einmal die neueste training gemacht, neu gezeigt und die Problem gelöst. Geh ich wieder heim vor Weihnachten. A Woche bevor ich kam dieses mal hats geheißen nicht mehr da, ne. Und dann fängst du gleich von vorne wieder an, ne.[794]

792 See e.g. G/44/JV/BJ(38:3), G/31/JV/SHA(8:20), and exploratory interview G/45/JV/BJ(79:1).

793 G/44/JV/BJ(38:3).

794 B/57/WFOE/SHA(16:11).

[I trained him, showed him everything, all my knowledge regarding this project, in order to enable it to really function smoothy, I was always frustrated as he said 'yes, yes, we are in' but he did nothing. But this doesn't matter, this is the Chinese way, isn't it. And then I came here last time, was here, provided him once again with the newest training, showed him again how to solve the problem. Then I went home for Christmas. A week before coming back, I heard that he is not here anymore, right. And then you immediately start from the beginning, right.]

Both the opportunities of employment and training did not seem to be well used from the point of view of German employees. Chinese employees did not make use of these opportunities to a sufficient extent or even rendered the efforts wasted when leaving the enterprise after a short time. Efforts to improve the employee's knowledge were offered by German employees, yet not fully reciprocated by Chinese employees.

After scrutinizing the Chinese perspective, the understanding of investing efforts into knowledge turns out to be different. The Chinese employees' investment of efforts began as soon as they being employed by the FIE. Having entered the FIE, they were positioned in a new context to which they have to adapt first in order to be able to pursue their work at all. Interestingly, the phase of adapting (适应)[795] to the workplace was a frequently raised issue in all interviews with Chinese employees.

In particular, this was a concern for new workforce entrants at the start of their first employment. Chinese new work force entrants regarded knowledge acquired at university as too superficial and theoretical for being immediately applied at work. This knowledge was seen as providing a certain background, but being hardly applicable in practical work.[796]

Accumulating experiences was seen as most conducive for adapting to a workplace as quickly as possible. The Chinese employees' focus was on accumulating experiences in as many *different* situations and with as many different people as possible.[797] Even when being only shortly – for instance for three month – with a certain employer, the employee could still gain insights on how people work in this environment. These were seen as valuable experience for future work. The more things were done and seen in practice, the more the employee could "adjust" (调整)[798] himself to changing circumstances in the current or future departments or enterprises. To a certain extent, an employee himself could put his efforts in raising the quantity of his experiences by, for example,

795 See e.g. C/28/WFOE/SHA(62:22), C/38/JV/JL(73:25), C/36/WFOE/BJ(20:15).
796 See e.g. C/25/WFOE/SHA(65B:13), C/40/JV/BJ(77:21), C/40/JV/JL(68:9).
797 See e.g. C/38/JV/JL(73:13), C/35/WFOE/SHA(44:21), C/27/WFOE/GD(3:37).
798 C/36/WFOE/BJ(20:15).

visiting four customers a day rather than only one.[799] Employees rather invested into efforts that culminated in a large amount of different experiences in order to adapt to different situations and people in a certain working environment. Adapting to the workplace thus also included accumulating basic experiences in communicating with colleagues or business partners, and was even implicitly regarded as a much greater challenge.

Linking experiences to the existing knowledge by figuring out which knowledge is relevant for work also required efforts during the adaptation phase.[800] In the course of this adaptation process, employees developed an awareness of their own knowledge and experiences, that is, what they needed at the workplace, what they actually possessed and what still had to be learned. A Chinese product manager at a WFOE, who has joined her FIE four years before, reflected on her adaptation phase as follows:

> 刚开始工作的时候，只是想如何。。。额。。。掌握你应该要做的这些事情，如何更快地去适应，［。。。］再回头去看之前的这些你会感觉，喔那些都是知识和经验。[801]

> [Just having started working, you have only thought about how to … uhm … master the things you had to do, how you could adapt more quickly, […] only in retrospect you realize that all this had been knowledge and experience.]

During the adaptation phase, she was only occupied with adapting to her new workplace. And only later on, she started to realize which parts were of value for her work. This figuring and sorting out of *relevant* knowledge was seen as belonging to the efforts put into work.

In order to make this basic accumulated experience and the adapted knowledge available for various practical and rather suddenly occurring situations, knowledge and experiences had to be regularly "summed up" (总结)[802]. Over time, the different experiences and knowledge were converted into abilities (能力)[803], enabling the employee to solve future problems by drawing parallels to past problems, and adapt even faster to new situations. Those abilities were ascribed to the person of the employee himself:

> 当然如。。。你。。。只有知识，比方说你学历很高，工作好多年，但你不善于总结，这也不行，你肯定要**总结**。。。从前面失败的例子当中或者看着别人

799 C/33/WFOE/JS(49:25,49:16).
800 See e.g. C/25/WFOE/SHA(48:27), C/38/JV/JL(73:7), C/34/JV/SHA(40:10).
801 C/33/WFOE/JS(49:25).
802 See e.g. C/38/JV/JL(73:24), C/35/WFOE/JS(66:22), C/34/JV/SHA(40:17).
803 See e.g. C/36/WFOE/BJ(20:15), C/28/WFOE/JS(14:14), C/40/JV/BJ(77:7).

> 好的地方你要总结总结，然后形成**你自个儿**的东西，这个东西**属于自个儿**的东西，我觉得就是**才能**。[804]
>
> [Of course, if … you … only have knowledge, for instance, your academic qualification is high, you have worked a good many years, this neither works out, you definitely have *to sum that up*… you have to sum up at times where you failed or look at where other people are good at, then form *your own things*, these things *belong to yourself*, I think, this is *ability*.]

This interviewee emphasized the efforts employees had to make in reflecting on the knowledge and experiences, including the observation of people in the environment. Through *individual* interaction with and reflection on the experiences of oneself and other people, abilities were build up which cannot be detached from the person and could only be built up by investing efforts oneself.

The majority of interviewees vividly explained how the knowledge adapted in university hardly helped them when pursuing their work. Especially in the beginning, they were strongly dependent on their colleagues for gathering knowledge. Implicit and tacit knowledge being intricately linked to employees was sharply differentiated from knowledge acquired from books. Book knowledge could quickly be learned when needed[805] and was not readily applicable anyway. Employees possessing only pure book knowledge (光有知识)[806] were not seen as having spent much effort in acquiring it, whereas an employee's individual abilities and the respective implicit and tacit knowledge only developed via a strenuous process. Applicable implicit and tacit knowledge was considered the employee's personal knowledge, which is seen as just being in his head, impossible to be separated from him, and existing through him.

Yet personal knowledge was not considered useful or meaningful as long as it was not *de facto applied in practice*.[807] For applying personal knowledge in practice, the employee expected to be *enabled* to "put his abilities to use" (发挥能力)[808] by the FIE. Thereby, the provision of training in the beginning of the employment was merely seen as a precondition to make the employee able to pursue the work for which he has been employed.[809] More significantly, the FIE was seen in the role of providing what is mostly expressed as an "opportunity" (机会) or as a "platform" (平台)[810]. This implies that employees are offered the

804 C/34/JV/SHA(40:10) [emphasis added].
805 See e.g. C/34/JV/JL(69:9), C/33/WFOE/JS(49:16), C/36/WFOE/SHA(13:10).
806 See e.g. C/36/WFOE/SHA(13:10), C/38/JV/JL(73:7), C/42/JV/JL(71:21).
807 See e.g. C/38/JV/JL(73:7), C/42/JV/JL(71:21), C/43/WFOE/BJ(76:1).
808 See e.g. C/30/JV/SHA(46:18), C/35/WFOE/JS(50:17), C/27/WFOE/GD(3:25).
809 See e.g. C/42/JV/JL(71:9), C/33/WFOE/JS(49:17,49:21), C/43/WFOE/BJ(76:11).
810 See e.g. C/40/JV/JL(68:27), C/28/WFOE/SHA(62:16), C/36/WFOE/GD(60:20).

possibility to pursue new tasks, allowing them to experience many different work situations, environments, and people, increasing the amount of *different* opportunities to put abilities to use.

The direct superior plays an essential role in this process.[811] He is expected to know the employee well enough to tap his full potential (知人善用)[812], enabling him to put his abilities to use to its full extent. The superior should encourage the employee in trying out new tasks and provide him with enough latitude to pursue the tasks largely autonomously without interfering too often.[813]

At the same time, the employee quickly feels overburdened with tasks with the result that he does not feel successful at all. This equally hinders him to fully unfold his abilities. Also, failures generate much pressure for an employee, giving him the feeling of having no choice but to opt for leaving the FIE for a new employer.[814] Encouragement and autonomy are thus expected to be carefully pursued by being well aware of the employee's abilities at a certain point in time.

Putting the abilities to use also means that the superior enables the employee to rotate within the FIE before the employee feels he has adequately understood a certain position. A rotation in intervals of one or two years was deemed necessary since the amount of knowledge that can be achieved at a certain position is generally seen as limited. This is the time seen as sufficient to develop to the utmost extent in a certain position.[815] A Chinese project manager at a JV expected his superior to know him well enough to *anticipate* the direction into which he can potentially develop even before he – the Chinese employee – himself was conscious about his potential:

> 因为有的员工［。。。］不会处理关系，你［领导］把他安到公关部，他就很头疼．［。。。］领导是**应该掌握**，比如[…]这个人［。。。]，很快就能拿到结果，就说明这个人，肯定他有自个儿有关系网，然后呢肯定人际关系处理得不错[。。。]，因此你[领导]就**必须知道**这个员工他喜欢做这个［。。。]。他［员工]可能也就也是无意识的［。。。]。[816]
>
> [Some employees cannot manage relationships, and if you [superior] transfer him to the public relations department, this is very troublesome. [...] The superior *should*

811 See e.g. C/28/WFOE/SHA(48:10), C/28/WFOE/SHA(54:20), C/34/JV/SHA(40:8).

812 C/34/JV/SHA(40:17).

813 See e.g. C/38/JV/JL(73:27), C/25/WFOE/GD(1:5), C/24/WFOE/SHA(61A:49).

814 See e.g. C/29/JV/SHA(9:3), C/30/JV/SHA(46:18), C/25/WFOE/GD(5:29). Only younger employees emphasize this point, showing that these might feel a stronger pressure to succeed than older employees.

815 See e.g. C/36/JV/SHA(43:6), C/28/WFOE/SHA(48:32), C/33/WFOE/SHA(49:20). But see C/33/WFOE/JS(45:23) (only after 2-3 years can abilities be used to its full extent). Yet the dominant opinion is to switch as often as possible in order to see and learn different things.

816 C/34/JV/SHA(40:17) [emphasis added].

> *understand well*, for example [...] that this person [...] can achieve results very quickly, which means that this person definitely has his own networks, and then he must be good at managing his relationships [...], and thus you [superior] *have to know* that this employee likes to do that [...]. He [employee] is maybe not conscious about that either.]

This interviewee saw the superior responsible for anticipating the abilities of the employee by closely observing and analyzing his work and drawing inferences about his abilities by the lapse of time he needs for achieving results. Observation and analyzing should be pursued before the employee is conscious about these abilities and wishes to use these abilities in another department or enterprise.

Paradoxically at first glance, to be granted certain autonomy was equally valued among the sampled Chinese employees. Especially when mediating with the business environment where their (German) superior was usually not engaged in, they needed certain autonomy, truly embracing their role as knowledge workers. Yet this is not to say that employees want the superior to retreat from accompanying their daily work. Employees still ascribed to the superior *the* crucial role for their professional development and career. Especially as the superior is decisive for evaluating their output of knowledge work which allows for developing more quickly, the employee depends on him for keeping an eye on even the smallest achievements and to assess their abilities accordingly. What follows is that Chinese employees can put their abilities to use in the best way as long as the superior invests sufficient efforts in achieving the adequate balance between attendance and autonomy for the respective employee.

For the most part of Chinese employees acting as knowledge workers it can be said that it is of utmost significance to see their abilities being put to *full* use *in practice*. In practice, abilities can adequately reflect the employee's personal value (体现自己的价值)[817]. The frequent usage of the relative term "value" (价值) elucidates that employees see themselves being exposed to strong competition from other employees. Especially when an employee is a new workforce entrant, he rarely is equipped with his own well-defined competitive advantage which distinguishes him from others. All have enjoyed a seemingly uniform education without any practice or mostly without foreign experiences. Seeing their value adequately reflected, which is necessary for coping with competition, Chinese employees mostly need an experienced superior who can exactly figure out the opportunities they need to be provided with within daily work. After the adaptation phase, the consciousness for the own personal value develops, and this value has to be permanently increased during the subsequent working life.

817 See e.g. C/36/WFOE/SHA(13:23), C/38/JV/JL(73:28), C/36/WFOE/GD(60:20).

Strongly acknowledging the efforts of both the employee and the FIE which are put into increasing the employee's value, some Chinese interviewees also pointed to the benefit for the FIE if their abilities are fully used.[818] A Chinese employee working as a researcher at a JV emphasized that the enterprise can use the employee also according to its needs:

> 我觉得这个，企业要思考清楚。然后也许他可以，然后协同各个方面考虑，那么可以按照他的要求，需要这个员工的话。。。那我可以给他更好，更好的平，平台发挥自己的能力。这样的话，对我企业也有好处，是吧，对这个员工也有好处，那他就不会离开这个企业了，是吧。[819]
>
> [I think this enterprise has to thoroughly reflect upon it. Then maybe it can coordinate and consider various aspects, and can according to its needs and requirements, concerning this employee … then I can give him a better plat…, platform for using his abilities. This way, this is an advantage for my enterprise, isn't it, and also advantageous for the employee. And then he will not leave this enterprise anymore, right?]

The enterprise was clearly expected to put much effort into the employee to benefit from him, yet can also take its own needs into account. Yet this employee implicitly said that if the employee left the enterprise, his knowledge would be lost. This knowledge in fact is only *indirectly* available to the FIE as it is inextricably linked to the person of the employee. The knowledge is only available for both as long as the employee is with the particular FIE.[820]

Knowledge workers in general are mobile by taking their means of production with them. Also, the need for keeping their knowledge up to date for countering labor market competition might be – among others – a reason for the high turnover rates especially in FIEs in China. Hence, if an employee does not see his abilities being put to use in an adequate way by the FIE and opts for switching to another employer, the valuable knowledge in the sense of abilities is ascribed to the (former) employee only.

For making knowledge *directly* available to the FIE, that is, being available independent of the person, the FIE is expected to put additional efforts in actively "taking out" (拿出来)[821] the employee's personal knowledge. For "taking" knowledge out of his head, the employee must be *willing* (愿意)[822] to directly contribute to the FIE. This willingness to contribute implies that the employee's sharing of his personal knowledge is valued as an additional contribution by the FIE.

818 See e.g. C/30/JV/SHA(46:18), C/34/JV/SHA(51:14), C/42/JV/JL(71:21).
819 C/30/JV/SHA(46:18).
820 See e.g. C/28/WFOE/SHA(48:31), C/25/WFOE/GD(5:3), C/32/WFOE/JS(63:18).
821 C/42/JV/JL(71:21).
822 See e.g. C/27/WFOE/GD(3:74), C/38/JV/JL(73:10), C/41/WFOE/JS(37:8).

In order to make the employee willing to contribute his knowledge, many interviewees indicated that it must be made clear to the employee that his additional contribution will be recognized. Making the employee's knowledge available within the FIE via sharing it with fellow employees was expected to be organized in a systematic manner. Chinese interviewees from various sampled FIE put forward examples, such as organization of a presentation or workshop by the FIE which provide the employee with an opportunity to share his knowledge.[823] In such a framework, the employee feels that his contribution is widely and openly recognized. If only sharing knowledge bilaterally or informally, the employee feels much uncertainty as only the colleague he shares knowledge with might benefit from his knowledge or even take advantage of him in the long run.

Furthermore, employees are more inclined to share knowledge when encouraged with monetary and mental rewards. Mental rewards are even preferred over monetary ones. Instead of receiving, for instance, some hundred RMB, being openly praised at a FIE event or in an internal newspaper has a greater effect. With the latter, the value of a person is more thoroughly reflected than by a one-time bonus.[824] While monetary rewards still function as encouragement, the interviews show that the need to see one's value reflected in comparison to others is an ever stronger concern.

Chinese employees further expressed to feel rewarded when their idea is made use of in the enterprise, when they receive feedback for an idea and the opportunity and encouragement to try out or realize the idea, or being rewarded with a task, a project, or even a promotion to be able to apply the abilities which have been revealed through the respective idea.[825] Again, the strife for mental rewards is striking as these are more directed toward the person and thus are capable of reflecting their personal value in a more sustainable way.

Chinese employees also expressed a concern that when making knowledge available or putting forward ideas their knowledge might be directly used by the FIE without reciprocation. As a precondition, they desired a leap of faith on the part of the FIE by showing that the knowledge of the employee is not used without any reciprocation. If this leap of faith is felt by the employee and knowledge transfer is successfully pursued, the relevant knowledge can be used by both regardless of the employees being with the FIE or not.

A further boundary for the usage of valuable knowledge was set by Chinese employees according to the *tangibility of the result*. Ideas recognized by the FIE for being of (measurable) value for the whole enterprise, such as ideas of saving costs or ideas which lead to innovations or even to registered intellectual proper-

823 C/40/JV/JL(68:10), C/32/JV/JL(51:22).

824 See e.g. C/40/JV/BJ(77:10), C/36/WFOE/SHA(13:8), C/38/JV/JL (73:12).

825 See e.g. C/36/WFOE/GD(60:20), C/29/JV/SHA(9:3,9:15), C/30/JV/SHA(46:7).

ty, were virtually completely ascribed to the FIE. Only to a lesser extent, if anything, were they ascribed to the employee.[826] Employees still expected to be rewarded for contributing to the tangible results in relation to the value they create for the FIE in order to have his personal value adequately reflected.[827] They did not see themselves, however, as authorized for *using* the results outside the FIE, especially during an employment in another enterprise.

Nevertheless, the knowledge, the idea or solution of a certain problem, which have led to an innovation were still considered to be in the employee's head.[828] A Chinese assistant plant manager at a WFOE emphasized that in line with all the knowledge an employee was able to acquire in the course of his employment this kind of knowledge is also inevitably taken along to the next employer:

> 如果是他个人能得到的知识，我觉得应该是属于个人吧。那，呃，就很简单。如果这个人他辞职了，那，知识还是在他脑中，还是属于我自己的。人家也不会说是吸走或者是拿走。[829]
>
> [If it is knowledge which he individually is able to acquire, then I find it should belong to the individual. That, uhm, is very easy. If this person resigns, then the knowledge is still in his head, still belongs to him personally. Other people would neither say that it is absorbed or taken away.]

To this Chinese employee it was self-evident that knowledge belongs to employees as long as they put efforts in acquiring it during the course of an employment. They can use it for themselves independently regardless of the employer. Although the interviewee was conscious about the intricate situation that an employee could potentially be blamed for leaking this specific knowledge, he was convinced that the knowledge is generally be seen as belonging to the respective person.

On the part of the Chinese employee, personal knowledge has more value to the employee than the tangible results he has achieved with the help of it. The reason is that his ultimate aim is to see his value reflected. Achieving something tangible with intangible knowledge can reflect his value only at a certain point in time. But the knowledge which has led to achieving the tangible result is even more decisive, and therefore can well be taken along to the next employer in order to achieve further tangible results. The property of the tangible results can be transferred between entities, whereas the intangible personal knowledge is something individually, intrinsically connected to the person of the employee.

826 See e.g. C/28/WFOE/SHA(48:9), C/25/WFOE/SHA(65B:10), C/35/WFOE/SHA(44:14).
827 See e.g. C/28/WFOE/SHA(48:10), C/33/WFOE/JS(45:15), C/25/WFOE/GD(5:21).
828 See e.g. C/28/WFOE/JS(14:14), C/45/JV/SHA(11:8,11:16), C/36/WFOE/GD(4:21).
829 C/27/WFOE/GD(3:25) [emphasis added].

The personal knowledge in the sense of individual abilities, the knowledge applied and built up through experiences and summed up during employment in fact accounts for the employee's personal value.

Without the FIE's efforts the Chinese employee would neither be able nor willing to put his personal knowledge to practical use to a significant extent. Therefore, from a Chinese point of view, the enterprise must be "*adept at* putting the employee's knowledge to use" (要善于去运用它)[830], and "hope" (希望)[831] that the employee's knowledge can be put to use or even be "taken out" in this particular enterprise. The achievement of tangible results, which signifies utmost applicability and utilization of the employee's knowledge, shows that the enterprise has invested significant efforts, and is thus seen as eligible of using the tangible results only.

German employees in FIEs also take the rationale of efforts as orientation to decide who is eligible in using valuable knowledge. Their focus, however, tends to be on the efforts they invest into knowledge *input*, particularly in the provision of formalized training for employees, whereas Chinese employees focus on the (potential) knowledge output. Chinese employees rather regard the mainly theoretical input of special trainings as a precondition for doing their work. If such a specialized training only comprises theoretical input, which has not been applied yet, they do not even regard this training as particularly valuable. Training is also often short and lacks personal and permanent implementation. The above mentioned example with the British employee at a WFOE, who provided training to a Chinese employee who resigned a bit later, shows that pure training is not sufficient. Rather, the employee wishes to be accompanied when he really applies the learnt content within the project in question.

Most German employees tended to pay less attention to the efforts invested in adapting to the workplace and developing abilities by Chinese employees. German employees – at least those who have stayed in China for a certain period of time – were clearly aware of the fact that problems in applying theoretical knowledge exist and more guidance is needed in China. Some were even aware of the fact that employees strive to enhance their personal value.[832] Due to time constraints and other priorities, however, the continous engagement with these issues was often neglected. Also, the German employees' implicit point of departure was expecting the employee to actively use the platform provided by the employing FIE to accumulate experiences right from the start. Yet Chinese employees expected German employees, and especially their (German) direct supe-

830 C/42/JV/JL(71:21).
831 See e.g. C/28/WFOE/SHA(48:28), C/42/JV/JL(71:21), C/33/WFOE/JS(49:21).
832 See e.g. G/58/JV/SHA(57:11), G/31/JV/SHA(8:20), H/39/WFOE/SHA(17:2).

riors, to invest efforts during the course of their employment into fully putting the employee's abilities to practical use.[833]

At the same time, Chinese employees in FIEs were commonly perceived as not willing to take on responsibility, while, in fact, they were often willing, but lacked the adequate encouragement and feedback, which they needed to pursue their work in a relatively autonomous way. German employees were more or less unaware of the fact that these efforts into making knowledge indeed *applicable* were precisely seen as implicit criteria of knowledge being eligible for usage by the FIE. Against this background, the above-mentioned situation of employees leaving the FIE for another platform where they can better apply their knowledge and see their value reflected, seems logical.

Apart from the rationale of the (limited) personal competitive advantage, the rationale of a permanent evaluation of efforts also contributes to the widely perceived reluctance in knowledge sharing. For instance, if new information was available regarding a project with several employees, German employees expected this information to be reported to the project leader. A German head of production at a JV, for instance, needed to question his employees every day. He had to ask his employees repeatedly for figures that are supposed to be reported on a weekly basis:

> Und das sind eben halt Sachen, die man lernen muss, immer wieder abfragen, immer wieder ran, von alleine läuft hier wenig.[834]
>
> [And these are things which you have to learn, time and again requesting, time and again doing it, few things happen by themselves.]

After having stayed in China for years, German employees were clearly aware that knowledge in China is understood as something you have to actively grasp as needed. However, they still did not thoroughly understand that Chinese employees expect their additional efforts to be adequately recognized, permanently driven by the rationale of seeing their value adequately reflected.

The reluctance to share knowledge does not necessarily mean that knowledge is intentionally held back. It is possible to obtain information without any resistance by actively asking for it instead of waiting for it to be shared deliberately.[835] Thus, it is part of any superior's responsibility to actively ask for and "take out" the knowledge. Since employees themselves are used to searching for the information they need instead of being automatically provided with it, they rather focus on gathering information. This focus, in turn, gives rise to the Ger-

---

833 See e.g. G/44/JV/BJ(38:10), G/51/WFOE/JS(18:19), and exploratory interview G/45/JV/BJ (79:3).

834 G/58/JV/SHA(57:20).

835 See e.g. G/63/WFOE/GD(2:10), G/40/JV/SHA(59:27), G/31/JV/SHA(8:29).

man perception of Chinese employees as being keen on "hoarding knowledge"[836] for themselves without fully grasping the underlying rationale.

In sum, German employees focus on the FIE's efforts invested into the input of knowledge. These efforts make the enterprise eligible to benefit from the employee's knowledge. For Chinese employees, in contrast, the efforts invested by the FIE into the output of knowledge, meaning the application of their knowledge to its full extent, marks the boundary between their personal knowledge and the knowledge the FIE should benefit from.

8.3 Assessing and Convincing Counterparts

Conflicts surrounding the sharing and protection of knowledge are ubiquitous. From the perspective of most German employees, valuable knowledge should clearly be shared *within* the FIE. Employees are supposed to immediately share knowledge which could be of value for someone else in the organization. Yet as obversed in above sub-chapters already, knowledge is not that self-evidently made available within in the FIE.

A German senior project manager at a JV drew a comparison to Germany, concerning the access to information on the enterprise's server. He emphasized that while department managers anywhere in Germany can usually access any information concerning their department, the situation in China is different:

> Was auch auffällt ist, wir haben auf unserem Server, der inhaltlich bescheiden ist, ein außerordentlich strenges Reglement an Zugriffsrechten, was es so in Deutschland in der Form nicht gibt. [...] Sie können bei unserem Server klicken wo Sie wollen, Sie haben da keine Zugriffsrechte, da ist man wirklich ganz pigelig, obwohl man doch sonst mit Informationen... Meine Kollegen, die irgendwelche Projekte haben, die wissen untereinander, wer darauf zugreift. Das versteh ich nicht, weil es eigentlich nicht dazu passt, dass man andererseits mit Informationen so offen umgeht. Auch innerhalb der Firma ist die Kommunikation von Information irgendwie ziemlich kanalisiert an manchen Stellen. [...] Also da gibt es Dinge, die ich bisher nicht verstehe, also warum es an manchen Stellen eine andere Art gibt, mit Informationen umzugehen.[837]

> [What is also striking, regarding our server, the content of which is moderate, is that we have extraordinary strict access rights, which do not exist in Germany in this form. [...] You can click on our server wherever you want to, you do not have any access rights, you are really very meticulous here in this regard, although you otherwise deal with information... My colleagues, who have some projects, they know

836 G/51/WFOE/JS(18:13).

837 G/40/JV/SHA(59:11). Note that access rights might be handled even more severe in this employee's enterprise due to the type of ownership as JV.

> who has access. I don't understand that, as it does not really fit to the otherwise open handling of information. Within the company as well the communication of information is somewhat pretty canalized at some points. [...] Hence, there are things, which I haven't yet understood, meaning, why is dealing with information handled so differently sometimes?]

The German project manager perceived access rights as largely untransparent and was perplexed about the channeling of information within the enterprise on the one hand and the openness regarding the handling of information on the other. The whole situation was seemingly not compatible with his rationale of the internal sharing of knowledge and the external knowledge protection.

When questioned about drawing the boundaries within concrete knowledge interactions of employees within or outside the FIE, some Chinese interviewees emphasized the importance of one's unique personal goals. From the perspective of German employees this was at least somewhat remarkable. German employees tended to argue from a corporate angle. Accordingly, internal knowledge interactions were channeled to the goals of one's own enterprise. Regarding external knowledge interactions, the enterprise's interests were likewise supposed to be focused on. Chinese employees, however, more thoroughly took into account the personal aims of the counterpart in question (either a colleague of the same or a contact person at another enterprise). They emphasized that the interests of any employee in a certain enterprise were naturally different, which was not worth emphasizing for German employees. Chinese employees instead were much more sensitive in checking whether the – perceived as natural – personal aims were solely of a private nature or coincided with the goals of the counterpart's department and/or enterprise.

Indeed, many Chinese employees perceived personal interests of fellow employees as in conflict with the enterprise's goals. Personal interests did not necessarily mean private interests of the persons involved but the interests of departments or other groups within the enterprise. Since relationships within the enterprise were ubiquitous and enabled an employee to pursue his work (as pointed out in the next sub-chapter), employees often strive for acting in the interest of fellow employees in their own department.

These conflicting interests easily result in frequent barriers (障碍)[838] within communication and knowledge flows. When inquiring for information, some Chinese interviewees described how they received only vague answers and had to probe further for information. Most importantly, the validity of the information received had to be checked first, for example, by asking third parties. In the same manner, employees had to equally assess the situation and the person care-

838 See e.g. C/33/WFOE/JS(45:13), C/38/JV/JL(73:13), C/35/WFOE/JS(50:20).

fully in advance, if they were asked for information. Although this extra effort could be interpreted as a barrier, these barriers were nevertheless taken for granted and well known within and outside an enterprise. Similarily, the manifold interests at stake, which caused these barriers, were perceived as self-evident by the majority of Chinese employees.[839] As a consequence, the assessment of the interests of all parties involved is the implicit point of departure within any knowledge interaction.

If information was to be gathered, all Chinese employees tried to convince their counterpart that their intentions were conducive to the common goal. The counterpart could be convinced by exhibiting one's competencies, personal objectives, situation, background as well as reasons for inquiring. This process usually required several communication phases.[840] Questioned about the process of gathering information and related obstacles, a Chinese interviewee, working at the legal department of a WFOE, eleborated on how he convinced the counterpart that he dealt with knowledge in a way catering toward the FIE's goals:

> 因为据我工作经历，这么像这五年到六年的工作经历，我觉得我的工作障碍这方面还比较少。因为首先我能**说服**对方，我做这个，我要这个信息是**做什么**用的。我有一个明确的目的，不是我个人目的，而是公司目的。所以这块，应该还好。我觉得这可能跟个人的一个工作能力也有关系的。[841]

> [Due to my work experiences, these five or six years of work experiences, I think that my barriers at work in this regard are still quite small. Because at first I am able *convince* the counterpart *for which purpose* I actually ask for this information. I have a clear-cut objective, not a personal objective but the company's objective. Therefore, this should not be such an issue. I think that this is maybe also connected to one's personal working ability.]

By revealing his work experiences and abilities he has gained during the years, the interviewee was usually able to circumvent the barriers within knowledge interactions. Through his competencies he was able to convince the counterpart that exchanging certain information catered toward the FIE's aims and not (entirely) private purposes.

However, it is not the competencies which eventually convince the counterpart. When interviewees elaborated on the situation from the opposite perspective, it became clear that an implicit assessment of the employee requesting knowledge likewise takes place. During this assessment, it is indeed mainly the moral disposition rather than the competencies which is assessed. When describing the process of providing knowledge, interviewees frequently referred to con-

839 See e.g. C/33/WFOE/BJ(21:5), C/35/WFOE/JS(66:19), C/27/WFOE/GD(3:5).
840 See e.g. C/46/JV/JL(67A:3), C/32/WFOE/JS(63:23), C/45/JV/SHA(11:32).
841 C/28/WFOE/JS(14:46) [original emphasis].

cepts such as “innate character” (本质) or “nature” (本性), “inner qualities” (素质), “education” (文化), or “attainment in self-cultivation” (素养).[842] The meaning the interviewees ascribed to these concepts mostly pointed to the environment in which the employee requesting knowledge has grown up, such as in a rural or an urban area, which social strata he belonged to, and the length and quality of education he received. While most interviewees were of the opinion that – expressed in an exemplary manner – “man at birth is fundamentally good in nature” (人之初,性本善)[843], later in life humans are being exposed to very different environments and circumstances which provide them with very different characters and qualities.

The education received serves as the main point of reference for Chinese employees regarding how someone’s character has developed. If someone attended school and university, they assume that he is not only equipped with a basic (theoretical) education but that he has at least the preconditions for a moral disposition. This was emphasized by a Chinese employee working in after-sales at a WFOE:

> 你看有部门有自己的那个，那个，那个资位嘛。那你自己有自己该做的那个事情嘛。那你就不应该去接触人家的东西。[。。。] 如果你从小到大你一定有去 educated 你应该要做什么，不应该做什么。那你就**明白对与错**嘛。哦，是吧。所以是如果你没有这个的话，那这个概念本来就不存在你的，在里边啦，不存在，没有一个概念的话就不觉得有问题。[844]
>
> [You see that you have a department and your own position, right? And you yourself have your things which you should do. So you should not touch upon the things of others. […] If you, from childhood to adulthood, have been taught what you should do and what you should not do, then you *understand right and wrong*, right? Therefore, if you don’t have that kind of thing, this concept does not exist in your head, does not exist. If you don’t know about this concept, then you don’t think it is a problem.]

This quotation shows that it is mostly a basic *consciousness* of morality that is relevant for daily work behavior including knowledge interactions. It is not the basic education or environment *per se* which indicate how someone might deal with valuable knowledge. Even more important is the notion that a certain kind of education creates this consciousness. This also includes an upbringing, protected from the potentially negative influences of a society that is seemingly in disorder and does not foster the development of moral values.[845]

---

842 See e.g. C/36/WFOE/SHA(13:32), C/34/JV/SHA(40:18), C/28/WFOE/SHA(54:19).

843 C/36/WFOE/SHA(13:32). See also C/40/JV/BJ(77:15).

844 C/32/WFOE/GD(42:14,42:1) [emphasis added].

845 See e.g. C/28/WFOE/SHA(54:23), C/36/WFOE/GD(60:6), C/25/WFOE/GD(41:12).

Besides the consciousness, the *willingness* to deal respectfully with the knowledge received was seen as equally important by a significant number of interviewees. This was shown by the quantitatively and qualitatively strong emphasis of "attitude" (态度) within the interviews. The attitude can be judged from the general behavior at work. A positive, right, or correct attitude is assumed when it can be observed that the employee works diligently and conscientiously, being fully devoted to his work.[846] Furthermore, he is seen as an active person if he helps others immediately by providing information.[847] A negative, wrong, or deviating attitude, in contrast, is displayed if an employee does not seem to care about how his work is pursued or if he simply works as he pleases and provides information only reluctantly and slowly.[848] These kinds of work behaviors are deemed illuminating as to how the employee is not only conscious of his personal moral conviction within knowledge interactions, but is potentially willing to pursue them according to moral criteria.

While the ability of dealing with knowledge also plays a role during the assessment, the emphasis was clearly on the moral disposition. Most pointedly, the importance of someone's attitude over abilities was expressed by the Chinese proverb "态度决定一切"[849] [attitude determines everything]. If a skilled person does not have a positive attitude or character, he does not only not make use of his skills for an appropriate usage of knowledge but his skills can even prove devastating if channeled to an inappropriate usage of the knowledge disclosed.[850] Hence, only in the context of someone's moral disposition can abilities, personal knowledge, experiences, and skills unfold in a moral way. This is the reason why such a disposition was seen as the most profound indicator when assessing employees requesting knowledge.

An employee therefore has not only to convince his counterpart that he is a moral person with certain abilities, he also has to show that his interests correspond to his position within the enterprise. Most significantly, withing the context of "selfish departmentalism"[851] (本位主义) the counterpart of another department is to convince that the interests of one's own department are in line with the other department's and the FIE's interests.[852] Due to "selfish departmentalism" employees usually only carefully provide small pieces of knowledge,

846 See e.g. C/27/WFOE/GD(3:75), C/42/WFOE/JS(37:8), C/45/JV/SHA(11:32).
847 See e.g. C/33/WFOE/BJ(21:10), C/36/JV/SHA(43:3), C/34/JV/SHA(40:12,40:16).
848 See e.g. C/27/WFOE/GD(3:62), C/33/WFOE/JS(45:15), C/36/WFOE/GD(60:3).
849 C/33/WFOE/BJ(21:9), C/42/WFOE/JS(37:8).
850 See e.g. C/36/WFOE/SHA(13:32), C/ 46/JV/JL(67A:10), C/32/JV/JL(51:22).
851 C/36/JV/SHA(43:12), C/35/WFOE/SHA(44:5). See also C/28/WFOE/SHA(62:9).
852 See e.g. C/32/WFOE/JS(63:26), C/28/WFOE/SHA(48:23), C/38/JV/JL(73:26).

first taking the interests of their department into account. An engineer at a WFOE reflected on this as follows:

> 那你要就是说交流的话，这个里面可能会要掌握很多很多一些具体小的小的细节，是因为很多人他有一个本位主义，我第一个需要我第一个好的是我这个部门，我就是说并不愿意腾出很多我的精力啊资源啊什么我来帮你做这个些事情。[853]
>
> [In case you have to communicate, there can be many, many small and tiny concrete details to be grasped. This is due to the selfish departmentalism of many people, that is, my needs and my department come first, and so I am not at all willing to use up much of my energy and resources and the like to help you to get your things done.]

In order to overcome this departmentalism, some Chinese interviewees brought up a point which was that self-evident for German employees that it was not worth mentioning. Within a knowledge interaction, an employee may not necessarily view the situation from the other one's point of view, but must be convinced to a point where he "puts oneself in the other position" (站在他的立场) [854]. An employee is far more likely to share his knowledge if he can understand (理解) the counterpart, his position, and his needs, especially when their positions within the FIE are perceived as competing. Frequent communication was regarded as fundamental to raise an employee's willingness to understand various standpoints. Thus, only if employees are convinced to develop an understanding for their colleagues, both parties can actually benefit.

Eventually, this complex convincing and assessing of a the person *per se* as well as his position entails categorizing employees as good (善) and evil (恶) people, right (正确) and wrong (错误) people, as well as adequate (合适) and inadequate (不合适) people.[855] While good, right, or adequate counterparts provide accurate and reliable information or treat the shared information carefully, evil, wrong, or inadequate people are those who are likely to provide inaccurate information, do not support the flow of information or easily disclose information.[856] These categorizations are the result of an orientation within knowledge interactions along multiple criteria. These can often only be exposed through a constant communication process in which abilities are the vehicle to reveal one's morality. Only via this process different personal interests, which form the basis of the need to convince someone of his intentions, can be aligned and make way for knowledge

853 C/35/WFOE/SHA(44:5).
854 C/29/JV/SHA(9:35). See also C/ 46/JV/JL(67A:2), C/38/JV/JL(73:18).
855 See e.g. C/35/WFOE/JS(66:17), C/45/JV/SHA(11:32), C/40/JV/BJ(77:26).
856 See e.g. C/28/WFOE/SHA(48:22), C/45/JV/JL(72:6), C/40/JV/BJ(77:26).

flows, which are in the mutual interest of both parties involved in a knowledge interaction.

In contrast, most German employees did not feel the need to "convince" someone to share valuable knowledge within the FIE. Rather, fellow employees within the same organization were supposed to automatically share knowledge which could be of value for someone else within the organization. Although in reality asking people for information is a part of the daily routine, knowledge ideally is to be delivered automatically when necessary rather than having to be gathered. This notion made it especially difficult for German employees recently moved into the Chinese business environment. This was shown by their emphasis on the need to "nachbohren"[857] [probe] for information. When information was not immediately provided, they felt a certain reluctance on the part of Chinese employees. After several attempts, however, they still received the information. This can be interpreted as being part of the process during which they convince their counterpart that information can be provided without counteracting their own interests.

When being asked for valuable knowledge, German employees usually do not feel the necessity for such a deep assessment of the employee who requests information. They believe that – if anything – the competency should be assessed and do not take into account that the competency bears implications on someone's moral disposition. From the perspective of the sampled German employees, a certain moral disposition is taken for granted. The point of departure is ideally the objective of the enterprise and what members in their specific functions and positions contribute to it.

Chinese employees, in contrast, do not expect knowledge to be delivered automatically by members of the same organization. Instead, employees have to request knowledge within a communication process. There is a strong awareness that employees have to consider the interests of the respective counterpart, including his personal interests and interests related to his position in the FIE. This applies to counterparts within and outside the FIE, but mostly causes conflicts within the FIE where German employees have the expectation of automatic knowledge sharing according to the formal position and without any barriers.

This process of assessing and convincing illuminates why the German senior project manager quoted above in this sub-chapter observed that his Chinese colleagues not necessarily had access to all projects, but were well informed about who has access to which project. What in the eyes of the German employee seems to be an obscure system, with information being unequally distributed

857 See e.g. G/40/JV/SHA(59:27), G/31/JV/SHA(8:29), G/63/WFOE/GD(2:10).

within the enterprise, follows the logic of strongly taking the relevant counterpart into consideration.

After having spent a certain time in the Chinese business context, German employees appeared to pursue a more complex assessment. For instance, a German sales and marketing manager, being nearly three years with the JV as well as in China in general, implicitly used the moral attitude as a basis and provides sensitive information of which the German headquarters would not have approved:

> [...] ich durchaus mal hingehen kann, ihm was erzählen kann oder am Telefon, was ich schriftlich nie machen würde, was ich wohl auch nicht dürfte. Aber ich weiß, er kann mit umgehen.[858]

> [[...] I indeed can just go to him, tell him something or call him, which I would never do in writing, and what I might not be allowed to do. But I know that he can deal with it appropriately].

Implicitly, the German employees also assessed his Chinese colleague with the result that providing sensitive information to him caters to the common goal. Hence, the implicit cultural knowledge of assessing and convincing during a communication process might well be internalized by a significant part of German employees after a while.

8.4 Investigating Relationships and Networks

The assessment of counterparts prior to any knowledge interactions and the need to convince the counterpart to disclose information are strongly connected with the need to investigate the relationship or network involved. Relationships and networks are generally necessary for knowledge interactions and appear to be a significant component of knowledge work for Chinese and German employees alike. Yet the understanding of relationships and networks is a different one, which frequently leads to conflicts.

When talking about relationships in China, the expression *guanxi* is inevitably used. *Guanxi* 关系 is not only the Chinese expression for "relationship" but is loaded with a particular connotation in China, emphazing mutual obligations and trust. The Chinese expression *guanxi* is widely known among (non-Chinese speaking) foreign employees working in China. In order to avoid confusion and assess situations in a more neutral manner, relationships concerning the daily work of Chinese employees are simply referred to as "relationships" in the fol-

858 G/48/JV/SHA(10:7).

lowing. The term *guanxi* is intentionally employed when referring to the special meaning usually ascribed to relationships in China.

The conflict potential of *guanxi* in the eyes of all sampled German employees lies primarily in causing a lack of transparency in knowledge flows. From a German point of view, this lack was caused by knowledge interactions of Chinese employees being persued while strongly mixing business and private issues. By contrast, the German saying "Dienst ist Dienst und Schnaps ist Schnaps"[859] [there is a time and place for everything] pointed to a strict separation between formal working life and informal private life. This was seen as the complete opposite of the Chinese *guanxi* culture where everything seems to be interrelated including knowledge interactions. One example of mixing the formal and informal in China was having dinner with customers or suppliers, as well as having a network of former fellow students in partner or even competing enterprises.[860] Further, it was striking to German employees that relationships seem to have a value *per se* in China rather than being an informal add-on to the formal ways of communication as it is the case in Germany.[861] Hence, for German employees the formal/informal differentiation clearly implies that the use of formal channels is the point of departure for work, whereas the informal – as concerning the private life – is seen as a deviation from formal communication channels.

When probing into interpersonal relationships and networks during the interviews, most Chinese employees vividly emphasized their strong importance for their daily work without hesitation. Some others, in contrast, revealed an ambivalent understanding of relationships in regard to knowledge interactions in the current Chinese business environment. Most strikingly, these expressions of relationship and network were said to have "of course" (当然)[862] a negative meaning, while – at the same time – "of course"[863] are generally used in enterprises by all employees. Not only are these statements contradictory, but both meanings seemed to be self-evident for the interviewees. The negative perception of relationships at first made several interviewees uncomfortable when elaborating on these expressions. Or, they felt the need to at least stigmatize *guanxi* before they started to explain the indispensable meaning of relationships for their current knowledge work.

Those interviewees feeling uncomfortable at first either directly ascribed a negative meaning or at least a negative connotation to *guanxi* and networks,[864] or

859 G/31/JV/SHA(8:16).
860 G/31/JV/SHA(8:16,8:24), G/40/JV/SHA(59:6).
861 See e.g. G/36/JV/SHA(15:34), G/31/JV/SHA(8:16), G/34/JV/JL(53:10).
862 C/40/JV/BJ(77:12).
863 C/35/WFOE/SHA(44:16).
864 See e.g. C/45/JV/SHA(11:18), C/34/JV/JL(69:18), C/36/WFOE/GD(4:43).

more indirectly stated that these cannot be avoided or prevented.[865] The stigma they described is the following: *Guanxi* are being regarded as more important than the content of the work or as an end in itself, being based only on making profit for a certain group, and thus diminishing the efficiency of the enterprise.[866]

In that way *guanxi* were seen as typically unfolding in SOEs. There, *guanxi* were perceived as particularly "complicated" (复杂) as people are "locked in constant strife" (勾心斗角) over different interests. *Guanxi* with the direct superior or other people further up the hierarchy were inevitable, as people can hardly get promoted by their own efforts and without *guanxi*. This provokes pretending that an employee executed a certain piece of work by himself alone, and even not refraining from slandering others in front of the superior for gaining a personal advantage. Navigating through these complicated *guanxi* was found to distract from the actual work.[867] The interviewees elaborating on *guanxi* in SOEs had either been themselves in SOEs before switching to FIEs or learnt about the situation from other people who worked there. As distracting from work or benefitting only a few employees instead of the whole enterprise, the expression *guanxi* eventually implied behavior detrimental to the enterprise's interest.

Against the background of such an understanding, some interviewees made attempts to neutralize the expressions *guanxi* and network. The expressions were seen as being neither positive nor negative *per se*, but a "double-edged sword" (双刃剑)[868], allowing for doing both good and bad things. Therefore, it depended on how they are indeed made use of.[869] Most explicitly, the contradiction was dissolved by differentiating into "healthy" (健康) and "unhealthy" (不健康) relationships and networks.[870] With categorizing the above meaning as "unhealthy" relationships and the rest as "healthy" relationships, the expressions could be used not only in a more neutral way, but a positive function could also be ascribed to relationships and networks within the employees' daily knowledge interactions, which was not detrimental to the FIE's interest.

After having critically discussed *guanxi*, these interviewees elaborated on the importance of relationships just like all other interviewees who did so right away. Throughout all the interviews there was a common consensus that (healthy) relationships can make communication and work more efficient. Efficient means, for instance, that information can be received quickly without hesitation, fellow employees are more willing to help, and barriers due to conflicts of inter-

865 See e.g. C/28/WFOE/SHA(48:6), C/33/WFOE/BJ(21:10), C/46/JV/JL(67:15).
866 See e.g. C/36/WFOE/BJ(20:16), C/32/WFOE/JS(63:27), C/34/JV/JL(69:12).
867 See. e.g. C/25/WFOE/GD(1:24), C/36/WFOE/SHA(13:14), C/33/WFOE/JS(45:13).
868 C/33/WFOE/BJ(21:10).
869 See e.g. C/45/JV/SHA(11:18), C/35/WFOE/JS(66:17), C/42/JV/JL(71:11).
870 C/46/JV/JL(67:15), C/33/WFOE/BJ(21:10).

ests occur to a lesser extent. Accordingly, results can be received with much less effort.[871] While unhealthy relationships were socially not acceptable among the sampled employees, cultivating healthy relationships, in contrast, was perfectly acceptable.

Being aware of the above mentioned stigma inherent in *guanxi*, some interviewees favored to ascribe a supplementary function to relationships. Metaphorically expressed as tool, lubricant, or catalyst,[872] they preferred to explicitly rank relationships lower in importance than their work. Relationships were said to play a role but not the decisive role. Not too much energy should be put into building relationships, the work should still be finished first.[873]

Yet at the same time, relationships were even being viewed as essential for survival.[874] Strikingly, this was indicated by this same interviewee who used the metaphor of the catalyst.[875] These explicit contradictions within the interviews and even within the same part of an interview – like saying that relationships are necessary for survival while ranking them lower than work – are illuminating the whole complex situation concerning relationships and knowledge interactions.

Indeed, what implicitly comes to light within all interviews is that in the employees' current working environment *everything* depends somehow on the relationships involved. In fact, in daily practice, building up and dealing with relationships *is* the employee's work. *During* collaboration and communication with others, relationships with any counterparts, internally and externally, are continuously processed. Communication only happens within a relationship which is established and cultivated by communicating the relevant knowledge *concerning work*. Thus, it is not about whether or not *guanxi* exist *per se*, but about the very requirement to *deal with any relationship in an adequate way* within knowledge interactions. In this sense, the pragmatic function as a catalyst to achieve more efficiency – if dealt with in an adequate way – fits into the picture as well, yet should not be interpreted in a way that relationships are only a supplement that could artificially be separated from their work.

Against this ambiguous background of both the negative meaning of *guanxi(wang)* on the one hand and the indispensability of relationships on the other, the differentiation into healthy and unhealthy relationships implicitly provides a basic orientation for assessing whether or not a relationship or network in a FIE is utilized in the *interest* of the FIE. Only if utilized in the interest of the FIE (as opposed to the interests of the relationship or network itself), relation-

871 See e.g. C/28/WFOE/SHA(48:29), C/40/JV/JL(68:15), C/30/JV/SHA(46:11).
872 See e.g. C/30/JV/SHA(46:19), C/34/JV/SHA(40:18), C/32/WFOE/JS(63:27).
873 See e.g. C/36/WFOE/GD(4:36), C/38/JV/JL(73:13), C/34/JV/SHA(40:18).
874 C/24/WFOE/SHA(61A:36), C/32/WFOE/JS(63:22).
875 C/32/WFOE/JS(63:27).

ships and networks are seen as fruitful within knowledge interactions, that is, valuable knowledge can smoothly be accessed from or shared within these relationships or networks. Hence, any relationship or network is implicitly investigated within daily work.

As (healthy) relationships are ubiquitous within knowledge work, the need for a further differentiation arises in daily practice. Relationships are also differentiated according to their quality into "good relationships" (好的关系) and "bad relationships" (不好的关系). As stated above, (healthy) relationships *can* lead to communicating and a more efficient working environment. Yet just due to the fact that a (healthy) relationship exists, it is not necessarily an efficient one regarding knowledge interactions. As a Chinese project manager at a JV put it:

> 你不能说你知道对方关系了，人家就会乐意给你提供信息，你还要搞好人际关系。[876]
>
> [You cannot say that if you have a relationship with someone, that someone is happy to provide you with information. You still have to do a good job with interpersonal relationships.]

Fellow employees are only willing to provide information, if the relationship is dealt with in a good way. This implies that when an employee does *not* cultivate relationships at the workplace in a proper way, relationships can easily be impaired (搞坏)[877], and networks can quickly be destroyed (破坏)[878] by employees. This employee most likely faces barriers in communication within knowledge interactions.

Barriers could mean that a counterpart deliberately delays the provision of information or provides incomplete information, making things difficult for a fellow employee. A deteriorating relationship is likely to influence other relationships at the workplace as well, as described by a Chinese IT department manager at a WFOE, who came very close to personally experiencing the following szenario:

> 这个人际关系肯定要处理好，如果你，如果大家都说你不好了，你这个人就**不愿意跟你来说话了**，不愿意跟你做一些什么事情上的一些什么交割了，那你这个人也就算了，你这个人在这个地方肯定待不下了。[879]
>
> [You definitely have to properly deal with these interpersonal relationships, if you, if everyone says you are not good, then people are really *not willing to talk to you*, are

876 C/34/SHA/JV(40:12).
877 C/36/WFOE/SHA(13:14).
878 C/40/JV/BJ(77:12).
879 C/36/WFOE/SHA(13:14) [emphasis added].

> not willing to process a transaction with you, and then you can say good-bye to that, there is no way that you can stay at this place.]

For this IT department manager there has been no alternative but to actively cultivate good and efficient relationships at work which he finally managed. Against this background, striving for communication and work to be "smooth" (顺利)[880] attains a new quality. Not only should work be as smooth as possible but the harm arising from bad and inefficient relationships" should be anticipated and avoided. If the employee is not able to communicate knowledge and information due to bad relationships, he is under great pressure pursuing his work, ultimately having no other choice but to leave the enterprise immediately.[881]

Considering the high employee turnover rate, this is especially significant. Since the insufficient cultivation of relationships means that employees do not receive any information, employees find themselves easily in the situation of not being *able* to pursue their work any longer. Pursuing effective knowledge work is thus inextricably linked to the *quality* of relationships and to the permanent evaluation of relationships, distinguishing between effective ones or the ones detrimental to accessing and sharing knowledge and information.

For providing further orientation within knowledge interactions, (good) relationships were more sharply differentiated into "working relationships" (工作关系) and "private relationships" (私人关系). What was categorized as a "private relationship" was seen as helpful for accessing valuable knowledge which would not be possible to access through a "working relationship". In an exemplary case, a Chinese sales assistant working for a WFOE was pressed for the immediate delivery of electronic spare parts by one of the key customers. To save time, she sidestepped the contact person – who was originally supposed to deliver the information whether the goods are available – by directly asking the employee working in the warehouse. If a "relatively good private relationship" existed, there would be a high probability that the stocker was willing to provide the requested information quickly and actively and seriously payed attention to which kind of information was really helpful in this situation. In case of a less sophisticated private relationship, information might still be provided, yet not in the necessary time frame and perhaps even of lesser quality. The sales assistant, therefore, had to build up this information channel in the form of a private relationship in advance.[882]

Not only does the delivery-speed and the quality of information decisively increase due to private relationships, but receiving certain information at all is

880 See e.g. C/42/JV/JL(71:11), C/35/WFOE/JS(50:20), C/27/WFOE/GD(3:51).
881 C/33/WFOE/SHA(49:25).
882 C/28/WFOE/SHA(48:6).

only possible through the use of private relationships. This is illustrated by using the example of a Chinese purchasing manager at a WFOE who not only regarded private relationships as facilitating her work, but as necessary for receiving information about the supplier which she would not be able to gather elsewhere. With information on the production capacity and the financial situation of the supplier, the employee seeked to minimize the risk of a sudden stop of delivery of spare parts which would be detrimental to the production schedule of her FIE. This was seen as a risk particularly in China where the situation of a supplier can quickly change. As employees of the supplier itself did not go into detail about the financial situation, she approached "friends" in the sector for helping her to access this urgent information. Friends in this case were preferably employees at a competing enterprise of the supplier. The purchasing manager believed since the enterprises are competitors, they might probably have a more in-depth knowledge of each other.[883] Such a transfer of an enterprise's sensitive information – which are yet important for the own enterprise – can only be pursued via a private relationship since a contact person without the background of the relationship would see no reason to provide that information. The purchasing manager put it in a nutshell with the Chinese proverb "多一个朋友多一条路"[884] [the more friends, the more ways], every private relationship could present an additional information channel.

With good private relationships Chinese employees can potentially also receive valuable, sensitive information about the future development plans of a customer, which could provide a salient advantage over the competitor. In an exemplary case, a Chinese product manager at a JV explained that with the help of a private relationship he received information on the future development direction of a customer from his contact person at the customer's enterprise. This information helped to build a perfect prototype for the customer. Thus, he did not only profit from the head start but was also able to meet the customer's needs in every respect. If the customer is satisfied with their solution, the product manager's enterprise will most probably receive the order.[885] Private relationships, hence, are a means of getting closer to a particular person and increasing the speed and quality of receiving even sensitive information.

Yet the examples also show that having a private relationship *per se* is not sufficient for succeeding in receiving (sensitive) information at all or quicker and of better quality. Only because of the fact that someone is a "friend", the employee is not necessarily able to access information from that person, nor does it mean that the employee is more willing to disclose information to him. However,

883 C/25/WFOE/GD(5:17,5:32).
884 C/25/WFOE/GD(5:17).
885 C/29/JV/SHA(9:20).

such a relationship is increasing the likelihood of receiving the information. Cultivating good private relationships is thus not seen as panacea for being able to access valuable knowledge, but can remarkably increase the probability. A constant cultivation and investigation of one's relationships and networks thus remains necessary.

Some Chinese interviewees elaborated on the situation from the other angle – being the one who discloses information within a private relationship. They all thoroughly took their own needs, requirements, and goals into account before disclosing information. Before disclosing information to friends or a former fellow student at another enterprise, for instance, Chinese employees consider the requirements of the other person and check whether these requirements are similar to their own. They still have to consider the own needs before disclosing information. When further examining the different agendas involved, it becomes apparent that most employees' objectives reflect those of their FIE. The rationale behind this principle is the conviction that only if one's own enterprise is doing well, people are able to satisfy their own demands.[886] Even with a common background, such as having attended the same university, the success of the own FIE is rather in one's own interest than the success of the counterpart's enterprise.

Implicitly, a certain distance is kept within private relationships. This shows that in the Chinese business environment "private relationships" provide the opportunity of receiving information, but only as long as these are not detrimental to one's own interests. The own interests are – as being employed by the FIE and being also dependent on the performance of the FIE – more often than not in line with the interests of the FIE.

Chinese employees also intentionally kept a greater distance within relationships. In the above example with the necessity of receiving information about suppliers for minimizing the risk on the market, the Chinese purchasing manager also referred to the necessity of keeping a certain distance to other market players. Working in the purchasing department she found herself positioned in a sensitive place in which a certain distance is particularly necessary. While accessing information about supplier was inevitable, a certain distance to the suppliers themselves was carefully kept in order to avoid the impairment of the enterprise's interests.[887]

In other cases as well, the relationship to suppliers was intentionally limited to a fairly superficial level while helping each other out as good as possible. Yet the relationship did not go any deeper, which means it was still in the scope of authority of the FIE and catered to its interests. Being still in the scope of author-

886 C/40/JV/BJ(77:26), C/25/WFOE/GD(1:26), C/36/WFOE/GD(60:24).

887 C/25/WFOE/GD(5:32).

ity means not to answer morally controversial questions of the counterpart and to minimize private communication.[888]

In all these cases the relationship were seen as too close. The interviewees kept a distance and intentionally employed what is referred to as "work relationship" with the relevant counterpart. The notion of a "work relationship" therefore implies much more than the fact that people have to work with each other. It implicitly counterbalances the private relationship by intentionally keeping a distance in communication. With the private relationships as a necessary point of departure for effective knowledge interactions, Chinese employees *then* intentionally employ working relationships to put the proximity to employees – especially from other enterprises – in perspective. This balance of proximity and distance has to be intuitively approached and to be constantly readjusted.

German employees usually neither fully realize nor fully embrace relationships in this differentiated sense. For most of them, the mere existence of such relationships is the very point of concern. Their point of departure is the formal relationship at work.

Yet this is not to say that some informal interactions are not accepted among German employees. The following cases show how the boundary of what is acceptable is usually set: People are seen as behaving adequately if using formal communication channels. An invitation for a dinner, however, might still be followed in order to do business in a more personal way. Implicitly, it was indicated that dinners were already deemed inappropriate, but were still acceptable for doing business in a more personal way. This was, for instance, compared to American customers who appear to focus on business in a very impersonal way.[889] Ideally, interviewees *unintentionally* established relationships and managed only those relationships which were established by chance instead of treating them as valuable *per se*. It was seen as acceptable to passively engage in some informal relations like following a dinner invitation and to make use of relationships by chance. Hence, for most German employees whether or not people have relationships was the issue under consideration, while not sharply differentiating between the interests, quality, or degree of proximity of the existing relationships.

German employees' discursive point of departure carries strong ethical weight. Relationships were morally acceptable if people only passively use them in some specific cases. Approaching them in an active way was deemed opportunistic, cold, and calculating.[890] This moral rationale often implicitly came to

888 See e.g. C/35/WFOE/JS(66:17), C/34/JV/SHA(40:12), C/25/WFOE/GD(5:32).
889 G/48/JV/SHA(10:5).
890 G/48/JV/SHA(10:5).

light in the interviews with expressions such as "tun wir halt nicht"[891] [we just don't do it]. The moral boundary between the formal and the informal allows for drawing on a person in addition to formal channels, whereas resorting to somebody just for receiving information is deemed unethical.

Yet many interviews implicitly revealed that despite this moral point of departure relationships and networks unfold an increasing importance for German employees as soon as they are in the Chinese business context. Obviously, after just having arrived (especially in large FIEs), there is a necessity of building relationships with – ironically – *German* colleagues within the headquarters in Germany. Employed at the Chinese subsidiary, they relied on the provision of technical and other knowledge from the headquarters. Knowing the relevant contact persons personally was regarded as a huge advantage or even "necessary for survival"[892] for receiving knowledge. Especially in times of strict production schedules personal relationships with colleagues in the headquarters pay off for receiving information at all.[893]

Sooner or later German employees also realized the need to actively build up relationships with their Chinese colleagues or partners to get involved in knowledge interactions at all. In an extreme case at a large JV, German employees struggled to access what is termed "information networks" or "information circles". The fact that a German product manager at this JV did not refer to networks *per se* but to "information networks" is revealing in regard to his experiences with the circulation of information largely within information networks, especially during his first year with the JV. If German employees were not willing to build up relationships and earn the trust of the Chinese employees, they turned out to be ineffective for both the JV and the German headquarters. According to this interviewee, German employees often make the mistake to rely on formal hierarchies – or even on their German nationality – expecting to be "automatically" considered within knowledge interactions. As a result, they are quickly deprived of information to an extent that the interviewee refers to as "information bullying at work"[894]. In another case a German sales and marketing manager has worked more than two years at another JV at the time of the interview and has already build up some relationships and has become partly integrated into Chinese networks. Nevertheless, he still often felt like an "outsider", when noticing that his Chinese subordinates – in contrast to himself – are always

891 G/49/JV/SHA(12:43).
892 G/36/JV/SHA(15:25).
893 See e.g. G/31/JV/SHA(8:24), G/41/JV/JL(52:7), G/36/JV/SHA(15:25).
894 G/33/JV/JL(19:15,19:16). See also G/34/JV/JL(53:6).

very well informed.[895] As a matter of fact, German employees are easily and quickly isolated from knowledge flows at the workplace.

Eventually, some German employees managed to access information networks. Here, the earning of trust of Chinese employees was a basic condition. Most significantly, a leap of faith occurred when information flows were handled in an open manner. On the one hand, sharing knowledge in advance was seen as conducive. Especially in JVs where interests of two different enterprises are involved, German employees earned the trust of their Chinese colleagues by making their conversations with other German colleagues (or at least a large extent) transparent to the Chinese employees (for instance, via the loudspeaker function on the phone). On the other hand, earning the trust of Chinese employees likewise meant to handle their information in a confidential manner. In the eyes of German employees, Chinese employees may feel disadvantaged when information is transferred. As a consequence, some German employees made explicit to whom else or to which department the information (of the German side of the joint venture) is about to be transferred and discussed this with Chinese colleagues in advance rather than doing it straight away. This went so far that information was not transferred as long as the Chinese colleagues had not agreed. This mostly applied to JVs where both partner enterprises were large in size, as many departments in each of the enterprises with different interests were involved in knowledge flows. In turn, Chinese employees provided German colleagues even with sensitive information about the Chinese side of the joint venture which they were not supposed to receive.[896] Accordingly, if German employees *first* actively share their knowledge in a transparent manner, they are rather able to receive information of their subordinates as well as to access information networks at the workplace.

Regardless of how German employees managed to access information networks, the depth of Chinese networks was regarded to be unique. Even when having spent several years at a FIE and being integrated into relationships and networks to an extent seen as fruitful for daily work, German employees seemed to be never completely integrated. They still were not able to receive all information the Chinese employees –"being masters in building and maintaining networks"[897] – manage to access. In accordance with their Chinese employees, German employees perceived special communication skills and experiences as necessary for delving deeply into the networks.

German employees also perceived enterprises in China as closely intertwined with the market. Especially relations with customers and suppliers were

895 G/48/JV/SHA(10:40).

896 See e.g. G/33/JV/JL(19:1), G/49/JV/SHA(12:35), G/34/JV/JL(53:2).

897 G/49/JV/SHA(12:35). See also G/40/JV/BJ(39:2), H/40/WFOE/SHA(17:10).

perceived as much closer in China than in Germany, the US, Japan, or even in the whole world.[898] Customers and competitors, due to relationship and network ties, could be less clearly differentiated from each other in China. FIEs even refrained from suing competitors in China as these are also friends of their own customers, with whom a close relationship is maintained.[899] In such a dense social fabric, knowledge flows are much more fine-grained. This makes German employees aware of Chinese employees having gained valuable communication skills and being indispensable intermediaries for FIEs.

If relationships were recognized as valuable and were actually used by German employees depended to a certain extent on how long they had been working in China's foreign-invested manufacturing sector. For instance, a German purchasing manager at a JV who thought of *guanxi* as (only) going to dinner, has worked one year in China at the time of the interview, a comparatively short period of time which in this case could be an explanation for his superficial understanding of relationships. Strikingly, at the end of the interview when asked about his afterthoughts, he again related back to the topic of relationships, reflecting on the fact that the importance of relationships has just become clearer to him.[900] In contrast, a German sales department manager who has worked for about six years at a JV was able to internalize the implicit cultures of dealing with relationships as information channels in a differentiated way. In retrospect, he has adapted to the Chinese environment after having stayed for two years with the JV.[901] Often even the period of three years of working in China, which applies to most of the sampled German employees, was seen as a very short time for earning the trust of the employees and becoming integrated into networks. While the internalization of the implicit cultural knowledge of relationships was achieved at very different points in time, the probability of integration into networks is usually raised when staying longer in China.

In any event, after working for a certain time in China, relationships were normatively evaluated in a positive way by German employees. While still perceiving the social fabric as a barrier especially for receiving knowledge, they explicitly or implicitly stated that relationships played a fundamental role for their daily work. Some even reckoned that a stronger focus on relationships and contact persons would be important in Germany as well. In fact, relationships and the focus on the person were seen as equally important in Europe, but dealing with relationships in an adequate way usually is either not directly admitted

898 See e.g. G/40/JV/SHA(59:22), G/48/JV/SHA(10:5), H/40/WFOE/SHA(17:10).
899 G/48/JV/SHA(10:32).
900 G/31/JV/SHA(8:16). See also G/41/JV/JL(52:4).
901 G/49/JV/SHA(12:13).

or not *consciously* pursued.[902] As these were the information channels of importance, a German marketing and sales manager at a JV deemed the disregard of the importance of relationships as irrational: "Wir denken immer, wir sind so rational und sind es dann doch nicht"[903] [We usually think that we are so rational, but in fact we are not].

Apparently, the importance of relationships and networks became clear to these interviewees in a way that is free of moral constraints. In their eyes, due to the rapid development of the Chinese market, innovations have to be implemented much quicker which can only be done by having an effective network in place. Networks were seen as only as effective as the relationships involved. Otherwise, networks would be "artificial", when network members only check whether information is available or not. Yet having "good" relationships and networks, employees could almost be sure to have the exact and reliable information available within a certain time.[904] Hence, the investigation of relationships and their differentiation into good and bad relationships over time became relevant for some German employees as well.

Not only German employees had to get used to the differentiation of relationship and the need of constant investigation, also for new workforce entrants this rationale was not self-evident. This clearly came to light by interviewees referring to "entering society" (进入社会)[905], an expression used for university graduates joining their first employer who have to realize and handle the complex social situation at the workplace. The expression "entering society" connoted that one has to leave the protected space of family, school, and university for the society with its complicated social fabric. Just having graduated from university and suddenly being exposed to this social fabric, the focus was on developing knowledge, experiences, and professional skills, while awareness about the actual importance of relationships did hardly exist. Only during the adaptation phase in the working environment it became clear to the employee that the establishment and management of social relationships within the social fabric was indispensable for pursuing his work and that he needed adequate communication skills to be able to access society at all. Experiencing conflicts of interest and communication barriers mostly during the adaptation phase and later on, having one's own network of people was seen over time as an important, yet normal phenomenon for accessing knowledge "in society".

To summarize, relationships are permanently investigated by Chinese employees in regard to interests involved, their quality, as well as the degree of

902 See e.g. G/49/JV/SHA(12:43), G/36/JV/SHA(15:21), G/44/JV/BJ(38:4).
903 G/48/JV/SHA(10:5).
904 G/49/JV/SHA(12:35). See also G/36/JV/SHA(15:34).
905 C/33/WFOE/JS(45:27). See also C/30/JV/SHA(46:19), C/40/JV/BJ(77:17).

proximity. This differentiation takes place by employees mostly making use of their tacit knowing, as often being unable to clearly articulate how they indeed know about the interests, the quality, and the necessary proximity of a relationship. This is to a certain extent internalized by German employees who first only evaluate relationships along the lines of the formal/informal dichotomy. This thorough investigation and differentiation not only serves to draw the boundaries within knowledge interactions but transforms the conventional meaning of *guanxi* in the context of knowledge work in the foreign-invested manufacturing sector in China.

8.5 Preventing the FIE's Competitive Disadvantage

FIEs recruit Chinese employees first and foremost to access the Chinese market. Acting as intermediaries for the FIE, Chinese employees are naturally intertwined with the external environment during knowledge interactions. Yet this is precisely the area where conflicts are most severe in China's FIEs.

Conflicts between Chinese and German employees arise due to valuable information being perceived as flowing without any restrictions in the eyes of German employees. Statements such as "hier [in China] wird sich beliebig oft ausgetauscht"[906] [here [in China] exchange is pursued at random], "die Chinesen, die sprechen alle miteinander"[907] [the Chinese, they all talk to each other], "in China gibt es keine Geheimnisse"[908] [there are no secrets in China], "keine Geheimhaltungsdenke"[909] [no mindset of keeping secrecy], in China it is "tendenziell transparenter"[910] [more transparent by trend], "ist hier alles viel zu offen"[911] [everything is way to open here] and "völlige Offenheit"[912] [total openness] were all too frequently mentioned by German employees.

A German senior project manager at a JV was perplexed how sensitive information of a competitor was self-evidently used by his Chinese employees:

> Ja, wenn wir Projekte anbieten, dann machen wir das natürlich schon unter genauer Berücksichtigung dessen, was unsere Wettbewerber tun. Unser Verkäufer steht dann hier an der Tafel und schreibt auf, […] der und der Preis, die und die Entwicklungskosten. Und das ist erstaunlich hier, weil das in Deutschland kaum einer weiß […].

906 G/40/JV/SHA(59:10).
907 G/63/WFOE/GD(2:7).
908 G/50/JV/SHA(58:1).
909 G/40/JV/SHA(59:10).
910 G/50/WFOE/JS(78:3).
911 G/35/WFOE/JS(82:1).
912 G/40/JV/SHA(59:10).

> Diese ganzen Geschichten werden hier tatsächlich abgewogen aufgrund des Wissens, was man hat, und was man eigentlich nicht haben sollte.[913]
>
> [Yeah, when we offer a project, we do that of course with thorough consideration of what our competitors are doing. Our sales person stands here at the blackboard, writing down […] this and that price, this and that development costs. And this is astonishing here, since in Germany hardly anyone knows this […]. This whole thing is indeed weighted here against the background of the knowledge which one possesses, and which one actually should not have.]

Not only compared to Germany but also on a global level, this situation of uncontrolled information flows was said to be specific to China. The competitive advantage was thus perceived as being particularly threatened in China.

Yet there is a rationale behind these knowledge and information flows which comes to light by scrutinizing the Chinese perspective. While legal and moral criteria do provide an orientation for how to draw the boundary around the FIE's property, Chinese employees primarily orient themselves along the implicit rule of *preventing* a competitive *dis*advantage for the FIE.

Information, which is considered valuable by Chinese employees, does not start with secret information but with mundane insights. The sales techniques the customer accepts are such a valuable piece of information. In case the customer prefers business meetings in a rather "serious" (认真) way, meetings were held in the office, while being pursued at dinner in case he preferred meetings to be rather "lively" (热闹).[914] Any information on the current mood of customers was also regarded as conducive for the business.[915] These kinds of subtle information are not secret *per se* and can with little effort be known by any enterprise. Yet precisely as others can potentially access the information, this can easily become a disadvantage. Information being rather insensitive from the angle of sustaining an enterprise's competitive advantage unfolds its value when it comes to preventing a competitive disadvantage.

Strikingly, when exchanging knowledge with market players in the Chinese business environment also most subtle and vague pieces of market information were deemed very valuable by Chinese employees. Especially surrounding the cooperation with customers "any tiny hints or traces" (蛛丝马迹)[916] during personal meetings are strongly paid attention to. Engineers, product or marketing managers often accompany the sales employee to the customer in order to receive more direct and clear first-hand information or to access additional infor-

913 C/40/JV/SHA(59:10).
914 C/25/WFOE/GD(41:21).
915 C/45/JV/SHA(11:30).
916 C/45/JV/SHA(11:33). See also C/35/WFOE/SHA(44:5).

mation by chance from their different perspectives.[917] Not having these additional tiny hints can also lead to being disadvanted over other market players who also are able to use this method to grasp tiny details.

Regarding a more sensitive exchange of information, several exemplary cases show that legal and moral criteria play an additional role. In an exemplary case, the Chinese head of finance and controlling at a JV regularly arranges dinners with competitors. During the interview, the employee expressed in numerous ways that she regards meeting with the competitors as morally controversial behavior. This can, for instance, be seen from the use of the word "even" (甚至) when referring to the fact that "even" with the competitor knowledge is exchanged. Further, the interviewee felt the need to emphasize that no core knowledge of the enterprise is exchanged, but only circumstances all competitors equally face are discussed, such as how to cope with the tax office – seen as a grey area especially in China – or how to calculate the daily allowance for employees' business trips. She additionally pointed out that this is no illegal behavior.[918] The head of finance and controlling, hence, was clearly aware that she operates in a morally controversial way by disclosing internal information to someone to whom protection efforts are usually directed to and whose interests are diametrically opposed to the interests of one's own enterprise, and employs moral and legal criteria as orientation during information exchange. Yet preventing a competitive disadvantage for her enterprise still was her pivotal rationale to avoid a significant information disadvantage caused by not attending the dinners.

In another case, a Chinese engineer at a JV with many years of work experience expressed his desire to pay a visit to a competing enterprise (albeit within the same Chinese corporate group) in order to learn about quality control techniques. He suggested that some experiences might be useful for his JV and vice versa for employees of the other enterprise. Since every system had its strengths and weaknesses, pursuing mutual exchange and complementing experiences might be useful for both.

At the same time, the Chinese engineer was clearly aware that this was a critical endeavor. This was among others expressed by his attempt to emphasize that although knowledge is exchanged, "figures" should clearly rest with the respective enterprise. It was thus not astonishing for the engineer that the German parent enterprise appears to be strictly against such kind of exchange, whereas in China, in contrast, the preconditions for such an exchange "even" (甚至) exist. Chinese (and some foreign) enterprises with no German parent enterprise behind are, according to the interviewee, able to mutually exchange infor-

917 See e.g. C/28/WFOE/SHA(62:12), C/25/WFOE/SHA(65B:3), C/29/JV/SHA(9:24).
918 C/45/WFOE/BJ(76:21,76:22,76:25).

mation and experiences on quality analysis. Yet as this is the usual practice in China ("here you can actually find it out" (在这儿你实际可以了解)), the engineer was concerned that his German FIE – as not pursuing information exchange as detailed as other enterprises – could incur a competitive disadvantage on the market which could have easily been alleviated.[919]

Using concrete secret information of the customer also appears to be relevant to prevent a competitive disadvantage. A Chinese sales department manager evaluated a customer's secret information as being important for his own JV, but still would not intentionally ask for it:

> 就从我们本身来说，我们不会，呃，呃，**故意**去到对方的那些，呃，人员去，让他们讲一些**不应该讲的事情**，呃，我们可能也只是关心一下他一些，比较，不是很保密的那些信息啦，或者是一些常务，常务的一些信息啦。[笑]当然，如果他讲了，讲了的话，我们可能会提醒他，是善意地提醒他。以后这种东西，可能，**还是**要，**还是要注意下**。这样。因为我们，因为**我们不想让竞争对手抓住我们的把柄**。他也可能，以后会永远地攻击我们。[920]
>
> [... we would not, uhm, uhm, *deliberately* go to some, uhm, employees of our counterpart [the customer] to let him tell us some things you should not tell, uhm, maybe we just care for some of his, comparatively not very protected information, or some information on everyday, everyday business. [laughs] Of course, if he told us, we maybe would warn him in a benevolent way. Later this kind of things maybe *still* have to, *still have to be paid attention to.* That way. Because we, because *we do not want to let the competitor take a hold on us*. They later also might forever attack us.]

This sales manager would not actively ask for secret information and probably also warn the customer if he too carelessly discloses information. This shows that there is an implicit moral barrier in place which (potentially) prevents such behavior. Eventually, however, he would use the all of the information the customer reveals even if these are rather secret ones. The Chinese sales manager permanently feared an attack of the competitor who is most probably informed to a similar extent, and the secret information could prove useful in preventing the competitive disadvantage in advance.

The rationale of preventing a competitive disadvantage may take an even stronger priority than moral scruples. More sensitive information about the customer was also accessed by some interviewees. A Chinese product manager at a JV, for instance, actively gathered information on future development plans and prices of a customer, their changes in branding, design, or internal changes in order to prepare as early as possible the next order for the customer.[921] That the

919 C/40/JV/JL(68:19).
920 C/45/JV/SHA(11:27).
921 C/29/JV/SHA(9:24,9:21).

employee was nevertheless aware of acting morally questionable is among others indicated by using "even" (甚至). What made the employee still cross the boundary was the concern of being disadvantaged:

> 如果能找到客户的反馈的话，那我们就能［。。。］尽早地满足客户的需求。如果你行动晚的话，可能到最后你就落后了。[922]

> [If we are able to receive feedback from a customer, then we would be able to [...] satisfy his demand as soon as possible. If you acted late, you would get behind eventually.]

All this core information about the customer enabled the JV to supply the customer according to his demands as soon as possible before the competitor does so and thus preventing the enterprises's competitive disadvantage.

Sensitive information about a competitor is accessed as well. A Chinese product manager explicitly saw prices of the main competitor as belonging to his secret core information. Yet she still obtained these prices as otherwise this would disadvantage her WFOE:

> 这个价格的话可能就是你只能通过客户获得。那他也一样，他**肯定**也要通过这方面，他们也会知道我们的，这样的。[笑]理论上讲是秘密，但实际上是大家都，都，都，都可以知道这样。［。。。］应该来说还是**比较正常**的，因为他们获得，我也获得你这样子，对。[923]

> [For instance, this price can maybe only be obtained via the customer. But he [the competitor] also, he *definitely* will also use this channel; he will also know about ours. [laughs] Theoretically speaking this is a secret, but in fact everyone can get to know it this way. […] It should be said that this actually is *pretty normal*, as they obtain [my information], I likewise obtain yours, yes.]

This conscious deviation from legal regulations and the justification of this deviation confirm that legal and moral criteria both function as broad orientation in practice. During the interview, the product manager was clearly aware that deviating from legal criteria was a sensitive matter as can be seen from the fact that she lowered her voice when elaborating on this topic. At the same time, she clarified that the mutual accessing of core information about competitors had already become a usual business practice. Adhering to this business practice is necessary since one's own enterprise would otherwise be disadvantaged on the market.

While there is a focus on accessing information, the protection of knowledge is yet not neglected. Information is protected according to its degree

922 C/29/JV/SHA(9:21).
923 C/33/WFOE/JS(49:23) [emphasis added].

of secrecy. Concrete (具体)[924] or core (核心)[925] information was seen as having a high degree of secrecy (非常机密)[926]. This kind of information included registered intellectual property as well as technical, product-related know-how, such as elementary drawings of a product.[927] What was also often regarded as core knowledge was management information such as prices, and especially the discount for a certain customer.[928] The sampled Chinese employees were all aware of the fact that this information was required to be secret, and was to be respected as the intellectual property of the FIE and to be kept internally.[929] It was explicitly seen as illegal behavior to leak this kind of an enterprise's knowledge to external sources, for instance, by posting it on the internet and making it publicly available.[930]

From these kinds of information most Chinese employees distinguished information with a lower degree of secrecy which can be disclosed externally. What can or even should be disclosed is information being referred to as superficial,[931] not detailed,[932] or concerns the "scope" (外延类)[933] of information rather than its content *per se*. For instance, certain parts of drawings should be disclosed to suppliers in order to communicate technical problems.[934] Or, external access should be provided for rather superficial product-related technical information, such as videos and presentations, for acquiring new customers.[935] The concreteness of the information and the related degree of secrecy are thus basic criteria for orientation when drawing the boundaries.

Yet the examples put forward by some interviewees show that the decision what to protect and what to disclose is far from straightforward in daily practice. A large number of Chinese interviewees pointed out that rules on how an employee should behave toward business partners in knowledge interactions were scarcely made explicit in enterprise regulations or handbooks. When deciding what is to be disclosed to others within or outside the FIE, existing rules and regulations were considered far too vague for deciding what in fact could be

924 C/34/JV/JL(69:17).
925 See e.g. C/45/JV/SHA(11:25), C/29/JV/JL(70:5), C/38/JV/JL(73:15).
926 C/33/WFOE/JS(49:27). See also C/45/JV/SHA(11:27), C/40/JV/BJ(77:26).
927 See e.g. C/34/JV/JL(69:17), C/36/WFOE/BJ(20:18), C/36/JV/SHA(43:20).
928 See e.g. C/32/WFOE/GD(42:4), C/28/WFOE/SHA(48:15), C/25/WFOE/GD(41:17).
929 See e.g. C/40/JV/JL(68:19), C/27/WFOE/GD(3:17), C/45/JV/SHA(11:26).
930 See e.g. C/36/WFOE/GD(4:1), C/25/WFOE/GD(41:17), C/30/JV/SHA(46:24).
931 C/32/WFOE/GD(42:4).
932 C/36/JV/SHA(43:20).
933 C/35/WFOE/JS(66:24) (An expression from philosophical logique meaning scope of a word instead its concrete content (内涵)).
934 C/36/WFOE/GD(4:37,4:1).
935 C/33/WFOE/JS(49:27).

disclosed. Training in the beginning was hardly seen as helpful for orientation within the actual decision process in practice.[936]

The decision which valuable knowledge should be disclosed "largely depends on the employee's own initiative" (主要还是靠自觉)[937]. It is strongly subjective and formed by tacit knowledge developed intuitively in practice. During the interviews, some Chinese employees tried to describe this important boundary but proved not to be able to exactly describe how they indeed have come to draw it. This lack of explicit orientation became most apparent in an interview in the course of which the interviewee even asked the interviewers for advice on how to set the boundaries when disclosing information.[938]

Most pointedly, this intuitive boundary drawing is shown by a Chinese sales manager at a JV who accompanied new employees' first encounters with employees from other departments or from customers. He informed them in advance about his anticipation that sensitive information are about to be required soon and gave hints on how the new employee should draw the boundary of what should be exclusively known by the department or the JV at this point in time.[939] Apparently, instead of giving abstract explicit advice, the sales manager only was able to indicate how to set the boundary in regard to concrete situations, making use of his implicit knowledge. He was still not able to instruct other employees how to do it in a more abstract way. Apart from a practical situation where he himself was personally situated in, he himself only tacitly could know how to set the boundaries around the JV's or his department's internal valuable knowledge. Over time, this implicit and tacit knowledge was developed, providing guidelines of how to behave in practical situations, while not being able to explicitly tell what exactly triggered his decisions.

Tacit knowing thus helps in deciding which knowledge is sensitive and thus needs to be protected within the FIE or can be exchanged with the environment. Especially in the frequently occurring situation, when a customer requests information almost falling into the scope of secrets, these abilities are particular necessary for not answering all questions and only carefully disclosing what is regarded as adequate.[940]

These vague points of reference can also result in inner struggles of employees. When a customer requested a product certificate from the product manager quoted above, the product manager was aware of the fact that this secret document might end up with the competitor as soon as it is provided to the cus-

936 See e.g. C/42/JV/JL(71:11), C/33/WFOE/JS(49:23), C/27/WFOE/GD(3:70).
937 C/45/JV/SHA(11:33). See also C/33/WFOE/JS(49:23), C/43/WFOE/BJ(76:22).
938 C/29/JV/SHA(9:27).
939 C/45/JV/SHA(11:33).
940 See e.g. C/29/JV/SHA(9:25), C/40/JV/BJ(77:26), C/45/JV/SHA(11:33).

tomer and that the competitor via this channel might come to know the details and specificities of the product. She usually hesitates to forward the certificate and discusses the matter with the research and development department. She mentioned how making this decision bothers her:

> 确实我们有的时候会。。。心里边会比较挣扎，这个东西要不要给他。[941]
>
> [Indeed we sometimes go through … an inner struggle, whether we should give this to him or not.]

During this process of inner struggle, she often thought about the option of providing the customer only with a summary of the certificate in order to minimize the information which might end up with the competitor. Eventually, however, in case customers still request such information, she usually rather opts for providing it to him in order to prove that the enterprise really possesses this certificate.[942]

Disclosing these technical details to a customer is necessary to gain a (mostly timely) advantage over the competitor. When the customer receives the information quickly, he rather opts for placing an order with the enterprise which is able to deliver earlier. How much is disclosed depends on personal judgment of the employee, who decides when these boundaries regarding core information have to be crossed. This personal judgment is implicitly informed by legal and moral criteria. The rationale of preventing a competitive disadvantage, however, weighs more, which leads to the transcending of legal and moral boundaries in certain situations.

While drawing the boundaries of secret information in daily work, what affected the daily work of the sampled Chinese employees was not only the protection of knowledge, but the pressing need of actively and quickly exchanging more or less secret information. A Chinese purchasing manager at a WFOE saw too little communication as a threat to an enterprise's operations in the Chinese market:

> 如果不交流的话，你只你只是在你这一个好像井底之蛙，你只会看到你自己的东西，看不到外面的东西。[943]
>
> [If you do not communicate, you are only, you are only like a frog at the bottom of the well, you can only see your own things, and cannot see the things outside.]

It was also clearly expressed within the interviews that the need to communicate with the environment should not be hindered by too much focusing too much on

941 C/33/WFOE/JS(49:29).
942 C/33/WFOE/JS(49:27,49:29). See also C/45/WFOE/BJ(76:22).
943 C/25/WFOE/GD(5:46).

the protection of knowledge,[944] as most pointedly expressed by a Chinese sales manager at a JV:

> 你一个企业的发展不可能是一个孤立的环境中，你过分的保护你可能就是有有些封闭，有些，有些自闭这样的。[。。。]保护的话你觉得肯定会有一些，有一些自大有些封闭这样。[945]
>
> [Your enterprise cannot develop in an isolated environment, if you exaggerate protection, you are kind of shielding yourself off, kind of autistic. [...] Protection would definitely be a bit like arrogantly shielding yourself off.]

In the eyes of this interviewee, protection was indeed necessary, but should not be exaggerated. Too much protection very likely gives other market players a negative impression of the enterprise, which might make cooperation more difficult. If an enterprise does not actively communicate with the environment, it seemingly automatically ends up as being isolated from the market. This was seen as detrimental to the enterprise's objectives and thus the connection with the environment was deemed more important than protection.

Being isolated from the environment was seen as a threat especially to FIEs. As the FIE's competitive advantage more often than not arises from high quality products, Chinese employees have to reveal a few more technical details on the product in order to explain this special quality. This is most important when convincing Chinese customers that the quality is worth paying a higher price for. Even when employees were not exactly sure about the FIE's attitude toward disclosing technical specificities of a product (as there are no explicit rules available), they still disclosed some technical information in order to convince the customer that a higher investment into this product will turn out to be more profitable than purchasing a competitor's product. A close connection to the customer was regarded necessary in order to be able to convince the customer about the high quality. Having enough Chinese personnel available to constantly be in touch with all the customers was regarded as adequate especially for FIEs in the competitive manufacturing sector.[946] A constant connection to the environment can thus compensate for the FIE's potential competitive disadvantage of higher prices.

This connection to the environment including the accessing of even core information of other enterprises and disclosing some more or less secret knowledge of the own FIE is not only a concern of employees in outward-oriented departments. As can be seen from some examples above, Chinese employees of

944 See e.g. C/27/WFOE/SHA(61B:45), C/34/JV/JL(69:18), C/40/JV/JL(68:15).
945 C/45/JV/SHA(11:25).
946 See e.g. C/28/WFOE/SHA(54:35), C/40/JV/BJ(77:19), C/33/WFOE/JS(49:7).

different positions and departments engage in communication with the environment. Naturally, employees working in outward-oriented departments, like sales or purchasing, are more concerned by this. Still, employees of inward-oriented departments, like production or design, also often emphasized the exchange of knowledge with the environment.[947] Hence, preventing a competitive disadvantage is an implicit cultural understanding more or less concerning all non-manual Chinese employees of different departments.

The predominance of this rationale gains even more weight against the background that Chinese employees were clearly aware that they cross legal boundaries. Although they might not be informed on the concrete content of laws and regulations (neither is the average German employee), they intuitively anticipated a legal boundary. Nevertheless, the rationale of avoiding a disadvantage still prevailed.

This implicit point of reference contradicts the distinct focus of maintaining a competitive advantage employed by most German employees. Through the protection of the valuable knowledge (in part provided by the German headquarters), they seek to sustain the competitive edge not only of the FIE but of the German enterprise as a whole. This focus is apparently related to their positioning as expatriates. As expatriates they are more immediately connected to the German headquarters and its competitive advantage, which not least secures their workplace later in Germany again.

With this focus information seems to flow freely. This active exchange clearly crosses a moral boundary. This becomes evident by statements such as "das macht man einfach nicht"[948] [you just don't do that], or that people should not obtain concrete information at the expense of other market players, nor include them in the process of calculating development costs. In Germany, customers would not even try to ask for such internal information. Vice versa, for suppliers in Germany disclosing internal information to their customers about their competitors is considered an "absolute taboo"[949]. The moral boundary also prevents that when drinking a beer with a friend who works for an enterprise in the same sector, employees would still not engage in an intimate talk about secret information of one's enterprise.[950]

Yet moral constraints only prevent German employees from *actively* gathering market information. If information was received *by chance*, German employees likewise made use of them. Information is, for instance, received when occasionally sitting next to the competitor at the dinner table during an event within

947 See e.g. C/36/WFOE/GD(4:37), C/25/WFOE/SHA(65B:3), C/29/JV/SHA(9:24).
948 G/40/JV/SHA(59:10).
949 G/40/JV/SHA(59:10)
950 G/49/JV/SHA(12:35), G/40/JV/SHA(59:10).

the business sector. German employees drew a rather clear boundary when talking to competitors, that is, prices and current projects were not to be talked about. Nevertheless, certain management information, such as business models and payments methods, was openly discussed. These kinds of information were seen as valuable for both sides.[951]

In contrast to the Chinese view, however, it is an *additional* value not to be expected or even taken for granted. Chinese employees intentionally arrange dinners with competitors on a regular basis in order to gain this mutual value. Although both Chinese and German employees regard the exchange with competitors as a controversial issue, the boundaries are set differently. Chinese employees are more aware of the usefulness and even necessity of mutual exchange of more or less concrete management information, the neglect of which could cause a competitive disadvantage.

Such additional information includes also details about other market players. If German employees got their hands on information like price lists of other enterprises in the sector, they did not refrain from using this information.[952] A German managing director at a WFOE yet emphasized that this behavior is limited to passively taking notice of such information:

> Klar, wenn er mir das da auf den Tisch legt, würde ich mit Sicherheit nicht wegschauen, aber ich würde niemals, niemals das aktiv verfolgen, solche Informationen zu bekommen, entgeltlich oder unentgeltlich, also da ist bei mir eine moralische Grenze gesetzt.[953]
>
> [Of course, when he puts it on the table in front of me, I would surely not look the other way, but I would never ever actively seek to get such information, free of charge or not, in this case I am restricted by a moral boundary.]

This exemplary quotation expressed the inner resistance to *not actively* gather these kinds of information, while already having gained a feeling for the actual necessity of using such information in the competitive Chinese environment. This active, intentional, and regular exchange with the environment irritated German employees mainly at the beginning of their stay at a FIE. After working for a certain period of time in China, German employees became more inclined to make use of such market information, and not to only focus on maintaining the FIE's competitive advantage.

Conflicts also likely arise with the German headquarters whose employees even stronger focus on protecting knowledge. Although a FIE is in fact a subsid-

951 G/47/JV/SHA(10:11).

952 See e.g. G/34/WFOE/GD(7:30), G/49/JV/SHA(12:60), and exploratory interview G/64/JV/JS(81:1).

953 G/45/WFOE/BJ(83:1).

iary of its German headquarters, it was perceived as an external autonomous entity. All knowledge disclosed to the FIE was regarded as being automatically publicly available in China and therefore should only be transferred under certain conditions, such as licenses or access regulations. Strict legal and regulatory barriers toward the own subsidiary were employed to guarantee the utmost protection of their German enterprise's competitive advantage.

As a consequence, the majority of the sampled Chinese employees struggled with the strong hesitation to forward information on the part of the German headquarters while they had to meet their customer's needs adequately. The reluctance of the German headquarters often unfolded in a long approval or feedback process, which slowed down the information transfer. The Chinese employees accused their German colleagues at the headquarters of not knowing the Chinese market well enough. They argued that if the German colleagues knew the Chinese market better, they would know that time is of the essence concerning the handling of information. German employees at the headquarters seemed totally ignorant about the fact that customers might quickly and suddenly place an order and have to be individually cared for. They also did not seem to understand that if a customer does receive timely information on the feasibility of his order, he might opt for placing the order with the competitor. Similarly, one had to closely collaborate with suppliers, who also needed sufficient information and training in order to realize a certain order, sometimes this even includef training of staff regarding production processes. Chinese employees assumed that it was precisely the quickly changing Chinese market and the plans and requests of the Chinese employees changing accordingly that led to insufficient trust and the persistent impression of being less reliable.[954] Not being sufficiently informed by the headquarters or having to wait too long for approval of which part of knowledge can be disclosed to customers and suppliers, Chinese employees have significant difficulties in preventing a competitive disadvantage for the FIE.

Not only Chinese employees often found cooperation from the German headquarters insufficient, the missing support was also felt by some German employees within the FIE. A German engineer who stayed for four years at his JV said at the time of the interview:

> Wir Deutsche, [JV]-Deutsche [Mutterhäusler] sind denn sowieso immer noch in soner Mittelrolle, weil … ja, … wir sitzen zwischen den Stühlen, ne. Zum einen geht mir das so von der [Muttergesellschaft], das, das, das, dieses arrogante … Getue auf den Senkel und werde, muss dann die [JV], fange automatisch an, die [JV] zu schüt-

954 See e.g. C/29/JV/SHA(9:11,9:14,9:16,9:23,9:33), C/33/WFOE/JS(49:3), C/28/WFOE/SHA(48:14,48:35).

> zen. Und auf der anderen Seite machen wir so viel Blödsinn, dass ich immer nur sagen kann: Meine Güte Leute! Und muss dann wieder auch hier raufhauen.[955]
>
> [We Germans, [JV]-German [headquarterers] are anyway still in a an intermediary role, because ... yah, ... we are caught in the middle, right. On the one hand, I feel this on the part of the [headquarters], the, the, the, this arrogant attitude gets on my nerves and I will, must the [JV] then, I automatically start to defend the [JV]. And on the other hand, we get up to so much nonsense here that there is nothing left to say but: guys, oh my gosh! And then I have to put my foot down again.]

Germans fould themselves in an intermediary role while stronger identifying with the FIE the longer they stay with the enterprise. Having been with the JV for six years at the time of the interview, a German manager of a sales department complained about the scarce and slow transfer of knowledge:

> Ich ärgere mich ja *ständig täglich mehrmals* über meine deutschen Kollegen, warum jetzt das wieder nicht rüber kommt und das kommt nicht rüber und das kommt nicht.[956]
>
> [I *constantly* get angry *several times on a daily basis* about my German colleagues again not transferring this and then not transferred that and not providing this.]

The issue of the headquarters' reluctance concerning knowledge transfer comes up on a daily basis, and – if the FIE is a JV – always connotes the question which JV side one supports. The quoted German employee, as being employed by the JV, explained that he had no choice but to look at things from the vantage point of the JV when knowledge interactions were concerned, and only then considered the headquarters' motives. Prioritizing the JV's perspective involved the adoption of a focus on the market where the need of the customer ranks highest. Only this commitment to localization was eventually seen as benefitting the headquarters. Hence, the focus of this German employee has switched from maintaining a competitive advantage – which is still relevant, yet not the priority within his knowledge interactions anymore – to preventing a competitive disadvantage on the Chinese market.

Conflicts with Chinese employees arise as German employees are not engaged with the environment in the same way as Chinese employees are. Independent of their positions, they are rather focused on serving the German headquarters. Coming to China and having stereotypes of Chinese employees easily leaking knowledge in mind, the actions of Chinese employees are interpreted against them when seeing them randomly connecting with the environment. German employees often enough just do not understand the rationale behind

955 G/44/JV/BJ(38:2).

956 G/49/JV/SHA(12:41).

what they perceive as randomly leaking information to the business environment or hoarding all kinds of different information.

After a certain time at the FIE, however, they started seeing the value of being close to the market and focusing on gathering subtle, tiny, mundane, sensitive, and secret market information in view of a potential competitive disadvantage. Some even started to help their Chinese employees to convince the colleagues at the headquarters of providing information. German employees then themselves take an intermediary position, yet not between the FIE and the Chinese business environment, but between Chinese employees and the colleagues in Germany.

8.6 Acknowledging the FIE as a Stable Space

When drawing the boundaries of knowledge, German and Chinese employees alike distinguish between the inside of the FIE (*neibu* 内部) and the outside (*waibu* 外部).[957] At first glance, *neibu* and *waibu* differentiate between the physical interior of a FIE where valuable knowledge is to be shared among employees and the external business environment outside of the premises against which knowledge is to be protected. Yet this rather matches the understanding of German employees. What *neibu* and *waibu* indeed means for Chinese employees' knowledge interactions is not that straightforward.

Being implicitly embedded in the answers of the interviewees, the *neibu* of a FIE neither refers to the inside of the physical premises nor the employed persons. Rather, *neibu* implies the assumption of a space which provides stability for its members as opposed to the unstable *waibu*. This space does not exist *a priori*. The FIE providing explicit rules and regulations, stipulating processes and providing an organization chart with all formal members as well as slogans of a corporate culture is regarded significant for a preliminary orientation for knowledge interactions. As rules and the like can be amended immediately, they are regarded as rather superficial and unstable in the long term and are not sufficient for erecting boundaries between the internal and the external.[958] What is regarded as stable boundaries or as a clear *neibu/waibu* distinction of the FIE does not exist *per se*, but has to be manifested over time by the FIE and to be eventually acknowledged by the employees.

First of all, in the eyes of most Chinese employees a FIE's boundaries were manifested by implementing a sense of stability through the moral attitude of the FIE toward its employees. Chinese interviewees described a FIE holding an

957 See e.g. C/28/WFOE/SHA(48:15), C/35/WFOE/JS(50:26), C/25/WFOE/SHA(65B:11).

958 See e.g. C/34/JV/JL(69:13), C/28/WFOE/SHA(62:24), C/36/WFOE/SHA(13:18).

attitude of acting in the employee's interest and not only in self-interest as "genuine" (真正)[959] or "regular" (正规)[960] enterprise. Such a "genuine" or "regular" FIE develops from the angle of showing concern as well as caring for the employees and treating the employees in a human way (人性化)[961] instead of sacrificing employees' interests for short-term profits. What is regarded as a "regular" FIE should *first* think of its employees and *then* of its own interests, as pointedly expressed by a Chinese sales operator at a WFOE:

> 只有从关爱员工这个角度去发展的话，它才可以循序渐进地就是再回到公司它的本身。[962]
>
> [Only if [the enterprise] develops from the angle of showing concern and caring for the employee, only then the company can step by step come back again to itself.]

Yet more important for manifesting enterprise boundaries is not the FIE's attitude toward every single employee. Rather, it is evaluated whether the FIE successfully creates what can be referred to as a community, collective or – most suitably – as space, which is located on a higher level than the aggregate of individuals or the aggregate of all employer-employee relationships within the FIE. This was made explicit by the large majority of the sampled Chinese interviewees by emphasizing of what is expressed in terms of atmosphere (氛围), culture (文化), or spirit (精神) within the direct working environment.[963] The interviewees frequently mentioned these topics at the beginning of the interview which was not triggered by a related question. Compared to other items of organizational capital, they often thought of the corporate culture as the basic foundation for anything else. They were not able to eleborate on it much further, but feel or become aware of the existence of a culture, atmosphere, or spirit already when entering the FIE.[964]

Such an atmosphere or culture was seen as significant for active cooperation within the FIE including knowledge sharing behavior and overcoming communication barriers.[965] The atmosphere or culture could both be conducive and detrimental to knowledge sharing. This influence was pointed out by many interviewees, such as this Chinese manager of quality control at a JV:

959 C/40/JV/JL(68:10).
960 C/28/WFOE/SHA(54:13). See also C/27/WFOE/SHA(61B:56).
961 See e.g. C/41/WFOE/JS(37:6), C/33/WFOE/JS(49:10), C/43/WFOE/BJ(76:5).
962 C/28/WFOE/SHA(54:13).
963 See e.g. C/32/JV/JL(51:8), C/33/WFOE/JS(45:24), C/27/WFOE/GD(3:33).
964 See e.g. C/28/WFOE/SHA(54:19), C/36/WFOE/SHA(13:18,13:23), C/36/JV/SHA(43:5).
965 See also chapter 8.4.

> 我愿意来传授给，把我的知识，积累这么多年的知识来传授给徒弟，那么这种是**靠他对他自己公司这种热爱一种文化**，那我也可以不传授给你，或者把我的百分之五十我传授，我自己再留百分之五十，也，也可以，那不是不不可以，但是呢要想把这个我的经验很无私地这个传授给这个徒弟的话，我觉得更多的是靠一种，这种文化。[966]
>
> [If I am willing to pass [my knowledge] on to you, to pass on my knowledge to the apprentice which I gathered over so many years, *depends on this kind of adoration of this culture of the own company*. I can also pass it on to you or pass on 50% of mine and still keep 50% for myself, that is also possible, it not impossible though. However, if you think of very altruistically passing on this – my – experiences to this apprentice, I find that rather depends on a kind of, of this kind of culture.]

Chinese employees were strongly aware of their latitude in deciding what is passed on to colleagues. It is not only a question of sharing anything at all, but also the extent of sharing has to be considered by the employee. Especially the reference to the "many years" during which knowledge and experiences where accumulated shows that the efforts behind this gathering were still considered before passing the knowledge on to someone else.[967] For *nevertheless* deciding to share it to at least a certain extent, the kind of atmosphere or culture of the FIE was explicitly regarded as the decisive criterion. If the FIE succeeded in establishing such an atmosphere, it would be worth to share knowledge to its full extent.

The atmosphere can generate a certain knowledge sharing behavior which spreads quickly among the employees. The behavior of others is strongly in the focus of fellow employees, as expressed by a Chinese employee working in a WFOE's legal department: "If you do it this way, you are right, I also do it this way" (你是这么做的，你是对的，我也要这么做)[968]. It influences the extent to which an employee contributes his own knowledge and, conversely, is able to receive knowledge from fellow employees. A Chinese sales assistant even saw that atmosphere as able to initiate a virtuous circle of knowledge sharing in this WFOE:

> 这个环境决定了[要不要]把自己的知识贡献出来，这样会得到，从别人身上得到更多的知识，那么这个**环境决定**了这个良性的循环。[969]
>
> [This [working] environment determines if one contributes one's knowledge, this way one will receive more, from other people receive more knowledge, hence, *the environment determines* this virtuous circle.]

966 C/38/JV/JL(73:10) [emphasis added].
967 See also chapter 8.2.
968 C/36/WFOE/SHA(13:18). See also C/28/WFOE/SHA(54:20).
969 C/24/WFOE/SHA(61A:33) [emphasis added].

One the other hand, an environment with an atmosphere detrimental to knowledge sharing also quickly spreads from one employee to another. In an exemplary case, a competent employee who pursued his work successfully was not inclined to share knowledge. Even though he trained other employees, they in turn turned out to behave like him and did not share their knowledge with fellow employees either. As for this position it was essential to regularly share knowledge, the employee was relocated to a position where he could still unfold his competency, but where knowledge sharing was less essential.[970]

Apparently, not only the mere organizing of (regular) sharing of knowledge is sufficient. Although the employee shared his knowledge with some employees he also conveyed a culture detrimental to knowledge sharing. Hence, an atmosphere of knowledge sharing – with the sharer as a role model – has to be implemented from top to bottom, not to be stopped after sharing knowledge once. Through the spreading of this kind of atmosphere a vicious circle can be prevented and a virtuous one initiated by employees internalizing that atmosphere.

This quick spreading of an atmosphere conducive or detrimental to knowledge sharing leads to employees feeling either *able* or *unable* to share knowledge. The FIE was regarded to be responsible for creating an environment and thus enables or disables them to share knowledge. Two Chinese employees – a manager in a mechanical design department at a WFOE and one purchasing manager at a JV – both similarly referred to knowledge sharing between departments as follows:

> 这个部门之间的话，**能够协作**。它属于那种公司的这种，我们叫氛围吧。就这种环境是吧。[971]
>
> [Then these departments *are able to collaborate*. It belongs to this, we call it atmosphere, right. This is this kind of environment, right?]
>
> 公司在这方面的确也是给我们创造这么一个氛围，让员工**能够**，就是比较，比较积极的一种心态，比较合作这种氛围，比较有爱的这种氛围之间成长。[972]
>
> [The company in this regard indeed creates such an atmosphere for us, which *enables* the employees [having], that is, a quite, a quite active mentality, a quite cooperative atmosphere, to develop together within a quite benevolent atmosphere.]

Only against the background of a certain corporate culture or atmosphere, there is the *chance* that other employees also act in a way considering others and the

970 C/32/JV/JL(51:22).
971 C/36/WFOE/GD(4:19) [emphasis added]. See also C/29/JV/SHA(9:29) and C/36/WFOE/SHA (13:18).
972 C/36/JV/SHA(43:3) [emphasis added]. See also C/24/WFOE/SHA(61A:7) and C/34/JV/JL (69:6).

FIE, which, in turn, enables everyone to act in a moral way by altruistically sharing knowledge. If such an atmosphere does not exist, it is generally assumed that other employees do not behave in their most active, cooperative, or altruistic manner.

The most important function of this culture or atmosphere, which enables employees to cooperate, is the establishing of a sense of cohesiveness (凝聚力) [973] among the employees. Apparently, people within an enterprise are not seen as bounded together *per se* by the mere formal affiliation to the FIE, but by a sense of cohesiveness. A certain level of cohesiveness creates a space in which cooperation during knowledge interactions becomes possible. An interviewee implicitly referred to such a space by stating that "a certain cohesiveness binds such a bunch of people together *here*" (有一定的凝聚力就是把这样一批人凝聚**在这里**)[974].

Such an atmosphere was expected to be established through a shared belief, thinking or behavior pattern. Similar to a religion which guides the behavior, a relatively fix, clear, and strong shared belief established in an enterprise provides all the employees with a common reference for orientation and makes them feel that fellow employees all go into the same direction, that is, toward the common goal of the FIE.[975] Yet some interviewees strongly pointed out that a passive or abstract slogan being released from the upper management level is neither adequate nor credible as a basis for a shared belief or culture. Rather, every individual superior is expected to live out this active and concrete culture and to continuously remind and stimulate his employees to actively cooperate for the FIE's goals, and thus to create the cohesiveness within the respective team.[976]

Conversely, if the implementation of such a thinking was hardly or not permanently pursued within the enterprise – such as in small Chinese private enterprises (民营企业)[977] – all interviewed employees would less be inclined to share knowledge. If a FIE does not care about the cultural or moral rules that bind people together in the particular space and limits (约束)[978] thoughts detrimental to cooperation, moral knowledge sharing behavior cannot be expected of the employees, who assume that others do not act altruistically either. Only if a FIE succeeds in raising awareness for a common ground over time, employees will gain confidence to trust other employees acting accordingly. Only then they are willing to cooperate.

973 See e.g. C/42/JV/JL(71:24), C/25/WFOE/GD(41:14), C/33/WFOE/JS(49:10).
974 C/33/WFOE/JS(49:10) [emphasis added].
975 See e.g. C/45/JV/JL(72:3), C/46/JV/JL(67A:16), C/33/WFOE/BJ(21:5).
976 See e.g. C/28/WFOE/SHA(54:20,54:22), C/27/WFOE/GD(3:5,3:18), C/40/JV/JL(68:17,68:26).
977 C/35/WFOE/SHA(44:14).
978 C/24/WFOE/SHA(61A:41). See also C/38/JV/JL(73:10,73:29).

By adopting a view of its employees in the sense of a network rather than viewing them as representing different positions as expressed by the organization chart, a FIE can also contribute to establishing a stable space. A FIE can build and strengthen a network by filling free positions with current employees where relationships have proved to be harmonious instead of hiring new employees.[979] This network of people is seen as more stable as it has been built up over a long time and fulfills a "maintenance function" (维持作用)[980] for the FIE. An organization chart, in contrast, cannot depict the many *de facto* vague and not clearly separated responsibilities, and be changed immediately.[981] Within a network, however, people can navigate to find the suitable person for knowledge interactions and even when a few people change their positions and jobs, the stability of the network is still felt by Chinese employees.

Establishing an atmosphere of cohesiveness further includes that the FIE permanently "coordinates relationships" (协调关系)[982] within the network. Even if relationships in detail can only be managed between two persons, the large majority of interviewees deemed the management or superiors as vital in coordinating these relationships. It was proposed that this can be done by, for instance, establishing and coordinating work teams and departments not only according to processes but also according to how the people feel about each other and where knowledge can circulate without barriers.

In an exemplary case, the senior employees or "elders" (元老) at a WFOE were rated problematic by a Chinese IT department manager since they often blocked knowledge flows. His superior was expected to publicly delegate the relevant authority for a certain task or project to the employee:

> 因为每个公司都会有自己的元老在里头，可能会有些事情处理起来会比较困难[。。。]就不是说你没能力而是说你没办法去做。。。就是你[高层]想让他做这件事情的时候，你一定要**预计到**会有这样的问题发生，[。。。]必须要给他相关的权限。[983]

> [As there are senior employees within every company, it is not easy to handle some things […]. It is not to say that you cannot do it because of not having the ability […]. When you [the leaders] want to let him do this thing, you definitely have to *anticipate* that such a problem will be about to happen, […] and you necessarily have to give him the relevant authority.]

979 See e.g. C/41/WFOE/JS(37:16), C/45/JV/SHA(11:34), C/25/WFOE/GD(41:29).
980 C/45/JV/SHA(11:18). See also C/25/WFOE/GD(41:29).
981 See e.g. C/36/WFOE/GD(4:35), C/42/JV/JL(71:11), C/36/JV/SHA(43:12).
982 See e.g. C/34/JV/SHA(40:16), C/34/JV/JL(69:12), C/27/WFOE/GD(3:21).
983 C/36/WFOE/SHA(13:11) [emphasis added]. See also C/40/JV/BJ(77:4) and C/34/JV/SHA(40:16).

In this case, only if barriers are anticipated by the superior, relationships can be coordinated in a way that the employee is able to pursue his knowledge work at all and gains confidence that he will be able to do so in future as well.

This atmosphere or stable space is clearly expected to be formed and initiated by the FIE, yet not imposed on the employees. Rather, an atmosphere which was regarded "as a very *natural* form of rules, which are not imposed" (很**自然**的一种规定一样，不是谁强迫的)[984] upon the employees provides stability. Such an enterprise culture should not only be mentioned once during the training for new entrants, but should continuously be implemented by superiors, and hence, being transferred and tightened from top to bottom. Every employee regardless of his position ideally develops an active consciousness for this atmosphere and profoundly understands and internalizes it.[985] Hence, orientation from above is needed, but only an atmosphere which seemingly emerges in a natural way was regarded as being able to provide a feeling of stability.

The establishing of this atmosphere was seen as a long-term process, lasting several years.[986] Although it is only an "imperceptible influence" (潜移默化)[987], due to the fact that it has grown over a long time, it was considered more stable than systems, processes, or procedures.[988] If the FIE does not initiate changes too quickly and invests time to cultivate a relatively stable and harmonious network of relationships between its employees, the FIE appears trustworthy. To strive for a common goal directed toward the FIE becomes possible. For instance, after having been employed by an enterprise for a longer period of time, an employee was more likely to internalize the notion that an idea should be shared with the FIE:

> 我作为我自己的话我肯定会提出来，提出来然后[。。。]我因为这个企业里面待了相对来说久了，我并不会刻意地说啊这个主意是我的。我应该获得就是说相应的一些概念啊，所以说应该还是最主要看**那个企业里面怎么样子考虑**吧。[989]
>
> [As far as I am concerned, I would definitely put forward [my idea]. After having put [it] forward [...], as I have stayed in this enterprise quite a long time, I would not say that this idea is strictly mine. I should have gained, that is, this kind of understanding, right. Thus, what should still be most important is *how this is thought over within that enterprise*, isn't it.]

984 C/42/JV/JL(71:23) [emphasis added]. See also C/36/WFOE/BJ(20:10) and C/28/WFOE/SHA (54:12).

985 See e.g. C/34/JV/SHA(40:16), C/33/WFOE/JS(45:24), C/34/JV/JL(69:13).

986 See e.g. C/34/JV/JL(69:13), C/36/WFOE/SHA(13:18), C/33/WFOE/JS(45:24).

987 C/36/WFOE/SHA(13:18). See also C/42/JV/JL(71:24).

988 See e.g. C/42/JV/JL(71:4), C/41/WFOE/JS(37:9), C/45/JV/SHA(11:19).

989 C/35/WFOE/SHA(44:14) [emphasis added].

Although the atmosphere is already felt when entering the FIE as a new workforce entrant and provides a certain orientation, it is consensus among the interviewees that only over time the thinking can be internalized and only then the sharing of ideas and knowledge indeed becomes quite natural. When most employees internalized moral rules and behave according to them within their knowledge interactions, the FIE was perceived as a stable space.

Paradoxically, employees perceived this space as stable because of its flexibility. While regulations were commonly regarded as being too inflexible to quickly handle new situations, an open and vivid atmosphere, in which people are generally willing and able to help, was seen as more flexible.[990] This vitality and mutual help was what qualified the space as stable.

When having stabilized the FIE internally, such a stable space at the same time strengthens boundaries to the outside by being in stark contrast to the external competitive business environment:

> 部门之间的斗争非常的激烈，就有的时候感觉不是说在，在市场上去做一些。。。这个打拼，还要呢跟公司内部要去做一些斗争，就感觉比较辛苦一点。[991]
>
> [The fighting between departments is very intense, so that sometimes you feel like … these struggles do not only take place on the, on the market, but you have to start fighting within the enterprise too, that makes you feel quite a bit exhausted.]

Most Chinese employees desired an atmosphere within the FIE which was clearly different from the daily struggles on the competitive market. This involves developing a feeling of stability by being assured that the FIE – and their workplaces – can last on this market. Implicitly, the employee demanded of the enterprise to assure him that the enterprise develops and has a future, also indicating in which direction it develops, and that the employee is needed for this development.[992]

The stable space (*neibu*) clearly distances itself and its employees from the Chinese social environment (*waibu*). It was widely assumed that due to the quick economic development, a strong belief or core values were still not that developed in contemporary Chinese society. A Chinese engineer at a WFOE referred to Chinese society by stating: "Our thinking is still comparatively backward" (我们这种观念还是比较那个落后的)[993]. A new employee had to be limited by values in the enterprise's stable space, which was stable through moral values which make up for the less developed values in society. When entering the

990 See e.g. C/25/WFOE/GD(41:31), C/28/WFOE/SHA(62:24), C/36/JV/SHA(43:12).
991 C/33/WFOE/JS(49:10).
992 See e.g. C/36/WFOE/SHA(13:23), C/45/JV/SHA(11:17), C/45/JV/JL(72:3).
993 C/35/WFOE/SHA(44:14). See also C/35/WFOE/BJ(84:1)

space, the different characters and attitudes of employees with different backgrounds and values are cultivated (培养)[994] by providing a certain atmosphere or culture, which they can grasp (可以抓得住)[995], and that provides guidance. Within society, this space has its own unique form,[996] and thus differentiates itself from society as a whole. Employees preferred such a stable point of reference through which they gain confidence to pursue knowledge interactions in the interest of the FIE and its employees.[997]

Most Chinese employees pointed out that if a FIE encouraged the establishment of a relatively stable, comprehensive and encompassing atmosphere, culture, or spirit, the FIE was more likely to be acknowledged (认同)[998] by its employees. Only in this working environment, employees are able and willing to pursue knowledge interactions by actually orienting themselves along the *neibu/waibu* distinctions. *Neibu* was clearly differentiated from *waibu*, and *waibu* was not only the competitor but society as a whole, which was definitely seen as the opposite of a stable space. If an employee acknowledged the enterprise and identified with it, he would be less likely to behave in an immoral way, such as selling the knowledge he acquired in the FIE,[999] since his aims overlapped with the FIE's objectives. If the FIE can be trusted to initiate and maintain a stable space (*neibu*), employees ultimately develop a "feeling of acknowledgment" (认同感)[1000]. Thus, knowledge sharing cannot only be pursued with softened barriers between employees of the same enterprise, since everyone is a part of this stable space. Even the outward differentiation from other enterprises and competitors is strengthend, which potentially reduces knowledge leaking to the outside to a minimum.

This process of acknowledging the stable space is opposed to the assumption of all German interviewees of fixed enterprise boundaries existing *a priori*. Within the interviews this attitude was shown by German employees only referring to the enterprise's corporate culture when asked about it. Although acknowledging the importance of a corporate culture, they did not emphasize it as much as their Chinese colleagues. A German general manager at a WFOE even believed that a corporate culture can hardly be implemented in enterprises in China:

> Sie können, grundsätzlich bin ich der Meinung, Sie können keine Corporate Culture hier richtig reinsetzen, das macht keinen Sinn. […] das funktioniert hier nicht. Glaub ich nicht. Vielleicht gibt es Unternehmen, die es schaffen. […] Warum wollen Sie

994 See e.g. C/27/WFOE/GD(3:18), C/28/WFOE/JS(54:13), C/36/WFOE/GD(4:15).
995 C/34/JV/JL(69:13).
996 C/35/WFOE/JS(50:22), C/24/WFOE/SHA(61A:41).
997 See e.g. C/28/WFOE/SHA(54:12), C/28/WFOE/SHA(54:12), C/32/JV/JL(51:8).
998 See e.g. C/28/WFOE/SHA(48:25), C/45/JV/JL(72:9), C/34/JV/JL(69:14).
999 C/24/WFOE/SHA(61A:41).
1000 C/36/WFOE/GD(60:9).

denn die Kultur hier ändern, die 5000 Jahre alte, meinen Sie, die können Sie ändern? Ja, die können Sie anpassen, anpassen ja, aber nicht ändern, das war mein Punkt, ändern. Weil viele Unternehmen, und so kamen wir auch, ein bisschen blauäugig und sagen, ja wir machen Corporate Culture hier, ne. Ja, was ist denn das?[1001]

[You can, basically, I am of the opinion that corporate culture cannot truly be inserted here, this makes no sense. […] this doesn't work out here. I don't believe that. Maybe there are enterprises which achieve it. […] Why would you want to change the culture here, this 5000 year old culture, do you think you can change it? Yeah, you can adapt it, adapt it yes, but not change it, that was my point, change it. Since many enterprise, including us, came here a little starry-eyed and say, yes we do corporate culture here, right. Yeah, what is it really?]

This German employee assumed that due to a long persisting Chinese culture an enterprise culture which differs from the Chinese culture was virtually impossible to establish. He referred to his own enterprise which had tried to transfer the corporate culture from the German headquarters, but had failed completely. Apparently, he did not see any alternative and was strongly convinced that foreign enterprises are generally bound to fail in China in terms of corporate culture.

Other German employees also rather pointed to the general cultural environment than referring to the atmosphere of their own enterprise. They often referred to what they perceived as a moral vacuum outside of the enterprise. To emphazise the existence of this supposed moral vacuum, where everyone acted in an egoistic way, several interviewees referred to the traffic situation in China. A German manager of the planning department at a JV very pointedly compares the behavior of his fellow Chinese employees with the road users he bumps into every day:

Chinesen sind Egoisten, absolute Egoisten. Für die zählt nur ihr eigener, persönlicher Vorteil, und dann erst mal lange, lange, lange Zeit gar nichts. […] Das sehn se doch auf der Straße, da nimmt keiner auf den Anderen Rücksicht. Da hält doch nicht mal einer und lässt den Anderen vor. Das ist denen doch völlig egal. Die gucken Sie an und fahren vors Auto und fahren in aller Ruhe da rum und Sie müssen anhalten, das interessiert die gar nicht. Also das sind, die sind sehr egoistisch und überhaupt nicht rücksichtsvoll. Und das merken Sie auch hier [in der Firma] natürlich. Das ist aber, sagen wir mal, das ist halt ne kulturelle Geschichte.[1002]

[Chinese are egoists, absolute egoists. What counts for them is only their own personal advantage, and then nothing for a long time. […] You can see that on the street, where nobody is considerate of others. None of them would even stop and let the other one go first. These people are totally ignorant about this. They look at you and drive in front of your car and then, as if they had all the time in the world, drive

1001 G/51/WFOE/JS(18:16).
1002 G/50/JV/SHA(58:5).

> around and you have to stop. They do not pay attention at all. Um, well, this is, they are very egoistic and not considerate at all. And you notice that here [in the company] as well of course. But this is, let's say, this is just a cultural thing.]

Comparing the problematic knowledge sharing situation within the FIE with the chaotic traffic situation in China, the interviewees clearly ascribed the perceived egoism to Chinese society as a whole. Just like an employee was too egoistic to share his knowledge with others, he would not give way to another car.[1003]

This metaphoric comparison carries the assumption that if moral behavior cannot be observed in society, enterprises employing nationals of this society are likewise exposed to this behavior. The possibility is not (sufficiently) taken into account that moral norms can take hold in enterprises and that the enterprise can provide a stable space to its members with boundaries limiting the influence of the environment. Although the sampled German employees were all positioned at superior or management levels, most of them did not see the need for establishing enterprise boundaries by defining and transferring a distinguished culture or atmosphere wihtin the FIE. After all, the observed behavior in traffic seems to confirm the picture of the selfish Chinese people, and hence, they saw no obvious reason to question their observations.

The Chinese perspective on enterprises was a completely different one. Contrary to their German colleagues, who think of an enterprise as a formal organization, Chinese employees rather see a stable space which has to be created by the enterprise and acknowledged by the employees. Knowledge interactions are pursued while taking the flexible boundaries of this stable FIE space as a reference point. Germans usually do not realize that they themselves being superiors have to initiate and implement such an atmosphere.

Yet some German interviewees, having been in China for several years, realized that a certain atmosphere has to be established by them. A German plant manager, for instance, strongly observed the cooperation within different departments of his WFOE. In some cases he put people with different functions in one department, such as an employee for administration into the financial department. When he observed that an employee did not contribute much to the team and was not "stable", he soon searched for another person for that position in case the relationship with other employees in the department deteriorated. The plant manager was very aware to avoid the growing of anger or other obstacles between two or more employees, since these could spread quickly to other employees of a team or even the whole enterprise.[1004] This German employee has also realized the necessity for actively coordinating relationships within his team

1003 See e.g. G/50/JV/SHA(58:5), G/60/WFOE/SHA(55:4), G/51/WFOE/JS(18:15).
1004 G/34/WFOE/GD(7:38).

in China much earlier than he would have done in Germany and adopted the priority to establish stability within his teams.

But even this German employee, who keenly observed atmospheres, tendencies, struggles, and conflicts among his employees and coordinated relationships accordingly, did not observe the corporate culture and the establishing of a sense of belonging to a sufficient extent, as mentioned by one of his Chinese employees. After all, though the importance of an atmosphere for stabilizing the enterprise is felt by most German employees after a certain time, this appears to be much more important for Chinese employees who usually pay much more attention to it.

9 Discussion

> To build up the same factory with the same machines in the same way worldwide is possible. [...] However, just adding Chinese names into the organization chart won't make it work in China – and it is very hard to describe why not.[1005]

The present chapter endeavors to point out what this British interviewee at a WFOE in China failed to put in words. Among the difficulties involved when building up an enterprise in China, conflicts surrounding valuable knowledge are deemed most critical. Most importantly, knowledge is only scarcely shared within the FIE but unduly disclosed to other market players in the external business environment. German employees hardly find explanations why knowledge is handled in such a controversial way. More often than not it is pinned on an enigmatic "Chinese culture".

This study is about the actual role of culture within knowledge conflicts in China's FIEs. Discussing the findings in an interrelated manner and in view of the conceptual framework allows for carving out the inner logic of knowledge practices informing Chinese employees (9.1). These insights are discussed with regard to a German perspective and traced back to their root causes, illuminating the roots of Sino-German knowledge conflicts (9.2). Emanating from conventional explanatory approaches, it is found that "Chinese culture" also plays a role within the conflicts, yet in a different way than usually assumed (9.3). The insights gained in this discussion pave the way for solutions to the conflicts (9.4).

9.1 The Inner Logic of Knowledge Practices

The first research question of the present study is how Chinese employees draw the boundaries of knowledge in FIEs. The drawing of knowledge boundaries is informed by six practices. These have been identified in the preceding empirical chapter (see also Figure 5).

1005 B/57/WFOE/SHA(16:17).

Figure 5: Practices informing the drawing of knowledge boundaries.

Source: Author's own illustration.

The identified practices inherently contribute to the overall objective of understanding the role of culture within knowledge conflicts in FIEs. First, the fact that practices can even be identified shows that Chinese employees do not draw the boundaries of knowledge in an arbitrary way. Rather, their actions are informed by common criteria beyond individual motives.

Second, these common criteria do not operate detached from the employees, but *indeed* proves relevant for guiding their behavior. The empirical study reveals the criteria and strategies which employees really need as orientation during knowledge interactions. In contrast to the usually ascribed collectivist culture or assertions such as "intellectual property is absolutely counterintuitive to Chinese"[1006], these criteria are not just ascribed to Chinese employees and their observed behavior at work. Instead, these criteria and strategies emerged through an inductive investigation. Chinese employees, for instance, opting for assessing their counterparts has not formed a hypothesis at the outset but appeared to be an important and strongly emphasized component of knowledge interactions, actively having been put forward by the interviewees. The link between the individual and the social could thus be established in the present study.

Third, these common criteria are located on a rather practical and more tacit level rather than existing as clear artifact, such as explicit rules and norms. The implicitness of these criteria was shown by the fact that the interviewees had difficulties in defining them. In daily work, there was no necessity or no incentive to reflect on these criteria. Yet when the employees reflected on the subject during the interviews, they summed it up using phrases such as "this is your core competitiveness"[1007]. The common criteria could also be read between the lines of the interviews, for instance, by pointing out the efforts when accumulating knowledge which implicitly justify the personal use of this knowledge.

Fourth, these criteria cannot be thought of in terms of Hofstede's "collective programming of the mind"[1008]. The flexibility of the criteria of each practice shows that practices do not determine actions in a rigid culture-as-system sense. The empirical data also show that the behavior of the sampled employees does not resemble Geertz' metaphor of animals passively being "suspended in webs"[1009]. Rather, employees actively draw on practices when pursuing knowledge work in a way adequate for a concrete situation. Hence, practices can rather be thought of as a resource, providing employees with manifold criteria allowing for orientation as well as tactfulness and timing within knowledge interactions, such as noticing and interpreting the subtlest hints from a customer and acting according to his current mood.

These insights into the role of culture not only contribute to the main concern of this research endeavor, they also give rise to further questions. Each practice has its own implicit criteria which provide the know-how for judging practical situations and being able to respond in an adequate way. Yet *what* is adequate from the point of view of the employee? When cultivating one's own competitive advantage, what makes one decide to what extent this competitive advantage is adequately limited and how small the own knowledge monopoly indeed can be? Or, what determines the extent to which distances within relationships are adequately kept?

1006 Li Luo 2010: 277. See also Shao Ke 2006.
1007 C/36/JV/SHA(43:19).
1008 Hofstede 1984: 82.
1009 Geertz 2008: 31.

For answering these questions, the spatial dimension of the practices is to be considered. Practices in this study appear in the form of integrated practices. Integrated practices occupy a certain domain of social life. They are integrated in the same spatial nexus, in which the employees are physically situated. If one acknowledges the practices to be integrated in the same spatial nexus, the question is what induces Chinese employees in the same spatial nexus to judge situations in socially coherent and non-arbitrary ways, overcoming the manifold contingencies of social life? What "coordinates" or "aligns" the various practices in a way that they are socially congruent? What makes this particular social world function at least to an extent which leads – despite all contingencies – to social (as opposed to individual) phenomena coming into existence and developing to a niveau that they can be identified and categorized as social phenomena at all?

These questions point to a common background against which the diverse subtle strategies and criteria make sense for the sampled Chinese employees. An even deeper underlying rationale at the roots of the practices ensures that the practices fit in with the actions of all employees acting together in a consensual way. This tacit consensus channels the application of implicit criteria and subtle strategies into a direction which makes sense in practice. Or, in other words, Chinese employees are provided with a lens through which the subtle strategies make practical sense in their social world.

This is reminiscent of Bourdieu's research in the Province of Béarn,[1010] in which the subtle strategies of the parents prevent the family property from being split among all children. What underlies and connects all strategies and determines the extent to which the subtle strategies and criteria inform the parents in each practical situation is the underlying rationale of protecting the family property. Similarly, a tacit common thread appears which connects all the subtle strategies and criteria for judgment applied by Chinese employees. Whereas each implicit strategy was already pointed out in the above analysis of the empirical data, this underlying rationale only emerges when the practices are analyzed in an overarching manner.

Taking the practice of cultivating a limited personal competitive advantage as an example, the question arises to which extent the protection of this competitive advantage is limited by moral standards. The knowledge kept for oneself should just suffice to secure a certain core competitiveness over others, but the remainder should be shared. But why is this limit instituted at all and how is its extent determined? It is argued that the answers can be found in the striking connection with the practice of acknowledging the FIE as a stable space. This practice entails that knowledge sharing depends on a certain culture or atmos-

1010 See chapter 2.3.

phere of stability within the enterprise. Only against this background, there is a *chance* that other employees also act in a considerate way toward others and the FIE. Only the conviction of others sharing the same attitude enables an employee to act in a moral way by altruistically sharing knowledge. If such an atmosphere does not exist, it is generally assumed that other employees do not behave in their most active, cooperative, or altruistic manner. Whether the protection of a personal competitive advantage is limited by moral standards and to which extent thus depends on how the FIE implements this "limit". Only then this limit comes into effect at all. And only then employees have a reason to reconsider these limits instead of strategically keeping their knowledge. Alhough the altruistic ideal of sharing exists as a general idea, it is very likely that nothing is shared if the FIE is perceived as unstable or if it does not implement values to a sufficient extent. Knowledge is only seen as worth to be shared within a stable space as an employee can be relatively sure that fellow employees also act in an altruistic way conducive to the FIE. Although the sharing of 100% of one's knowledge is extremely unlikely, it is the FIE's implementation of an atmosphere of stability which can encourage the employees to share the greater part of their knowledge.

The extent to which the FIE is acknowledged as a stable space also serves as a tacit benchmark for the evaluation of the FIE's efforts. When evaluating the efforts of the FIE, that is, the efforts the FIE puts into the application of the employee's knowledge via the relevant superiors, the employee's ultimate aim is to be able to fully put his abilities to use. Only when these are fully put to use in this particular enterprise, the employee perceives his value as being adequately reflected. Due to the fact that Chinese employees regard their abilities as being best put to use by often pursuing new tasks and being in different positions, the employee strongly depends on various fellow employees sharing their knowledge relevant for this new task or position and thus enabling the employee to pursue his daily work. The superior plays a decisive role in paying attention to the relationships in the department where the employees is transferred to and has to coordinate them in a way that ensures smooth knowledge interactions. That means that the extent to which an employee is able to adapt to new tasks and positions strongly depends on his superior. The employee tacitly assumes that the (future) behavior of the superior as well as of other colleagues is cooperative in line with the extent to which the FIE has implemented a common moral reference providing everyone with a reason to act in a way conducive to the common aim. Only when the FIE was successful in creating a relatively stable space with well manifested boundaries, an employee can be confident to be situated in an environment which allows for using his abilities to the utmost extent. It is thus not only the efforts of the superiors toward the employees which provide the employee with sufficient confidence that abilities are used to the full extent. It is the stability of the FIE's space against which efforts are evaluated in terms of their reliability and sustainability.

When assessing a fellow employee within the FIE in order to find out whether knowledge can be disclosed to him and whether he will act in the interest of both, a careful review of his moral disposition is most decisive. The empirical findings reveal that a background check is pursued including the abilities, competencies, and experiences of the counterpart which serve as a vehicle for estimating his moral disposition. The attitude someone displays at work is seen as the most important indicator regarding the willingness to act in the common interest. The attitude is judged by how one pursues one's work and how one helps out fellow employees with knowledge. It can be argued that the way one pursues his work and the extent to which one helps other employees is contingent on the enterprise's atmosphere. If there is a sense of cohesiveness prevailing in an enterprise where the knowledge interaction takes place, employees are more inclined to mutually help each other by providing knowledge. Through this atmosphere of cohesiveness the assessment of a counterpart leads to a rather positive result. In case the counterpart of a certain knowledge interaction is an employee of another enterprise, his likely behavior is estimated judging from the atmosphere in his respective working environment. Hence, the results of an assessment of one's counterpart depend to a great extent on the immediate work environment he is situated in. The extent to which it forms a stable space eventually determines the extent to which knowledge can be disclosed to the requesting employee.

Not only is the counterpart taken into account but also the relationship with him as well as the networks he is involved in. The findings suggest that cultivating healthy, good, and private relationships with colleagues or business contacts can remarkably increase the probability of accessing valuable knowledge. The failure to cultivate and distinguish relationships, by contrast, can even lead to being unable to pursue one's work. At the same time, investigating a person's relationships and networks can indicate whether someone can be entrusted with certain information. It can be argued that deciding about the nature of relationships mostly happens against the background of the enterprise's atmosphere of stability, either of the own enterprise if the relationship to a colleague is concerned or the contact person's enterprise, respectively. An enterprise is considered as relatively stable, if its superiors usually engage in the coordination of relationship and the stabilization of networks. The more stable an enterprise in this sense, the more likely can a relationship or network be considered a healthy one. Depending on the enterprise's stability, relationships can be cultivated in an efficient way. Also, the enterprise's stability can indicate whether a relationship has the potential to evolve into a private relationship in which information are provided in a timely manner. The investigation of relationships and networks hence very likely yields positive results in terms of healthy, good, and private relationships and networks as long as the enterprise(s) involved is perceived as a stable space.

Similarly, when guided by the market and preventing the FIE's competitive disadvantage, employees face a complex social fabric of particularly close external relationships. The findings reveal that a close connection to the market and close exchange is not considered an advantage over others but rather assure not to be *dis*advantaged. Within these relationships one has to provide more knowledge in advance to employees of other enterprises. Otherwise competitors might use this window of opportunity for the own business. Many subtle pieces of information are seen as important but even what is categorized as secrets – and seen as morally controversial when being disclosed externally – still has to be regularly exchanged with the environment. In the light of this necessarily close connection to the environment and the careful exchange of valuable knowledge, it can be argued that a stable space allows for very distinctly pursuing communication with the outside, gathering the subtlest information and carefully disclosing what is at the boundary or even in breach of the boundaries of what can be disclosed. Only if a stable space strengthens the boundaries of a space, binding together employees and shielding them away from the struggling external environment, these employees have the incentive to protect this stable entity by preventing a competitive advantage by pursuing sensitive knowledge interactions in the most careful way. Eventually, it is the stable space which tacitly provides employees with a reason to pursue knowledge interactions directed toward the interest of what they perceive as a stable enterprise now and in the future.

The practice of acknowledging the FIE as a stable space takes center stage among the knowledge practices. Within each practice of cultivating, assessing, evaluating, investigating, and preventing the stable space provides an unconscious foil against which actions take place. It is argued that the FIE as a stable space tacitly ties together all the practices of the domain (see Figure 6). A FIE's stable space *provides the lens* which determines the extent to which Chinese employees apply all the subtle strategies. Although stability is explicitly stated in the interviews, the significant role the FIE can play via providing a stable space and the relation to the implicit criteria for knowledge interactions remains tacit. This relation between the FIE as a stable space and the remaining practices enables the social world to function.

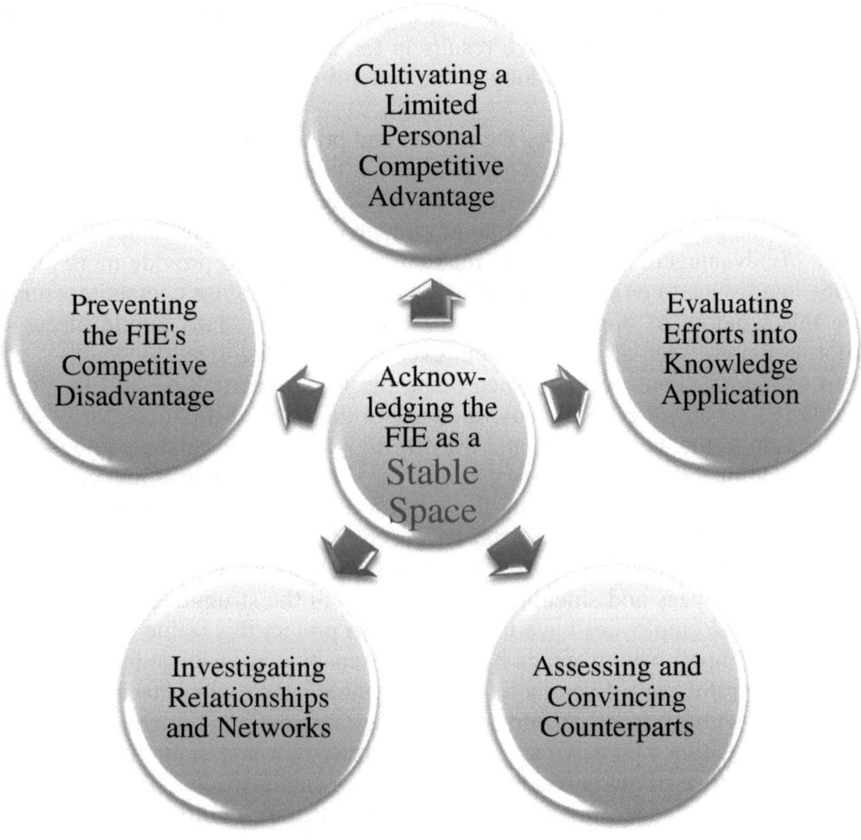

Figure 6: The relation between the practices.

Source: Author's own illustration.

Had the people in the Béarn-study consciously and explicitly stated that the younger children are in fact being exploited in order to protect the family property, the system would not be able to persist any longer. This fact has thus to remain tacit in order to make the social world function. Similarly, as a stable space is something which can hardly be explicitly judged or implemented, employees can only vaguely make it explicit by referring to the enterprise's atmosphere. It can be argued that as soon as stability as an underlying rationale is made explicit, every knowledge interaction would be consciously judged according to the FIE's stability. But this endeavor would be bound to fail as effective stability can only be felt. If employees began to consciously reflect on it, they would not have adequate benchmarks at hand. Not having adequate benchmarks at hand, people would come to the inevitable conclusion that there is no real stability. By *remaining tacit*, this logic inherent in practices leads to the evolving of all the implicit criteria. This tacit logic also directs their application in a certain way. In this study, all Chinese employees unconsciously orient their knowledge-related strategies to *the approaching* of stability.

Furthermore, the data set strikingly reveals that stability is considered to be fragile. When reflecting upon the relevant data it becomes clear that precisely the element of fragility ensures a relative stability for the interviewees. Even when manifested over time, stability is never absolute as it essentially depends on the behavior of people, relationships, and networks rather than on formal explicit structures. Chinese employees in their role as knowledge workers depend on the enterprise for applying their knowledge and at least must rely on a preliminary – or even more pointedly fictional – stability. Only then a relative stability has the chance to develop. Although absolute stability cannot be achieved, it is precisely this flexible stability which provides employees with a feeling of security and enables to quickly adapt to new situations inside and outside of the FIE. Externalizing this rationale and explicitly questioning (absolute) stability (and hence questioning the enterprise as such) would, in turn, destroy the social order, as the enterprises would right from the start not have any chance to establish a stable island in an unstable environment.

The inner logic of Chinese employees' knowledge practices in FIEs unfolds when considering the relation between the practices. Culture in terms of this inner logic thus can also be thought of as an adhesive: it makes the social world function in a way which makes sense for the employees.

9.2 The Roots of Sino-German Knowledge Conflicts

How do the practices of Chinese employees' knowledge practices with their inner logic cause such conflicts with German employees? Why is so much knowledge exchanged externally and so little shared internally? The cultural glue in the form of a stable space holding the social world of Chinese employees in FIEs together only makes sense for Chinese employees. When German employees enter FIEs in China, the understanding of a clear differentiation of inside/outside existing *a priori* has obviously been transferred from the German context in an unchanged manner to the Chinese context. It is taken for granted as common and overarching absolute reference point for employees in any enterprise regardless of the enterprise's location. In contrast, knowledge interactions are much more contingent in the eyes of the sampled Chinese employees. What is striking is that the subtle strategies within the practices of Chinese employees are in essence evaluating, investigating, assessing, and the like. This shows that knowledge is handled in a very *deliberate* way involving several criteria. Sharing or disclosing knowledge only happens *under certain conditions*, subjected to some sort of situational and subjective assessment in advance. Within each unique knowledge situation a latent “Why should I?” seems to appear in the back of the mind of Chinese employees. This “Why should I?” unconsciously depends on the underlying rationale of how stable the FIE’s space is perceived at this specific point in time.

But what are the roots of such conflicting points of departure? The core difference between the sampled Chinese and German employees reminds of the Chinese sociologist Fei Xiaotong. In the 1940s, Fei observed and analyzed basic differences in the social organization of Chinese society compared to Western societies.[1011] He depicted Western societies as structured by organizations with distinct boundaries which are recognized by their members. Organizations are formed by individuals with identical relationships to the organization. If relationships are different in terms of organizational hierarchy, the different positions are being individually agreed upon and specified by clear organizational rules. In contrast, Chinese social structure is described as concentric circles with everyone being in the center of their own circles. Metaphorically described as a stone being thrown into water forming one circle after another, one becomes interrelated with different circles at different times and places. Rather than individualism there is *egocentrism* with the self at the center. The way Fei depicts Western organizations from a Chinese perspective pointedly shows that thinking in such abstract organizational ways has been fairly uncommon in China.

Evidence for a deep-rooted tendency toward orientation along concentric circles versus fixed organizational structures can be found in other historical records. As premodern Chinese history shows, late Imperial China’s social structure was much more complex than that of Medieval Europe with its rigid class boundaries. Chinese people were at one time affiliated to families, clans, guilds, and native place associations. When pursuing knowledge interactions, the adherence to several groups provided people with different points of reference rather than an abstract overarching reference system, which could have been used as unitary orientation in society.

The individual acting from an egocentric perspective depicts what can still be observed as the point of departure for the sampled Chinese employees: The points of reference for orientation within knowledge interactions depart from the self (“Why should I?”), rather than departing from an abstract organizational

1011 Fei Xiaotong 1992: 60-70.

point of view. Most significantly, the requisite to cultivate certain personal core competitiveness at all times clearly puts the self at the center. Also, for new workforce entrants it is crucial to first adapt to their immediate work environment (the first circle at the workplace) to gather information and use their knowledge before thinking in terms of the whole organization (a weaker and more distant circle) within any knowledge interaction. The point of departure when investigating relationships or assessing counterparts – at least in the beginning – can only be seen as their own subjective assessment in order to be able to pursue their work. This concerns the inside as well as the outside of the FIE where cultivating relationships is essential for avoiding the FIE's disadvantage on the market. Finally, employees do not recognize the FIE as a predetermined collective to which the relation is clearly set right from the beginning. It rather gets acknowledged by each employee individually. The legacy of orientation along concentric circles as observed by Fei Xiaotong is thus still visible in contemporary China.

This study argues that Fei Xiaotong's observations reappear in a particular domain in contemporary China: the domain of knowledge work in China's foreign-invested manufacturing sector. At first, being positioned among the 50 million knowledge workers in China, the characteristics of the knowledge worker concept appear to be particularly consequential. The specifity of the concept is that knowledge is not communicated in an abstract organizational way (according to Taylorian principles) and along formal hierarchies. This was the situation in the West when the concept was coined, drawing attention to the kind of work that did not fit into traditional organizational structures. Instead, knowledge is communicated according to what the knowledge worker deems necessary himself. Only he can decide when with whom and how communication is pursued. Within this communication process, the egocentric perspective particularly comes to the fore. When having entered the FIE the immediate working environment and the supervisor are most decisive for daily communication of knowledge, followed by other departments and other market players. These multiple points of reference require Chinese employees to strongly make use of the latitude knowledge workers have *per definionem*.

The characteristic of knowledge as being strongly embedded in its context from which it cannot be artificially detached is particularly visible within knowledge work in this particular domain. Without the practical context, development or transfer of knowledge would generally be impossible. In the domain under investigation, the social context provides *the* important criteria for orientation within knowledge interactions. While in the West, organizational boundaries and structures more strongly frame communication processes, the social context judged by the respective individual functions as orientation. Employees cannot but actively manage relationships in their immediate working environment to ensure that they can pursue their (communication) work including the sharing and disclosing of knowledge. How this is pursued and how knowledge is configured thereby is largely influenced by this immediate social context as well as the larger social context of the FIE and the business environment.

The relationship between a Chinese knowledge worker and his enterprise is not just a horizontal one as proposed by the knowledge worker concept, but far more complex. Considering that at the outset the immediate working environment is more important to the employee than the enterprise as such, the relationship of the Chinese knowledge worker to the enterprise has to be built up over time instead of existing *a priori*. It is not seen as a (vertical or horizontal) relationship to an abstract organization, but as a network of people which are banded together in a certain space. Depending on how the enterprise establishes stability in this space, a relationship of reciprocal nature can be built up with the enterprise.

This building up of a reciprocal relationship can be further sustained by the implicit cultural rationale of evaluating the efforts put into the application of knowledge. Chinese employees evaluate the efforts the enterprise puts into the application of knowledge as a means of production and how their potential can be unfolded. The perceived efforts of the FIE influences the efforts the Chinese employees puts in, for instance, the sharing of knowledge. The relationship is thus not vertical as is with the conventional manual worker. It can neither be adequately described as a purely horizontal one, but rather as one of a reciprocal nature.

Knowledge also is endowed with a special meaning for Chinese knowledge workers. Knowledge as his means of production does not only need to be permanently updated to enable an employee to do his work. Against the background of a more theoretical Chinese education system, to apply knowledge in practice is regarded as essential for being able to pursue work and for one's career. To make their knowledge more productive, Chinese knowledge workers even stronger claim the application of their knowledge in practice. Middle-aged employees with several years of work experience where they had the opportunity to apply their knowledge are most well positioned on the Chinese labor market.

Furthermore, with regard to perception of a competitive Chinese labor market, knowledge gains even more importance. To stay competitive, Chinese knowledge workers strongly focus on their abilities to be unfolded to their full potential and strongly compare their "value" with that of their peers. As the term "value" suggests, employees strongly compare the own abilities to others. The permanent increase of their value helps them to differentiate themselves from other employees. This also explains the special meaning of the superior in the Chinese work context, which is confirmed by this study. To apply the knowledge at the workplace employees particularly rely on people such as the superior to use their potential – which is largely unknown to themselves – to the fullest extent. Only the superior is potentially informed about the employee's competencies in such a detailed way that he can ensure the constant unfolding of an employee's value. This sheds a new light on the understanding of employees as "assets".

Knowledge work has a special meaning in China not only due to the competitive situation on the labor market but also due to the social competition. Even though knowledge workers belong to the upper strata of Chinese society, the social competition is nevertheless – or precisely due to this fact – very strong. A general distrust prevalent in society is another obstacle for knowledge workers in particular who have to permanently communicate within this distrustful Chinese society. Nowadays, Chinese society does not provide a strong common reference suitable to function as orientation but a complicated social fabric, such as colleagues, peers, contact persons in other enterprises, and market actors with whom trust has constantly to be maintained. When "entering society" – as it is expressed by new workforce entrants – they are mostly exposed to this current mentality of Chinese society. The competitive mentality of everyone striving to increase their own value as compared to the value of others lets Chinese employees focus even more on increasing their own value as well as their personal competitive advantage. As fellow employees strive for the same, communication barriers at the workplace easily appear. Knowledge is not easily gathered, since one has to constantly convince others about one's motives and also carefully assess and investigate the counterpart's intentions. Such a social environment can be characterized as erratic and unstable especially from a knowledge worker's perspective.

Second, apart from knowledge workers in China, Fei Xiaotong's observations are particularly relevant for employees in FIEs. Besides being employed by the FIE, Chinese employees appear to be strongly connected to the market with enterprise boundaries becoming increasingly blurry. In their position as intermediaries, they have a particular latitude in communicating knowledge as foreign managers cannot connect on a similar strong level with external actors.

Their position between the FIE and the market strongly reminds of the institution of the comprador in modern Chinese history. For foreign enterprises not having a good comprador constituted a serious disadvantage. Even betrayal by the comprador was tolerated, since he had been useful in terms of preventing a competitive disadvantage.

Although nowadays – in contrast to the beginning of the comprador époque – German employees more and more engage with the Chinese language and customs and vice versa, for the intricate connection to the market intermediaries prove *nevertheless* indispensable. As it was the case in premodern China, where "one got nowhere until a relationship of trust had been established"[1012], business transactions today can still not be pursued offhandedly but against the background of a certain trustful connection. Although the role of intermediaries was particularly strong at the beginning of the economic transition, the increasing competition and need for more profound and detailed knowledge of the business environment is increasing to this day. Due to the dense social fabric, the non-transparency still characterizes the Chinese business environment in the current phase of transition. Even employees who have stayed for years in China cannot fully delve into the social fabric. This dense social fabric will very likely persist even after the transition-phase. To still be at the forefront of competition, intermediaries remain necessary.

Especially as FIEs usually produce high quality products, a lot more information has to be communicated and a lot more interactions with suppliers and customers are necessary. Close interaction with market players is necessary to not be disadvantaged in competition. Chinese employees acting as intermediaries in FIEs are particularly dependent on quick information flows from the headquarters. Yet these information flows are usually slow precisely due to the German employees' fear of disclosure of valuable knowledge to competitors on the Chinese market. Hence, Chinese employees depend much more on searching for solutions for the customers by searching for help in their own concentric circles.

Third, Fei Xiaotong's observations appear to be particularly relevant regarding the Chinese manufacturing sector. The manufacturing sector is perceived as competitive and is subjected to quick changes. The market situation makes quick and constant communication vital. Chinese employees emphasized the importance of maintaining a close connection to the market – including regular exchange with competitors – in order to prevent isolation, which would automatically be the case if the connection failed. Employees are quickly disadvantaged when not sufficiently and timely informed, for example, on product details before the competitor steps in. Whereas customers are of importance to any business worldwide, detailed, tiny, and subtle pieces of information on the customer appear to be particularly valuable in China's manufacturing sector. It is not only the explicit details on a customer list *per se*, but much more so the tacit knowing and subtle information which the enterprise has gained during the personal interaction with the customer. Efforts put into the social interaction with the environment are not seen as an advantage, but as a necessary and basic condition for being able to access sufficient information to pursue the daily work and eventually pursue knowledge interactions for the FIE. As mirrored by both Chinese legal practice and work practice in enterprises, what is considered valuable

1012 van der Sprenkel 1977: 620.

knowledge is very strongly connected to personal interactions between employees and market players including competitors.

This entails to be strongly connected to the market in order to know when one has to gather or deploy certain information, even if this requires the crossing of legal boundaries. This implies that the sampled Chinese employees exchange secrets with other market players while being aware of their secret status. They know that by disclosing them there is a good chance that these secrets might end up with a competitor. Careful and deliberate disclosure of knowledge in the way it is done is not due to missing legal awareness but precisely due to the fact that this legal consciousness exists.

This is contrary to what has been observed in Chinese legal practice, where making the employee aware of the concrete content of trade secrets is very much emphasized and at first glance points to a lower awareness. These contradicting results might point to the fact that employers – especially in China – often fail to explicitly inform their employees about the concrete content and scope of trade secrets and thus fail to meet the statutory element of adopting secrecy measures. Although the Chinese employees are not informed about the exact wording of legal statutes (neither are their German counterparts), employees still prove to be intuitively aware of core know-how and sensitive information. Nevertheless, they still exchange information in line with what appears to be usual business practice especially in the manufacturing sector.

Scholars and practitioners alike often come to the cursory conclusion that the disclosure of valuable knowledge is based on a barely existent legal consciousness in China – judged from the scarce implementation and enforcement of law.[1013] They thus take for granted that the exchange of knowledge cannot but mean a missing awareness and respect of valuable knowledge. More often than not the argument is brought forward that intellectual property only has a short history of less than three decades in China in which a basic understanding and consciousness for legally protected private property of knowledge could not have developed. Yang[1014], for instance, in her widely-cited study on intellectual property and doing business in China, concludes that the intellectual property system in China "will take time and effort to evolve and to make the whole society have the ideology of private rights protection"[1015]. Against the background of an intricate Chinese business reality with its own cultural criteria (which do not contra-

1013 Such as local protectionism, the dependency of the judiciary on local governments, and the qualification of judges (see e.g. Tao Jingzhao 2007: 107-108, Kong Qingjiang 2005: 60, Lardy 1994: 81, Mertha 2005: 3-4).

1014 Yang Deli 2003.

1015 Yang Deli 2003: 243.

dict legal awareness), the conventional diagnose of a missing legal consciousness in China seems rather short-sighted.

Fourth, especially in contemporary China's knowledge economy Fei Xiaotong's egocentric circles can be applied, yet in a different way. As Naughton[1016] puts it: contemporary China's economy "carries with it parts of the traditional, the socialist, the modern, and the market, all mixed up in a jumble of mind-boggling complexity"[1017]. Industrial enterprises in China have grown in size and numbers only with reform and opening up, and Chinese employees increasingly take over functions in enterprises which fall under the definition of knowledge work. The differentiation into knowledge and manual work happens when both the knowledge era is under way and industrialization takes place in a mostly agrarian country. Organizations are of different ownership type with often being not clearly privately or state-owned. Clear organizational structures and clear rules to serve as orientation are not self-evident against the background of such a transitional economy.

In this transitional (knowledge) economy with its rapidly changing conditions, an even quicker knowledge exchange and more communication with an even stronger need of personal interaction than before are needed. This increased need of personal interaction sheds a new light on the *guanxi* discourse. Instead of being only a substitute for institutional shortcomings, the empirical findings reveal that relationships are *ubiquitous* for the daily handling of valuable knowledge for Chinese employees. Knowledge interactions cannot be disentangled from the relationships between the persons involved. Communication only happens against the background of relationships and during communication relationships are continuously defined. This creatively transforms the nature of relationships in the domain under investigation.

As a matter of fact, Chinese employees positioned as knowledge workers and intermediaries in FIEs draw on such traditional cultural resources in a different way than usually expected. They not just use the *guanxi* they have as a facilitator for knowledge interactions, as argued by several studies,[1018] but closely investigate relationships within each knowledge interaction. This implies that just because of "having *guanxi*" with someone one would not receive information or easily share or disclose information. Relationships have to be continuously cultivated to be able to access information and share knowledge. At the same time, the proximity and distance has to be balanced and constantly readjusted where knowledge exchange could be critical to one's own interest, which mostly overlap with the interests of the FIE (subject to the FIE as a stable space). While the essentialized meaning of

1016 Naughton 2007.
1017 Naughton 2007: 4.
1018 See e.g. Munier and Huan Cao 2010, Huang Qian et al. 2008, Yin Hongjuan et al. 2011.

guanxi in the form of mutual obligations, which facilitate knowledge flows, rests on a discursive level, a new particular relevance of relationships among Chinese employees in FIEs can indeed be found.

This particular relevance of relationships in this particular domain resonates with Yang[1019] who argues that *guanxi* transforms itself in different spheres. *Guanxi* again flourishes in certain business domains while its impact is declining in domains of social life. It is constantly revised in the reform process and thus does not constitute an unchanging essence, which has already been formed prior to the capitalist process. Yao[1020] similarly asserts that *guanxi* is constructed in contexts, "even though it has all the aura of timeless, historical generality"[1021]. This is in stark contrast to the wide-spread assumption of a zero-sum game of the decline of *guanxi* in line with the development of capitalist institutions.[1022] In the domain under investigation, relationships are much more complex than the conventional rigid characterization of *guanxi* by irrevocable mutual obligations.

This study shows that the relationships underlying knowledge interactions do not resemble a traditional resource which fills a gap until other institutions come into effect. If this was the case, *guanxi* would not be the ideal way, and doing knowledge work along fixed organizational boundaries and institutions would be preferred. As the data show, knowledge interactions in the domain under investigation most likely do not develop into impersonal transactions governed by institutions. This becomes most apparent through the approaching of a stable space instead of formal institutions. Institutions in the form of rules and regulations cannot provide stability for Chinese employees when it comes to intricate knowledge interactions. With the upcoming knowledge era, the ever quicker and more fine-tuned exchange of ever more detailed pieces of knowledge within a complicated social fabric gives rise to a renewed and even stronger meaning of these traditional resources discursively referred to as *guanxi*.

With the upcoming knowledge era in China, the enterprise's role seems to gain in importance and appears to serve as an additional (relatively fixed) reference point. While egocentrism again appears to be the point of departure in the domain of knowledge work in China's foreign-invested manufacturing sector, the social fabric cannot strictly be thought of in terms of orderly concentric circles. Instead it constitutes more complicated and much more overlapping and fuzzy circles. Self-centered networks of social relationships are regarded as too complex within daily work. In fact, the sampled Chinese employees desire a

1019 Yang Mayfair Mei-hui 2002.
1020 Yao Souchou 2002.
1021 Yao Souchou 2002: 252.
1022 See e.g. Guthrie 1998, Barner-Rasmussen and Björkman 2007.

more *streamlined and stable orientation* to successfully navigate through the complex social fabric.

Considering the time of Fei Xiaotong's writing and the focus of his analysis resting on the rural society, social morality only made sense in terms of personal connections.[1023] Under these circumstances, orientation along the lines of one's concentric circles was most appropriate. Yet in today's knowledge economy, more orientation is needed. In the knowledge economy and especially in the domain of knowledge work the foreign-invested manufacturing sector in China, a quick exchange of subtle pieces of knowledge is necessary. Mediating knowledge workers need a point of reference which is valid for fellow employees as well. This more stable form of reference can arguably only be provided by organizations in the form of a stable space.

The desire of a manifestation and strengthening of organizational boundaries might at first glance be attributed to a strife for Western organizations as observed by Fei Xiaotong. Yet the organization, which is strived for as an orientation, is different. It is not the organization *per se* but the stability it provides through common moral references that is coming into focus. This kind of stability is never absolute, but can only be developed through personal interactions of its members in the long-term, establishing a sense of cohesiveness through an overarching common moral reference system, which should be exhibited and transferred by superiors. It differs from the perceived stability of Western organizations which results from fixed and more or less stable explicit rules. An organization in the form of a stable space counteracts potential influences from the unstable environment which changes all too quickly and which hardly can provide orientation for knowledge interactions.

In contrast to Fei Xiaotong, the manifestation of organizational boundaries shielding away the environment is seen as a source of stability rather than only navigating through the social fabric from an egocentric perspective. That involves being in a space which is clearly differentiated from the environment. Clear differentiation between *neibu* and *waibu* makes employees in *neibu* adhere to a common reference which is different from the complicated *waibu*. Such a space has manifested its boundaries, which are clearly structured but which are also still flexible enough to cope with different circumstances in the remaining social fabric and the market. Hence, there is a strong awareness of how organizations manifest their boundaries, alleviating the exposure to the complicated society which is often perceived as a moral void or moral vacuum.

Enterprises are apparently seen as being able to provide a veritable opportunity of providing orientation by establishing the basis for a communal spirit.

1023 Fei Xiaotong 1992: 71-79.

The enterprise constitutes an additional stable space which can alleviate much of the social struggle when entering society. It has the potential to provide a common reference for its employees which alleviates the complex orientation along their own concentric cirles. Thus, traditional cultural knowledge has not lost its meaning. In a modified way it is still applicable. As expressed by the Heraclitus' saying "you cannot step twice into the same river", cultural resources are constantly changing.

From a more theoretical point of view, this explicit cultural knowledge as observed by Fei Xiaotong intermingles with possibilities and limitations offered by other contexts the sampled Chinese employees have become entangled in (the Chinese national context, the Chinese economy and society, the Chinese manufacturing sector, and the FIE). Traditional explicit cultural knowledge of several contexts interacts with the cultural knowledge in a certain space at a certain point in time. To an extent, it is represented in an even more distinct way in the context of the upcoming knowledge economy in the Chinese foreign-invested manufacturing sector. This is the kind of knowledge which indeed informs the employees as seen by the empirical results.

German employees, by contrast, focus on organizational structures *a priori.* The strength of this structural reference point for German employees has first and foremost to be seen against the background of how the Western economy has been structured for more than a century. Organizations have constituted the backbone and structural principle of the Western economy. Work has been enormously structured and organized according to Taylorian mass production principles. Workers had a clear task with each step perfectly fitting into the whole organization. Work had – at that time – become structured to the strongest degree in history.

Most German employees in the sample regard their knowledge workers foremost as "employees" (*Arbeitnehmer*) with the relationship to the employer (*Arbeitgeber*) being clearly defined by a contract. The notion most important to them is that Chinese employees fulfill the contractually agreed work, which they get paid for. They still embrace a truly vertical relationship. As Adam and Oleksak confirm for the Western hemisphere,[1024] most entrepreneurs still do not know how to see beyond the individuals, and do not yet consider them as knowledge assets.

This vertical relationship implies that structures and rules are defined by the employer. These can be deviated from but are still the point of departure. German employees thus implicitly expect from an "employee" to put all his efforts into work right from the start and to automatically share all his knowledge.

1024 Adams and Oleksak 2010: 21.

The expectation of automatically sharing knowledge, however, is indeed not realistic toward knowledge workers in general, who have to carefully consider their means of production. To a certain extent, all knowledge workers critically evaluate the efforts an enterprise invests into their means production. What is most striking among the sampled Chinese employees is that they most succinctly and on a permanent basis evaluate the FIE's efforts into their knowledge as well as into establishing a stable space. They only see them as sufficient if their abilities are fully put to use and if their value can constantly increase in an environment perceived as stable.

The accusation of hoarding information has also to be evaluated against the background of knowledge workers in general. Chinese employees indeed are strongly occupied with seeking out information. Yet knowledge workers in general spend almost 40% of their working time searching for information.[1025] The findings reveal that gathering information externally and producing tailor-made products requires much information and exchange with customers. It is even seen as necessary for survival. Thus it necessarily appears to be strongly in the focus of Chinese employees acting as intermediaries.

Conflicts are reinforced by a situation in which German employees are often positioned in the upper management. They expect to automatically receive information and knowledge due to their superior positions. Chinese employees, in contrast, expect their direct superior of actively asking for the required information and putting efforts in applying their knowledge as well as providing a space in which his knowledge work can be adequately pursued.

Strikingly, even though the knowledge era is much longer under way in Western economies, truly pursuing knowledge work still proves difficult. A survey of the recruitment service provider Hays[1026] pursued in enterprises in Germany, Austria, and Switzerland points to the fact that knowledge work increasingly requires increased exchange and communication. Exchange and communication processes were also found to be increasingly complex. The participants saw a need to increase the exchange with colleagues, customers, and suppliers within their daily work. Especially the external exchange is emphasized facing an ever more fragmented value chain.[1027] This study implicitly reveals that the functional and structural approach of German-speaking countries is not compatible anymore with the current knowledge economy.

This inevitably raises the question of whether conflicts might be more pronounced with Germans working in China compared to other foreigners in China. Yet it is well outside the scope of the present study to determine whether the

1025 McDermott 2005: 15.
1026 Stiehler et al. 2011.
1027 Stiehler et al. 2011: 7.

Sino-German conflicts are relevant only for German-invested enterprises as opposed to other FIEs. As already reflected upon in the research design and methods section, German-enterprises are largely representative for FIEs from other (Western) countries in terms of valuable knowledge, yet in terms of culture generalizations they require more caution.

Judging from available country-level data, conflicts in German-invested enterprises might indeed be more pronounced than within FIEs in general. According the widely-cited GLOBE study,[1028] which was pursued in over sixty countries, Germans tend to be driven by abstract principles which are used as (often absolute) guidelines that need to be executed even if particular cases merit another treatment.[1029] If these data were taken at face value, the ever more communication-intense knowledge economy in general and in China in particular would pose most challenges on employees from Germany.

Still, these country-level data should be used *with utmost caution*. Especially since the present study argues that culture requires a more thorough approach than relying on country-level data only.[1030] While acknowledging the amount of data captured in such studies which can be a valuable data source when used with caution, they also run the risk of furthering counterproductive essentializations. Thorough research within FIEs of other origins might further contribute to filling this gap.

9.3 The Role of "Chinese Culture"

As can be seen in the previous sub-chapter, the roots of most knowledge conflicts are cultural ones. Yet this culture is different from the "Chinese culture" usually ascribed to the controversies surrounding the handling of valuable knowledge. The present study argues that this conventional "Chinese culture" is to be differentiated from the role culture actually plays for knowledge conflicts.

In studies touching upon the intersection of valuable knowledge and culture, culture is often loosely defined as traditional ethical or philosophical thoughts, overwhelmingly with certain parts of Confucianism. Yet in contrast to what existing studies on the topic assert,[1031] the empirical investigation shows that Chinese employees neither directly nor indirectly draw upon the assumed philosophical resources. Despite a close exchange of valuable knowledge with the environment, it is self-evident that core know-how belongs to the enterprise and

1028 House et al. 2004.
1029 Brodbeck and Frese 2008: 165.
1030 See chapter 9.3. See also Poerner 2014.
1031 See e.g. Alford 1995, Qu Sanqiang 2012: xliv-xlvi, Li Luo 2010. See also chapter 1.3.

has to be protected. The Chinese employees all proved to have a thorough understanding of knowledge being property ascribed to a certain entity, a thinking which is *not* "incompatible"[1032] with Chinese thought as commonly assumed. Valuable knowledge within daily work is seen as valuable for individual entities, either the FIE or the individual employee. It is even clearly sorted out who is seen as eligible in using this valuable knowledge.

As can be seen when tracing knowledge property in Chinese philosophy, it is unlikely that Chinese philosophy has provided any concrete orientation for knowledge interactions of ordinary Chinese people. Rather, philosophers were concerned with state affairs and public matters of society. Historical records of premodern China confirm as well that private knowledge protection was an issue regulated among citizens and groups such as guilds themselves according to the logic of private interests. This confirms the results of studies which question the relevance of Chinese philosophical thoughts for the handling of valuable knowledge in the form of intellectual property.[1033]

The scarce relevance of the philosophical resources viewed from a knowledge angle, however, should not be equalized with an absence of moral values *per se* – the so-called "moral void"[1034]. This study's empirical data show many moral points of reference which provide orientation for Chinese employees. For instance, contrary to the German employee's assumption of Chinese employees being "absolutely egoistic"[1035], the personal competitive advantage is not unlimited by moral constraints. Also, moral criteria are necessary points of reference for judging the behavior of others and being able to decide how to behave during knowledge interactions. Eventually, the attitude and behavior of the enterprise is also judged according to moral criteria.

Yet the relevance of these moral criteria cannot simply be derived from the existence of philosophical resources in China as a whole. Rather, their relevance is strongly depended on the immediate environment. Only as long as they are implemented and maintained by a certain entity – in this case the enterprise – do they appear to be relevant for orientation within knowledge interactions. This is necessary as the environment is seen as unstable, subject to frequent changes, and thus unpredictable. In an unstable environment such an entity is unconsciously in focus and has to provide a common reference, drawing boundaries within which cohesiveness among its members can be developed. It is in fact this morality which makes the social world stable. The most basic strife for stability which tacitly informs all knowledge interactions is intricately linked with morali-

1032 Lehman 2006: 1.
1033 See e.g. Yu Peter K. 2012, Ivanhoe 2005, Shi Wei 2006. See also chapter 1.3.
1034 Lim and Blanchard 2013. See also chapter 7.1.
1035 G/50/JV/SHA(58:5). See also chapter 8.1 and 8.6.

ty. Hence, there is no such thing as a "knowledge hoarding culture" having developed in a "moral void" but there is a culture of implicitly applying moral criteria regarding any person involved in knowledge interactions. The application of criteria largely depends on whether the FIE is successful in creating a stable space in an unstable (yet not morally void) environment.

Other studies tackling the nexus of valuable knowledge and culture also draw on another popular component of "Chinese culture": collectivism.[1036] They argue that a collectivist orientation, that is, sharing knowledge with regard to an (in-)group's interest rather than according to self-interest, is a decisive factor for knowledge sharing. Most often, Hofstede's "individualism/collectivism dimension" is applied. Hofstede's notion of individualism represents a preference for a loosely knit social framework in which individuals are expected to take care of only themselves and their immediate families. Collectivism, by contrast, presupposes a tightly-knit framework in society in which individuals can expect their relatives or members of a particular in-group to look after them in exchange for unquestioning loyalty. While in individualist societies, people's self-image is defined in terms of "I", the self-image in collectivist society is characterized by a colletive "we".[1037] China ranks low in the individualism score, even compared to other Asian nations, whereas Germany – as it is typically the case in Western countries – ranks relatively high.[1038] It is presumably these handy either-or results which prompt scholars, publishing in English language business management journals, to use this dimension as a tool of analysis for Chinese knowledge sharing behavior.

Yet none of the studies can provide the link between the supposed cultural influence and the employees' behavior. Although the studies are of an empirical nature they only survey how knowledge is shared instead of digging deeper into possible motives behind this behavior. In order to explain the results, the authors draw on available explicit cultural knowledge such as the individualism/collectivism dimension. Yet whether the assumed collectivist culture really provides orientation for the employee is still open to question.

The empirical findings of the present study reveal an "individualist orientation" at first glance. This is mostly shown by the fact that Chinese employees are eager to cultivate their own competitive advantage. Paying attention to the efforts the FIE puts into the application of their knowledge further shows that they equally contribute their knowledge to the FIEs, if their knowledge is applied. Also, the judgment of others is an indispensable component of knowledge inter-

1036 See e.g. Michailova and Hutchings 2006, Shin et al. 2007, Wilkesmann et al. 2008. See also chapter 1.3.
1037 Hofstede 1984: 83.
1038 Hofstede 2005: 78-79.

actions. Prior to any knowledge interaction they first assess the counterpart with regard to whether he or she is suitable to be provided with knowledge. They also evaluate relationships inside and outside the FIE in terms of whether or not they are suitable for exchanging information. These judgments are at first informed by the rationale of "Why should I?". Any knowledge interaction is deliberately pursued from an individual point of view instead of taking a collective – such as a department, enterprise, or other social group – as the point of departure.

Yet to evaluate this point of departure as merely individualist would be short-sighted. When taking the most tacit underlying logic into account, it becomes clear that this seemingly individualist "Why should I" is not sparked by a completely subjective judgment but by a tacit social consensus. This inner logic reveals the desired collectivist unit which ties all members together. Hence, Chinese employees do not act in a collectivist way *a priori*, meaning, they do not act in favor of an ingroup from the outset. Rather, they subjectively assess situations considering their own benefit, and only on a very tacit level they are informed by the desire of a common point of reference as a guide for their subjective judgments.

These findings shed further light on Hofstede's individualism/collectivism dimension. Culture does not simply unravel into collectivism and individualism in a dichotomous way. Even when the FIE does provide a (relatively) stable space, Chinese employees cannot expect other members of this particular "in-group" to look after them in exchange for "unquestioning loyalty" in a Hofstedian sense. On the contrary, the stability is always relative and fragile and thus has constantly to be questioned. "Unquestioning loyalty" is not even given in the so-called in-groups within an enterprise which the studies have found to be a unit in which knowledge is shared. Neither premodern Chinese economy and society with their various group affiliations and complicated social fabric nor the empirical data of the present study with the multiple points of reference can confirm a collectivist attitude.

Interestingly, empirical studies within *Chinese* academic literature rightly indicate a more complex way than the typical cultural dimension suggests. They point to individually oriented persons as socially embedded in relationships and to the importance of superiors and the contingency of behavior within the organization. This comes close to the point of departure from an egocentric perspective and the attention paid to the FIE as a stable space. A collectivist orientation can thus not be applied as an explanation for controversial knowledge interactions and rankings of national culture should be used with caution.

The notion of collectivism is closely connected to the accusation of nationalism being at the roots of insufficient knowledge sharing inside the FIE and excessive knowledge leakage to the outside. When titles such as "Yellow

Spys"[1039] accuse of nationalism, they imply the assumption of Chinese individuals having an "unquestioning loyalty" to the Chinese population as a whole collective entity. Yet Chinese sources display a more diverse picture. At the beginning of the 20th century when nationalist tendencies in China were strong, the comprador was among the first being blamed to be anti-nationalist. He had such a bad reputation that even his title had been amended by foreign merchants into "Chinese manager".[1040] As the available sources reveal, few compradors actually acted in "imperialist interests" and some rather engaged in nationalist activities. But the large majority was clearly only following their own private interests.

As to what concerns the sampled Chinese employees, who were in a similarly critical position, neither displayed a nationalist attitude nor were they concerned of such accusations by their fellow countrymen. Their focus clearly was on being able to pursue their work and to keep up with the social and labor market competition they were specifically exposed to in their roles of knowledge workers. This competition induced them to cultivate a (limited) competitive advantage as well as the need to see their abilities put to use to the fullest extent and see their value adequately reflected within the respective enterprise. This ubiquity of competition between Chinese employees themselves, the social pressure and the general low trust level within Chinese society made a collective nationalist thinking at the workplace less likely. Also, the communication barriers existing between them clearly confirm that the sharing of knowledge was not only a problem toward German employees. This virtually rules out the possibility of a nationalist rationale inducing Chinese employees to keep knowledge for themselves instead of sharing it with fellow employees or their FIE. Nationalist sentiments in contemporary China might foremost erupt within extreme cases with a strong political dimension, such as the Japanese protests or the Rio Tinto case concerning a strategic state sector.[1041]

These results confirm one of the few existing studies in the realm of knowledge work in China in which foreign managers wrongly believed that technology has to be protected against Chinese engineers who might leak knowledge motivated by nationalism. In fact, the Chinese employees proved to have relatively few ties to the propaganda but were driven by rational economic decisions.[1042] The own interest and that of the immediate environment rather than the interest of the Chinese nation are usually seen as most important and hence inform Chinese employees within knowledge interactions.

1039 *Der Spiegel* 2007.
1040 See chapter 4.3.
1041 See chapter 5.3 and 7.3.
1042 Kessler 2007. See also chapter 1.3.

What is further strinking is that all these explanations of Confucianism, collectivism, and nationalism locate "Chinese culture" at the level of the *nation state*. China is considered a "cultural container"[1043] which is internally homogenous and can be clearly differentiated from other nations. Chinese people are considered to be automatically subject to the influence of this culture. In the empirical investigation, the sampled German interviewees similarly referred to a culture which is relevant for China as a whole, using statements such as "the Chinese way"[1044]. Controversial knowledge interactions are interpreted with locating culture at a national level.

Yet the *de facto* relevant explicit cultural knowledge discussed in the previous sub-chapter is not automatically to be put on a national level as spatial unit of reference. This study argues that the relevant explicit cultural knowledge appears to be of special relevance *only* in the domain of knowledge work in China's foreign-invested manufacturing sector rather than for China as a whole. This drawing on these explicit cultural resources for orientation in daily life proves to be particularly necessary for the protagonists of this study: those Chinese employees employed by FIEs who act as knowledge workers and intermediaries. Being entangled as a mediating knowledge worker in this unique combination of contexts – the Chinese national context, in Chinese economy and society, the foreign-invested manufacturing sector, the own enterprise – the cultural resources of the national context unfolds its particular relevance. It is not only the Chinese employee's positioning in China *per se* which draws upon historically and socially conditioned possibilities within knowledge interactions. Most significantly, the positioning of the employees as both knowledge worker and intermediary in the competitive manufacturing sector in China makes the drawing on these historical resources relevant and at the same time transforms them in an adequate way. It is thus this particular group of Chinese employees which draws on the national cultural resources to orient themselves in the complex world with its different contexts.

If the identified cultural knowledge was understood to appear only at the level of the nation state, the phenomenon of the controversial handling of knowledge could be quickly characterized as an ethnical or inherently cultural one. Yet this is not the case. The findings indicate that the national context of origin is not only the decisive one for the sampled German employees. German employees did not strictly adhere to the cultural knowledge they were exposed to while growing up. Over time, most of them internalized the cultural knowledge in China to a certain extent.

1043 Beck 1998: 13-14.
1044 B/57/WFOE/SHA(16:11). See also chapter 8.2 and 8.6.

This internalization becomes most apparent within the practice of investigating relationships. The ubiquity of relationships as being a part of their work unconsciously took hold in their daily working practices. This necessitated the assessment and differentiation of relationships instead of purely considering their existence or absence. Relationships were more actively used for gathering subtle information instead of only unintentionally using them by chance. Also, while having been still focused on the competitive advantage of the FIE in line with the expectations of the colleagues at the headquarters, they started to embrace the importance of connecting to the environment in order to prevent a quickly arising competitive disadvantage on the Chinese market. After a certain time, German employees did not expect automatic knowledge sharing from their Chinese colleagues anymore but actively asked for the needed information. Having internalized this cultural knowledge, which proves necessary for orientation in China's foreign-invested manufacturing sector to a certain extent, they increasingly took over an intermediary role between the headquarters and the Chinese employees.

This internalization is yet not equally observable among all sampled employees. While some German employees appear to not have internalized the cultural knowledge at all, others did so to varying degrees. The timespan they spent in the context can serve as an indicator on how strong this internalization is. At least for the sampled German employees, it appears that the longer they were in the domain of knowledge work in China's foreign-invested manufacturing sector, the more it is reflected in the interviews that they were exposed to the practices of this domain and the cultural background knowledge informing them. Apart from the time spent in this domain, the speed with which they internalized the cultural knowledge is surely also contingent on the individual combination of the other manifold spatial and temporal contexts they have become entangled in during their lifetime.

There is evidence in the data set according to which German employees never *fully* internalized the cultural knowledge. Even after several years the depths of the networks compared to those of their Chinese colleagues could not be reached. This points to the fact that German employees were not positioned as knowledge workers and intermediaries in the same way as Chinese employees. Although the German employees were knowledge workers as well, they were not knowledge workers in Chinese society and thus not exposed to the particular social pressure. They also acted as intermediaries, but they rather mediated between Chinese colleagues and German colleagues and were not that connected to the Chinese business environment.

Further evidence of cultural knowledge being particularly relevant in the domain of knowledge work in China's foreign-invested manufacturing sector rather than being based on the national context of origin is provided by new workforce entrants. These Chinese employees were not exposed to practices in the domain before having entered the FIE as their first workplace. They were not apt to navigate through the social fabric only due to the fact that they grew up in the Chinese environment. Before having entered the FIE they were in the protected domains of the family, school, and university, where the drawing on traditional cultural resources did not prove as relevant as in the domain under investigation. “Entering society” involves learning how to cope with the dense and complicated social fabric and to navigate through it. In this domain, a new significance has been ascribed to the social fabric and its relationships and networks especially when working with knowledge in the quickly changing business environment. This has to be embraced by Chinese employees entering the business world in a similar vein as German employees.

This is also sustained by overseas returnees or *haigui* who have grown up in China and have gathered experiences in the business world of other (Asian or Western) countries.[1045] Like university graduates or foreign employees, *haigui* first have to adapt to the Chinese social and cultural environment. In a comprehensive survey on overseas returnees conducted by Beijing University’s Guanghua School of Management, social and cultural barriers have been exposed as the most important obstacles by the majority of returnees. Social and cultural barriers among others refer to complicated interpersonal relationships within enterprises.[1046] Only after a certain time, *haigui* have managed their “relocalization”.[1047] Even when having stayed abroad only for a few years and still being relatively young and flexible, *haigui* experience barriers when they return and start working in an enterprise in China, which is often a FIE.

The fact that *haigui* have gathered work experiences and communication skills in foreign countries but still struggle when entering the domain of the (foreign-invested) manufacturing sector in China elucidates a unique spatial cultural knowledge, which is different from business domains in other countries. This is sustained by the fact that the *haigui* in the survey returned from many different societies including Asian countries, where the social fabric generally differs from Western societies as well. Yet this cultural knowledge is only prevalent in this special domain rather than being inherently Chinese since even Chinese themselves – as new work entrants or *haigui* – have to adapt to it despite having grown up in the Chinese environment.

Although the discursive “Chinese culture” of Confucianism (in terms of knowledge propery), collectivism, and nationalism is not drawn upon by interviewees, it is nevertheless somehow relevant in practice. Ironically, the typical

1045 For more details on *haigui* as part of China’s knowledge workforce refer to chapter 6.2.
1046 Lu Jiangyong et al. 2012: 27-32, see *Xinhuawang* 2012.
1047 Lu Jiangyong et al. 2012: 104-112, *Xinhuawang* 2012.

"Chinese culture" seems to provide orientation for German employees rather than for Chinese employees. The Confucius dogma is referred to only by German employees. Even without being asked about any philosophical reasons for the ambiguous handling of valuable knowledge, some of the sampled German employees referred to Confucius and the typical "copying your master"-thesis. The data confirm what has become commonly accepted among foreigners when it comes to knowledge, creations, innovations, and the like in China.

The highly emotional discourse on knowledge and inventions in general might well have stirred these arguments. Mostly, this discourse surrounds the particularly emotional topics of copyright in literature and art. It is no coincidence, that the debate on intellectual property infringements in China is often backed by arguments from the realm of art and literature. Indeed, many intriguing works on this topic illuminate an arguably unique understanding of creativity in China. For instance, in Chinese art, as shown by Ledderose[1048] using the example of the Terracotta Warriors in Xi'an, creativity stemmed from small changes through reproduction and combination. Original and reproduction have not been as categorically distinguished as it is the case in the West. For the field of literature, Stone[1049] illustrates on the basis of the *Zuo Documentary* (*Zuozhuan* 左传), the complex, implicit and often original allusion that necessitated an intricate process of identifying the source and continuous determination of meaning on the part of the educated reader. He asserts that this is distinctly different from Western borrowing, where the recognition of the original source would not that profoundly influence the understanding of a text. Henningsen's[1050] study on contemporary literature such as Harry Potter also shows that the employing, reworking, or modifying of existing works results in new creations. Imitation thus becomes an instrument of creativity itself blurring the boundaries between the original and the fake.

From a Western perspective, this arguably unique understanding of creativity might indeed seem disrespectful against the background of the natural rights movement within the European Enlightenment, where the author was the "creative individual" contributing his original personality to a book. Producing something original by himself, he naturally owned all property rights concerning his work. Intellectual property at the time was considered as more naturally constituting the property of an individual as compared to the property of tangible objects.[1051] The "creative individual" and "romantic originality" of the natural rights tradition were passionately and fiercely fought for over decades by Euro-

1048 Ledderose 2000.
1049 Stone 2008.
1050 Henningsen 2008.
1051 Hesse 2002: 33-35, Siegrist 2006: 68.

pean writers. The immateriality of a book was sacred und inviolable, even higher than the material value.

The matter of copyright is still passionately fought over. Copyright also stretches – through its convenient usage – to other branches of intellectual property, making the debate highly symbolic. The ongoing discussion about copyright (with references to art and literature) contributes to purporting that a certain unique "Chinese culture" toward knowledge property is persistent enough to be generally relevant today, even for knowledge being totally different in nature and being used in a totally different setting. Yet to back up the "Chinese cultural" argument with evidence from the arts and literature does not explain the problem of the handling of valuable knowledge within enterprises. Rather, this "evidence" potentially strengthens the impression of the existence of a general "traditional culture" influencing "the Chinese" and leading to a certain disrespect of knowledge of all kinds.

As a matter of fact, the "Confucius argument" prevails, having become a highly symbolic and essentialized component of the intellectual property discourse. The widely-cited saying of Confucius to "transmit rather than create" (述而不作)[1052] is highly suggestive. The frequent use of the more symbolic word "create" for the Chinese word "zuo" (作) strengthens the impression of a despise of creations. However, famous sinologists have translated "zuo" in a less symbolic way, for instance into "maker" by James Legge ("A transmitter and not a maker […]"[1053]) in 1960, or into "machen" [make] by Richard Wilhelm ("Beschreiben und nicht machen [...]"[1054]) in 2005, and similarly into "I have 'transmitted what was taught to me without making up anything of my own' […]"[1055] by Arthur Waley as early as 1938. Also when tracing its roots back a bit further, the "Confucius argument" neither forms part of cultural knowledge rooted in social and historical facts, nor had related evidence been found in the empirical data set. The argument thus exists only – albeit persistently – on a discursive level, with Confucius as a "convenient scapegoat"[1056] for intellectual property infringements in China.

For German employees, the argument still becomes relevant in a way that the focus is constantly on this discursive "Chinese culture" in the Chinese business environment. This might well be fostered by guidebooks on intellectual property as well as countless popular accounts in Western media which perpetu-

---

1052 *Lunyu* VII,1. Brought forward as argument in the intellectual property debate e.g. by Alford 1995: 9 and 25, Nie Jianqiang 2006: 178, Qu Sanqiang 2012: xlvi.
1053 Legge 1960: 195.
1054 Wilhelm and van Ess 2005: 56.
1055 Waley 1938: 123.
1056 Shi Wei 2006: 12.

ally publish topics such as counterfeiting, economic espionage, and theft of ideas relating to China, even without a current incident.[1057] The resulting strong awareness of these topics might prevent German employees from digging deeper into the matter. Rather, German employees prove to interpret the deliberate and careful (rather than automatic) sharing as well as cases of excessive disclosure of knowledge against these pre-existing perceptions as is often the case with stereotypes.[1058] Thereby, these tenacious perceptions are seemingly confirmed and maintained.

And here the actual conflict which is caused by such a "Chinese culture" comes to light: whereas German employees focus on a "Chinese culture" in the *environment*, Chinese employees focus on the *enterprise* and how it provides a stable space. For Chinese employees the need for stability is located at the level of the enterprise rather than at the level of the nation state. The enterprise (or the space) is the entity against which any judgment occurs. It is the enterprise as a sub-society which serves as a new reference after university. Yet the crucial point leading to conflicts is that German employees focus on the environment for explaining the knowledge behavior of their Chinese colleagues. Germans are distracted by a cursory "Chinese culture" spreading in the national environment in which the enterprise is located.

This is also shown by the frequent reference to Chinese history or, most pointedly, by the fact that the seemingly chaotic traffic situation in China was often mentioned by German interviewees when asked about their daily work experiences with Chinese employees. Apparently, German employees tend to look to the outside for explaining the behavior inside, shifting "Chinese culture" to a national level. Virtually all sampled German employees are convinced that a traditional "Chinese culture" leads to the controversial handling of knowledge.

This "Chinese culture" is clearly seen – confirming Ross' study[1059] on foreign managers in China – as a "cultural burden". Also in line with the numerous English language studies on knowledge sharing,[1060] culture is rather viewed as a barrier by the sampled German employees. This is in stark contrast with the Chinese employees in Ross' study, the Chinese language studies in the area of knowledge sharing as well as the sampled Chinese employees in the present study, who perceive culture as an enabler of pursuing their daily work.

The German focus on a "Chinese culture" all too easily turns out to fuel self-fulfilling prophecies. One example of such a case can be found in Kessler's

1057 Richter and Gebauer 2010: 62 und 182.
1058 Stangor 2000: 13-14.
1059 Ross 2007.
1060 See chapter 1.3.

study[1061] on management strategies in FIEs. The foreign managers investigated in Kessler's study believed that Chinese engineers were leaking sensitive technologies due to a nationalist attitude and accordingly put measures in place to protect the enterprise. These measures, in turn, led to a restriction of the Chinese engineers' opportunities within the enterprise and provoked employees even more to leave the enterprise. Since with leaving the enterprise the risk of knowledge leakages becomes even higher, the fear of the foreign employees created a self-fulfilling prophecy.

What is identified as implicit and tacit cultural knowledge in the empirical chapter draws on explicit cultural knowledge as manifested in the past and present Chinese economy and society. The "Confucius argument", the "yellow spys", and other conventional explanations or stereotypes appear to be only relevant for German employees. They rest on a discursive level or at most falsely inform German employees when interpreting the dubious knowledge interactions of their Chinese colleagues against this explicit cultural knowledge. This kind of culture – if anything – could take the form of explicit cultural knowledge on a discursive level. The empirical data reveal that there is no link (as suggested by the reviewed studies on the topic) to the actual handling of knowledge. It is thus argued that the role of "Chinese culture" is to distract from the fact that Chinese employees' handling of knowledge can well be influenced.

This distracting effect might be fostered by the intercultural advice books and intercultural trainings. Most often, intercultural advice books on China refer to the approaches of Edward T. Hall, Geert Hofstede, Fons Trompenaars, and Alexander Thomas.[1062] These approaches have in common that they all locate cultural differences on the level of the nation state, which can as a seemingly homogenous cultural Other easily be differentiated from the "cultural dimensions"[1063] or "cultural standards"[1064] of other nation states. These studies further serve as basic material for many of the intercultural training sessions provided by consultants usually preparing expatriates for working in a Chinese subsidiary. Without delving too much into the actual situation, foreign employees are given some intuitive categories at hand, which can be used as quick explanation for culturally-induced conflicts which otherwise would be hard to describe.

It can be argued that quick explanations are especially problematic in the case of China. If there is anything that the vast majority of China scholars, Chinese scholars, and observers in and outside the country agree upon it is the fact

1061 Kessler 2007.

1062 For further details see Poerner's (2009: 117) investigation on intercultural advice books on China.

1063 Hofstede 1984, Hall 1989, Trompenaars and Hampden-Turner 1997, House et al. 2004.

1064 Thomas 2005.

that China is heterogeneous in many respects, most notably in terms of geography and people. Especially in the current phase of transition in the economic and social sphere, people draw on a more diverse and multifaceted cultural knowledge. The present study confirms that no unitary cultural orientation for the group under investigation could be found instead there are different cultural rationales which operate mostly on a subtle level.

Rather than being occupied with further essentializations, the present study captures the cultural dynamics and complexities including the link to the *de facto* cultural roots. Through its thorough empirical research it presents an alternative to swiftly ascribing static, fixed, and overessentialized traditional cultural attributes to the observed knowledge conflicts between Chinese and German employees. The actual culture of the present study does not arise from conventional reference systems,[1065] but from historical and current social and economic circumstances which have become newly and differently relevant *in a certain domain* at a certain point in time *on an implicit and tacit level*. The present study thus contributes to showing that culture only *in all its complexity* deserves to be entrusted with explanatory power for complex phenomena.

The way culture is treated in the present study carries theoretical and methodological implications for studying social phenomena in China from a cultural angle. Such as the theoretical perspective of cultural sociology provides fertile ground for studying the phenomenon of the controversial handling of knowledge in China, other phenomena could also be impartially investigated by applying this perspective. The perspective helps to analyze where culture indeed comes into effect within the social phenomenon under investigation. Rather than taking actions for granted or "natural", cultural sociology endeavors to illuminate the unconscious reasons and instincts of people and aims to "bring the unconscious cultural structures that regulate society into the light of the mind"[1066]. In this study, the behavior of Chinese employees is not seen as "naturally determined" by conventional "cultures", such as collectivism, influencing them in a compulsory way. The explanatory power of culture understood in this way is much more distinct than that of generalized meaning structures. It therefore is more adequate for researching the ever more complicated, contradictory, fragmented, flawy, and pluralistic social reality.[1067]

1065 Note that only Confucianism in regard to knowledge property is denied to have an influence. The author acknowledges that other findings such as the ubiquity of relationships or the model of the concentric circles again relate to Confucianism. Yet in this study these parts of Confucianism are seen as a reflection of the historical economic and social realities in China. These realities are regarded as more relevant for shaping the actual culture.

1066 Alexander 2003: 3-4.

1067 Eberle 2011.

This perspective presents an alternative to the conservative tendency within social sciences that builds on the nostalgia of a solid traditional culture.[1068] The said tendency can be observed within China studies as well as in other disciplines pursuing research on China, especially in business studies, which all too often refer to the mysteries of the Chinese culture.[1069] The phenomena of intellectual property infringements and insufficient knowledge sharing provide a prime example as these are commonly explained with a seemingly coherent and generalized traditional Chinese cultural system. Considering that the daily (working) life of many Chinese people is ever more complex, a more multi-faceted orientation is surely needed. Even regarding other areas of Chinese people's lives, this alternative perspective on culture as a discrete, local, and specific resource, might prove to be more adequate than the assumption of overall coherent cultural knowledge stocks.

For future research, it is recommended to use such a thorough theoretical perspective for bringing the unconscious cultural criteria to light rather than simply ascribing proposed cultural categories. Thus, the risk of being concerned with "assembling the values, communicative devices, actions, and aesthetics which fit in with favored explanations"[1070] can be avoided. Only then can China be researched from the inside in the spirit of the very essence of China studies.

The study's approach also carries methodological implications. The most apparent flaw of studies using "Chinese culture" as explanation is still that they adhere to a positivist deductive paradigm, treating culture as an exogenous variable for the sake of providing practical managerial advice. This neglects how culture is actually connected to human beings and vice versa. No empirical evidence is given whether this variable indeed influences Chinese people's thinking nowadays. In the present study, by contrast, the actual link between the individual and the social could be provided.

For future research, it is recommended to consider the Chinese perspective as far as possible applying a largely inductive dissection of alternative roles of culture. Where research is less deductively pursued, the results might not simply be a product of traditional "Chinese culture". Nor are they a reflection of Western assumptions with the real cultural mechanism remaining unnoticed.

A limitation is to be acknowledged concerning the analysis of the "role of 'Chinese culture'" in this study. The identified cultural knowledge is found to be only relevant to a particular domain as opposed to China as a whole. Yet it can only be proven to a limited extent that the culture is indeed only relevant for this domain. The examples of German employees, new workforce entrants, and over-

1068 Alexander 2003: 9.
1069 Goodman 2007: 175.
1070 Shurmer-Smith 2002: 14.

seas returnees only provide evidence for cultural knowledge not being inherently Chinese as is often suggested when treating nations as homogeneous "cultural containers". This, however, does not rule out the possibility that these cultures might be found in other domains in China. It can just be assumed that the probability of other domains being informed by the cultural knowledge investigated is rather low since it is precisely the combination of the positionings as knowledge workers and intermediaries in the contexts of China's contemporary economy and society and the FIE which make this cultural knowledge most relevant for orientation.

9.4 Solutions for Sino-German Knowledge Conflicts

How can these conflicts surrounding valuable knowledge be solved? The notion of an inherent "Chinese culture" at a national level suggests that nothing can be done about it. Yet precisely the opposite holds true: German managers *can* do something to prevent these kinds of conflicts.

From a corporate perspective, knowledge conflicts and their possible solutions touch upon many functions and positions rather than only being consequential for an enterprise's knowledge management which would probably seek to solve conflicts in an instrumental way. As a matter of fact, "knowledge management" is an awkward term in itself simply as knowledge cannot be managed. Knowledge cannot be regarded as detached from its context as commonly claimed by conventional knowledge management approaches. Rather, it is strongly connected to the persons involved. This is particularly obvious in China where knowledge is handled in a complicated and dense social fabric.

Considering that knowledge management in general and in China in particular rather requires the management of the context in which valuable knowledge is embedded, the term of *knowledge context management* is proposed. As Alvesson notes, "the managerial aspect is not too self-evident: *creating an environment* is not something that a management can do on its own, and it is definitely difficult to address in an instrumental way"[1071]. Creating a context or an environment for knowledge to be handled properly is thus not to be attempted by the management alone without involving employees and surely not only by applying classical (knowledge) management instruments.

This study shows that the context in which knowledge conflicts happen unfolds into a macro and a micro level context. These are strongly interrelated as each of these proves useless without taking the other into account. Knowledge context management on the macro level considers the enterprise as a whole. The

1071 Alvesson 2004: 169 [emphasis added].

senior management team ideally frequently asks the following questions: what holds the enterprise together? What is the common reference of the enterprise? How can a *stable* enterprise be created?

The precondition for the senior management to come to pose such questions at all rests on the *understanding* that knowledge conflicts are *not* caused by a fixed and unchangeable "inherent Chinese culture" which inevitably pervades the FIE, but that the actually relevant cultural knowledge makes Chinese employees precisely focus on the FIE as a stable entity. Without this acknowledgment, knowledge conflicts can hardly be solved.

Emphasizing a common reference reminds of what can be found as "corporate personality" or "organizational identity" in the business management literature.[1072] Such concepts draw attention to the deeper patterns of meaning or the core values as well as to the spirit, soul, or ideology which provides an enterprise – in the same manner as a person – with individuality and uniqueness. These intrinsic character "traits" give the enterprise its specificity, coherence, and stability especially in rapidly changing business environments.[1073] An enterprise with a coherent and strong character serves the general need for orientation which is naturally desired by any individual.

In the domain under investigation, however, the need for orientation particularly surrounds the feature of stability. To clearly differentiate the FIE with its various actors from the ever more complicated and unstable Chinese business and social environment in the upcoming knowledge economy, a common reference for guiding communication and behavior within knowledge interactions in *a stable way* is urgently needed by Chinese employees in FIEs. It is thus most essential that employees in this space can feel a certain kind of common identity from the beginning.

No matter whether the reference system is labeled as an enterprise's values, mission, vision, or philosophy or even if it is not clearly categorized, for the domain under investigation it is most important that is does not only exist on a discursive level. Explicit slogans offered by the management by putting up banners in every department or spreading it through the enterprise via intranet are not sufficient. These points of references are not perceived as stable since they can be amended anytime or fellow employees might just discard them. An enterprise can only claim that such a reference system exists when it is indeed understood and internalized by a certain number or the "critical mass"[1074] of its employees.

The reference system at the macro level cannot come into existence without employees at the micro level. To be perceived as *stable* this reference must be

1072 See Cornelissen (2008: 67-70) for a summary.
1073 Cornelissen 2008: 68.
1074 Ball 2004.

lived out by the employees, most importantly by those in management positions. On the part of superiors, the immediate work environment of every single employee deserves utmost attention. Here, *only* the direct superior is able to pursue this to a sufficient extent, as he represents the enterprise from the subordinates' point of view.

At the micro level, the superior is to create stability by, for instance, regularly providing information about the economic situation of the enterprise. In the fast changing Chinese environment this is seen as inextricably linked to the employees' future. Equally important (but more challenging) is the constant information for every single employee about his personal situation in the enterprise. This involves to continuously show the personal development possibilities in the enterprise and to encourage employees individually according to their personal abilities. The precondition is that the superior *continuously* observes the employees and even anticipates the direction which suits their talents. These efforts on the part of the enterprise are expected by the employees and directly connected to the efforts they invest into the enterprise themselves.

The superior is of particular significance for new workforce entrants who are first and foremost occupied with the struggle to adapt to the new work environment. Having just "entered society", new workforce entrants struggle to come to terms with their new responsibilities and their new colleagues, slowly acquiring indispensable communication competences at the workplace. They further have to figure out which kind of knowledge is required for their job and how acquired theoretical knowledge can be adapted in practice. While this might well be the case for new workforce entrants all over the world, this issue appears to produce particular uncertainties among the new workforce entrants in enterprises in China, where the stable space can be built up only over time. With so much uncertainty involved at the beginning of their work life, they particularly need the superior to provide a stable environment.

Superiors should also take action regarding employees who have gathered work experience of at least some years as these are most keen on increasing their value on the labor market. The concern especially about employees frequently switching employers should not prevent investing resources into them. On the part of Chinese employees, high turnover rates in China are definitely to be seen as a means for advancing the career. Yet what would be wise for superiors to take into account is that Chinese employees in their identity as knowledge workers strongly need the enterprise. As knowledge workers they are mobile and able to take their means of production with them, yet especially in China knowledge workers need an enterprise which is particularly adept in reflecting their value. The FIE appears to be a significant platform where employees can apply and upgrade their personal knowledge. As workplaces become more and more specialized, the employee can only apply this knowledge in a certain kind of enterprise and hence depends on this platform. Due to the need to succeed in a competitive environment, the suitability of the platform to distinctly reflect the individual employee's value is urgently needed.

Taking the stability of this platform into account is thus of utmost importance for Chinese employees in the framework of an upcoming knowledge economy in an unstable environment. The enterprise is such a potential source of stability. It is not so much the "corporate culture" itself, unfolding in events organized for employees or other tangible efforts (though this is might help as well), that provides stability. Rather, stability is felt within a culture where the employees realize that the enterprise cares for their knowledge now and in the future. There should be an understanding that this knowledge and abilities have to be fostered and unfolded to their full extent.

The task of *continuously* observing the immediate work environment of the respective employee and how he is embedded in the complex relations at the workplace *from the employee's perspective* should be taken very seriously by any superior. Although corporate culture starts at the top, it is the direct superiors who should shoulder the responsibility of establishing an atmosphere within the direct work environment of their employees which makes them willing to share knowledge. If, for example, a conflict of interest between departments arises and an employee has to decide what knowledge he will share and to what extent, the stability of his work environment greatly influences his descision. The direct superior should convince the employees that no negative consequences arise from sharing, and he should indeed ensure that such consequences cannot come into effect. Here again, it is the task of the direct superior to provide this stable environment and to anticipate such possible conflicts. The employee should be encouraged to share, making him confident that sharing will not result in a personal disadvantage. In this case, employees can be sure that their behavior is supported by the person who is directly responsible for them.

Direct superiors at best encourage their employees to share their knowledge in a way that makes them realize the benefits of sharing – not only for the company in general but for the efficiency of their own individual work as well. New ideas, for example, could be published in a company magazine or elsewhere to value the *individual* contribution to the company's success. The precondition is that the employee can rely on the direct superior who ensures that no one else reaps the benefits of certain knowledge items or ideas. Only then can an employee perceive his working environment as stable and be assured that his potential will be unfolded.

Regarding the disclosure of valuable knowledge to other market players, disclosure of a certain, limited extent should be accepted as a necessary concession. Managers also need to show confidence in their employees' knowledge handling experience and intuition – at least up to a certain extent. Employees' experience and intuition appear to be crucial for doing business on the Chinese market in general and for assessing counterparts and investigating relationships in particular. Here again, a common reference is helpful which provides employees with a stable background against which knowledge interactions with other enterprises can carefully be pursued.

Barriers within communication make work difficult for Chinese employees, putting much pressure on them and eventually impeding them from carrying out their tasks properly. They themselves – and not only the enterprise – in the first instance suffer from the reluctance of others to share knowledge and from the competitive mentality observed in the sampled enterprises. The direct superior at best identifies barriers and establishes a supporting work atmosphere for any of his employees while taking the information and communication channels they rely on into consideration. Although the employees are very much aware of the fact that they themselves have to cultivate relationships, they additionally expect the direct superior to coordinate these relationships in order to enable the employees to smoothly carry out their work. This is ideally to be pursued on a *continuous* basis.

For coordinating relationships, the direct superior might focus on the layout of the offices and locate employees according to how they can efficiently cooperate instead of strictly arranging them according to position, function, or department. For any superior, keeping an "informal organization chart" in mind could be of great help. This resonates with the requirements of the knowledge economy, where information only seldomly runs along the lines of formal work processes and functions. The exchange across departments and positions in an informal way can be most fruitful.

Regarding the communication with the headquarters, German employees better embrace the intermediary function between the FIE and their colleagues in Germany to improve the communication with the headquarters and increase a rapid and smooth flow of information. As being intermediaries, too, they at best feel responsible for raising awareness at the headquarters for the specific Chinese business environment where knowledge interactions follow their own subtle logic. Not providing this knowledge and failing to secure competitiveness would neither be in the interests of the German enterprise as a whole. Only with the German headquarters gaining in understanding, the pressure on Chinese employees to adapt to the constantly changing market conditions could be relieved.

German employees in the role of the direct superior naturally have the expectation of employees sharing their knowledge since they are used to being provided with information automatically. This expectation runs counter to the implicit rules in China according to which employees rather focus on assessing the counterpart and the relationship involved before sharing knowledge. As such, German employees ideally not just remain stuck in their expectations, but take the time to actively ask for information, being sensitive for "taking out" the knowledge of the employee. Knowledge sharing should be formally organized as this helps to openly recognize this contribution before someone else comes up with a similar idea. Rather than taking the contribution for granted, such a stable foundation for knowledge sharing has to be established first.

Since the direct superior plays such an important role in actively encouraging different groups of employees and providing an adequate work atmosphere and environment, the frequent rotation of foreign expatriates more often than not proves detrimental. Not only are they most likely unable to gain the trust of the employees or become aware of all the informal knowledge flows and conflicts within the environment. First and foremost, they suffer from not being provided with the most basic information themselves as they – besides possible language barriers – are not able to enter the information networks which have been established within the company for long time. The worst scenario is when the predecessor has not come to terms with the employees. Then the expatriate replacing him will face even more hurdles. How can he get the employees to share when they themselves have problems to get any information about what is going on in the company? After all, stability for Chinese employees involves a stable network of employees. A frequent rotation is thus detrimental to stability as such – also in the light of the fact that turnover among Chinese employees already threatens the stability.

Much more exchange among German employees in the FIE (both currently and formerly employed) is also desirable. The insight that cultural knowledge of this particular domain can be internalized can be made use of in enterprises. Regular exchange would help to gather different perspectives as everyone has presumably internalized the cultural knowledge of the domain to a different degree.

Finally, the challenges of knowledge work in China are ideally to embrace. It would be helpful to acknowledge that the structured thinking from an organizational perspective is a legacy of the Western industrial era. In the knowledge economy in general, knowledge can not be controlled and organized in a rational manner. Especially the domain under investigation is a prime example of how contextual knowledge in fact is and of how complex knowledge interactions are with so many criteria involved.

The notion of a "Chinese culture" should not divert the attention from the pressing issue of the stability the own FIE can provide. In being seen as a barrier, "Chinese culture" indeed becomes a barrier on the part of German employees in the sense of diverting attention from the own enterprise. Turning a blind eye on the cultural knowledge underlying the behavior within knowledge interactions is not adequate for the knowledge economy in general and even less for China's upcoming knowledge economy.

German employees do not have to helplessly stand by and let an assumed "Chinese culture" pervade their FIEs. They can focus on a common reference for orientation at the level of the enterprise and ensure that this is indeed lived out by the employees. Any superior could be a knowledge context manager by building up an atmosphere of stability. While considering the viewpoint of every single employee might be a challenging endeavor, it is definitely worth a try. The odds are surely against managers who quickly resort to blaming Confucius for the handling of knowledge.

10 Conclusions

For foreign businesses investing in China, the handling of valuable knowledge is most challenging. Critical issues are the excessive leakage of knowledge and insufficient knowledge sharing. Explanations for the controversial handling of knowledge are usually sought in the realm of "Chinese culture", most prominently referring to Confucianism or collectivism. This convenient usage of conventional cultural explanations for knowledge conflicts comes at a time where knowledge increasingly replaces low production costs as the crucial factor for the competitiveness of foreign businesses in China. It was unclear so far, whether such conventional cultural attributes indeed do inform the actors. This study's overall objective was to foster an understanding of the role culture actually plays within knowledge conflicts in China's FIEs.

Four major conclusions can be drawn from the present study. First, when drawing the boundaries of knowledge in FIEs, Chinese employees orient themselves along multiple criteria which are tacitly directed to the approaching of a stable space. Chinese employees thus do not draw the boundaries of knowledge in an arbitrary way but are informed by cultural knowledge beyond the individual. This cultural knowledge does not operate detached from the employees, but indeed proves relevant for the employees. Instead of ascribing cultural attributes, six practices emerged through an inductive investigation, allowing for indeed establishing the link between the individual and the social.

The cultural knowledge is located on a practical rather than discursive level, which is shown by the interviewees not being readily able to or being used to making them fully explicit. Furthermore, the practices do not determine actions in a rigid culture-as-system sense. Rather, employees actively draw on practices when pursuing knowledge work in a way adequate for a concrete situation. Practices thus can rather be thought of as a resource, providing employees with manifold criteria allowing for orientation as well as tactfulness and timing within knowledge interactions.

An underlying rationale alines the various practices to function in a non-arbitrary and socially concruent way in the domain the Chinese employees are positioned in. This underlying rationale is the FIE as a stable space tacitly tying together all practices. Within each practice of cultivating, assessing, evaluating, investigating, and preventing the stable space ensures channels the application of implicit criteria and subtle strategies into a direction which makes sense in the employees' social world. When the enterprise is acknowledged as being stable, employees have the incentive to limit the personal competitive advantage, to evaluate the superior's efforts into his knowledge application as reliable and sustainable, to yield positive results when assessing and investigating counterparts, relationships, and networks as well as to be careful when preventing a competitive disadvantage of the FIE during their close knowledge interactions with the business environment. This underlying rationale of stability can be seen as functioning as a contrasting foil to an unstable and volatile Chinese business and social environment.

The second main conclusion is that knowledge conflicts have their roots in differing points of departure. Whereas for Chinese employees the FIE as an entity has to be manifested over time to serve as a point of reference within knowledge interactions, the FIE *a priori* provides orientation for German employees. German employees take formal organizational structures as a point of departure. Chinese employees, in contrast, handle knowledge in a very *deliberate* way involving a situational and subjective assessment of the social fabric in advance.

This core difference of organizational structures versus social concentric circles has already been observed by the Chinese sociologist Fei Xiaotong in the 1940s. This deeply rooted cultural knowledge becomes relevant again in a distinct manner for Chinese employees positioned in the particular domain of knowledge work in China's foreign-invested manufacturing sector. In this domain it is a bunch of fuzzy and vague, oscillating and erratic, mixed and sometimes conflicting criteria, which at first necessitate the departure from an (unchanging) egocentric perspective. Yet to align all the contingent criteria a more streamlined point of reference is to be tacitly approached at the level of the FIE in form of a stable space.

The stability of the space, which can only be built up over time, yet contradicts the German employees' focus on organizational structures to guide knowledge interactions from the start. Against the background of how the Western economy has been structured for more than a century, adapting this structural viewpoint to the demands of quick and situational communication of the knowledge economy is a long process. The conflicting views are reinforced by a situation where German employees are often in an upper management position and demand employees to act upon organizational processes before providing the necessary stability.

The third main conclusion is that culture does not play a role in the conventional sense and that what is commonly referred to as "Chinese culture" distracts from the actually relevant culture. The actually relevant culture does not arise from conventional reference systems such as philosophy but from cultural resources being derived from historical and current social and economic circumstances which have become newly and differently relevant in a certain domain at a certain point in time on an implicit and tacit level. Culture only in all its complexity deserves to be entrusted with an explanatory power for certain phenomena.

In contrast to conventional explanations resorting to Confucianism, collectivism, and nationalism, which locate "Chinese culture" in the sense of an internally homogeneous "cultural container" at the level of the *nation state*, the identified culture only plays a role in the domain of knowledge work in China's foreign-invested manufacturing sector. The drawing on these cultural resources for orientation in daily life proves to be particularly necessary for the protagonists of this study: those Chinese employees employed by FIEs who act as knowledge workers and intermediaries. If one would leave the identified cultural knowledge at the level of the nation state, the phenomenon of the controversial handling of knowledge could be understood as an ethnical or inherently cultural one. German employees, however, potentially internalize the cultural knowledge after a certain period of time and Chinese new workforce entrants and overseas returnees themselves struggle with relationships and networks at the workplace. This shows that the cultural knowledge is particular relevant in the domain under investigation rather than for China as a whole.

It is the commonly accepted notion of "Chinese culture" which indeed causes the knowledge conflicts: whereas German employees focus on a "Chinese culture" in the environment, Chinese employees focus on the enterprise and how it provides a stable space. The practical relevance of "Chinese culture" is only found among German employees, referring all too often to the environment for an explanation. German employees tend to look to the outside for explaining the behavior inside. The role of the conventional "Chinese culture" actually is to distract from the fact that Chinese employees' handling of knowledge can well be influenced.

The fourth main conclusion is that managers in FIEs indeed can contribute to solving the conflicts surrounding valuable knowledge. The precondition is to understand that "Chinese culture" is not "inherently Chinese" and that the actual cultural roots mostly induce Chinese employees to focus on the enterprise and its stability. Rather than taking the enterprise as it is for granted right from the start and being only focused on the environment in the search for explanations for knowledge conflicts, managers could well endeavor to strengthen the stability of their FIE.

The stability of the FIE can mostly be ensured by what is termed knowledge context management in this study. Knowledge context management at a macro level is pursued by the senior management which ideally provides a common reference and ensures that it is lived out by a sufficient number of employees. On a micro level, knowledge context management is at best pursued by every superior in the FIE. Superiors would do well in focusing on the direct working environment of their employees from their individual perspective. This calls for coordinating relationships and networks, for alleviating barriers within communication, and ensuring that the employee's individual contribution is recognized. The careful exchange with knowledge with the environment should be acknowledged and the background against which these interactions are pursued should continuously be observed. German employees also ideally embrace their role as intermediaries between their Chinese colleagues and the German headquarters, learn from each other, and try to extend their stay in China. The challenges of knowledge work the domain of knowledge in China's foreign-invested manufacturing sector ideally are embraced by enhancing the thinking from a structural angle with a focus on the actual context in which knowledge interactions take place. In any event, this is indispensable for the ever more dynamic knowledge economy in general and for the Chinese one in particular.

German managers definitely do not have to stand by helplessly when an alleged "Chinese culture" of the Chinese environment seemingly pervades their FIEs. It is the stability at the level of the enterprise which should be the point of concern – rather than simply blaming Confucius.

References

Adams, Mary and Oleksak, Michael (2010): *Intangible Capital: Putting Knowledge to Work in the 21st-Century Organization*, Santa Barbara: Praeger.

Alexander, Jeffrey C. (2003): *The Meanings of Social Life: On the Origins of a Cultural Sociology*, New York: Oxford University Press.

Alford, William P. (1995): *To Steal a Book is an Elegant Offense: Intellectual Property Law in Chinese Civilization*, Stanford: Stanford University Press.

Alpermann, Björn (2012): "Qualitative Interviewforschung in China", in: Jan Kruse, Stephanie Bethmann, Debora Niermann, Christian Schmieder (eds.): *Qualitative Interviewforschung in und mit fremden Sprachen: Eine Einführung in Theorie und Praxis*, Weinheim: Beltz Juventa, pp. 169-189.

Alvesson, Mats (2004): *Knowledge Work and Knowledge-Intensive Firms*, Oxford: Oxford University Press.

American Chamber of Commerce in the People's Republic of China (2006): "Comments on the Draft Labor Contract Law of the People's Republic of China", *anchamshanghai.org*, April 19, 2006.

American Chamber of Commerce in the People's Republic of China (2007): "Comments on the Second Deliberated Draft Labor Contract Law of the PRC", *anchamshanghai.org*, Feb 12, 2007.

Apco Worldwide (2010): *Market Analysis Report: China's Automotive Industry*, November 2010, http://www.israeltrade.org.cn/hebrew/APCO%20Market%20Study%20for%20IEICI%20Automotive%20-%20For%20Embassy.pdf (accessed May 5, 2012).

Arayama, Yuko and Miyoshi, Katsuya (2004): "Regional Diversity and Sources of Economic Growth in China", *World Economy*, Vol. 27 No. 10, Hoboken, pp. 1583-1607.

Ariely, Gil (2008): "Intellectual Capital and Knowledge Management", in: Murray E. Jennex (ed.): *Knowledge Management: Concepts, Methodologies, Tools and Applications*, New York: Hershey, pp. 2965-2975.

Bai, J. Benjamin and Da, Guoping (2011): "Strategies for Trade Secrets Protection in China", *Northwestern Journal of Technology and Intellectual Property*, Vol. 9 No. 7, Spring 2011, Chicago, pp. 351-375.

Bai, Yunfei 白云飞 and Jia, Yuping 贾玉平 (1997): "Lun shangye mimi ji qi lifa baohu" [论商业秘密及其立法保护/ Discussing trade secrets and their legislative protection], *Faxuejia*, 02/1997, Beijing, pp. 39-44.

Baidu 百度 (2013): "Shehui jingzhengli" [社会竞争力/ Social competitiveness], *Baidu baike*, http://baike.baidu.com/view/2087218.htm (accessed May 20, 2013).

Ball, Philip (2004): *Critical Mass: How one thing leads to another*, London: Random House.

Barboza, David (2009): "Danone Exists China Venture After Years of Legal Dispute", *The New York Times online*, Sept 30, 2009, http://www.nytimes.com/2009/10/01/business/global/01danone.html?_r=0 (accessed June 10, 2013).

Barboza, David (2010): "China Sentences Rio Tinto Employees in Bribe Case", *The New York Times online*, March 29, 2010, http://www.nytimes.com/2010/03/30/business/global/30riotinto.html?pagewanted=all&_r=0 (accessed Feb 15, 2013).

Barner-Rasmussen, Wilhelm and Björkman, Ingmar (2007): "Social Capital and Knowledge Transfer between Subsidiaries of Foreign MNCs and Local Organizations: Comparing the Cases of China and Finland", in: Stewart Clegg, Karen Wang and Mike Berrell (eds.): *Business Networks and Strategic Alliances in China,* Cheltenham: Edward Elgar, pp. 77-98.

Beck, Ulrich (1998): "Wie wird Demokratie im Zeitalter der Globalisierung möglich? – Eine Einleitung", in: Ulrich Beck (ed.): *Politik der Globalisierung*, Frankfurt am Main: Suhrkamp, pp. 7-66.

Beijing Higher People's Court (2007): "Li Yong deng yu yatai dianzi youxian gongsi qinfan shangye mimi jiufen shangsuan" [李勇等与亚太电子有限公司侵犯商业秘密纠纷上诉案/ Dispute appeal case for infringement of trade secrets of Li Yong et al. and Rosenberger Asia Pacific Electronic Co., Ltd.], Book of Civil Cases Judgments, 184/2007, *Beida fabao*, http://www.pkulaw.cn/fulltext_form.aspx?Db=pfnl&Gid=117521663&keyword=%E7%BD%97%E6%A3%AE%E4%BC%AF%E6%A0%BC&EncodingName=&Search_Mode=accurate (accessed Jan 16, 2013).

Bell, Daniel (1974): *The Coming of Post-Industrial Society: A Venture in Social Forecasting*, London: Heinemann.

Bell, Daniel A. (2003): "Confucian Constraints on Property Rights", in: Daniel A. Bell and Hahm Chaibong (eds.): *Confucianism for the Modern World*, Cambridge: Cambridge University Press, pp. 218-235.

Berger, Peter and Luckmann, Thomas (2007): *Die gesellschaftliche Konstruktion der Wirklichkeit*, 21st edition, Frankfurt am Main: Fischer.

Bergère, Marie-Claire (1968): *La Bourgeoisie Chinoise et la Révolution de 1911*, Den Haag and Paris: Mouton & Co.

Bergère, Marie-Claire (1986): *L'Âge D'Or de la Bourgeoisie Chinoise 1911-1937*, Paris: Flammarion.

Bernard, Russell H. (2006): *Research Methods in Anthropology: Qualitative and Quantitative Approaches*, 4th edition, Lanham et al.: Altamira Press.

Bernard, Russell H. and Ryan, Gery W. (2010): *Analyzing Qualitative Data: Systematic Approaches*, Thousand Oaks, CA: SAGE.

Bian, Yanjie (1994): *Work and Inequality in Urban China*, Albany: State University of New York Press.

Bielinski, Juliane (2010): *Forschungs- und Entwicklungstätigkeiten von multinationalen Unternehmen in China: Eine empirische Analyse der deutschen Automobil-, Chemie- und Elektronikindustrie*, Frankfurt am Main: Peter Lang.

Bourdieu, Pierre (1977): *Outline of a Theory of Practice*, Cambridge: Cambridge University Press.

Bourdieu, Pierre (1987): *Sozialer Sinn: Kritik der theoretischen Vernunft*, Frankfurt am Main: Suhrkamp.

Bourdieu, Pierre (1994): *Raisons Pratiques: Sur la théorie de l'action*, Paris: Editions du Seuil.

Bramall, Chris (2009): *Chinese Economic Development*, Abingdon: Routledge.

Brandt, Loren and Rawski, Thomas G. (2008): "China's Great Economic Transformation", in: Loren Brandt and Thomas G. Rawski (eds.): *China's Great Economic Transformation*, New York: Cambridge University Press, pp. 1-26.

Breznitz, Dan and Murphree, Michael (2011): *Run of the Red Queen: Government, Innovation, Globalization and Economic Growth in China*, New Haven: Yale University Press.

Brodbeck, Felix C. and Frese, Michael (2008): "Societal Culture and Leadership in Germany", in: Jagdeep S. Chhokar, Felix C. Brodbeck and Robert J. House (eds.): *Culture and Leadership Across the World: The GLOBE Book of In-Depth Studies of 25 Societies*, New York and Abingdon: Taylor & Francis, pp. 147-214.

Buckley, Peter J., Clegg, Jeremy and Tan, Hui (2010): "Cultural Awareness in Knowledge Transfer to China: The Role of *Guanxi* and *Mianzi*", in: Buckley, Peter J. (ed.): *Foreign Direct Investment, China and the World Economy*, Hampshire: Palgrave MacMillan, pp. 165-191.

Burrows, Glen R., Drummond, Damon L. and Martinsons, Maris G. (2005): "Knowledge Management in China", *Communication of the ACM*, Vol. 48 No. 4, April 2005, New York, pp. 73-76.

Cai, Fang (2010): "Labor Market Development and Expansion of Rural and Urban Development", in: Fang Cai (ed.): *Transforming the Chinese Economy*, Leiden: Brill, pp. 85-114.

Cai, Fang, Park, Albert and Zhao, Yaohui (2008): "The Chinese Labor Market in the Reform Era", in: Loren Brandt and Thomas G. Rawski (eds.): *China's Great Economic Transformation*, New York: Cambridge University Press, pp. 167-214.

Cao, Wenjuan 曹文娟 (1996): "Xu Run" [徐润], in: Xu Mao 徐矛 (ed.): *Zhongguo shi maiban* [中国十买办/ China's ten compradors], Shanghai: Shanghai renmin chubanshe, pp. 1-41.

Cappai, Gabriele (2008): "Einleitung. Die empirische Erforschung des Fremden. Ein interdisziplinärer Ansatz", in: Gabriele Cappai (ed.): *Forschen unter den Bedingungen kultureller Fremdheit*, Wiesbaden: VS Verlag für Sozialwissenschaften, pp. 9-38.

Chai, Joseph C.H. (2011): *An Economic History of Modern China*, Cheltenham: Edward Elgar.

Chan, Anita (2001): *China's Worker Under Assault: The Exploitation of Labor in a Globalizing Economy*, Armonk: M.E. Sharpe.

Chan, Cheris Shun-ching (2007): "Honing the desired attitude: Ideological work on insurance sales agents", in: Ching Kwan Lee (ed.): *Working in China: Ethnographies of labor and workplace transformation*, Abingdon: Routledge, pp. 229-246.

Chan, Chris King-Chi (2010): *The Challenge of Labour in China: Strikes and the Changing Labour Regime in Global Factories*, Abingdon: Routledge.

Chan, Kai Yiu (2006): *Business Expansion and Structural Change and Pre-War China: Liu Hongsheng and His Enterprises, 1920-1937*, Hong Kong: Hong Kong University Press.

Chang, Jiankun 常建坤 and Li, Shichun 李时椿 (2006): *Chuangye jiaocheng* [创业教程/ Entrepreneurship Tutorial], Beijing: Qinghua daxue chubanshe.

Chang, Leslie T. (2009): *Factory Girls: From Village to City in a Changing China*, New York: Spiegel & Grau.

Chelala, Cesar (2012): "Overwork extracts a high price", *China Internet Information Center*, Nov 28, 2012, http://www.china.org.cn/opinion/2012-11/28/content_27247895.htm (accessed May 13, 2013).

Chen, Chunlai (2011): *Foreign Direct Investment: Location Determinants, Investor Differences and Economic Impacts*, Cheltenham: Edward Elgar.

Chen, Hefang 陈和芳 (2008): "Shilun wo guo gudai zhishi chanquan baohu zai shijieshang de lingxianxing" [试论我国古代知识产权保护在世界上的领先性/ Attempting to discuss China's global leading position in traditional intellectual property protection], *Jingjishi*, 06/2008, Taiyuan, pp. 57-58.

Chen, Jiagui and Wang, Qin (2010): "The Reform, Opening, and Development of China's Industrial Economy", in: Fang Cai (ed.): *Transforming the Chinese Economy*, Leiden: Brill, pp. 39-83.

Chen, Longxin 陈龙鑫 (2009): "Qinfan shangye mimi fanzui xianzhuang yu lifa wanshan: yi lituoan wei querudian" [侵犯商业秘密犯罪现状与立法完善：以力拓案为切入点/ Current situation of and legislature improvement for trade secret infringement offenses: with the Rio Tinto case as starting point], *Fanzui yanjiu*, 05/2009, Shanghai, pp. 40-46.

Chen, Shuang-Ye (2012): "Contributing knowledge and knowledge workers: the role of Chinese universities in the knowledge economy", *London Review of Education*, Vol. 10 No. 1, London, pp. 101-112.

Chen, Yu 陈玉 (2010): "Qiantan wo guo qiye shangye mimi de baohu" [浅谈我国企业商业秘密的保护/ Brief discussion of enterprises' trade secrets protection in China], *Fazhi yu jingji*, 04/2010, Beijing, pp. 99-101.

Cheng, Li (2010): "Chinese Scholarship on the Middle Class: From Social Stratification to Political Potential", in: Li Cheng (ed.): *China's Emerging Middle Class: Beyond Economic Transformation*, Washington, DC: Brookings Institution Press, pp. 55-83.

Cheng, Tsung-Mei (2012): "A great leveller", *South China Morning Post online*, March 17, 2012, http://www.scmp.com/portal/site/SCMP/template.printACopy/page%E2%80%A6printacopy/vgnextoid=f5ec4d4da1b16310VgnVCM100000360a0a0aRCRD (accessed 18 March 2012).

Chi, Wei (2007): "The Role of Human Capital in China's Economic Development: Review and New Evidence", *China Economic Review*, Vol. 19 No. 3, Amsterdam, pp. 421-436.

Child, John (2007): "Performance in International Joint Ventures in China: Critical Factors", in: Stewart Clegg, Karen Wang and Mike Berrell (eds.): *Business Networks and Strategic Alliances in China,* Cheltenham: Edward Elgar, pp. 290-316.

Child, John and Warner, Malcolm (2003): "Culture and Management in China", in: Malcolm Warner (ed.): *Culture and Management in Asia*, London and New York: RoutledgeCurzon, pp. 24-47.

China Daily (2010): "White-collar workers are China's newest underclass", *China Daily online*, June 23, 2010, http://www.chinadaily.com.cn/opinion/2010-06/23/content_10009579.htm (accessed May 28, 2012).

China Daily (2011): "Industries to remain world's competitive", *China Daily online*, Dec 13, 2012, http://www.chinadaily.com.cn/business/2011-12/13/content_14257422.htm (accessed May 5, 2012).

China Daily (2012): "Do you qualify as a white-collar worker?", *China Daily online*, May 16, 2012, http://europe.chinadaily.com.cn/business/2012-05/16/content_15311917.htm (accessed June 11, 2012).

China Institute of Applied Jurisprudence of the Supreme People's Court (CIAJ) 最高人民法院中国应用法学研究所 (1992-2011): *Renmin fayuan anlixuan* [人民法院案例

选/ Selected Cases of the People's Court], Vol. 1-78, Beijing: Renmin fayuan chubanshe.

China International Conference on Positive Psychology (2012): "An Interview with Kaiping Peng: 'From Driving Happiness with Development' to 'Driving Development with Happiness'", Oct 31, 2012, http://www.happy-sci.net/en/news/97.html (accessed May 22, 2013).

China Labor Bulletin (2006): "Death from Overwork in China", Aug 11, 2006, http://www.clb.org.hk/en/content/death-overwork-china (accessed May 13, 2013).

Chou, Justin A. and Ratner, Mitchell (2011): "The influence of Confucius on intellectual property rights in China", *Journal of Emerging Markets*, Vol. 15 (2011) No. 3, New York, pp. 8-16.

Chow, Chee W., Deng, Johnny F. and Ho, Joanna L. (2000): "The Openness of Knowledge Sharing within Organizations: A Comparative Study of the United States and the People's Republic of China", *Journal of Management Accounting Research*, Vol. 12, Sarasota, pp. 65-95.

Chow, Gregory C. (2004): *Knowing China*, Singapore: World Scientific.

Christians, Clifford G. (2005): "Ethics and Politics in Qualitative Research", in: Norman K. Denzin, Yvonne S. Lincoln (eds.): *The SAGE Handbook of Qualitative Research*, 3rd edition, London et al.: SAGE, pp. 139-164.

Clarke, Donald, Murrell, Peter and Whiting, Susan (2008): "The Role of Law in China's Economic Development", in: Loren Brandt and Thomas G. Rawski (eds.): *China's Great Economic Transformation*, New York: Cambridge University Press, pp. 375-428.

Clegg, Stewart, Wang, Karen and Berrell, Mike (2007): "Business Networks and Strategic Alliances in China: An Introduction", in: in: Stewart Clegg, Karen Wang and Mike Berrell (eds.): *Business Networks and Strategic Alliances in China*, Cheltenham: Edward Elgar, pp. 3-27.

Cochran, Sherman (2000): *Encountering Chinese Networks: Western, Japanese, and Chinese Corporations in China, 1880-1937*, Berkeley and Los Angeles, CA: University of California Press.

Cooke, Fang Lee (2005): *HRM, Work and Employment in China*, Abingdon: Routledge.

Cooke, Fang Lee (2010): "The changing face of human resource management in China", in: Chris Rowley and Fang Lee Cooke (eds.): *The Changing Face of Management in China*, Abingdon: Routledge, pp. 28-51.

Cooney, Sean, Biddulph, Sarah, Li, Kungang and Zhu, Ying (2007): "China's New Labour Contract Law: Responding to the Growing Complexity of Labour Relations in the PRC", *UNSW Law Journal*, Vol. 30 No. 3, Sydney, pp. 786-801.

Cornelissen, Joep (2008): *Corporate Communication: A Guide to Theory and Practice*, 2nd edition, London: SAGE.

Cortada, James W. (1998a): "Introducing the Knowledg Worker", in: James W. Cortada (ed.): *The Rise of the Knowledge Worker*, Boston, MA: Butterworth-Heinemann, pp. xiii-xviii.

Cortada, James W. (1998b): "Where Did Knowledge Workers Come From?", in: James W. Cortada (ed.): *The Rise of the Knowledge Worker*, Boston, MA: Butterworth-Heinemann, pp. 3-21.

Cua, Antonio S. (2009): "The emergence of the history of Chinese philosophy", in: Bo Mou (ed.): *Routledge History of World Philosophies: History of Chinese Philosophy*, Abingdon and New York: Routledge, pp. 43-68.

Cucco, Ivan (2008): "The professional middle classes: Management and politics", in: David S. G. Goodman (ed.): *The New Rich in China: Future rulers, present lives*, Abingdon: Routledge, pp. 126-147.

Cui, Xuesong 催雪松 (2008): "Jianlun wo guo shangye mimi de goucheng yaojian" [简论我国商业秘密的构成要件/ Brief discussion of the constituent elements of trade secrets in China], *Jingji yanjiu daokan*, 16/2008, Harbin, pp. 60-61.

Dahlkamp, Jürgen, Rosenbach, Marcel, Schmitt, Jörg, Stark, Holger and Wagner, Wieland (2007): "Prinzip Sandkorn", *Der Spiegel*, 35/2007, Hamburg, pp. 19-34.

Dahlman, Carl J. and Aubert, Jean-Eric (2001): *China and the Knowledge Economy: Seizing the 21st Century*, Washington, D.C.: The World Bank.

Davenport, Thomas H. (2005): *Thinking for a Living: How to Get Better Performance and Results from Knowledge Workers*, Boston: Harvard Business School Press.

Davies, Howard, Leung, Thomas K.P., Luk, Sherriff Ting-kwong and Wong, Y.H. (2003): "*Guanxi* and Business Practices in the People's Republic of China", in: Ilan Alon (ed.): *Chinese Culture, Organizational Behavior, and International Business Management*, Westport: Praeger, pp. 41-55.

Davies, Ken (2013): "China Investment Policy: An Update", *OECD Working Papers on International Investment*, 2013/01, http://www.oecd.org/china/WP-2013_1.pdf (accessed July 12, 2013).

Deng, Ziliang (2011): *Foreign Direct Investment in China: Spillover effects on domestic enterprises*, Abingdon: Routledge.

Der Spiegel (2007): *Die Gelben Spione: Wie China deutsche Technologie ausspäht*, Hamburg, 35/2007.

Dong, Ying 董颖 (2007): "Cong shangye mimi anli toushi qiye guanli" [从商业秘密案例透视企业管理/ A trade secret case perspective on corporate management], *China Intellectual Property*, Vol. 21, 12/2007, Hongkong, http://www.chinaipmagazine.com/journal-show.asp?id=294 (accessed Jan 15, 2013).

Dou, Xingya 窦醒亚 (2007): "Jiexi shangye mimi zhong heli de baomi cuoshi" [解析商业秘密中合理的保密措施/ Analyzing reasonable secrecy measures for trade secrets], *Dianzi zhishi chanquan*, 08/2007, Beijing, pp. 65-66.

Drepper, Thomas (2007): "Organisation und Wissen", in: Schützeichel, Rainer (ed.): *Handbuch Wissenssoziologie*, Konstanz: UVK, pp. 588-612.

Drucker, Peter F. (1959): *The Landmarks of Tomorrow*, New York: Harper & Brothers.

Drucker, Peter F. (1969): *The Age of Discontinuity: Guidelines to our Changing Society*, London: Heinemann.

Drucker, Peter F. (1990): *Neue Realitäten: Wertewandel in Politik, Wirtschaft und Gesellschaft*, 2nd edition, Düsseldorf: ECON.

Drucker, Peter F. (1999): *Management Challenges for the 21st Century*, New York: Harper Business.

Du, Jingjing 杜静静 and Tang, Youjun 唐友军 (2012): "Qianxi zhishi gongzuozhe de zhiyuanxing zai qiye guanlizhong de jiazhi" [浅析知识工作者的志愿性在企业管理中的价值/ Primary Analysis of the Value of Voluntary Participation of Knowledge Workers in Enterprise Management], *Jiazhi gongcheng*, 11/2012, Shijiazhuang, pp. 108-109.

Du, Ningning 杜宁宁 (2012): "Qiye shangye mimi baohu de falü wenti yanjiu: Yi shangze mimiquan yu laodongzhe zheqingquan de chongtu wei shejiao" [企业商业秘密保护的法律问题研究：以商业秘密权与劳动者知情权的冲突为视角/ Research on legislative problems of enterprises' trade secret protection: With the conflict of the right on trade secrets and the worker's right on information as perspective], *Lanzhou xuekan*, 09/2012, Lanzhou, pp. 165-168.

Duan, Yu 段玉 (2012): "Zhongguo haigui zhichang shengtai: '2012 haigui jiuyeli diaocha baogao'" [中国海归职场生态: '2012 海归就业力调查报告'/ The career ecology of China's overseas returnees: '2012 investigation of overseas returnees' strength of starting a career], *China Internet Information Center*, Oct 22, 2012, http://www.china.com.cn/education/zhichang/2012-10/22/content_26867739.htm (accessed April 29, 2013).

Eberle, Thomas S. (2011): "Cultural Sociology", in: Dietmar Treichel and Claude-Hélène Mayer (eds.): *Lehrbuch Kultur: Lehr- und Lernmaterialien zur Vermittlung kultureller Kompetenzen*, Münster et al.: Waxmann, pp. 72-78.

Economist (2012): "From brawn to brain: In China is to excel at innovation, the state must give entrepreneurs more freedom", *The Economist online*, March 10, 2012, http://www.economist.com/node/21549938 (accessed June 1, 2012).

Editorial Office 'Yearbook of Industry and Commerce Administration of China' '中国工商行政管理年鉴'编辑部 (1996-2011): *Zhongguo gongshang xingzheng guanli nianjian* [中国工商行政管理年鉴/ Yearbook of Industry and Commerce Administration of China], Beijing: Zhongguo gongshang chubanshe.

Edvinsson, Leif (2003): "The Intellectual Capital of Nations", in: Clyde W. Holsapple (ed.): *Handbook on Knowledge Management 1: Knowledge matters*, Berlin: Springer, pp. 153-163.

Eriksson, Päivi and Kovalainen, Anne (2008): *Qualitative Methods in Business Research*, London et al.: SAGE.

Ess, van, Hans (2003): *Der Konfuzianismus*, München: C.H.Beck.

EU-China IPR2 (2011): *Roadmap for Intellectual Property Protection in China: Trade Secrets Protection in China*, http://www.ipr2.org/storage/EU-Trade_secrets_in_China-EN1001.pdf (accessed Jan 15, 2013).

European Commission (2013): *Report on EU customs enforment of intellectual property rights: Results at the EU border 2012*, http://ec.europa.eu/taxation_customs/resources/documents/customs/customs_controls/counterfeit_piracy/statistics/2013_ipr_statistics_en.pdf (accessed Dec 15, 2013).

European Union Chamber of Commerce in China (2006): "Re: Comments of the European Union Chamber of Commerce in China on the Draft Labour Contract law", *the Danish parliament's official website*, April 18, 2006, http://www.ft.dk/samling/20061/spoergsmaal/s710/svar/292131/325381.pdf (accessed May 17, 2012).

European Union Chamber of Commerce in China (2012): *European Business in China: Business Confidence Survey 2012*, http://www.rolandberger.com/media/pdf/Roland_Berger_China_Business_Confidence_Survey_20120531.pdf (accessed Dec 15, 2013).

Fairbank, John King and Goldman, Merle (2006): *China: A New History*, 2nd edition, Cambridge: Harvard University Press.

Fan, C. Cindy (2009): "Flexible work, flexible household: Labor migration and rural families in China", in: Ching Kwan Lee (ed.): *Working in China: Ethnographies of labor and workplace transformation*, Abingdon: Routledge, pp. 377-408.

Fei, Xiaotong (1992): *From the Soil: The Foundations of Chinese Society. A Translation of Fei Xiaotong's Xiangtu Zhongguo*, Berkeley and Los Angeles, CA: University of California Press.

Feng, Sue (2009): "China's Graduates: An Ant's Life", *The Wall Street Journal online*, Nov 5, 2009, http://blogs.wsj.com/chinarealtime/2009/11/05/chinas-graduates-an-ants-life/ (accessed May 28, 2012).

Fischer, Doris (2002): "What's in a number? The role of statistics in China's contemporary economic research and economic policies", in: Doris Fischer and Andreas Oberheitmann (eds.): *China im Zeichen von Globalisierung und Entwicklung: Festschrift zum 70. Geburtstag von Ernst Hagemann*, Berlin: Duncker & Humblot, pp. 25-40.

Fleisher, Belton, Li, Haizheng and Zhao, Min Qiang (2010): "Human Capital, Economic Growth, and Regional Inequality in China", *Journal of Development Economics*, Vol. 92 No. 9, Amsterdam, pp. 215-231.

Fleisher, Belton and Wang, Xiaojun (2004): "Skill Differentials, Return to Schooling, and Market Segmentation in a Transition Economy: The Case of Mainland China", *Journal of Development Economics*, Vol. 73 No. 1, Amsterdam, pp. 315-328.

Flick, Uwe (2007a): *Designing Qualitative Research*, London: SAGE.

Flick, Uwe (2007b): *Managing Quality in Qualitative Research*, London: SAGE.

Frank, Sergey (2008): "Die wichtigsten China-Regeln", *manager magazin online*, July 16, 2008, http://www.manager-magazin.de/unternehmen/karriere/a-562640-3.html (accessed July 12, 2010).

Fu, Ping Ping, Wu, Rongxian and Yang Jun Ye, Yongkang (2008): "Chinese Culture and Leadership", in: Jagdeep S. Chhokar, Felix C. Brodbeck and Robert J. House (eds.): *Culture and Leadership Across the World: The GLOBE Book of In-Depth Studies of 25 Societies*, New York and Abingdon: Taylor & Francis, pp. 877-908.

Fu, Zhengyuan (1996): *China's Legalists: The Earliest Totalitarians and Their Art of Ruling*, Armonk, NY and London: M.E. Sharpe.

Fuchs, Hans Joachim (ed.) (2006), *Piraten, Fälscher und Kopierer: Strategien und Instrumente zum Schutz geistigen Eigentums in der Volksrepublik China*, Wiesbaden: Gabler.

Fung, Yu-Lan (1947): *The Spirit of Chinese Philosophy*, Boston: Beacon Press.

Gale, Barden N. (1978): "The Concept of Intellectual Property in the People's Republic of China: Inventors and Inventions", in: *The China Quarterly*, No. 74, June 1978, Cambridge, pp. 334-355.

Geertz, Clifford (2008): "'Thick Description: Toward an Interpretive Theory of Culture'", in: Timothy S. Oakes and Patricia L. Price (eds.): *The Cultural Geography Reader*, Abingdon: Routledge, pp. 29-39.

Gelepithis, Petros A. M. and Parillon, Nicole (2008): "Knowledge Management: Analysis and Some Consequences", in: Murray E. Jennex (ed.): *Knowledge Management: Concepts, Methodologies, Tools and Applications*, New York: Hershey, pp. 1480-1490.

German Chamber of Commerce in China (2007): "German Business Expansion in China: 2008-2010: Results of a Survey Conducted among German Operations in China Focussing on Market Potential, Barriers to Doing Business and Future Business Outlook", *BusinessForum China*, http://www.kooperation-international.de/fileadmin/public/cluster/Xuzhou/GermanBusinessStudy.pdf (accessed May 21, 2014).

GIC German Industry & Commerce (2007): "Arbeitsvertragsgesetz der VR China: Ein Überblick über die wichtigsten Regelungen", July 16, 2007, http://www2.china.ahk.de/download/news/isheet_Arbeitsvertragsgesetz.pdf (accessed May 12, 2012).

Giddens, Anthony (1984): *The Constitution of Society: Outline of a Theory of Structuration*, Cambridge and Malden, MA: Polity Press.

Gisclair, Jessica (2008): "The Dissonance between Culture and Intellectual Property in China", *Southeast Review of Asian Studies*, Vol. 30 (2008), Ashland, pp. 182-187.

Golas, Peter J. (1977): "Early Ch'ing Guilds", in: G. William Skinner (ed.): *The City in Late Imperial China*, Stanford, CA: Stanford University Press, pp. 555-580.

Goodman, David S.G. (2007): "Narratives of Change: Culture and Local Economic Development", in: Barbara Krug and Hans Hendrischke (eds.): *The Chinese Economy in the 21st Century: Enterprise and Business Behaviour*, Cheltenham: Edward Elgar, pp. 175-201.

Gov.cn 中华人民共和国中央人民政府门户网站 (2005): "Zhonghua renmin gongheguo laodongfa" [中华人民共和国劳动法/ Labor Law of the PRC], *the Chinese government's official website*, Aug 5, 2005, http://www.gov.cn/banshi/2005-08/05/content_20688.htm (accessed May 21, 2012).

Gov.cn 中华人民共和国中央人民政府门户网站 (2007): "Zhonghua renmin gongheguo zhuxiling" [中华人民共和国主席令/ Order of the President of the PRC], *the Chinese government's official website*, June 26, 2007, http://www.gov.cn/flfg/2007-06/29/content_669394.htm (accessed June 8, 2012).

Gov.cn (2012): "Constitution", *the Chinese government's official website*, 2012, http://english.gov.cn/2005-08/05/content_20813.htm (accessed Sept 6, 2011).

Grewal, Bhajan and Sun, Fiona (2002): "Foreign markets and foreign capital: The role of trade in China's economic transformation", in: Bhajan Grewal, Lan Xue, Peter Sheehan and Fiona Sun (eds.): *China's future in the knowledge economy: Engaging the new world*, Melbourne: Centre for Strategic Economic Studies, pp. 194-211.

Griffiths, Michael B. (2010): "Lamb Buddha's Migrant Workers: Self-Assertion on China's Urban Fringe", *Journal of Current Chinese Affairs*, Vol. 39 No. 2, Hamburg, pp. 3-37.

Groeger, Christian (2010): "Learning by Doing: There are a Number of Ways to develop Technical Talent in China", *BusinessForum China*, Oct 2010, http://www.businessforum-china.com/management_article_detail.html?articleid=86 (accessed May 2, 2012).

Guo, Shoukang and Zuo, Xiaodong (2007): "Are Chinese intellectual property laws consistent with the TRIPs Agreement?", in: Paul Torremans, Hailing Shan and Johan Erauw (eds.): *Intellectual Property and TRIPS Compliance in China: Chinese and European Perspectives*, Cheltenham: Edward Elgar, pp. 11-28.

Guowuyuan 国务院 (1988): "Guowuyuan pizhun guojia kewei guanyu keji renyuan yeyu jianzhi ruogan wenti de yijian" [国务院批准国家科委关于科技人员业余兼职若干问题的意见/ The State Council approves the opinion of the State Commission of Science and Technology on the several problems with the spare time jobs of scientific and technical personnel], *Falü tushuguan*, Jan 18, 1988, http://www.law-lib.com/law/law_view.asp?id=49080 (accessed May 12, 2012).

Guowuyuan 国务院 (1993): "Zhonghua renmin gongheguo fan bu zhengdang jingzhengfa" [中华人民共和国反不正当竞争法/ Law against Unfair Competition of the PRC], *Guowuyuan Gongbao*, 21/1993, pp. 983-988.

Gupta, Jatinder N. D., Sharma, Sushil K. and Hsu, Jeffrey (2008): "An Overview of Knowledge Management", in: Murray E. Jennex (ed.): *Knowledge Management: Concepts, Methodologies, Tools and Applications*, New York: Hershey, pp. 1-22.

Guthrie, Doug (1998): "The Declining Significance of Guanxi in China's Economic Transition", *The China Quarterly*, No. 154 (June 1998), Cambridge, pp. 254-282.

Halas, Elzbieta (2010): *Toward the World Culture Society: Florian Znaniecki's Culturalism*, Frankfurt am Main: Peter Lang.

Hall, Edward T. (1989): *Beyond Culture*, New York: Anchor Books.

Hamilton, Gary G. and Lai, Chi-kong (1986): "Jinshi zhongguo shangbiao yu quanguo dushi shichang" [今世中国商标与全国都市市场/ Trademarks and the National Urban Market in Late Imperial China], in: *Proceedings of the Conference on Regional Studies of Modern China*, Taipei: Academia Sinica.

Hamilton, Gary G. and Lai, Chi-kong (1989): "Consumerism without Capitalism: Consumption and brand names in late imperial China", in: Henry J. Rutz and Benjamin S. Orlove (eds.): *The Social Economy of Consumption: Monographs in Economic Anthropology, No. 6*, Lanham, MD and London: University Press of America, pp. 253-279.

Han, Dekuan 韩德宽 (2012): "Shangye mimi zhi shiyongxing qianxi" [商业秘密之实用性浅析/ Brief analysis of the practicality of trade secrets], *Zhongguo faming yu zhuanli*, 02/2012, Beijing, pp. 31-32.

Hannum, Emily, Behrman, Jere, Wang, Meiyan and Liu, Jihong (2008): "Education in the Reform Era", in: Loren Brandt and Thomas G. Rawski (eds.): *China's Great Economic Transformation*, New York: Cambridge University Press, pp. 215-249.

Hanser, Amy (2006): "Serving the state, serving the people: work in a post-socialist department store", in: Jacob Eyferth (ed.): *How China Works: Perspectives on the twentieth-century industrial workplace*, Abingdon: Routledge, pp. 91-109.

Hao, Yenping (1970): *The Comprador in Nineteenth Century China: Bridge between East and West*, Cambridge, MA: Harvard University Press.

He, Dan (2013): "Confucius' lessons still relevant, Xi says", *China Daily online*, Nov 27, 2013, http://usa.chinadaily.com.cn/china/2013-11/27/content_17133357.htm (accessed Dec 11, 2013).

He, Junjian 和军建 (2011): "Lun guojia mimi yu shangye mimi de qubie" [论国家秘密与商业秘密的区别/ Discussing the difference between state secrets and trade secrets]", *Fazhi yu shehui*, 03/2011, Kunming, p. 262.

He, Saiying 何赛瑛 (2002): "Qiye shangye mimi de baohu" [企业商业秘密的保护/ Protection of enterprises' trade secrets], *Guancha yu sikao*, 03/2002, Hangzhou, pp. 26-27.

Hebel, Jutta and Schucher, Günter (2007): "Beschäftigungsstrukturen und Arbeitsmärkte", in: Doris Fischer and Michael Lackner (eds.): *Länderbericht China: Geschichte – Politik – Wirtschaft – Gesellschaft*, Bonn: Bundeszentrale für politische Bildung, pp. 284-301.

Hebel, Jutta and Schucher, Günter (2009): "The Emergence of a 'Socialist' Market Labour Regime in China", in: Thomas Heberer and Gunter Schubert (eds.): *Regime Legitimacy in Contemporary China: Institutional Change and Stability*, Abingdon: Routledge, pp. 222-244.

Heberer, Thomas (1999): "Erwerbstätigkeit im Privatsektor: Self-Employment, Unternehmertum und vergessene Gruppen", in: Jutta Hebel and Günter Schucher (eds.): *Der chinesische Arbeitsmarkt: Strukturen, Probleme, Perspektiven*, Hamburg: Institut für Asienkunde, pp. 151-176.

Heilmann, Sebastian and Perry, Elizabeth J. (2011): "Embracing Uncertainty: Guerrilla Policy Style and Adaptive Governance in China", in: Sebastian Heilmann and Elizabeth J. Perry (eds.): *Mao's Invisible Hand: The Political Foundations of Adaptive Governance in China*, Cambridge: Harvard University Asia Center, pp. 1-29.

Hein, Christoph (2009): "China und die Investoren: Verhaftungen, Unterstellungen, Volkszorn", *Frankfurter Allgemeine online*, Aug 11, 2009, http://m.faz.net/aktuell/wirtschaft/wirtschaftspolitik/china-und-die-investoren-verhaftungen-unterstellungen-volkszorn-1841153.html (accessed Feb 15, 2013).

Hendrischke, Hans (2007): "Networks as Business Networks", in: Barbara Krug and Hans Hendrischke (eds.): *The Chinese Economy in the 21st Century: Enterprise and Business Behaviour*, Cheltenham: Edward Elgar, pp. 202-222.

Henningsen, Lena (2010): *Copyright Matters: Imitation, Creativity and Authenticity in Contemporary Chinese Literature*, Berlin: Berliner Wissenschafts-Verlag.

Hesse, Carla (2002): "The rise of intellectual property, 700 B.C. – A.D. 2000: an idea in balance", *Daedalus*, Spring 2002, Cambridge, pp. 26-45.

Heuser, Robert (2002): *Einführung in die chinesische Rechtskultur*, Hamburg: GIGA Institute of Asian Studies.

Heuser, Robert (2009): "‚Sozialistisches Recht' in der Erprobung: Entwicklungen der chinesischen Rechtsordnung (1949-2009)", *Zeitschrift für Chinesisches Recht*, 3/2009, Göttingen, pp. 247-261.

Hewitt Associates (2007): "China's Labor Contract Law and Implications for Workforce Management: Draft II", *Hewitt Global Report*, Special Edition April 2007.

Hofmann, Jeanette and Katzenbach, Christian (2006): "Einführung", in: Jeanette Hofmann (ed.): *Wissen und Eigentum: Geschichte, Recht und Ökonomie stoffloser Güter*, Bonn: Bundeszentrale für politische Bildung, pp. 9-20.

Hofstede, Geert (1984): "Cultural dimensions in management and planning", *Asia Pacific Journal of Management*, Vol. 1 No. 2, January 1984, New York, pp. 81-99.

Hofstede, Geert (2009): "Geert Hofstede Cultural Dimensions", http://www.geert-hofstede.com/geert_hofstede_resources.shtml (accessed Jan 12, 2010).

Hofstede, Geert and Hofstede, Gert Jan (2005): *Cultures and Organizations: Software of the Mind*, New York.

Hörning, Karl H. (2004): "Kultur als Praxis", in: Friedrich Jäger, Burkhard Liebsch, Jörn Rüsen and Jürgen Straub (eds.): *Handbuch der Kulturwissenschaften*, Band 1, Stuttgart: Metzler, pp. 139-151.

Hörning, Karl H. and Reuter, Julia (2004): "Doing Culture: Kultur als Praxis", in: Karl H. Hörning and Julia Reuter (eds.): *Doing Culture: Neue Positionen zum Verhältnis von Kultur und sozialer Praxis*, Bielefeld: Transkript, pp. 9-15.

Hou, Zhigang 后志刚 (1996): "Chen Lianbo" [陈廉伯/ Chen Lianbo], in: Xu Mao 徐矛 (ed.): *Zhongguo shi maiban* [中国十买办/ China's ten compradors], Shanghai: Shanghai renmin chubanshe, pp. 317-332.

House, Robert J., Hanges, Paul J., Javidan, Mansour, Dorfman, Peter W. and Gupta, Vipin (eds.) (2004): *Culture, Leadership, and Organizations: The GLOBE Study of 62 Societies*, London: SAGE.

Howell, Jude (1999): "Workers in Foreign-Invested Enterprises", in: Jutta Hebel and Günter Schucher (eds.): *Der chinesische Arbeitsmarkt: Strukturen, Probleme, Perspektiven*, Hamburg: Institut für Asienkunde, pp. 135-150.

Hsu, Carolyn L. (2005): "A taste of 'modernity': Working in a western restaurant in market socialist China", *Ethnography*, Vol. 6 No. 4, New York, pp. 543-565.

Hsu, Carolyn L. (2007): *Creating Markt Socialism: How Ordinary People Are Shaping Class and Status in China*, Durham and London: Duke University Press.

Hsu, Sonya; Mykytyn, Peter P. (2008): "Intellectual Capital", in: Murray E. Jennex (ed.): *Knowledge Management: Concepts, Methodologies, Tools and Applications*, New York: Hershey, pp. 2047-2056.

Hu, Albert G.Z. and Jefferson, Gary H. (2008): "Science and Technology in China", in: Loren Brandt and Thomas G. Rawski (eds.): *China's Great Economic Transformation*, Cambridge: Cambridge University Press, pp. 286-336.

Huang, Qian, Davison, Robert M. and Gu, Jibao (2008): "Impact of personal and cultural factors on knowledge sharing in China", *Asia Pacific Journal of Management*, Vol. 25, New York, pp. 451-471.

Huang, Yifeng 黄逸峰, Jiang, Duo 姜铎, Tang, Chuansi 唐传泗 and Chen, Jiang 陈绛 (1982): *Jiu zhongguo de maiban jieji* [旧中国的买办阶级/ Ancient China's comprador class], Shanghai: Shanghai renmin chubanshe.

Hunter, Laurie (2006): "A management perspective", in: Derek Bosworth and Elizabeth Webster (eds.): *The Management of Intellectual property,* Cheltenham: Edward Elgar, pp. 66-84.

Hurst, William (2014): "Urban China: Change and Contention", in: William A. Joseph (ed.): *Politics in China: An Introduction*, 2nd edition, Oxford: Oxford University Press, pp. 320-341.

Hutchings, Kate and Michailova, Snejina (2007): "Re-examining knowledge sharing in an intercultural context: findings from the transition economies of China and Russia", in: Kate Huchings and Kavoos Mohannak (eds.): *Knowledge Management in Developing Economies: A Cross-Cultural and Institutional Approach*, Cheltenham: Edward Elgar, pp. 72-89.

Ivanhoe, Philip J. (2002): *Ethics in the Confucian Tradition: The Thought of Mengzi and Wang Yangming*, 2nd edition, Indianapolis, IN: Hackett.

Ivanhoe, Philip J. (2005): "Intellectual Property and Traditional Chinese Culture", in: Joseph Keim Campbell, Michael O'Rourke and David Shier (eds.): *Law and Social Justice*, Cambridge, MA and London: MIT Press, pp. 125-142.

Jamison, Dean T., Lau, Lawrence J. and Wang, Jia (2010): "The Contribution of Health and Education to Economic Growth in China", in: Gordon G. Liu, Shufang Zhang and Zongyi Zhang (eds.): *Investing in Human Capital for Economic Development in China*, Singapore: World Scientific Publishing, pp. 19-41.

Jarrett, Kenneth and Wendholt, Amy (2010): "Transferring Technology to Transform China – Is It Worth It?", *The China Business Review online*, March-April 2010, Washington.

Jiang, Ruqin 蒋汝勤 (2009): "Jiang Ruqin: Lituo anjian zheshechu shenme" [蒋汝勤：力托案件折射出什么/ Jiang Ruqin: What the Rio Tinto case shows], *Xinlang caijing*, Aug 8, 2009, http://finance.sina.com.cn/review/yjfx/20090808/19546591085.shtml (accessed June 10, 2013).

Jincao.com 中国企业集成 (2013): "Zhonghua renmin gongheguo laodong hetongfa (cao'an)" [中华人民共和国劳动合同法（草案）/ Labor Contract Law of the People's Republic of China (draft)], http://www.jincao.com/fa/12/law12.65.htm (accessed Feb 21, 2013).

Joseph, Richard (2005): "The knowledge worker: a metaphor in search of a meaning?", in: David Rooney, Greg Hearn and Abraham Ninan (eds.): *Handbook on the Knowledge Economy*, Cheltenham: Edward Elgar, pp. 245-254.

Junghans, Lida (2006): "Industrial involution: recruitment and development within the railway system", in: Jacob Eyferth (ed.): *How China Works: Perspectives on the twentieth-century industrial workplace*, Abingdon: Routledge, pp. 74-90.

Kakabadse, Nada K., Kakabadse, Andrew and Kouzmin, Alexander (2003): "Reviewing the knowledge management literature: toward a taxonomy", *Journal of Knowledge Management*, Vol. 7 No. 4, Bingley, pp. 75-91.

Keane, Michael (2007): *Created in China: The Great New Leap forward*, Abingdon: Routledge.

Kessler, Dimitri (2007): "Nationalism, theft, and management strategies in the information industry of mainland China", in: Ching Kwan Lee (ed.): *Working in China: Ethnographies of labor and workplace transformation*, Abingdon: Routledge, pp. 209-228.

Kisgen, Stefanie (2005): "Der Schutz von Geschäftsgeheimnissen", in: Robert Heuser (ed.): *Beiträge zum chinesischen Zivil- und Wirtschaftsrecht*, Hamburg: Institut für Asienkunde, pp. 99-146.

Klett, Alexander R., Sonntag, Matthias and Wilske, Stephan (2008): *Intellectual Property Law in Germany: Protection, Enforcement and Dispute Resolution*, München: C.H. Beck.

Knoblauch, Hubert (2005): *Wissenssoziologie*, Konstanz: UVK.

Kong, Qingjiang (2005): *WTO, Internationalization and the Intellectual Property Regime in China*, Singapore: Marshall Cavendish Academic.

Kotte, Jacqueline and Li, Wei (2007): *Geschäftlich in China: Verhaltensweisen verstehen und erfolgreich umsetzen*, Augsburg: Wißner.

Kroeber, Alfred L. and Kluckhorn, Clyde (1963): *Culture: a critical review of concepts and definitions*, New York: Vintage Books.

Krotoschak, Eva and Kleine, Zarah (2010): "What do you want from me? Employers in China Need to Better Understand How to Retain Staff", *BusinessForum China*, Oct 2010, http://www.businessforum-china.com/management_article_detail.html?article id=85 (accessed 2 May 2012).

Krug, Barbara (2007): "Enterprise Ground Zero in China", in: Barbara Krug and Hans Hendrischke (eds.): *The Chinese Economy in the 21st Century: Enterprise and Business Behaviour*, Cheltenham: Edward Elgar, pp. 113-144.

Krug, Barbara and Kuilman, Jeroen (2007): "Whom are We Dealing With? Shifting Organizational Forms in China's Business Sector", in: Barbara Krug and Hans Hendrischke (eds.): *The Chinese Economy in the 21st Century: Enterprise and Business Behaviour*, Cheltenham: Edward Elgar, pp. 223-243.

Kruse, Jan (2014): *Qualitative Interviewforschung: Ein integrativer Ansatz*, Weinheim Basel: Beltz.

Lai, Karyn L. (2008): *An Introduction to Chinese Philosophy*, Cambridge et al.: Cambridge University Press.

Land, Frank, Nolas, Sevasti-Melissa and Amjad, Urooj (2008): "Theoretical and Practical Aspects of Knowledge Management", in: Murray E. Jennex (ed.): *Knowledge Management: Concepts, Methodologies, Tools and Applications*, New York: Hershey, pp. 23-31.

Lardy, Nicholas R. (1994): *China in the World Economy*, Washington: Institute for International Economics.

Lardy, Nicholas R. (2002): *Integrating China into the Global Economy*, Washington: Brookings Institution Press.

Ledderose, Lothar (2000): *Ten Thousand Things: Module and Mass Production in Chinese Art*, Princeton: Princeton University Press.

Lee, Ching Kwan (2007a): *Against the Law: Labor Protests in China's Rustbelt and Sunbelt*, Berkeley: University of California Press.

Lee, Ching Kwan (2007b): "The unmaking of the Chinese working class in the northeastern rustbelt", in: Ching Kwan Lee (ed.): *Working in China: Ethnographies of labor and workplace transformation*, Abingdon: Routledge, pp. 15-37.

Lee, Lai To (1986): *Trade Unions in China*, Singapore: Singapore University Press.

Lee, Thomas H. C. (2000): *Education in Traditional China: A History*, Leiden: Brill.

Legge, James (1960): *The Chinese Classics: Confucian Analects, The Great Learning, The Doctrine of the Mean*, 3rd edition, Hong Kong: Hong Kong University Press.

Lehman, John A. (2006): "Intellectual Property Rights and Chinese Trandition Section: Philosophical Foundations", *Journal of Business Ethics*, 69/2006, New York, pp. 1-9.

Lei, Guang (2007): "Rural 'guerrilla' workers in home renovation in urban China", in: Ching Kwan Lee (ed.): *Working in China: Ethnographies of labor and workplace transformation*, Abingdon: Routledge, pp. 56-76.

Lemley, Mark A. (2008): "The Surprising Virtues of Treating Trade Secrets as IP Rights", *Stanford Law Review*, Vol. 61, Nov 2008, Stanford, pp. 311-353.

Li, Cheng (2000): "'Credentialism' Versus 'Entrepreneurism': Interplay and Tensions between Technocrats and Entrepreneurs in the Reform Era", in: Chan Kwok Bun (ed.): *Chinese Business Networks: State, Economy and Culture*, Singapore: Pearson Education Asia, pp. 86-111.

Li, Cheng (2010): "Introduction: The Rise of the Middle Class in the Middle Kingdom", in: Li Cheng (ed.): *China's Emerging Middle Class: Beyond Economic Transformation*, Washington, DC: Brookings Institution Press, pp. 3-31.

Li, Chunling 李春玲 (2012): "Daxue biyesheng jiuye nanti wenti de xin bianhua" [大学毕业生就业难题问题的新变化/ New changes of university graduates' difficulties and problems of starting a career], in: Lu Xueyi 陆学艺, Li Peilin 李培林 and Chen Guangjin 陈光金 (eds.): *Shehui lanpishu: 2013 nian zhongguo shehui xingshi fenxi yu yuce* [社会蓝皮书：2013 年中国社会形势分析与预测/ Blue Book of China's Society: Society of China Analysis and Forecast (2013)], Beijing: Shehui kexue wenxian chubanshe, pp. 164-176.

Li, Luo (2010): "How has Chinese Traditional Culture an Impact onChina's Intellectual Property Legal System? Would this Influence be a Problem in the Protection of Folklore by the Intellectual Property Legal System?", *The International Journal of Interdisciplinary Social Sciences*, Vol. 5 No. 1, Champaign, pp. 269-282.

Li, Meng and Gao, Fei (2003): "Why Nonaka highlights tacit knowledge: a critical review", *Journal of Knowledge Management*, Vol. 7 No. 4, Bingley, pp. 6-14.

Li, Peilin 李培林 (2004): "Huashuo shehui fencing" [话说社会分层/ To recount social stratification], Li Peilin 李培林, Li Qiang 李强 and Kong Liping 孙立平 et al. (eds.): *Zhongguo shehui fencing: Social Stratification in China Today* [中国社会分层: Social Stratification in China Today/ China's Social Stratification: Social Stratification in China Today], Beijing: Shehui kexue wenxian chubanshe, pp. 1-15.

Li, Raymond (2012): "Graduates like 'security' of state jobs: Survey finds nearly half prefer to join state-owned companies or civil service", *South China Morning Post online*, June 27, 2012.

Li, Sheng 李生 and Yu, Jun 于君 (2009): "Wuxing ziben zhiliang de hanyi, yingxiang yinsu ji pingjia biaozhun" [无形资本质量的含义，影响因素及评价标准/ Content, influencing factors and evaluation criteria of intangible capital quality], *Caihui yuekan*, 05/2009, Wuhan, pp. 13-14.

Li, Shenxue and Scullion, Hugh (2006): "Bridging the distance: Managing cross-border knowledge holders", *Asia Pacific Journal of Management*, Vol. 23 No. 1, Singapore, pp. 71-92.

Li, Shoushuang (2007): *The Legal Environment and Risks for Foreign Investment in China*, Heidelberg: Springer.

Li, Wei, Ardichvili, Alexander, Maurer, Martin, Wentling, Tim and Stuedemann, Reed (2007): "Impact of Chinese Culture Values on Knowledge Sharing Through Online Communities of Practice", *International Journal of Knowledge Management*, Vol. 3 No. 3, San Diego, pp. 94-107.

Li, Wenzhong 李文忠 and Wang, Liyan 王丽艳 (2013): "Guanxi xinren dui zhishi fenxiang dongji ji fenxiang xingwei de yingxiang" [关系信任对知识分享动机及分享行为的影响/ Influence of *guanxi* trust on knowledge sharing motivation and sharing behavior], *Jingying yu guanli*, 02/2013, Tianjin, pp. 101-105.

Li, Yi (2005): *The Structure and Evolution of Chinese Social Stratification*, Lanham et al.: University Press of America.

Li, Yiqiong and Sheldon, Peter (2011): "Skill shortages: Where labour supply problems meet employee poaching", in: Peter Sheldon, Sunghoon Kom, Yiqiong Li and Macolm Warner (eds.): *China's Changing Workplace: Dynamism, diversity and disparity*, Abingdon: Routledge, pp. 129-143.

Li, Yiqiong, Sheldon, Peter and Sun, Jian-Min (2011): "Education, training and skills", in: Peter Sheldon, Sunghoon Kom, Yiqiong Li and Macolm Warner (eds.): *China's Changing Workplace: Dynamism, diversity and disparity*, Abingdon: Routledge, pp. 111-128.

Li-Hua, Richard and Peng, Jian (2007): "Tacit Knowledge and Inter-firm Learning in China", in: Stewart Clegg, Karen Wang and Mike Berrell (eds.): *Business Networks and Strategic Alliances in China,* Cheltenham: Edward Elgar, pp. 133-153.

Liang, Xiaosheng 梁晓声 (2010): *Zhongguo shehui ge jieceng fenxi* [中国社会各阶层分析/ Analysis of each stratum of Chinese society], Beijing: Wenhua yishu chubanshe.

Liang, Zhao 梁钊 (2012): "Yao heli bawo kehu mingdan zuowei shangye mimi baohu de jiexian" [要合理把握客户名单作为商业秘密保护的界限/ The boundary for protection customer lists as trade secrets must be reasonably grasped], *SIPO's official website*, Dec 21, 2012, http://www.sipo.gov.cn/mtjj/2012/201212/t20121220_780981.html (accessed Jan 20, 2013).

Liao, Chun (2009): *The Governance Structure of Chinese Firms: Innovation, Competitiveness, and Growth in a Dual Economy*, Dordrecht: Springer.

Lieberthal, Kenneth (1995): *Governing China: From Revolution Through Reform*, New York: W. W. Norton & Company.

Lim, Benjamin Kang and Blanchard, Ben (2013): "Xi Jinping hopes traditional faiths can fill moral void in China: sources", *Reuters online*, Sept 29, 2013, http://www.reuters.com/article/2013/09/29/us-china-politics-vacuum-idUSBRE98S0GS20130929 (accessed Dec 11, 2013).

Lin, Jing and Sun, Xiaoyan (2010): "Higher Education Expansion and China's Middle Class", in: Li Cheng (ed.): *China's Emerging Middle Class: Beyond Economic Transformation*, Washington, DC: Brookings Institution Press, pp. 217-242.

Lin, Thunghong and Wu, Xiaogang (2009): "The Transformation of the Chinese Class Structure, 1978-2005", in: Kwok-Bun Chan, Agnes S. Ku and Yin-Wah Chu (eds.): *Social Stratification in Chinese Societies*, Leiden and Boston: Brill, pp. 81-112.

Liu, Chao 刘超 and Fu, Jinmei 付金梅 (2012): "Zhuguan fufuquan shineng dui xiashu shizhi fenxiang yingxiang jizhi de tanjiu" [主管副赋权使能对下属知识分享影响机制的探究/ Investigation of the mechanisms of superior's empowerment influencing subordinate's knowledge sharing], *Keji guanli yanjiu*, 20/2012, Guangzhou, pp. 187-199.

Liu, Gang 刘钢 (2011): "Dui 'zhongguo gudai youwu zhishi chanquan zhidu' zhengyi de sikao" [对'中国古代有无知识产权制度'争议的思考/ Reflecting on the 'if ancient China did or did not have an intellectual property system' controversy], *Shiyan zhiye jishu xueyuan xuebao*, Vol. 24 No. 6, 2011, Shiyan, pp. 36-39.

Liu, Jinghui (2007): "Das Bildungswesen in der Volksrepublik China: ein struktureller und statistischer Überblick", in: Doris Fischer and Michael Lackner (eds.): *Länderbericht China: Geschichte – Politik – Wirtschaft – Gesellschaft*, Bonn: Bundeszentrale für politische Bildung, pp. 513-522.

Liu, Jisheng 刘冀生(2003): *Qiye zhanlue guanli* [企业战略管理/ Strategic Enterprise Management], Beijing: Qinghua daxue chubanshe.

Liu, Rong (2008): "Focus on trade secret – GE vs. Jiuxiang (I)", *China Intellectual Property*, Vol. 24, June 2008, Hongkong, http://www.chinaipmagazine.com/en/journal-show.asp?id=388 (accessed Feb 18, 2013).

Liu, Siân Victoria (2007): "'Social positions': Neighborhood transitions after *danwei*", in: Ching Kwan Lee (ed.): *Working in China: Ethnographies of labor and workplace transformation*, Abingdon: Routledge, pp. 38-55.

Liu, Xiaohai (1999): *Rechtsschutz von Unternehmensgeheimnissen: Vergleichende Untersuchung zum Schutzniveau des chinesischen Rechts im Vergleich mit dem deutschen und amerikanischen Recht*, Frankfurt am Main: Peter Lang.

Liu, Xiaohai (2011): "Unfair competition/trade secrets/know-how (2)", in: Kariyawasam, Rohan (ed.): *Chinese Intellectual Property and Technology Laws*, Cheltenham and Northampton, MA: Edward Elgar, pp. 127-161.

Liu, Yingqun 刘英群 (2008): "Dui wo guo shangye mimi baohu de falü sikao" [对我国商业秘密保护的法律思考/ Law analysis regarding China's trade secret protection], *Fazhan*, 09/2008, Lanzhou, pp. 43-44.

Liu, Yunsheng 刘云生 (2007): "Chuantong zhongguo zhihui caichanzhong de quanli yisihi yu jiazhi duizhi" [传统中国智慧财产中的权利意识与价值对峙/ Value opposition and legal consciousness within traditional China's intellectual property], *Zhengzhou daxue xuebao*, Vol. 40 No. 2, 2007, Zhengzhou, pp. 54-57.

Liu, Yunsheng 刘云生 (2009): "Chuantong zhihui caichan quanli shengcheng lujing ji qi gongneng shibie" [传统智慧财产权利生成路径及其功能识别/ Generating methods and distinguished functions of traditional intellectual property rights], *Huadong zhengfa daxue xuebao*, 04/2009, Shanghai, pp. 10-16.

Lu, Hanlong (2010): "The Chinese Middle Class and *Xiaokang* Society", in: Li Cheng (ed.): *China's Emerging Middle Class: Beyond Economic Transformation*, Washington, DC: Brookings Institution Press, pp. 104-131.

Lu, Jiangyong 路江涌, Lin, Daomi 林道谧 and Zhang, Xiru 张曦如 (2012): "Zhongguo haigui fazhan yanjiu baogao (2012)" [中国海归发展研究报告 (2012)/ Research report on the development of China's overseas returnees (2012)], Chuangxin chuangye yanjiu baogao xilie, Beijing daxue guanghua guanli xueyuan chuangxin chuangye zhongxin.

Lu, Xueyi 陆学艺 (ed.) (2002): *Dangdai zhongguo shehui jieceng yanjiu baogao* [当代中国社会阶层研究报告/ Research Report on Contemporary China's Social Strata], Beijing: Shehui kexue wenxian chubanshe.

Lu, Xueyi 陆学艺 (ed.) (2004): *Dangdai zhongguo shehui liudong* [当代中国社会流动/ Social Mobility in Contemporary China], Beijing: Shehui kexue wenxian chubanshe.

Lu, Xueyi 陆学艺 (ed.) (2010): *Dangdai zhongguo shehui jiegou* [当代中国社会结构/ Social Structure of Contemporary China], Beijing: Shehui kexue wenxian chubanshe.

Luo, Minyan and Müller, Constanze (2011): "Imitation oder Innovation? Das *shanzhai*-Phänomen in der Debatte um Geistiges Eigentum in China", in: Joachim Freimuth, Renate Krieg, Minyan Luo, Constanze Müller and Monika Schädler (eds.): *Geistiges Eigentum in China: Neuere Entwicklungen und praktische Ansätze für den Schutz und Austausch von Wissen*, Wiesbaden: Gabler, pp. 47-68.

Machlup, Fritz (1962): *The Production and Distribution of Knowledge in the United States*, Princeton: Princeton University Press.

Machlup, Fritz (1980): *Knowledge: Its Creation, Distribution, and Economic Significance*, Volume I: Knowledge and Knowledge Production, Princeton: Princeton University Press.

Marvasti, Amir B. (2004): *Qualitative Research in Sociology*, Thousand Oaks, CA: SAGE.

Mason, Jennifer (2002): *Qualitative Researching*, 2nd edition, Thousand Oaks, CA: SAGE.

Maxwell, Joseph A. (2013): *Qualitative Research Design: An Interactive Approach*, 3rd edition, Thousand Oaks, CA: SAGE.

Mayer-Kuckuk, Finn (2010): "Fallbeispiel Gildemeister: Deutsche Industrie muss chinesischer werden", *Handelsblatt online*, June 14, 2010.

McDermott, Michael (2005): "Knowledge Workers: You can gauge their effectiveness", *Leadership Excellence*, Vol. 22, Aurora, p. 15.

Mei, Liumei 梅刘谜 (2012): "Liuxuesheng jiuye diaocha, jinling haigui de mimi" [留学生就业调查，金领海归的秘密/ Survey on employment of students studying abroad, the secret of golden collar returnees], *Liuxuewuyouwang*, July 9, 2012, http://www.liuxue51.net/611/ONewsDetail-17384.html (accessed April 29, 2013).

Mertha, Andrew C. (2005): *The Politics of Piracy: Intellectual Property in Contemporary China*, Ithaca: Cornell University Press.

Michailova, Snejina and Hutchings, Kate (2006): "National Cultural Influences on Knowledge Sharing: A Comparison of China and Russia", *Journal of Management Studies*, Vol. 43 No. 3, May 2006, Hoboken, pp. 383-405.

Michelson, Ethan (2007): "The practice of law as an obstacle to justice: Chinese lawyers at work", in: Ching Kwan Lee (ed.): *Working in China: Ethnographies of labor and workplace transformation*, Abingdon: Routledge, pp. 169-187.

Michelson, Ethan (2009): "Gender Inequality in the Chinese Legal Profession", in: Lisa Keister (ed.): *Work and Organizations in China after Thirty Years of Transition*, Bingley: Emerald, pp. 337-376.

Mills, C. Wright (1951): *White collar: the American middle classes*, New York: Oxford University Press.

Ministry of Human Resources and Social Security of the PRC 中国人民共和国人力资源和社会保障部 (2011): "2010 niandu renli ziyuan he shehui baozhang shiye fazhan tongji gongbao" [2010 年度人力资源和社会保障事业发展统计公报/ Announcement on the development statistics of human resources and social security activities in 2010], *official website of the Ministry of Human Resources and Social Security of the PRC*, July 20, 2011, http://www.mohrss.gov.cn/SYrlzyhshbzb/zwgk/szrs/ndtjsj/tjgb/201107/t20110720_69907.htm (accessed June 6, 2013).

Mop.com 猫扑 (2012): "Zenme shiying shehui jingzheng" [怎么适应社会竞争/ How to adapt to social competition], http://dzh.mop.com/whbm/20120508/0/5gSzS5I29939e9F3.shtml (accessed May 22, 2013).

Morgan, W. John and Wu, Bin (2011): "Introduction", in: W. John Morgan and Bin Wu (eds.): *Higher Education Reform in China: Beyond the expansion*, Abingdon: Routledge, pp. 1-10.

Morse, Hosea Ballou (1910): *The International Relations of the Chinese Empire: Vol. I: The Period of Conflict 1834-1860*, London: Longmans, Green & Co.

Morse, Hosea Ballou (1918): *The International Relations of the Chinese Empire: Vol. II: The Period of Submission 1861-1893*, London: Longmans, Green & Co.

Morse, Hosea Ballou (1920): *The Trade and Administration of China*, 3rd edition, London: Longmans, Green & Co.

Morse, Hosea Ballou (1967): *The Gilds of China: With an Account of the Gild Merchant or Co-Hong of Canton*, 2nd edition, New York: Russell & Russell.

Morse, Hosea Ballou and MacNair, Harley Farnsworth (1967): *Far Eastern International Relations*, Vol. II, New York: Russell & Russell.

Müller, Constanze and Schädler, Monika (2009): "Restriktion und Entwicklung wertvollen Wissens: Umgang mit Unternehmensgeheimnissen in China", *ChinaContact*, 11/2009, Münster, pp. 46-48.

Müller, Constanze and Sprick, Daniel (2011): "Unternehmensgeheimnisse in China: Rechtliche Grundlagen und betriebliche Praxis", in: Joachim Freimuth, Renate Krieg, Minyan Luo, Constanze Müller and Monika Schädler (eds.): *Geistiges Eigentum in China: Neuere Entwicklungen und praktische Ansätze für den Schutz und Austausch von Wissen*, Wiesbaden: Gabler, pp. 145-177.

Munier, Francis and Huan, Cao (2010): "Guanxi and the Business Environment in China: An Innovative Network as a 'Process of a Knowledge-based Economy'", in: Blandine Laperche, Paul Sommers and Dimitri Uzunidis (eds.): *Innovation Networks and Clusters: The Knowledge Backbone*, Brussels: Peter Lang, pp. 89-100.

National Bureau of Statistics of the PRC 中华人民共和国国家统计局 (1989): *Zhongguo laodong tongji nianjian 1989* [中国劳动统计年鉴 1989/ China Labor Statistical Yearbook 1989], Beijing: Zhongguo tongji chubanshe.

National Bureau of Statistics of the PRC 中华人民共和国国家统计局 (2002-2009): *Zhongguo laodong tongji nianjian 2002* [中国劳动统计年鉴 2002/ China Labor Statistical Yearbook 2002], Beijing: Zhongguo tongji chubanshe.

National Bureau of Statistics of the PRC 中华人民共和国国家统计局 (2010a): *Zhongguo laodong tongji nianjian 2010* [中国劳动统计年鉴 2010/ China Labor Statistical Yearbook 2010], Beijing: Zhongguo tongji chubanshe.

National Bureau of Statistics of the PRC 中华人民共和国国家统计局 (2010b): *Zhongguo maoyi waijingji tongji nianjian 2010* [中国贸易外经济统计年鉴 2010/ China Trade and External Economic Statistical Yearbook 2010], Beijing: Zhongguo tongji chubanshe.

National Bureau of Statistics of the PRC 中华人民共和国国家统计局 (2011a): *Zhongguo tongji nianjian 2011* [中国统计年鉴 2011/ China Statistical Yearbook 2011], Beijing: Zhongguo tongji chubanshe.

National Bureau of Statistics of the PRC 中华人民共和国国家统计局 (2011b): *Zhongguo laodong tongji nianjian 2011* [中国劳动统计年鉴 2011/ China Labor Statistical Yearbook 2011], Beijing: Zhongguo tongji chubanshe.

Naughton, Barry (2007): *The Chinese Economy: Transitions and Growth*, Cambridge: The MIT Press.

Neuman, William Laurence (2000): *Social Research Methods: Qualitative and Quantitative Approaches*, 4th edition, Boston: Allyn & Bacon.

Nie, Jianqiang (2006): *The Enforcement of Intellectual Property Rights in China*, London: Cameron May.

Nie, Winter, Xin, Katherine and Zhang, Lily (2009): *Made in China: Secrets of China's Dynamic Entrepreneurs*, Singapore: John Wiley & Sons.

Nolan, Peter (2011): "China and the Global Economy", in: David Shambaugh (ed.): *Charting China's Future: Domestic and International Challenges*, Abingdon: Routledge, pp. 44-53.

Nonaka, Ikujiro and Takeuchi, Hirotaka (1997): *Die Organisation des Wissens: Wie japanische Unternehmen eine brachliegende Ressource nutzbar machen*, Frankfurt am Main: Campus.

North, Klaus and Güldenberg, Stefan (2008): *Produktive Wissensarbeit(er): Antworten auf die Management-Herausforderung des 21. Jahrhunderts*, Wiesbaden: Gabler.

North, Klaus (2011): *Wissensorientierte Unternehmensführung: Wertschöpfung durch Wissen*, 5th edition, Wiesbaden: Gabler.

Oakley, Sheila (2002): *Labor Relations in China's Socialist Market Economy: Adapting to the Global Market*, Westport, Conn.: Quorum Books.

OECD (2011): "Education Attainment", in: *OECD Factbook 2011-2012: Economic, Environmental and Social Statistics*, OECD Publishing, http://dx.doi.org/10.1787/factbook-2011-85-en (accessed May 5, 2013).

OECD (2012): "Foreign direct investment", in: *OECD Factbook 2011-2012: Economic, Environmental and Social Statistics*, OECD Publishing, http://www.oecd-ilibrary.org/sites/factbook-2011-en/04/02/01/index.html?itemId=/content/chapter/factbook-2011-38-en (accessed June 6, 2013).

Ordish, Rebecca and Adcock, Alan (2008): *China Intellectual Property – Challenges & Solutions: An Essential Business Guide*, Singapore: John Wiley & Sons.

Ostrom, Elinor and Ahn, T.K. (2009): "The meaning of social capital and its link to collective action", in: Gert Tinggaard Svendsen and Gunnar Lind Haase Svendsen (eds.): *Handbook of Social Capital*, Cheltenham: Edward Elgar, pp. 17-35.

Ou, Xiuping 欧修平 (2006): "Shangye mimi de sifa baohu" [商业秘密的司法保护/ Judicial protection of trade secrets], *Dongguan government's official website*, http://www.dg.gov.cn/http://www.dgsme.gov.cn/dgsme/zw_v3/470/2/50195.html (accessed Feb 18, 2013).

Patulny, Roger (2009): "The sociability of nations: international comparisons in bonding, bridging and linking social capital", in: Gert Tinggaard Svendsen and Gunnar Lind Haase Svendsen (eds.): *Handbook of Social Capital*, Cheltenham: Edward Elgar, pp. 402-427.

Pelzer, Nils (2012): "Die Anfänge des Urheberrechts in China", in: Lena Hennigsen and Martin Hofmann (eds.): *Tradition? Variation? Plagiat? Motive und ihre Adaption in China*, Wiesbaden: Harrassowitz, pp. 15-31.

Peng, He (2012): "Counterproductive Work Behavior Among Chinese Knowledge Workers", *International Journal of Selection and Assessment*, Vol. 20 No. 2, June 2012, pp. 119-138.

Pernicka, Susanne, Lasofsky-Blahut, Anja, Kofranek, Manfred and Reichel, Astrid (2010): *Wissensarbeiter organisieren: Perspektiven kollektiver Interessenvertretung*, Berlin: edition sigma.

Poerner, Michael (2009): "China-Knigge für deutsche Geschäftsleute? Die Darstellung Chinas in interkultureller Ratgeberliteratur", *Interculture Journal: online-Zeitschrift für Interkulturelle Studien*, 8/9, pp. 111-130.

Poerner, Michael (2014): "Intercultural Communication Studies and the Problem of Chinese Exceptionalism", in: Saila Poutiainen (ed.): *Theoretical Turbulence in Intercultural Communication Studies*, Newcastle upon Tyne: Cambridge Scholars Publishing, pp. 121-136.

Polanyi, Michael (1966): *The Tacit Dimension*, New York: Doubleday.

Polanyi, Michael (1985): *Implizites Wissen*, Frankfurt am Main: Suhrkamp.

Potter, Pitman B. (2011): "The Future of China's Legal Regime", in: David Shambaugh (ed.): *Charting China's Future: Domestic and International Challenges*, Abingdon: Routledge, pp. 67-73.

Probst, Gilbert, Raub, Steffen and Romhardt, Kai (2006): *Wissen managen: Wie Unternehmen ihre wertvollste Ressource optimal nutzen*, 5th edition, Wiesbaden: Gabler.

Pun, Ngai (2005): *Made in China: Women Factory Workers in a Global Workplace*, Hong Kong: Duke University Press.

Pun, Ngai and Li, Wanwei (2008): *Dagongmei: Arbeiterinnen aus Chinas Weltmarktfabriken erzählen*, Berlin: Assoziation A.

Pyöriä, Pasi (2005): "The concept of knowledge work revisited", *Journal of Knowledge Management*, Vol. 9 No. 3, Bingley, pp. 116-127.

Qian, Minhui 钱民辉 (2011): *Shehui redian mian dui mian* [社会热点面对面/ Face to face with society's hot topics], Vol. 2, Beijing: Renmin ribao chubanshe.

Qian, Xiaolei and Smyth, Russell (2006): "Growth Accounting for the Chinese Provinces 1990-2000: Incorporating Human Capital Accumulation", *Journal of Chinese Economic and Business Studies*, Vol. 4 No. 1, London, pp. 21-37.

Qu, Sanqiang (2012): *Intellectual Property Law in China*, Alphen aan den Rijn: Kluwer Law International.

Rainey, Lee Dian (2010): *Confucius & Confucianism: The Essentials*, Chichester: John Wiley & Sons.

Ramasamy, B., Goh, K.W. and Yeung, Matthew C.H. (2006): "Is Guanxi (relationship) a bridge to knowledge transfer", *Journal of Business Research*, Vol. 59, Amsterdam, pp. 130-139.

Raphael, Lutz (2004): "Habitus und sozialer Sinn: Der Ansatz der Praxistheorie Pierre Bourdieus", in: Friedrich Jäger and Jürgen Straub (eds.): *Handbuch der Kulturwissenschaften, Bd. 2: Paradigmen und Disziplinen*, Stuttgart: J. B. Metzler, pp. 266-276.

Rawski, Thomas G. (1989): *Economic Growth in Prewar China*, Berkeley: University of California Press.

Reckwitz, Andreas (2004): "Die Kontingenzperspektive der 'Kultur'. Kulturbegriffe, Kulturtheorien und das kulturwissenschaftliche Forschungsprogramm", in: Friedrich Jaeger, Burkhard Liebsch, Joern Ruesen and Juergen Straub (eds.): *Handbuch der Kulturwissenschaften*, Band 3, Stuttgart: Metzler, pp. 1-20.

Reckwitz, Andreas (2010): "Auf dem Weg einer kultursoziologischen Analytik zwischen Praxeologie und Poststrukturalismus", in: Monika Wohlrab-Sahr (ed.): *Kultursoziologie: Paradigmen – Methoden – Fragestellungen*, Wiesbaden: VS Verlag für Sozialwissenschaften, pp. 179-205.

Redding, S. Gordon (1990): *The Spirit of Chinese Capitalism*, New York and Berlin: Walter de Gruyter.

Reinhardt, Rüdiger, Bornemann, Manfred, Pawlowsky, Peter and Schneider, Ursula (2001): "Intellectual Capital and Knowledge Management: Perspectives on Measuring Knowledge", in: Meinolf Dierkes, Ariane Berthoin Antal, John Child and Ikujiro Nonaka (eds.): *Handbook of Organizational Learning and Knowledge*, Oxford: Oxford University Press, pp. 794-820.

Ren, Jingrong 任景荣 (2005): "Qinfan shangye mimi zhi qianxi" [侵犯商业秘密之浅析/ Brief analysis of trade secret infringements], *Jiage yuekan*, 09/2005, Nanchang, pp. 45-46.

Renminwang 人民网 (2004): "Lianggao tuichu zhishi chanquan baohufa jieshi" [两高推出知识产权保护司法解释/ Two Supremes publish an interpretation on law of intellectual property protection], Dec 8, 2004, http://www.people.com.cn/GB/shehui/1060/3071298.html (accessed Feb 18, 2013).

Renminwang 人民网 (2006): "Guojia zhongchangqi kexue he jishu fazhan guihua gaiyao" [国家中长期科学和技术发展规划纲要/ Outline of the National Medium- and Long-term Program for Science and Technology Development], Feb 9, 2006, http://politics.people.com.cn/GB/1026/4089311.html (accessed May 29, 2012).

Renminwang (2007): "China supreme court issues guide for unfair competition cases", Jan 18, 2007, http://english.peopledaily.com.cn/200701/18/eng20070118_342499.html (accessed Jan 15, 2013).

Richter, Carola and Gebauer, Sebastian (2010): *Die China-Berichterstattung in den deutschen Medien*, Berlin: Heinrich-Böll-Stiftung.

Rooney, David and Schneider, Ursula (2005): "The material, mental, historical and social character of knowledge", in: David Rooney, Greg Hearn and Abraham Ninan (eds.): *Handbook on the Knowledge Economy*, Cheltenham: Edward Elgar, pp. 19-36.

Ross, Andrew (2007): "Outsourcing as a way of life? Knowledge transfer in the Yangtze Delta", in: Ching Kwan Lee (ed.): *Working in China: Ethnographies of labor and workplace transformation*, Abingdon: Routledge, pp. 188-208.

Röttgers, Kurt (2010): "Das Eigentum am Text", in: Thomas R. Eimer, Kurt Röttgers and Barbara Völzmann-Stickelbrock (eds.): *Die Debatte um geistiges Eigentum: Interdisziplinäre Erkundungen. Rechtswissenschaft – Politikwissenschaft – Philosophie*, Bielefeld: transcript, pp. 181-210.

Rozman, Gilbert (2012): "Chinese National Identity: A Six-Dimentional Analysis", in: Gilbert Rozman (ed.): *East Asian National Identities: Common Roots and Chinese Exceptionalism*, Stanford, CA: Stanford University Press, pp. 73-99.

Schanz, Günther (2006): *Implizites Wissen*, München: Rainer Hampp.

Scharping, Thomas (2003): "Sozialwissenschaftliche Chinaforschung", in: Brunhild Staiger, Stefan Friedrich and Hans-Wilm Schütte (eds.): *Das große China-Lexikon*, Darmstadt: Wissenschaftliche Buchgesellschaft, pp. 693-695.

Scharping, Thomas (2007): "Bevölkerungspolitik und demographische Entwicklung", in: Doris Fischer and Michael Lackner (eds.): *Länderbericht China: Geschichte – Politik – Wirtschaft – Gesellschaft*, Bonn: Bundeszentrale für politische Bildung, pp. 50-71.

Schatzki, Theodore R. (1996): *Social Practices: A Wittgensteinian Approach to Human Activity and the Social*, Cambridge: Cambridge University Press.

Schatzki, Theodore R. (2001): "Introduction: Practice theory", in: Theodore R. Schatzki, Karen Knorr Cetina and Eike von Savigny (eds.): *The Practice Turn in Contemporary Theory*, London: Routledge, pp. 1-14.

Schilcher, Christian (2006): *Implizite Dimensionen des Wissens und ihre Bedeutung für betriebliches Wissensmanagement*, Darmstadt: Technical University of Darmstadt.

Schnettler, Bernt (2007): "Thomas Luckmann", in: Rainer Schützeichel (ed.): *Handbuch Wissenssoziologie und Wissensforschung*, Konstanz: UVK, pp. 161-170.

Schucher, Günter (2006): "Chinas neues Arbeitsvertragsgesetz – Stärkung der Schwachen oder nur Beruhigungspille", *China aktuell*, 4/2006, Hamburg, pp. 47-65.

Schucher, Günter (2009): "China's Employment Crisis: A Stimulus for Policy Change?", *Journal of Current Chinese Affairs*, Vol. 38 No. 2, Hamburg, pp. 121-144.

Schüller, Margot (2008): *Technologietransfer nach China: Ein unkalkulierbares Risiko für die Länder der Triade Europa, USA und Japan?*, Berlin: Friedrich-Ebert-Stiftung.

Seffert, Birte (2003): "China auf dem Weg zur Wissensgesellschaft: Entwicklungen und Probleme im Pflichtschulbereich", *China aktuell*, Mai 2003, Hamburg, pp. 578-591.

Sewell, William, Jr. (2008): "The Concept(s) of Culture", in: Timothy S. Oakes and Patricia L. Price (eds.): *The Cultural Geography Reader*, Abingdon and New York: Routledge, pp. 40-49.

Shaffer, Lynda (1981): "Modern Chinese Labor History", *International Labor and Working Class History*, No. 20, Fall 1981, Cambridge, pp. 31-37.

Shambaugh, David (ed.) (2011): *Charting China's Future: Domestic and International Challenges*, Abingdon: Routledge.

Shan, Hailing (2007): "Protection of know-how in Chinese enterprises and employment relationships", in: Paul Torremans, Hailing Shan and Johan Erauw (eds.): *Intellectual Property and TRIPS Compliance in China: Chinese and European Perspectives*, Cheltenham: Edward Elgar, pp. 153-174.

Shan, Hailing (2008): *The Protection of Trade Secrets in China*, Alphen aan den Rijn: Kluwer Law International.

Shanghai Daily (2012a): "MNCs struggle to find local Chinese talent", *Shanghai Daily online*, Jan 11, 2012, http://www.shanghaidaily.com/Opinion/china-knowledge-wharton/MNCs-struggle-to-find-local-Chinese-talent/shdaily.shtml (accessed Oct 14, 2013).

Shanghai Daily (2012b): "China's talent war: Demand far exceeds pool of qualified talent", *Shanghai Daily online*, July 3, 2012, http://shanghaidaily.com/Opinion/china-knowledge-wharton/Chinas-talent-war-Demand-far-exceeds-pool-of-qualified-talent/shdaily.shtml (accessed Oct 14, 2013).

Shao, Ke (2006): "What May Validate Intellectual Property in a Traditional Chinese Mind? Examining the U.S.-China IP Disputes through a Historical Inquiry", *ELJ – Journal of Information Law & Technology*, 2006 (1), Coventry, http://www2.warwick.ac.uk/fac/soc/law/elj/jilt/2006_1/shao (accessed Dec 15, 2013).

Shenkar, Oded (2005): *The Chinese Century: The Rising Chinese Economy and Its Impact on the Global Economy, The Balance of Power, and Your Job*, Upper Saddle River: Wharton School Publishing.

Shi, Wei (2006): "Cultural Perplexity in Intellectual Property: Is Stealing a Book an Elegant Offence?", *North Carolina Journal of International Law and Commercial Regulation*, Vol. 32 No. 1, 2006, Chapel Hill, http://papers.ssrn.com/sol3/papers.cfm?abstract_id=1685588 (accessed May 4, 2011).

Shin, Seung K., Ishman, Michael and Sanders, Lawrence G. (2007): "An empirical investigation of socio-cultural factors of information sharing in China", *Information & Management*, Vol. 44, Amsterdam, pp. 165-174.

Shurmer-Smith, Pamela (2002): "The Trouble with Theory", in: Pamela Shurmer-Smith (ed.): *Doing Cultural Geography*, London: SAGE, pp. 11-18.

Siegrist, Hannes (2012): "Geistiges Eigentum und Piraterie in historischer Perspektive", *APUZ: Aus Politik und Zeitgeschichte*, 48/2012, Bonn , pp. 16-21.

Siemons, Mark (2011): "Moral in China: Wo wir unser Herz verloren haben", *Frankfurter Allgemeine online*, Oct 26, 2013, http://www.faz.net/aktuell/feuilleton/debatten/moral-in-china-wo-wir-unser-herz-verloren-haben-11503674.html (accessed Dec 11, 2013).

Skinner, G. William (1977a): "Introduction: Urban Social Structure in Ch'ing China", in: G. William Skinner (ed.): *The City in Late Imperial China*, Stanford, CA: Stanford University Press, pp. 521-553.

Skinner, G. William (1977b): "Cities and the Hierarchy of Local Systems", in: G. William Skinner (ed.): *The City in Late Imperial China*, Stanford: Stanford University Press, pp. 275-351.

Solinger, Dorothy J. (2009): "The phase-out of the unfit: keeping the unworthy out of work", in: Lisa Keister (ed.): *Work and Organizations in China after Thirty Years of Transition*, Bingley: Emerald, pp. 307-336.

Sollberger, Bettina A. (2006): *Wissenskultur: Erfolgsfaktor für ein ganzheitliches Wissensmanagement*, Bern: Haupt.

Sonobe, Tetsushi, Hu, Dinghuan and Otsuka, Keijiro (2004): "From Inferior to Superior Products: An Inquiry into the Wenzhou Model of Industrial Development in China", *Journal of Comparative Economics*, Vol. 32 No. 3, Amsterdam, pp. 542-563.

Spegele, Brian and Nakamichi, Takashi (2012): "Anti-Japan Protests Mount in China", *The Wall Street Journal online*, Sept 16, 2012, http://online.wsj.com/article/SB10000872396390443720204578000092842756154.html# (accessed June 7, 2013).

Spence, Jonathan D. (1990): *The Search for Modern China*, New York: W. W. Norton & Company.

Sprenkel, van der, Sybille (1977): "Urban Social Control", in: G. William Skinner (ed.): *The City in Late Imperial China*, Stanford, CA: Stanford University Press, pp. 609-632.

Staiger, Brunhild (2007): "Bildung und Wissenschaft", in: Doris Fischer and Michael Lackner (eds.): *Länderbericht China: Geschichte – Politik – Wirtschaft – Gesellschaft*, Bonn: Bundeszentrale für politische Bildung, pp. 523-541.

Stangor, Charles (2000): "Volume Overview", in: Charles Stangor (ed.): *Stereotypes and Prejudice: Essential Readings*, Ann Arbor, MI: Edwards Brothers, pp. 1-16.

State Intellectual Property Office of the PRC (SIPO) 中华人民共和国国家知识产权局 (2000-2011): *Zhongguo zhishi chanquan nianjian 2000* [中国知识产权年鉴 2000/ China Intellectual Property Yearbook 2000], Beijing: Zhishi chanquan chubanshe.

Stiehler, Andreas, Schabel, Frank and Alich, David (2011): *Fachbereiche im Wandel: Wie Wissensarbeit die Unternehmen verändert*, published by Hays, Mannheim, http://www.hays.de/mediastore/pressebereich/Studien/pdf/HAYS-Studie_Fachbereiche_im_wandel_wissensarbeit.pdf (accessed July 12, 2013).

Stone, Charles R. (2008): "What plagiarism was not: Some preliminary observations on classical Chinese attitudes toward what the West calls intellectual property", *Marquette Law Review*, Vol. 92 No. 1, Milwaukee, pp. 199-230.

Stone, Leslie (2011): "Preparing for the twenty-first century: Liberal education and undergraduate educational reform at Sun Yat-sen University", in: Janette Ryan (ed.): *China's Higher Education Reform and Internationalization*, Abingdon: Routledge, pp. 69-85.

Süddeutsche (2012): "Chinesisches Geld und deutsche Flitzer bescheren VW Gewinnsprung", April 26, 2012, http://www.sueddeutsche.de/wirtschaft/autokonzern-legt-quartalszahlen-vor-chinesisches-geld-und-deutsche-flitzer-bescheren-vw-gewinnsprung-1.1342263 (accessed Jan 23, 2013).

Sun, Baiyang 孙白杨, Cao, Bangying 曹邦英, Li, Hong 李虹 (2008): "Guanyu yunzuo wuxing ziben tishen qiye wenhua jingzhengli de tantao" [关于运作无形资本提升企业核心竞争力的探讨 / Investigation on the raising of the enterprise's competitiveness through the operation of intangible capital], *Tongji yu zixun*, 5/2008, Harbin, pp. 14-15.

Swider, Sarah (2011): "Permanent Temporariness in the Chinese Construction Industry", in: Sarosh Kuruvilla, Ching Kwan Lee, Mary E. Gallagher (eds.): *From Iron Rice Bowl to Informalization: Markets, Workers, and the State in a Changing China*, Ithaca, NY: Cornell University Press, pp. 138-154.

Szanton, David L. (2004): "Introduction: The Origin, Nature, and Challenges of Area Studies in the United States", in: David L. Szanton (ed.): *The Politics of Knowledge: Area Studies and the Disciplines*, Berkeley and Los Angelos, CA: The University of California Press, pp. 1-33.

Taipei Times (2007): "The self-made Chinese entrepreneur who refuses to back down", July 8, 2007, http://www.taipeitimes.com/News/bizfocus/archives/2007/07/08/2003368682 (accessed June 10, 2013).

Tan, Yinglan (2011): *Chinnovation: How Chinese Innovators are Changing the World*, Singapore: John Wiley & Sons.

Tang, Beibei (2011): "Change and continuity in China's urban workforce: Recent trends", in: Peter Sheldon, Sunghoon Kom, Yiqiong Li and Macolm Warner (eds.): *China's Changing Workplace: Dynamism, diversity and disparity*, Abingdon: Routledge, pp. 71-92.

Tang, Kemin 唐克敏 (1996): "Tang Tingshu" [唐廷枢/ Tang Tingshu], in: Xu Mao 徐矛 (ed.): *Zhongguo shi maiban* [中国十买办/ China's ten compradors], Shanghai: Shanghai renmin chubanshe, pp. 42-56.

Tang, Wenfang and Parish, William L. (2009): "Life Chances: Education and jobs", in: Andrew Kipnis, Luigi Tomba and Jonathan Ungar (eds.): *Contemporary Chinese Society and Politics, Vol. III (Urban China)*, Abingdon: Routledge, pp. 99-121.

Tanigawa, Shinichi (2005): *The Cultural Revolution and Educational Stratification: Revolution in Education Revisited*, Creation of New Contemporary Asian Studies, Working Paper, July 2005, Waseda University.

Tanner, Harold M. (2009): *China: A History*, Indianapolis: Hackett Publishing Company.

Tao, Jingzhao (2007): "Problems and new developments in the enforcement of intellectual property rights in China", in: Paul Torremans, Hailing Shan and Johan Erauw (eds.): *Intellectual Property and TRIPS Compliance in China: Chinese and European Perspectives*, Cheltenham: Edward Elgar, pp. 107-124.

Taubmann, Wolfgang (2007): "Naturräumliche Gliederung und wirtschaftsgeographische Grundlagen", in: Doris Fischer and Michael Lackner (eds.): *Länderbericht China: Geschichte – Politik – Wirtschaft – Gesellschaft*, Bonn: Bundeszentrale für politische Bildung, pp. 15-49.

Teo, Stephen T.T. and Wang, Karen (2007): "Human Capital, Social Capital and Firm Performance in Chinese SMEs", in: Stewart Clegg, Karen Wang and Mike Berrell (eds.): *Business Networks and Strategic Alliances in China,* Cheltenham: Edward Elgar, pp. 230-251.

Thaler, Wolfgang (2009): *Die rechtliche Abwehr von Marken- und Produktpiraterie*, Innsbruck: Innsbruck University Press.

Thoegersen, Stig (2007): "Bildungstradition", in: Brunhild Staiger, Stefan Friedrich and Hans-Wilm Schütte (eds.): *Das große China-Lexikon*, Darmstadt: Wissenschaftliche Buchgesellschaft, pp. 102-103.

Thomas, Alexander (2005): "Kultur und Kulturstandards", in: Alexander Thomas, Eva-Ulrike Kinast and Sylvia Schroll-Machl (eds.): *Handbuch interkulturelle Kommunikation und Kooperation*, Göttingen: Vandenhoeck & Ruprecht, pp. 19-31.

Todeva, Emanuela (2007): "Business Networks in China: Legacies and Practice", in: Stewart Clegg, Karen Wang and Mike Berrell (eds.): *Business Networks and Strategic Alliances in China,* Cheltenham: Edward Elgar, pp. 252-271.

Tomba, Luigi (2011): "Remaking China's working class: *Gongren* and *nongmingong*", in: Peter Sheldon, Sunghoon Kom, Yiqiong Li and Macolm Warner (eds.): *China's Changing Workplace: Dynamism, diversity and disparity*, Abingdon: Routledge, pp. 144-159.

Travers, Max (2001): *Qualitative Research through Case Studies*, Thousand Oaks, CA: SAGE.

Trompenaars, Fons and Hampden-Turner, Charles (1997): *Riding the Waves of Culture: Understanding Diversity in Global Business*, Maidenhead: Mcgraw Hill Book.

Tse, Edward (2010): *The China Strategy: Harnessing the Power of the World's Fastest-Growing Economy*, New York: Basic Books.

Tsui, Anne S. (2012): "Contextualizing research in a modernizing China", in: Xu Huang, Michael Harris Bond (eds.): *Handbook of Chinese Organizational Behavior: Integrating Theory, Research and Practice*, Cheltenham and Northampton, MA: Edward Elgar, pp. 29-47.

US-China Business Council (2006): "Comments on the Draft Labor Contract Law of the People's Republic of China (Draft of March 20, 2006)", April 19, 2006, https://www.uschina.org/public/documents/2006/04/uscbc-comments-labor-law.pdf (accessed May 15, 2012).

US-China Business Council (2011): *USCBC 2011 China Business Environment Survey Results: Market Growth Continues, Companies Expand, But Full Access Elusive for Many*, https://www.uschina.org/public/documents/2011/10/membership_survey_english.pdf (accessed May 2, 2012).

US-China Business Council (2012): *USCBC 2012 China Business Environment Survey Results: Continued Growth and Profitability; Tempered Optimism Due to Rising Costs, Competition, and Market Barriers,* https://www.uschina.org/info/members-survey/2012/pdfs/uscbc-2012-member-survey-results.pdf (accessed Dec 8, 2012).

Voelpel, Sven and Zheng, Han (2005): "Managing knowledge sharing in China: The case of Siemens ShareNet", *Journal of Knowledge Management*, Vol. 9 No. 3, Bingley, pp. 51-63.

Waley, Arthur (1938): *The Analects of Confucius*, London: George Allen & Unwin.

Wang, Dan 王丹 and Yang, Heqing 杨河清 (2012): "Zhishi gongzuozhe guodu laodong de xingcheng jizhi tanxi" [知识工作者过度劳动的形成机制探析/ Exploring and analyzing the formation mechanism of knowledge workers' overwork], *Zhongguo renli ziyuan kaifa*, 01/2012, Beijing, pp. 96-99.

Wang, Gungwu (2003): *Anglo-Chinese Encounters since 1800: War, Trade, Science and Governance*, Cambridge: Cambridge University Press.

Wang, Haiyan, Appelbaum, Richard P., Degiuli, Francesca and Lichtenstein, Nelson (2009): "China's New Labour Contract Law: is China moving toward increased power for workers?", *Third World Quarterly*, Vol. 30 No. 3, London, pp. 485-501.

Wang, Haiyao 王辉耀 (2012): "Zhongguo haigui chuangye fazhan baogao" ['中国海归创业发展报告 2012' 综述/ Report on the development of China's overseas returnees' enterpreneurship], *FT Zhongguowang*, Jan 16, 2013, http://www.ftchinese.com/story/001048502 (accessed April 29, 2013).

Wang, Hongyi (2011): "Chinese professionals prefers domestic firms", *China Daily online*, http://www.chinadaily.com.cn/china/2011-06/09/content_12661892.htm (accessed May 3, 2012).

Wang, Jianying and Davis, Deborah (2010): "China's New Upper Middle Classes: The Importance of Occupational Disaggregation", in: Li Cheng (ed.): *China's Emerging Middle Class: Beyond Economic Transformation*, Washington, DC: Brookings Institution Press, pp. 157-176.

Wang, Junxiu 王俊秀 (2011): "Guanzhu renmin de zunyan he xingfu, cujin shehui de gongzheng yu hexie: 2010-2011 nian zhongguo shehui xintai yanjiu baogao" [关注人民的尊严和幸福，促进社会的公正与和谐：2010~2011 年中国社会心态研究报告/ Caring about the people's status of dignity and well-being, moving toward a just and harmonious society: report on social mentality in China, 2010-2011], in: Wang, Junxiu 王俊秀, Yang, Yiyin 杨宜音 (eds.): *Shehui xintai lanpishu: zhongguo shehui xintai yanjiu baogao (2011)* [社会心态蓝皮书: 中国社会心态研究报告 (2011) / Blue Book of Social Mentality: annual Report on Social Mentality of China (2011)], Beijing: Shehui kexue wenxian chubanshe, pp. 1-23.

Wang, Junxiu 王俊秀 (2013): "Guanzhu shehui qingxu, cujin shehui rentong, ningju shehui gongshi: 2012-2013 nian zhongguo shehui xintai yanjiu baogao" [关注社会情绪，促进社会认同，凝聚社会共识：2012~2013 年中国社会心态研究报告/ Paying close attention to social emotion, improving social identity, uniting social consensus: Report on social mentality in China, 2012-2013], in: Wang, Junxiu 王俊秀, Yang, Yiyin 杨宜音 (eds.): *Shehui xintai lanpishu: zhongguo shehui xintai yanjiu baogao (2012-2013)* [社会心态蓝皮书: 中国社会心态研究报告 (2012-2013)/ Blue Book of Social Mentality: Annual Report on Social Mentality of China (2012-2013)], Beijing: Shehui kexue wenxian chubanshe, pp. 1-25.

Wang, Lijun 王立军 (1996): "Dulake tan: shijie jingji yu qiye de zouxiang" [杜拉克谈：世界经济与企业的走向/ Drucker discusses the direction of the global economy and enterprises], *Zhongwai guanli*, 11/1996, Beijing, pp. 40-42.

Wang, Xi 王希 (2012): "Lun rencai liudongzhong de shangye mimi baohu" [论人才流动中的商业秘密保护/ Discussing trade secrets protection and employee turnover], *Qianhai*, 04/2012, Hohhot, pp. 93-95.

Wang, Xiufang (2003): *Education in China since 1976*, Jefferson: McFarland.

Wang, Yan and Yao, Yudong (2003): "Sources of China's Economic Growth: 1952-99: Incorporating Human Capital Accumulation", *China Economic Review*, Vol. 14 No. 1, Amsterdam, pp. 32-52.

Wang, Yu 王瑜 (2006): "Rencai liudong yu qiye shangye mimi" [人才流动与企业商业秘密/ Talent turnover and enterprises' trade secrets], *Zhongguo shichang*, 05/2006, Beijing, pp. 16-17.

Watson, Burton (2003): *Han Feizi: Basic Writings*, New York: Columbia University Press.

Webster's Revised Unabridged Dictionary (1913): "implicit", Springfield, MA: C. & G. Merriam Co, p. 736.

Wen, Haiming (2012): *Chinese Philosophy*, Cambridge: Cambridge University Press.

Wermke, Matthias, Kunkel-Razum, Kathrin and Scholze-Stubenrecht, Werner (eds.) (2006): "implizit", in: Wermke et al. (eds.): *Duden: Das Fremdwörterbuch*, Berlin: Bibliographisches Institut, p. 443.

Wexler, Alexandra (2011): "Goodyear's Toughest Fight Is the Fight for Talent", *The Wall Street Journal online*, Aug 8, 2011, http://online.wsj.com/article/SB100014240 53111903454504576487593768691666.html (accessed July 3, 2012).

Whyte, Martin King (2010): *Myth of the Social Volcano: Perceptions of Inequality and Distributive Injustice in Contemporary China*, Stanford, CA: Stanford University Press.

Wilhelm, Richard and Ess, Hans van (2005): *Konfuzius: Gespräche*, München: C.H.Beck.

Wilkesmann, Uwe, Wilkesmann, Maximiliane and Fischer, Heike (2008): "Wissenstransfer auf Chinesisch: Besonderheiten in Hongkong", *Wissensmanagement*, Vol. 8, Neusäß, pp. 28-30.

Williams, Brad and Mihalkanin, Danielle (2011): "Intellectual Property: China's Special Campaign to Combat IPR Infringement", *China Business Review online*, October-December 2011.

Willke, Helmut (1998): *Systemisches Wissensmanagement*, 1st edition, Stuttgart: UTB.

Willke, Helmut (2001): *Systemisches Wissensmanagement*, 2nd edition, Stuttgart: UTB.

Willke, Helmut (2007): *Einführung in das systemische Wissensmanagement*, 2nd edition, Heidelberg: Carl-Auer-Systeme.

Witte, Christina Maren (2010): "Risikoeffizienz und Wirksamkeit betriebswirtschaftlicher Schutzmaßnahmen gegen Produktpiraterie", in: Carsten Fussan (ed.): *Managementmaßnahmen gegen Produktpiraterie und Industriespionage*, Wiesbaden: Gabler, pp. 23-105.

World Bank (2010): "Foreign Direct Investment – The China Story", July 16, 2010, http://www.worldbank.org/en/news/feature/2010/07/16/foreign-direct-investment-china-story (accessed Feb 19, 2013).

World Trade Organization (WTO) (2013): "Part I – General Provisions and Basic Principles", http://www.wto.org/english/docs_e/legal_e/27-trips_03_e.htm (accessed Feb 3, 2013).

Wu, Ming 吴明 (2008): “Lun shangye mimi de goucheng yaojian” [论商业秘密的构成要件/ On the constituent elements of trade secrets], *Anhui gongye daxue xuebao*, Vol. 25 No. 5, 09/2008, Ma’anshan, pp. 90-91.

Wu, Wei-ping (2000): “Transaction Cost, Cultural Values and Chinese Business Networks: An Integrated Approach”, in: Chan Kwok Bun (ed.): *Chinese Business Networks: State, Economy and Culture*, Singapore: Pearson Education Asia, pp. 35-56.

Xiao, Junming 萧俊明 (1996): “Buerdi’e de shijian lilun yu wenhua zaisheng lilun” [布尔迪厄的实践理论与文化再生理论/ Bourdieu’s practice theory and culture reproduction theory], *Guowai shehui kexue*, 04/1996, Beijing, pp. 49-55.

Xiao, Yunduan 肖云端 (2010): “Jingji quanqiuhua beijingxia jiaqiang shangye mimi baohu de lifa tanxi: guanyu ‘lituoan’ de fansi” [经济全球化背景下加强商业秘密保护的立法探析：关于‘力拓案’的反思/ Strengthening exploration and analysis of trade secrets protection legislation against the background of economic globalization: Rethinking the ‘Rio Tinto case’], *Jiangsu shanglun*, 06/2010, Nanjing, pp. 150-152.

Xie, Wei and Li-Hua, Richard (2009): “What will China make an innovation-oriented country?”, *Journal of Knowledge-based Innovation in China*, Vol. 1 No. 1, 2009, Amsterdam, pp. 8-15.

Xie, Yu, Lai, Qing and Wu, Xiaogang (2009): “*Danwei* and social inequality in contemporary urban China”, in: Lisa Keister (ed.): *Work and Organizations in China after Thirty Years of Transition*, Bingley: Emerald, pp. 283-306.

Xing, Lujia 邢璐佳 and Hong, Min 洪慜 (2010): “Qiantan shangye mimi de falü jiuji ji qiye de fangfan cuoshi” [浅谈商业秘密的法律救济及企业的防范措施/ Brief discussion on legal protection of trade secrets as well as enterprises’ protection measures], *Fazhi yu shehui*, 02/2010, Kunming, p. 108.

Xinhuawang 新华网 (2012): “Haiwai rencai guiguohou hui yudao na xie zhang’ai? Haigui de xin jiyu” [海外人才归国后会遇到哪些障碍? 海归的新机遇/ Which barriers will overseas talents face after returning to China? New opportunities for overseas returnees], Nov 30, 2012, http://news.xinhuanet.com/fortune/2012-11/30/c_124025846.htm (accessed April 29, 2013).

Xu, Dixin 许涤新 and Wu Chengming 吴承明 (2003): *Zhongguo zibenzhuyi fazhanshi* [中国资本主义发展史/ History of Chinese capitalism’s development], Vol. II, Beijing: Renmin chubanshe.

Xu, Feng (2000): *Women Migrant Workers in China’s Economic Reform*, London: MacMillan Press.

Xu, Xiaoqun (2004): *Chinese Professionals and the Republican State: The Rise of Professional Associations in Shanghai 1912-1937*, Cambridge: Cambridge University Press.

Yan, Hairong (2009): "Rurality and labor process autonomy: The waged labor of domestic service", in: Ching Kwan Lee (ed.): *Working in China: Ethnographies of labor and workplace transformation*, Abingdon: Routledge, pp. 145-165.

Yang, Deli (2003): *Intellectual Property and Doing Business in China*, Oxford: Elsevier Science.

Yang, Deli and Clarke, Peter (2005): "Globalisation and intellectual property in China", *Technovation*, No. 25, pp. 545-555.

Yang, Keming (2007): *Entrepreneurship in China*, Hampshire: Ashgate.

Yang, Mayfair Mei-hui (2002): "The Resilience of *Guanxi* and its New Deployments: A Critique of Some New *Guanxi* Scholarship", *The China Quarterly*, Vol. 170 No. 2, Cambridge, pp. 459-476.

Yang, Ping 杨萍 (2009): "Cong 'liguoan' toushi wo guo shanye mimi de baohu" [从'力拓案'透视我国商业秘密的保护/ China's trade secret protection from the perspective of the 'Rio Tinto case'], *Fazhi yu shehui*, 09/2009, Kunming, pp. 143-144.

Yang, Wanchun 杨万春 (1981): "Yi ben gei ren qifa de guanli zhuzuo: youxiao de guanlizhe" [一本给人启发的管理著作：有效的管理者/ An Inspiring Management Book: The Effective Executive], *Shijie jingji*, 08/1981, Beijing, pp. 73-76.

Yang, Yao (2013): "President Xi touts moral models", *China Daily online*, Sept 27, 2013, http://www.chinadaily.com.cn/china/2013-09/27/content_16997938.htm (accessed 11 Dec, 2013).

Yao, Souchou (2002): "*Guanxi*: sentiment, performance and the trading of words", in: Thomas Menkhoff and Solvay Gerke (eds.): *Chinese Enterpreneurship and Asian Business Networks*, Abingdon: Routledge, pp. 233-254.

Yi, Jicang 易继苍 (2006): "Maiban yu Shanghai jinrong jindaihua" [买办与上海金融近代化/ The comprador and the modern financial history of Shanghai], Beijing: Zhishi chanquan chubanshe.

Yin, Hongjuan 尹洪娟, Yang, Jing 杨静, Wang, Zheng 王铮, Li, Chen 李琛 (2011): "'Guanxi' dui zhishi fenxiang yingxiang de yanjiu" ['关系'对知识分享影响的研究 / Research on the influence of 'guanxi' on knowledge sharing], *Guanli shijie*, 06/2011, Beijing, pp. 178-179.

Yin, Pumin (2012): "An Ambitious Objective: Building world-class universities is a long-term project", *Beijing Review online*, Feb 27, 2012, http://www.bjreview.com.cn/nation/txt/2012-02/27/content_427985.htm (accessed June 4, 2012).

Yu, Dan (2009): *Konfuzius im Herzen: Alte Weisheit für die moderne Welt*, München: Droemer.

Yu, Liping 俞利平 and Yin, Xianying 尹显英 (2007): " Qinfan shangye mimicui de rending ji qi fangfan" [侵犯商业秘密罪的认定及其防范/ Determining and preventing trade secrets infringements], *Zhongguo renmin gongan daxue xuebao*, 01/2007, Beijing, pp. 13-20.

Yu, Mi 于米 (2011): "Geren/jiti zhuyi qinxiang yu zhishi fenxiang yiyuan zhijian de guanxi yanjiu: Zhishi huoxing de tiaojie zuoyong" [个人/集体主义倾向与知识分享意愿之间的关系研究：知识活性的调节作用/ Research on the relation between individualism/collectivism orientation and the willingness to knowledge sharing: the regulating function of knowledge-related activity], *Nankai guanli pinglun*, Vol. 14 No. 6, Tianjin, pp. 149-157.

Yu, Peter K. (2012): "The Confucian Challenge to Intellectual Property Reforms", *WIPO Journal*, Vol. 4 (2012), London, pp. 1-9.

Yueh, Linda (2013): *China's Growth: The Making of an Economic Superpower*, Oxford: Oxford University Press.

Zang, Yunxiao 臧云霄 (2010): "Rencai liudongzhong de shangye mimi baohu" [人才流动中的商业秘密保护/ Trade secrets protection and employee turnover], *Shanghai xinxihua*, 06/2010, Shanghai, pp. 48-51.

Zhang, Chunhu 张春虎 (2013): "Zuzhi qifen yingxiang yuangong zhishi fenxiang de jili yanjiu" [组织气氛影响员工知识分享的机理研究/ Research on mechanisms of organizational atmosphere influencing employees' knowledge sharing], *Jishu jingji yu guanli yanjiu*, 03/2013, Taiyuan, pp. 59-64.

Zhang, Dainian (2002): *Key Concepts in Chinese Philosophy*, New Haven and London: Yale University Press.

Zhang, De 张德 (2001): *Renli ziyuan kaifa yu guanli* [人力资源开发与管理/ Human Resources Development and Management], 2nd edition, Beijing: Qinghua daxue chubanshe.

Zhang, Jiaqing 张家庆 (2011): "Cong lituoan kan guojia mimi yu shangye mimi zhi jiexian" [从力拓案看国家秘密与商业秘密之界限/ Setting the boundary between state secrets and trade secrets from the angle of the Rio Tinto case], *Zhongxiao qiye guanli yu keji*, 05/2011, Shijiazhuang, pp. 137-138.

Zhang, Lijia (2011): "How can I be proud of my China if we are a nation of 1.4bn cold hearts?", The Guardian online, Oct 22, 2011, http://www.theguardian.com/commentisfree/2011/oct/22/china-nation-cold-hearts#start-of-comments (accessed Dec 11, 2013).

Zhang, Pingying and Van Deusen, Cheryl (2010): "French Danone and Chinese Wahaha: Yet another example of an unsuccessful international joint venture", *International Business: Research, Teaching and Practice*, 2010/4(1), http://www.aibse.org/www.aibse.org/wp-content/uploads/2012/02/ZhangVanDeusen2010.pdf (accessed June 10, 2013), pp. 82-100.

Zhang, Wenxian, Wang, Huiyao and Alon, Ilan (eds.) (2010): *Entrepreneurial and Business Elites of China: The Chinese Returnees who have Shaped Modern China*, Bingley: Emerald.

Zhang, Xueyuan and Reinmoeller, Patrick (2007): "Foreign Firms in China: Success by Strategic Choices", in: Barbara Krug and Hans Hendrischke (eds.): *The Chinese Economy in the 21st Century: Enterprise and Business Behaviour*, Cheltenham: Edward Elgar, pp. 42-70.

Zhao, Shuming (2005): "Changing structure of Chinese enterprises and human resource management practices in China", in: Russell Smyth, On Kit Tam, Malcolm Warner and Cherrie Jiuhua Zhu (eds.): *China's Business Reforms: Institutional challenges in a globalized economy*, Abingdon: RoutledgeCurzon, pp. 106-123.

Zheng, Chengsi (1987): *Chinese Intellectual Property and Technology Transfer Law*, London: Sweet & Maxwell.

Zheng, Chengsi and Pendleton, Michael D. (1991): *Copyright Law in China*, North Ryde: CCH International.

Zheng, Tiantian (2007): "From peasant women to bar hostess: An ethnography of China's karaoke sex industry", in: Ching Kwan Lee (ed.): *Working in China: Ethnographies of labor and workplace transformation*, Abingdon: Routledge, pp. 124-144.

Zheng, Tiantian (2009): *Red Lights: The Lives of Sex Workers in Postsocialist China*, Minneapolis: University of Minnesota Press.

Zhou, Junqiang 周俊强 (2008): "Zhishi chanquan gainianzhong 'zhishi' hanyi bianxi" [知识产权概念中'知识'含义辨析/ Differentiating and analyzing the hidden meaning of 'knowledge' within the concept of intellectual property], *Anhui shifan daxue xuebao*, Vol. 36 No. 2, 2008, Wuhu, pp. 180-184.

Zhou, Xueguang (2004): *The State and Life Chances in Urban China: Redistribution and Stratification, 1949-1994*, Cambridge: Cambridge University Press.

Zhu, Bo 祝波 (2012): "Mubiao guanli shi dui zhishi gongzuozhe de youxiao jili" [目标管理是对知识工作者的有效激励/ Management by objectives is the effective motivation for knowledge workers], *Shanghai qiye*, 03/2012, Shanghai, pp. 76-77.

Zhu, Miaochun 朱妙春 and Wang, Xiaobing 王小兵 (2009): "Cong lituoan kan qiye shangye mimi de baohu: jiantan lituoan dai gei waiguo qiye de qishi" [从力拓案看企业商业秘密的保护：兼谈力拓案带给外国企业的启示/ Viewing enterprises' trade secret protection from the angle of the Rio Tinto case: additionally discussing the illumination the Rio Tinto case brought about for foreign enterprises], *Zhongguo faming yu zhuanli*, 11/2009, Beijing, pp. 14-16.

Zhuang, Xulong 庄绪龙 (2010): "She waishangye fubai fancui shiyong wo guo xingfa ruogan wenti yanjiu: yi shanghai 'Lituoan' wei luoji qidian" [涉外商业腐败犯罪适用我国刑法若干问题研究：以上海'力拓案'为逻辑起点/ Research on several problems regarding the application of China's criminal law for corruption crimes of foreign businesses: the Shanghaier 'Rio Tinto case' as a logical starting point]", *Fazhi yanjiu*, 2010/02, Hangzhou, pp. 84-90.

360doc.com (2012): "Shenmeyang de rencai cai neng shiying shehui jingzheng?" [什么样的人才才能适应社会竞争?/ What kind of talents only could adapt to social competition?], May 6, 2012, http://www.360doc.com/content/12/0506/06/7712863_208957418.shtml (accessed May 22, 2013).

Appendices

Appendix 1: List of Interviewees

Nationality	Date of Interview	Enterprise	Place of Interview[1075]	Int.-No. (Atlas.ti)
German	2009-09-07	WFOE 1	Shanghai	55
German	2009-09-07			56A
Chinese	2009-09-07			56B
German	2010-03-02	WFOE 2	Beijing	83
Chinese	2010-03-02			84
Chinese	2010-03-08	WFOE 3	Guangdong	1
Chinese	2010-03-08			60
Chinese	2010-03-09			41
German	2010-03-09			2
Chinese	2010-03-11	WFOE 4	Guangdong	3
German	2010-03-11			4
Chinese	2010-03-11			42
Chinese	2010-03-12			5
German	2010-03-12			7
German	2009-09-09	JV 1	Shanghai	59
German	2010-03-15			8
Chinese	2010-03-15			9
German	2010-03-15			10
Chinese	2010-03-15			43
Chinese	2010-03-15			11
German	2010-03-15			12
Chinese	2010-03-16	WFOE 5	Shanghai	61A
Chinese	2010-03-16			61B
Chinese	2010-03-16			44
Chinese	2010-03-16			13
Chinese	2010-03-16			62
Chinese	2010-03-17	WFOE 6	Jiangsu	63
Chinese	2010-03-17			64
Chinese	2010-03-17			14

1075 In order to preserve the anonymity of the interviewees only the level of provinces or municipalities is provided.

Nationality	Date of Interview	Enterprise	Place of Interview[1075]	Int.-No. (Atlas.ti)
Chinese	2010-03-17			45
Chinese	2010-03-22			49
German	2010-03-22			78
German	2009-09-08	JV 2	Shanghai	57
German	2010-09-08			30
Chinese	2010-03-18			40
German	2010-03-18			15
Chinese	2010-03-18			46
British	2010-03-19	WFOE 7	Shanghai	16
Hungarian	2010-03-19			17
Chinese	2010-03-19			48
Chinese	2010-03-19			54
Chinese	2010-03-19			65A
Chinese	2010-03-19			65B
German	2010-03-26	WFOE 8	Jiangsu	18
Chinese	2010-03-26			37
Chinese	2010-03-26	WFOE 9	Jiangsu	66
Chinese	2010-03-26			50
German	2010-03-26			82
Chinese	2010-03-30	JV 3	Jilin	67A
Chinese	2010-03-30			67B
Chinese	2010-03-30			51
Chinese	2010-03-30			69
German	2010-03-30			52
Chinese	2010-03-30			68
Chinese	2010-03-30			70
Chinese	2010-03-31			71
Chinese	2010-03-31			72
German	2010-03-31			19
German	2010-03-31			53
Chinese	2010-03-31			73
German	2010-03-31			74
Chinese	2010-04-01	WFOE 10	Beijing	20
Chinese	2010-04-01			21
Chinese	2010-04-01			76
German	2010-04-01			75
German	2010-04-02	JV 4	Beijing	38
German	2010-04-02			39
Chinese	2010-04-02			77

Appendix 2: Topic Guide

Part I: Interviewee	• Position, function, department • Age, qualification, career, how long in the enterprise • Daily work and tasks[1076]
Part II: Valuable knowledge	• Main daily knowledge flows *(→ drawing main flows)* • Obstacles with handling knowledge • Protection and exchange of knowledge • Knowledge belongs to whom[1077]

Part III: Intangible capital[1078]	• Reflection upon intangible capital (→ *commenting on cards*)[1079]
	  o Intellectual capital (green): invention (发明)[1080], creativity (创新能力)
	  o human capital (blue): experiences (经验), knowledge (知识), ability (才能)
	  o social capital (yellow): relationships (人际关系), networks (关系网)
	  o structural capital (orange): routines (日常常规), production processes/ management procedures (生产流程/管理程序), corporate structure (企业结构), corporate culture (企业文化)
	• Role of each for daily knowledge interactions
	• Importance of each for the enterprise
	• Comparative significance (→ *card sorting*)

1076 The rationale was threefold: to receive information on the person and his/her position, to get him/her to talk, and to acquire first indications of criteria for communicating valuable knowledge should be given by the interviewee himself before asking more concretely.

1077 For these more sensitive questions vignettes were used, such as "Imagine two employees together developed a new product. How would you treat them if you were their manager? How would you desire being treated being one of the employees?". The answers illuminated that the employee's knowledge input still forms part of their knowledge which has to be adequately rewarded instead of being perceived as automatically belonging to the enterprise.

1078 Intangible capital is a concept to estimate the market value of an enterprise with its non-physical sources of future benefit (see chapter 2.2). Reflecting on the role of each for knowledge interactions serves as a point of departure for accessing possible (semi-)conscious criteria of sharing and disclosing knowledge.

1079 Eleven cards each conveying one component of intangible capital in German, English and Chinese, every interviewee was asked to reflect upon. The cards with the components belonging to the same category were in the same color and were put on the table at once.

1080 The terms for each component were chosen according to the concepts chapter including Chinese language academic literature (see e.g. Li Sheng and Yu Jun 2009: 13, Sun Baiyang et al. 2008: 15) as well as through discussions with Chinese native speaking business actors, ensuring that the terms are commonly used in the Chinese business environment.

Part IV: Enterprise[1081]	• Enterprise's strength and core competencies • Relationship to the enterprise • Sense of belonging to enterprise, department, networks

1081 In the last part, probing into the role of the enterprise (department/network) for providing orientation within knowledge interactions was pursued.

Appendix 3: Total Knowledge Workers 2002-2010 (1)

Year	Total Population 总人口 (persons)	Employment 全国就业人员 (persons)	Unit Head 单位负责人 (%)	Unit Head 单位负责人 (persons)	Professional and Technical Personnel 专业技术人员 (%)	Professional and Technical Personnel 专业技术人员 (persons)	Clerk and Related Workers 办事人员和有关人员 (%)	Clerk and Related Workers 办事人员和有关人员 (persons)	**KW1 (persons)[1]**	**KW2 (persons)[2]**
2002	1,284,530,000	737,400,000	1.7	12,535,800	6.0	44,244,000	7.0	51,618,000	**108,397,800**	**56,779,800**
2003	1,292,270,000	744,320,000	1.8	13,397,760	6.9	51,358,080	7.7	57,312,640	**122,068,480**	**64,755,840**
2004	1,299,880,000	752,000,000	1.7	12,784,000	7.2	54,144,000	7.6	57,152,000	**124,080,000**	**66,928,000**
2005	1,307,560,000	758,250,000	1.5	11,373,750	7.5	56,868,750	3.7	28,055,250	**96,297,750**	**68,242,500**
2006	1,314,480,000	764,000,000	1.2	9,168,000	5.7	43,548,000	3.4	25,976,000	**78,692,000**	**52,716,000**
2007	1,321,290,000	769,900,000	1.2	9,238,800	5.6	43,114,400	3.7	28,486,300	**80,839,500**	**52,353,200**
2008	1,328,020,000	774,800,000	1.1	8,522,800	5.4	41,839,200	3.8	29,442,400	**79,804,400**	**50,362,000**
2009	1,334,740,000	779,950,000	1.0	7,799,500	5.8	45,237,100	4.0	31,198,000	**84,234,600**	**53,036,600**
2010	1,340,910,000	761,050,000	1.8	13,698,900	6.8	51,751,400	4.3	32,725,150	**98,175,450**	**65,450,300**

Source: *China Labor Statistical Yearbooks* (National Bureau of Statistics of China 2003-2011).

[1] The knowledge worker group referred to as KW1 comprises unit heads, professional and technical personnel and clerks and related workers.

[2] The knowledge worker group referred to as KW2 comprises unit heads as well as professional and technical personnel.

Appendix 4: Total Knowledge Workers 2002-2010 (2)

Year	Unit Head (college degree and above/ 大专以上) (%)	Unit Head (大专以上) (persons)	Professional and Technical Personnel (大专以上) (%)	Professional and Technical Personnel (大专以上) (persons)	Clerk and Related Workers (大专以上) (%)	Clerk and Related Workers (大专以上) (persons)	**KW3 (persons)[1]**	**KW4 (persons)[2]**
2002	41.1	5,152,213.8	37.4	16,547,256.0	30.8	15,898,344.0	**37,597,813.8**	**21,699,469.8**
2003	41.8	5,600,263.7	38.7	19,875,577.0	32.8	18,798,545.9	**44,274,386.6**	**25,475,840.6**
2004	43.7	5,586,608.0	38.1	20,628,864.0	34.5	19,717,440.0	**45,932,912.0**	**26,215,472.0**
2005	36.6	4,162,792.5	42.1	23,941,743.8	42.6	11,951,536.5	**40,056,072.8**	**28,104,536.3**
2006	36.4	3,337,152.0	53.1	23,123,988.0	44.2	11,481,392.0	**37,942,532.0**	**26,461,140.0**
2007	34.6	3,196,624.8	51.9	22,376,373.6	43.2	12,306,081.6	**37,879,080.0**	**25,572,998.4**
2008	31.3	2,667,636.4	53.7	22,467,650.4	43.1	12,689,674.4	**37,824,961.2**	**25,135,286.8**
2009	32.9	2,566,035.5	52.7	23,839,951.7	45.5	14,195,090.0	**40,601,077.2**	**26,405,987.2**
2010	39.4	5,397,366.6	61.3	31,723,608.2	47.4	15,511,721.1	**52,632,695.9**	**37,120,974.8**

Source: *China Labor Statistical Yearbooks* (National Bureau of Statistics of China, 2003-2011).

[1] The knowledge worker group referred to as KW3 comprises unit heads, professional and technical personnel and clerks and related workers holding a college degree or higher.

[2] The knowledge worker group referred to as KW4 comprises unit heads as well as professional and technical personnel holding a college degree or higher.

Appendix 5: Explanatory Notes to Figure 2

The fluctuations of the absolute numbers of China's knowledge workers between 2002 and 2010 (see figure 2) are scrutinized in more detail in the following. The increase in 2003 was nearly equally caused by an absolute increase of total employed persons and the absorption of employed persons from non-knowledge work occupational categories.[1082] The increase of total employed persons might in part have resulted from the first expansion of higher education enrollment in 1999 as a strong increase of bachelor graduates in the categories of professional and technical personnel as well as clerks and related workers can be observed. In contrast, persons of the non-knowledge work categories might have rather been absorbed by the lower qualifications of knowledge work occupations.

Most obvious, in the years 2002 to 2004, KW1 was not only larger than in subsequent years but significantly larger than all other groups. This was caused by the number of clerks and related workers accounting for twice as much compared to 2005. This is not only reflected by the absolute numbers but also by the simultaneous increase in this time span of KW2 and KW4 which both do not include clerks. The sudden relevant decrease of clerks and related workers in 2005 might well have occurred due to an adjustment of criteria of who was eligible to be included in this rather vague category.

Several observations sustain this assumption. In 2005, the category "others" decreased from 7.8 to 0.3%. Compared to the preceding and following years, this was an unparalled decrease. This might be an indication for the rendering of the criteria for all categories more precisely in that year. Furthermore, the only slight decrease of KW3 (including clerks and higher qualifications) shows that mostly the clerks with degrees lower than college have not been included in the category of clerks anymore.[1083] These might have been classified into non-knowledge worker occupations in 2005, all of which show a relative increase.[1084] Moreover, the numbers of clerks in both clerk-including KW1 and KW3 stayed relatively constant in the years following 2005. As such, the decrease might indeed have been caused by an adjustment of criteria rather than a *ceteris paribus* change of occupations. Following the adjustment, a higher proportion of higher qualified clerks and related workers have been included in the group of KW1, alleviating the significant quantitative difference to the other groups.

1082 NBS 2003: 47 and 3, NBS 2004: 63 and 3 (Exemplary calculation of KW1: Increase of 13,670,680 persons between 2002 and 2003; increase of total employed persons of 6,920,000 persons; corresponding decrease between 2002 and 2003 of non-knowledge worker occupational categories).

1083 The absolute number confirms that more than two thirds with a degree lower than college are not included in the category of clerks in 2005 anymore.

1084 NBS 2005: 71, NBS 2006: 71.

In 2006, all four groups decreased in numbers. Whereas in KW3 and KW4 the decrease was relatively equally distributed among the respective occupational categories, the decrease in the KW1 and KW2 can mainly be attributed to the category of professional and technical workers. This category shows that professional and technical workers with degrees below college have become less included in this occupational category since 2006. As constant numbers can be observed in the subsequent years, this occupational category also very likely followed the trend of adjustment toward higher qualifications.

The renewed rise of all four groups between 2009 and 2010 was mainly due to an increase in the categories of unit heads as well as professional and technical personnel. The increase of the latter and the slight increase of clerks consisted of persons with qualifications of college degree and above. It was only the unit heads who were still fairly represented in various qualifications. The increase of knowledge workers within this period was also due to adjustments following the population census in 2010.[1085] While total employment decreased by nearly 19 million persons, agricultural laborers alone decreased by more than 80 million persons, and the remaining knowledge and non-knowledge worker occupational categories all saw a respective increase in numbers.[1086]

1085 See e.g. NBS 2010a: 3, NBS 2011b: 2 (retrospectively displaying a lower figure of total employment for 2009 than NBS 2010a does).
1086 NBS 2010a: 60 and 3, NBS 2011b: 59 and 2.

Appendix 6: Knowledge Workers (urban) 2002-2010 (1)

Year	Total Urban Population 城镇人口 (persons)	Urban Employment 城镇就业人员 (persons)	Unit Head 单位负责人 (urban) (%)	Unit Head 单位负责人 (urban) (persons)	Professional and Technical Personnel 专业技术人员 (urban) (%)	Professional and Technical Personnel 专业技术人员 (urban) (persons)	Clerk and Related Workers 办事人员和有关人员 (urban) (%)	Clerk and Related Workers 办事人员和有关人员 (urban) (persons)	**KW1 (urban) (persons)[1]**	**KW2 (urban) (persons)[2]**
2002	502,120,000	247,800,000	4.0	9,912,000	13.8	34,196,400	16.9	41,878,200	**85,986,600**	**44,108,400**
2003	523,760,000	256,390,000	4.1	10,511,990	15.1	38,714,890	18.2	46,662,980	**95,889,860**	**49,226,880**
2004	542,830,000	264,760,000	3.9	10,325,640	15.1	39,978,760	17.5	46,333,000	**96,637,400**	**50,304,400**
2005	562,120,000	273,310,000	2.9	7,925,990	12.7	34,710,370	8.0	21,864,800	**64,501,160**	**42,636,360**
2006	577,060,000	283,100,000	2.7	7,643,700	12.3	34,821,300	8.0	22,648,000	**65,113,000**	**42,465,000**
2007	593,790,000	293,500,000	2.4	7,044,000	11.9	34,926,500	8.4	24,654,000	**66,624,500**	**41,970,500**
2008	606,670,000	302,100,000	2.1	6,344,100	11.2	33,835,200	8.2	24,772,200	**64,951,500**	**40,179,300**
2009	621,860,000	311,200,000	2.0	6,224,000	11.5	35,788,000	8.6	26,763,200	**68,775,200**	**42,012,000**
2010	669,780,000	346,870,000	3.4	11,793,580	13.0	45,093,100	8.7	30,177,690	**87,064,370**	**56,886,680**

Source: *China Labor Statistical Yearbooks* (National Bureau of Statistics of China 2003-2011).

[1] The knowledge worker group referred to as KW1 comprises unit heads, professional and technical personnel and clerks and related workers in urban areas.

[2] The knowledge worker group referred to as KW2 comprises unit heads as well as professional and technical personnel in urban areas.

Appendix 7: Knowledge Workers (urban) 2002-2010 (2)

Year	Unit Head (college and above/ 大专以上) (urban) (%)	Unit Head (大专以上) (urban) (persons)	Prof. (大专以上) (urban) (%)	Prof. (大专以上 (urban) (persons)	Clerk (大专以上) (urban) (%)	Clerk (大专以上) (urban) (persons)	**KW3 (urban) (persons)**	**KW4 (urban) (persons)**
2002	46.5	4,609,080.0	44.5	15,217,398.0	34.5	14,447,979.0	**34,274,457.0**	**19,826,478.0**
2003	47.6	5,003,707.2	46.1	17,847,564.3	36.5	17,031,987.7	**39,883,259.2**	**22,851,271.5**
2004	50.8	5,245,425.1	45.9	18,350,250.8	38.9	18,023,537.0	**41,619,213.0**	**23,595,676.0**
2005	44.2	3,503,287.6	55.3	19,194,834.6	46.4	10,145,267.2	**32,843,389.4**	**22,698,122.2**
2006	41.0	3,133,917.0	58.0	20,196,354.0	47.2	10,689,856.0	**34,020,127.0**	**23,330,271.0**
2007	39.9	2,810,556.0	57.1	19,943,031.5	46.2	11,390,148.0	**34,143,735.5**	**22,753,587.5**
2008	35.6	2,258,499.6	58.7	19,861,262.4	46.1	11,419,984.2	**33,539,746.2**	**22,119,762.0**
2009	37.8	2,352,672.0	57.9	20,721,252.0	48.9	13,087,204.8	**36,161,128.8**	**23,073,924.0**
2010	43.4	5,118,413.7	65.8	29,671,259.8	50.5	15,239,733.5	**50,029,407.0**	**34,789,673.5**

Source: *China Labor Statistical Yearbooks* (National Bureau of Statistics of China 2003-2011).

[1] The knowledge worker group referred to as KW1 comprises unit heads, professional and technical personnel and clerks and related workers in urban areas holding a college degree or higher.

[2] The knowledge worker group referred to as KW2 comprises unit heads as well as professional and technical personnel in urban areas holding a college degree or higher.

Appendix 8: Knowledge Workers (urban) per Age Group (2010)

Age Groups	Unit Head 单位负责人 (urban) (persons)[1]	Professional and Technical Personnel 专业技术人员 (urban) (persons)[1]	Clerk and Related Workers 办事人员和有关人员 (urban) (persons)[1]	**KW1 (urban) (persons)**	Total employment by edu. attainm. (%)[2]	Total employment by edu. attainm. (persons)	Total employed persons with college and above (% of age group)[3]	Total employed persons with college and above (persons)	Total employed persons with college and above (% of total)[4]	**KW3 (urban) (persons)[5]**	KW3 (urban) (%)	Knowledge workers without tertiary Education (urban) (persons)
16-19	35,380.74	360,744.80	301,776.90	**697,902.44**	3.2	24,377,977.98	1.3	316,913.71	0.41	**207,212.67**	29.69	490,689.77
20-24	471,743.20	4,419,123.80	2,836,702.86	**7,727,569.86**	11.1	84,561,111.11	12.5	10,570,138.89	13.81	**6,911,239.88**	89.44	816,329.98
25-29	1,238,325.90	8,297,130.40	4,496,475.81	**14,031,932.11**	11.1	84,561,111.11	20.7	17,504,150.00	22.88	**11,445,013.24**	81.56	2,586,918.87
30-34	1,698,275.52	7,801,106.30	4,345,587.36	**13,844,969.18**	11.0	83,799,299.30	16.5	13,826,884.38	18.07	**9,040,648.92**	65.30	4,804,320.26
35-39	2,170,018.72	7,665,827.00	4,647,364.26	**14,483,209.98**	13.7	104,368,218.22	11.6	12,106,713.31	15.82	**7,915,922.46**	54.66	6,567,287.52
40-44	2,217,193.04	6,628,685.70	4,345,587.36	**13,191,466.10**	14.7	111,986,336.34	8.4	9,406,852.25	12.29	**6,150,629.91**	46.63	7,040,836.19
45-49	2,004,908.60	5,366,078.90	4,164,521.22	**11,535,508.72**	12.2	92,941,041.04	7.9	7,342,342.24	9.60	**4,800,758.92**	41.62	6,734,749.80
50-54	1,096,802.94	2,660,492.90	2,685,814.41	**6,443,110.25**	8.0	60,944,944.94	5.4	3,291,027.03	4.30	**2,151,823.88**	33.40	4,291,286.37
55-59	684,027.64	1,442,979.20	1,780,483.71	**3,907,490.55**	7.4	56,374,074.07	3.2	1,803,970.37	2.36	**1,179,518.27**	30.19	2,727,972.28
60-64	129,729.38	270,558.60	362,132.28	**762,420.26**	4.0	30,472,472.47	0.7	213,307.31	0.28	**139,470.07**	18.29	622,950.19
65+	47,174.32	180,372.40	211,243.83	**438,790.55**	3.5	26,663,413.41	0.5	133,317.07	0.17	**87,168.79**	19.87	351,621.76
Total				**87,064,370.00**	99.9	761,050,000.00		76,515,616.57	100.00	**50,029,407.00**		37,034,963.00

Source: *China Labor Statistical Yearbook* (National Bureau of Statistics of China, 2011b).

[1] NBS 2011b: 70. Only figures for age groups of urban occupational categories are available.

[2] NBS 2011b: 54. Educational attainment not available for occupational categories; only available for total employment. Urban employment is neither available.

[3] NBS 2011b: 53. Figures present the sum of percentages of college, bachelor and master graduates.

[4] Variables for calculating KW3 (urban). Calculation with "Total employed persons with college and above" (76,515,616.57) = 100. As variables are used for calculating the *proportion* for each age group, the fact that employment is not available specifically for urban areas is not significant.

[5] The Part of KW1 (urban) with college degree and above is the equivalent of KW3 (urban).

Appendix 9: Knowledge Workers (urban) per Educational Attainment (2010)

Age Group	Unit Head 单位负责人 (urban) (persons)[1]	Professional and Technical Personnel 专业技术人员 (urban) (persons)[1]	Clerk and Related Workers 办事人员和有关人员 (urban) (persons)[1]	**KW1 (urban) (persons)**	born between (urban) (year)	Entering primary school (urban) (year)	Entering primary school (urban) (%)[2]	Entering primary school (urban) (persons)	Entering lower middle school (urban) (year)	Entering lower middle school (urban) (%)[2]	Entering lower middle school (urban) (persons)	Entering upper middle school (urban) (year)[2 3]	Entering upper middle school (urban) (%)[2]	Entering upper middle school (urban) (persons)[4]
16-19	35,380.74	360,744.80	301,776.90	697,902	1991-1994									
20-24	471,743.20	4,419,123.80	2,836,702.86	7,727,570	1986-1990									
25-29	1,238,325.90	8,297,130.40	4,496,475.81	14,031,932	1981-1985									
Total 16-29				**22,457,404**										
30-34	1,698,275.52	7,801,106.30	4,345,587.36	13,844,969	1976-1980	1982-1986			1988-1992			1991-1995	41%	
35-39	2,170,018.72	7,665,827.00	4,647,364.26	14,483,210	1971-1975	1977-1981			1983-1987			1986-1990	40%	
Total 30-39				**28,328,179**										
40-44	2,217,193.04	6,628,685.70	4,345,587.36	13,191,466	1966-1970	1972-1976			1978-1982			1981-1985	42%	
45-49	2,004,908.60	5,366,078.90	4,164,521.22	11,535,509	1961-1965	1967-1971			1973-1977			1976-1980	55%	
50-54	1,096,802.94	2,660,492.90	2,685,814.41	6,443,110	1956-1960	1962-1966			1968-1972			1971-1975	50%	
Total 40-54				**31,170,085**										
55-59	684,027.64	1,442,979.20	1,780,483.71	3,907,491	1951-1955	1957-1961	92%	3,594,892	1963-1967	80%	2,875,914	1966-1970	28%	805,256
60-64	129,729.38	270,558.60	362,132.28	762,420	1946-1950	1952-1956	90%	686,178	1958-1962	72%	494,048	1961-1965	30%	148,214
65+	47,174.32	180,372.40	211,243.83	438,791	until 1945	until 1951	88%	386,136	until 1957	65%	250,988	until 1960	32%	80,316
Total 55+				**5,108,702**										**1,033,786**

Sources: *China Labor Statistical Yearbook* (National Bureau of Statistics of China, 2011b), Tanigawa 2005.

[1] NBS 2011b: 70. Only figures for age groups of urban occupational categories are available.

[2] Figures taken from Tanigawa (2005: 12-14) who calculates the proportion of urban lower middle school graduates who entered upper middle school. Where age groups do not correspond, average values of Tanigawa's age groups are used.

[3] Exact calculation possible as age groups from the *China Labor Statistical Yearbook* 2011 and those used by Tanigawa exactly correspond.

[4] These figures reveal that only 1,033,786 senior knowledge workers entered upper middle school *directly* after graduating from lower middle school, while the majority of 4.1 million either at most completed lower middle school or had their formal education disrupted.

MIX
Papier aus verantwortungsvollen Quellen
Paper from responsible sources
FSC® C105338

If you have any concerns about our products,
you can contact us on
ProductSafety@springernature.com

In case Publisher is established outside the EU,
the EU authorized representative is:
Springer Nature Customer Service Center GmbH
Europaplatz 3, 69115 Heidelberg, Germany

Printed by Libri Plureos GmbH
in Hamburg, Germany